H.M.S. RODNEY

Other books in the Warships of the Royal Navy series by Iain Ballantyne

WARSPITE
H.M.S. LONDON

With Jonathan Eastland

H.M.S VICTORY

Also by Iain Ballantyne

STRIKE FROM THE SEA

All titles published by Pen & Sword Books

WARSHIPS of the ROYAL NAVY

H.M.S. RODNEY

Iain Ballantyne

Pen & Sword
MARITIME

First published in Great Britain in 2008 by
PEN & SWORD MARITIME
an imprint of
Pen & Sword Books Ltd
47 Church Street, Barnsley
South Yorkshire, S70 2AS

ISBN: 978-1-84415-406-7

A CIP catalogue record for this book
is available from the British Library.

Typeset in 10/12pt Palatino by
Concept, Huddersfield, West Yorkshire

Printed and bound in England by
CPI UK.

Pen & Sword Books Ltd incorporates the imprints of
Pen & Sword Aviation, Pen & Sword Maritime, Pen & Sword Military,
Pen & Sword Select, Pen & Sword Military Classics,
Leo Cooper and Wharncliffe Local History.

For a complete list of Pen & Sword titles please contact
PEN & SWORD BOOKS LIMITED
47 Church Street, Barnsley, South Yorkshire, S70 2AS, England
E-mail: enquiries@pen-and-sword.co.uk
Website: www.pen-and-sword.co.uk

CONTENTS

H.M.S. RODNEY

Motto

'Eagles do not breed doves'

Battle Honours

QUEBEC 1759
SYRIA 1840
CRIMEA 1854
NORWAY 1940
ATLANTIC 1940–1
BISMARCK ACTION 1941
MALTA CONVOYS 1941–2
NORTH AFRICA 1942–3
SICILY 1943
SALERNO 1943
MEDITERRANEAN 1943
NORMANDY 1944
ENGLISH CHANNEL 1944
ARCTIC 1944

This is my story
This is my song
Been in commission far too long
Roll out the Rodney, *the* Nelson, *the* Hood
This two-funnelled bastard is no bloody good

Salty sea ditty sung by sailors of smaller vessels, such as destroyers, in the early days of the Second World War, expressing their defiant longing for the allegedly softer, easier life to be found in a capital ship like HMS *Rodney*. The story related on the following pages proves that perception was a little wide of the mark.

This book is dedicated to the remarkable generation of men who defended freedom and democracy during the Second World War.

Also in memory of the late Syd Goodman:
friend and colleague,
but, above all,
a tireless advocate of warship history
who did not suffer fools gladly.

FOREWORD

by

Commander R.W. Morris OBE, Royal Navy (Retd), who served in HMS Rodney *as a Midshipman from September 1943 to December 1944*

As a boy I always knew that my destiny was a life at sea. This was nurtured by family holidays at Sennen Cove on the tip of England's Cornish peninsula. Fishing with my father, trolling for mackerel and then selling them to the fishermen's wives for a penny each to feed their visitors are among my most treasured memories. Our last holiday at Sennen was in August 1939, when war clouds were gathering and I vividly remember seeing the ships of the Home Fleet steaming northwards from their Channel ports in an endless stream. My father reluctantly said it was time to go home. What a sad day that was. Within a few days Britain was at war with Germany.

I was determined to join the Navy and, after three years training as a cadet, I was appointed to HMS *Rodney*. I was thrilled to be going to the battleship that had played such a key role in sinking the *Bismarck* just a few years earlier. I was seventeen-and-three-quarter-years-old and a lowly Midshipman. It was all, of course, a huge adventure, starting, in September 1943, with myself sailing in an escort ship, riding shotgun on a troop convoy to Algiers, then on to Malta, to join the mighty battleship. I was not disappointed, the massive 16-inch guns looming over me were simply awe-inspiring in their majesty and menace; I first glimpsed them from a pinnace taking me to the ship.

The land campaign was still very much alive, but the war at sea in the Mediterranean was subsiding, the Italian Fleet having surrendered. Therefore, after a very brief period of time, we sailed for the UK. Soon *Rodney* was bombarding Normandy and, after a foray to the Channel Islands, accompanied a Russian convoy in a bid to draw *Tirpitz*, sister ship of *Bismarck*, out of a Norwegian fjord. These were the twilight days of *Rodney*'s life but she was still very much a ship of war right to the end.

Now, more than sixty years on, we have this most absorbing and comprehensive telling of not only battleship *Rodney*' story but also that of her forebears. In recounting the amazing events of battleship *Rodney*'s war career, the author has drawn on my own midshipman's journal. Reading quotes taken from it – in particular the amazing, almost cinematic, descriptions of action during the battle to break out from the Normandy beachhead in the summer of 1944 – I am struck by how lyrical my younger self could be. But, we lived very fast in those days; the teenager that I was back then was more often excited than afraid. The main achievement of this book is to bring alive the human experience in the mighty *Rodney*, and I am honoured to have played my part in helping breathe life into this epic yarn.

It is, above all else, a magnificent and detailed account of the fighting life of the huge dreadnought that displaced 42,000 tons at the peak of her powers. It is not a name that today seems likely to grace a warship, but in her day *Rodney* reigned supreme; she was respected by her own side and feared by the opposition. The

An ink drawing of *Rodney* at sea. *HMS* Rodney *Association.*

battleship's record in the Second World War was second to none. *Rodney* may have been broken up in the late 1940s, but the spirit of the men who sailed her did not vanish. The HMS *Rodney* Association was formed. Annual Meetings were invariably held in HMS *Drake*, the naval barracks at Devonport, followed by a dinner in the Chief and Petty Officers' mess, and there would be a church service the next day. The first President was Vice Admiral Sir William Crawford, who had been *Rodney*'s gunnery officer during the *Bismarck* action. The Association disbanded several years ago, because of decreasing numbers, and no one was willing to take on the onerous task of Secretary. None of us was getting any younger. I was President for a couple of years, which was a great honour, and of which I am particularly proud. Too bad it had to finish; such ships are sadly gone forever, while those who manned them are fewer every day. This book means that *Rodney*, and the experiences of her men, live on.

ACKNOWLEDGEMENTS

The genesis of this book can be traced back nearly four years, to a dinner party in Plymouth, hosted by Andrew Pearce and his wife Sharon. Knowing my background as an author of books about famous British warships, Andy mentioned that his dad, Derrick, had been Secretary of the HMS *Rodney* Association (disbanded in 2001). Anyone with even a passing interest in naval history knows that *Rodney* helped destroy *Bismarck* and supported the D-Day invasion and I remarked that she would certainly be worthy of a book at some stage. Soon, packages of material from what remains of the HMS *Rodney* Association archive started arriving, brought up to my house by Sharon, whenever she came up to go running with my wife, Lindsey. And that is how this marathon started, with only a detour to write HMS *Victory*, third in Pen & Sword's 'Warships of the Royal Navy' series, with Jonathan Eastland, in time to be published during the Trafalgar 200 anniversary year. Derrick Pearce has proved an invaluable point of reference at various stages and the material he provided, especially the names and addresses of around 150 Association members, formed a key starting point. The researching and writing of HMS *Rodney* has absorbed a significant proportion of downtime from my day job, editing *WARSHIPS International Fleet Review* magazine, and I am indebted to Derek Knoll and HPC Publishing for allowing me the freedom to squeeze this project in.

I often say to my long-suffering wife – by way of an apology for periodically abandoning her and my children – that I have to write this kind of book now, in order to incorporate fresh eyewitness accounts. For, and I am sure the veterans of the Second World War won't mind me saying this, if I were to ease off now, by the time I come back (perhaps when I am retired) there will not be any veterans left alive. It is the chance to capture in print previously untold stories that gives this book, and previous titles in the series – *Warspite* (2001) and HMS *London* (2003) – their principal value. HMS *Victory* was obviously an exception. My letters to HMS *Rodney* Association members led to responses from veterans living not only in the UK, but also in Australia, Canada, the USA and South Africa. Some wrote long, detailed letters, others offered a few background notes and both published and unpublished documents. In many cases I followed up initial contact with one, or more, interviews, either by telephone or (depending on time available and distance) in person. Large or small, mentioned specifically or not, interviewed or incorporated in some other way, they all informed and educated me and therefore propelled the narrative of the book as well as providing vivid stories to enliven proceedings. In some cases, both veterans and their families were involved in helping me out. I would like to extend my thanks to them all and the following in particular:

Jack Austin, Charles Barton, Tom Brock, Harry G. Farmer, Phil Fordham, Ken and Brian George, Ian Hamilton, Rupert Hardwell, Robert G. Jackson, Ernie Johnson, Arthur and Simon Kavanagh, Phil Lancett, Bill MacKinlay, James McLean, Roger

Morris, Len Nicholl, Tony Robinson and his daughter Lindy Pritula, Les Sadler, Alan and Nigel Sharp, Allan and Jack Snowden, Frank Summers, Rev. Gordon Taylor, John and Peter Wells-Cole.

Jack Austin mailed me a richly detailed 21-page letter, from his home in New South Wales, which ended, appropriately enough, with a rather salty sentence:

> *Iain, you have cost me a bloody fortune in tea bags and smokes but the memories were worth it.*

I hope all the veterans will agree that Jack's tea and cigarettes were worth it.

Roger Morris deserves a further mention for writing the excellent Foreword to this book, and also allowing full access to his impressive Midshipman's Journal, from which I extracted quotes and illustrations. Roger's patience and willingness to support the cause over the past few years have been the epitome of indefatigability. Similarly deserving of an extra salute, is Allan Snowden who, like Roger, never failed to answer my questions as fully (and cheerfully) as he could, plus also forwarded a sizeable amount of material from his own *Rodney* archive. Canadian Paul Maddison has been a staunch supporter throughout, his British grandfather Clifford Woolley having served in the battleship during the Second World War. Paul very generously offered the use of photographs from his family's private collection, as well as helping me with obtaining an image from a Canadian archive. He also provided assistance with some areas of research, including a Crew List for the ship. Paul runs a superb HMS *Rodney* web site (see Appendices). Among those veterans and others connected with the HMS *Rodney* Association, whom I would like also to thank for helping me one way or the other are: Dennis Berry, Bob S. Bright, Barbara Dadds, Stuart Fletcher, Diane Jackson, Ron Kingdon, W. MacJean, Mike Mackay, George Paddon, Keith Parker, Mr W.G. Phillips, Mrs E. Pink, Mrs M.E. Skidmore, R. Thomas, Henry L. Thompson.

As regards all those others who responded, but whom I have inadvertently forgotten to mention, please accept my sincere apologies and heartfelt thanks.

Rodney veteran Peter Staveley, some of whose papers are lodged in the Imperial War Museum's Department of Documents, very kindly provided supplementary material for which I am extremely grateful. Sadly, some who started out on the journey have not made it, including Ted Russ, whom I interviewed in Plympton one cold November evening and who provided me with some excellent research material and a couple of photographs. Sadly he passed away before this book could be published, as did fellow *Rodney* veterans Hugh Cooley, Bob Pink and Bill Skidmore. Another casualty was Syd Goodman, my good friend and naval history adviser, but, like the veterans, he lives on in the spirit of this book. Some of battleship *Rodney*'s deceased shipmates made their contributions via their children, who have kept the flame of memory burning bright, most notably: Kevin Byers, who supplied me with his father Tommy's very vivid accounts of his time in *Rodney*, also forwarding relevant photographs; Lesley Evetts and Geoff Myers, who graciously agreed to provide not only their father Bill's unpublished memoirs, but also photographs from their family's private collection; W. Gordon Campbell, who included his dad's recollections in a wonderful document he has lovingly crafted on battleship *Rodney*. Mrs Mary Watson sent an evocative photograph of her late father, James Thoirs, taken during the period that he served in *Rodney*. She also passed on a few memories of *Rodney* connections.

Ray Faulkner went to a considerable amount of trouble to photograph his late father's 'Crossing the Line' certificate from 1942, which is reproduced in the plates. John Faulkner's favourite story of his time in *Rodney* sprung from the ship's 1941 refit at Boston, when, according to Ray, an American family 'took him to an ice cream parlour and he saw what was to him the world's biggest Knickerbocker Glory.' And he ended up getting it for free for the family, by managing to eat two of them.

It goes to prove that often *Rodney*'s men blotted out the blood and thunder of other episodes with happy memories, many of which they have passed on to me, helping to bring alive their incredible stories. When it comes to illustrating this book, there are a number of other people who I should also thank: Stephen Courtney, Curator of Photographs at the Royal Naval Museum in Portsmouth; photographers Nigel Andrews, Dave Billinge and Stephen J. Borg; Kevin and Denise Goodman, for allowing images from the Goodman Collection to be used. It is an honour indeed to include a painting of *Rodney* by Paul Wright ARSMA (www.paulwrightmaritimeartist.co.uk), whose enthralling work has previously graced books by luminaries such as Patrick O'Brian. Museums, libraries and archives played their part in bringing this project to fruition and I would like to take this opportunity to extend my gratitude to the staffs of: National Maritime Museum; Imperial War Museum; Royal Naval Museum; Portsmouth and Plymouth city libraries; Wirral Archives Services (particularly Ava Wieclawska); Merseyside Maritime Museum; Nova Scotia Archives and Records Management; US Naval Historical Center; *Western Morning News*. The US Naval War College granted me permission to quote from Admiralty signals contained within the book *On His Majesty's Service* by Rear Admiral Joseph H. Wellings, USN (Retd).

With reference to material that was sourced in the Department of Documents at the Imperial War Museum (and listed in Sources) every effort has been made to trace copyright holders of the papers of E.L. Brown, G. Conning, Rear Admiral G.C. Ross and Captain D.C. Woolf. The author and the Imperial War Museum would be grateful for any information that might help to trace those whose identities or addresses are not currently known. I accessed quotes from *Lord Blayney's Narrative*, in order to breathe life into the story of the Napoleonic Wars era *Rodney*, via John Schneider of the Napoleonic Literature web site (see Sources). Some interesting material on Admiral Tovey's life was available from Ian Donald Gardiner in New Zealand. Others who deserve my thanks for helping bring the book together are: Mrs Georgina Barnard, whose late husband wrote the excellent book *Building Britain's Wooden Walls* about the shipbuilding family that constructed the 74-gun *Rodney*; Stephan Barnard who runs a web site inspired by the same volume (www.woodenwalls.co.uk); Trevor Davenport and Terry Gander, who have researched battleship *Rodney*'s fire mission against Alderney; Richard Coltart, whose Royal Navy sailor uncle painted *Rodney* in the late 1920s and early 1930s; Roger Busby and Melanie Bowran of the Sea Cadet Corps HQ in London, who helped track down SCC units named after *Rodney*; the staff of the public relations office and others at Devonport Naval Base, Plymouth, the *Rodney*'s old base port, who helped tie up some loose ends. Last, but by no means least, I would like to extend my thanks to friends and colleagues Dennis Andrews (who has again created some superb illustrations), Martin Robinson (who proved invaluable in helping me to proof read the book), Jonathan Eastland and Peter Hore (both for general support and encouragement). Brigadier Henry Wilson, Publishing Manager of Pen & Sword Books, surely deserves a tribute for his patience and perseverance during the extended climb to the summit of this particular mountain, which turned out to be more of a challenge than either of us could have imagined at the outset of the ascent.

The long trek to completion started with Derrick and Andy Pearce, plus what remained of the HMS *Rodney* Association archive. They deserve my special thanks, for without them a fascinating and exciting story of warships named *Rodney* could not have been told.

AUTHOR'S INTRODUCTION

***Rodney*'s official ship's crest.**
HMS Rodney *Association.*

The Forgotten Battleship

This 'she' was named in honour of Admiral Sir George Rodney who, in the twilight of his life, saved Britain and the Royal Navy from disgrace and disaster and then was sacked by an ungrateful government. Elevated by the more appreciative general public to the status of national hero, the 18th Century legend was, as you will soon learn, later awarded a princely annual pension of £2,000 by way of apology. By 1948, it was with similar ingratitude that HMS *Rodney* had been discarded in the aftermath of a great victory.

Even during the Second World War, the battleship was more than once ignored when she should have been acclaimed to the rafters. While *Rodney* was the vessel that did most to destroy the Nazi battleship *Bismarck*, even at the time other ships, which had arguably done far less damage than her, grabbed the headlines. Three years later *Rodney*'s decisive bombardments of German troop concentrations in Normandy, which helped save the Allied beachhead from disaster, were largely overlooked. This book aims to restore *Rodney* – in many ways the forgotten battleship of British naval history – to her rightful position. Perhaps part of the problem is that people love nothing better than a heroic disaster at sea, which might explain why the *Hood* and *Bismarck*, both doomed vessels, have consistently garnered more attention than *Rodney*, which came through the war with a superb record of success, but without suffering major damage or casualties. Today the sheer awe which battleship *Rodney* inspired – along with sister ship *Nelson* the most modern capital ships Britain possessed on the outbreak of war in September 1939 – is long forgotten. For a while, in the pre-nuclear age, they were considered by many to be the most powerful man-made destructive force on the face of the planet. However, it is better they are remembered for carrying the hopes and fears of humanity in the battle against the tyranny of Hitler's odious Nazi regime.

Resigned by the late 1940s to being a cold and silent shell, awaiting the end of days, *Rodney* was inevitably destined for the breakers' yard rather than a watery grave. But what days they had been. For twenty years her mess decks thronged with humanity, metal locker doors banging as matelots dressed for the working day, with jokes traded and insults too (some friendly, some not). At mealtimes the ordinary sailors who were the lifeblood coursing through her steel veins would sit around a huge table in each mess to chew over the day's happenings, cursing the officers who had botched another job, discussing the latest piece of rumour and maybe bolting down a supper of liver and bacon.

Plates and cutlery cleared away, off-watch the sailors engaged in noisy banter, enjoyed entertaining games or lost themselves in a book. Some found a haven in writing letters to loved ones back home while others respectfully avoided reading over their shoulder. At the other end of the ship, quite literally, the officers enjoyed their pink gins and schoolboy hi-jinks in the wardroom or gunroom. It is for sure *Rodney*'s part in all their lives was deeply embedded in the hearts and souls of the flesh and blood cogs that made the battleship such a mighty machine of war.

In this book, which is the first to attempt a proper, full-blooded history of all British warships to carry the name HMS *Rodney*, we travel through great dramas of war between 1759 and 1945 from the waters of the St Lawrence in the fabled 'Year of Victories', when Wolfe made his assault on the Heights of Abraham, to a rare surrender by British naval forces, in the Caribbean, in 1782; through the forgotten role of the Royal Navy in securing Wellington's victory over Napoleon in the Iberian Peninsula, to a bitter winter for *Rodney*'s men besieging Sevastopol. It is, of course, the mighty battleship *Rodney*, constructed between the two world wars of the twentieth century, that provides the main focus, being one of just two capital ships built for Britain between 1922 and the late 1930s, a time when the UK Armed Forces were starved of cash by governments that struggled to cope with huge social problems, regarding the Royal Navy in particular as a drain on resources. The population at large doubted the relevance of the Navy and was largely pacifist. Few ships were in service, fuel was scarce, even people were in short supply – economy was the order of the day. Aware that it would not get any more battleships for many years, if at all, *Rodney* and *Nelson* were designed by the Royal Navy as cutting-edge vessels, with as much capability as possible packed into them. These are all familiar elements to anyone aware of the state of the Royal Navy in the early twenty-first century, which faces exactly the same challenges (and attitudes). It is likewise coping with too few ships for its many tasks, and experiencing difficulties in retaining personnel. Few in UK society today comprehend the enduring crucial relevance of the British fleet, which is once again pinning its hopes on a mere two capital ships, the future aircraft carriers HMS *Queen Elizabeth* and HMS *Prince of Wales*. The cost to the British taxpayer of these new leviathans amounts to some £3.9 billion, or £1.95 billion each. Further worthwhile comparison between today and the cash-strapped 1920s is provoked by the similarity in cost – in today's money *Rodney* alone would cost £1.6 billion to construct.

In the 1920s technology sometimes overwhelmed the practice of good man management, which led to trouble in *Rodney*'s lower deck, during the mutiny at Invergordon. In this book the reader will also experience events during that notorious episode and sail in *Rodney* through ill-fated adventures off Norway in the early days of the Second World War. The story of the ship's ignored key role in deterring Hitler's troops from invading Britain is also presented. We will, of course, take part in the pursuit and destruction of Hitler's most powerful battleship and witness *Rodney* as saviour of Allied troops fighting desperately in the D-Day beachhead. It is appropriate a ship named after an admiral who found both fame and disappointment in war should have a close association with other senior naval commanders who also experienced the highs and lows of a career at sea. Her pre-war captains included Andrew Cunningham, Britain's Second World War 'Nelson', who would be the victor of Matapan in the Second World War and mastermind the Allied naval campaign that defeated the Axis in the Mediterranean. Another of her pre-war Commanding Officers was Admiral Sir John Tovey, who later commanded the Home Fleet in its pursuit of the *Bismarck* and watched *Rodney*'s guns batter the German behemoth from the bridge of his flagship, the newer, but less well-armed, HMS *King George V*. However, it is the stories of junior officers and inhabitants of the 'lower deck', insomuch as they were intertwined with the legendary fighting lives of the various *Rodneys*, which find pride of place in the following pages.

They are the unsung heroes, the stars of this epic tale ordinary men caught up in extraordinary events.

Iain Ballantyne
Plymouth, 2008

H.M.S. Rodney = Xmas 1944

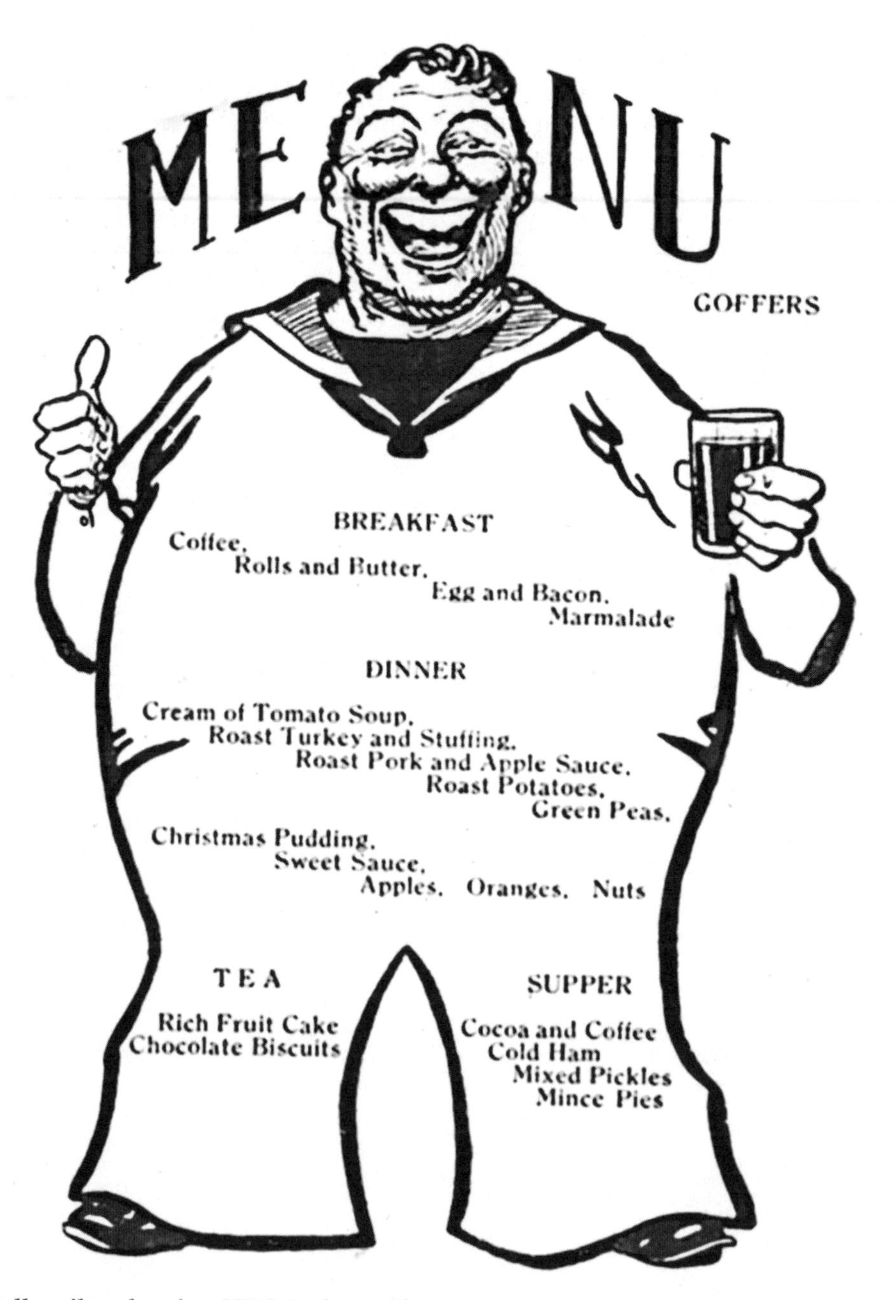

A jolly sailor advertises HMS *Rodney*'s Christmas Day 1944 ship's menu. 'Goffers' is naval slang for a non-alcoholic drink, a necessary precaution, as the battleship was standing by for action. *HMS* Rodney *Association*

Chapter One

OF SHOOTING, SLAYING AND SINKING

The man that British naval ships called *Rodney* were named after enjoyed a mixed reputation. On one hand, he was considered by many subordinates to be coldly arrogant, famously admonishing one officer under his command, following an ill-judged display of initiative, that 'the painful task' of thinking in battle should belong to the Admiral alone. On the other, George Brydges Rodney was also regarded as a firm but popular ship's captain, capable of dishing out severe punishment and showing extraordinary kindness. Following the Battle of Martinique, in 1780, during which his ship HMS *Sandwich* fought three French warships on her own, Rodney learned that, against regulations, a sailor's wife[1] had helped crew a 24-pdr gun. Calling the exhausted woman to his cabin – she had been up through the night tending to the wounded – Rodney told her off but then expressed 'warm thanks' by giving her ten pounds.[2] Some years earlier, when Governor of Greenwich Hospital, Rodney castigated a junior officer for complaining about money spent on coats for impoverished naval pensioners. Rodney reminded the offending officer he had risen from the lower deck and ought therefore to have more consideration. At the same time, Rodney was visiting gambling houses in London where he recklessly threw away his fortune. He would make controversial decisions when appointed once again to a war-fighting command, using military operations to regain financial solvency. That unseemly pursuit of money ultimately mired his reputation as a fighting admiral.

While there is no record of Rodney's date of birth, he was baptised on 13 February 1718 at the church of St Giles-in-the-Fields, London, where, curiously enough, battleship *Rodney's* last naval chaplain would be rector for 50 years following the Second World War.

Having first gone to sea in the summer of 1732, Rodney the man, descended from a knight who fought alongside Richard the Lionheart at Acre, was promoted from midshipman to Lieutenant in 1739 and appointed to HMS *Dolphin*. Service in various ships in the English Channel, North Sea and Mediterranean followed. He became a Post Captain at the age of twenty-five, in 1743, after bringing the 60-gun HMS *Plymouth* home for repair. In early 1746, Rodney became master and commander of the 60-gun HMS *Eagle*, a ship that involved him in many scrapes and brought much good fortune, in one thirteen-month stretch participating in the capture of sixteen enemy vessels.[3] In October 1747 Rodney saw action in *Eagle* at the Second Battle of Cape Finisterre, against the French, his time in command ending at Plymouth in August 1748. He could consider himself well pleased, as his total prize money of £15,000 today would represent nearly £2 million.

By March 1749 Rodney was in command of HMS *Rainbow*, 50-guns, in North American waters, his presence leading to the commissioning of the first vessel to bear his name.

Subsequently appointed Governor of Newfoundland, Rodney had 'secret orders to support the colonists against the encroachments of the French in Nova Scotia'.[4]

Newfoundland, which was where John Cabot made his first landfall in North America, in 1497, was jealously guarded. Large numbers of settlers from the south-west of England and Ireland flooded into Newfoundland and it was perhaps in recognition of wise stewardship of their province that our first *Rodney* was named in Captain Rodney's honour. Possibly the *Rodney* initially served as a fisheries patrol cutter off Newfoundland, as Captain Rodney introduced into service a number of small boats for such missions, to ensure quotas for cod were not abused. Some remote communities were also at risk of being squeezed out by the aggressive French. Curiously, Admiralty records do not list the cutter *Rodney* as the first ship to bear the name, even though she – ships are by tradition considered female even if bearing the name of a man – is generally regarded as being initiator of the line. While our story encompasses six *Rodneys*, officially only four British warships have borne the name, the first 'official' being a ship of the line commissioned in 1810, which we will soon meet. Bearing in mind the Admiralty's reluctance to recognise the cutter, it is strange the earliest battle honour attributed to *Rodney* comes from that vessel, which, a decade after Captain Rodney's governorship of Newfoundland, garnered the tribute 'Quebec 1759'. The *Rodney* cutter supported General Wolfe's brilliant assault on Quebec and while she carried a mere four guns, they were adequate enough for the job of carrying despatches to and from the scene of battle. However, while the cutter earned the battle honour she was not believed to have been present when Wolfe scaled the Heights of Abraham to confront Montcalm, the British general losing his life in the process of achieving a great victory, ending French hopes of establishing control over much of Canada.

During the Quebec campaign *Rodney* was commanded by Lieutenant the Honourable Philip Tufton Perceval, an aristocrat of Irish descent. His father was John Perceval, 2nd Earl of Egmont, at one time tipped to be a future Prime Minister of Britain but who, instead, became First Lord of the Admiralty, in 1763 and 1766.

The *Rodney*'s commander was born on 10 March 1741, his mother being Catherine Cecil, a daughter of the Earl of Salisbury. Lieutenant Tufton Perceval was therefore not even nineteen when he took charge of *Rodney*; he was made a Master and Commander on 5 September 1759, receiving his promotion, and captaincy of *Rodney*, eight days before the climactic battle for Quebec.[5] After his time in command of the cutter, Tufton Perceval no doubt moved on to larger ships, but does not seem to have distinguished himself greatly in his subsequent naval career, dying at the age of 54, on 21 April 1795.[6] His half brother, Spencer, found greater success, as a politician, but in 1812, while serving as Prime Minister, was assassinated in the House of Commons.

In the same year the *Rodney* cutter sailed the St Lawrence, the man she was named after received promotion to Rear Admiral of the Blue and an appointment to command a naval force charged with containing a French invasion force in Le Havre. By this time Rodney's reputation was mixed, to say the least. In 1762 he had ignored Army claims that Martinique could not be taken from the French and landed troops with Royal Navy guns and gunners to take the island's chief stronghold, Fort Royal. The British soon subdued the fortress; a notable triumph achieved against the odds.

Following the end of the Seven Years War, in August 1764 Rodney was made a baronet and, aside from serving as Governor of Greenwich Hospital for five years, entered politics. It was not his first such venture, for Rodney had been elected MP for Saltash in 1751, a borough just up the River Tamar from Plymouth Dock, today known as Devonport and future home port of the Second World War-era battleship *Rodney*. Rodney the man was by 1761 MP for Penryn, another Cornish constituency.

Rodney's campaign to be elected MP for Northampton in 1768, while successful in that it gained him the seat, was ruinously expensive and, taken together with his addiction to gambling, plunged him into dire financial straits.[7] An appointment to command in Jamaica did not solve his money problems and, when he retired from the Caribbean in 1775, Rodney sought refuge in France to avoid the indignity of a spell in a debtors' prison. The admiral lived in Paris until May 1778 when, with hostilities about to break out between Britain and France over the latter's support for rebels in North American colonies, Rodney went home, able to pay off his debts thanks to a very generous loan from a French general. Ironic then, that Rodney's return would eventually lead to a defeat that brought ruin upon France's designs to enrich herself by taking British colonies. Rodney was appointed to command in the Leeward Islands in 1779, mainly because, although not universally admired, he was the best available at a time when talent was thin on the ground, partly because the Keppel-Palliser affair[8] had prompted many senior naval officers to refuse service at sea. On the way to his new posting, Rodney was tasked with relieving the siege of Gibraltar, the resulting victory in the 'moonlight battle' of January 1780 raising his reputation to a new high. Once he arrived in the West Indies, Admiral Rodney was hopefully preoccupied with saving Jamaica from Franco-Spanish invasion. With lingering financial problems that a share in lucrative captures might solve, he was particularly keen on ships under his command taking prizes. This motive cast further disrepute on Rodney's name, for it is reckoned money-seeking prompted him to organize an operation to seize the island of St Eustasius from the Dutch. Although this venture yielded a lot of treasure, various legal issues meant Rodney personally benefited little. Most serious was the fact that it diverted him from providing a proper defence for Martinique, which was taken back by the French.

A combination of disgrace, over his putting lucre before securing British possessions, and ill health forced Rodney to resign in 1781 and return home, but, as is the way with such things, he was accorded the honorary rank of Vice Admiral of Great Britain in early November. Such was the poverty of talent among Britain's available sea-going admirals, Rodney was soon sailing again for the West Indies, returning to the post of Commander-in-Chief in mid-January 1782.

The next HMS *Rodney* was a 16-gun brig-sloop,[9] with a ship's company of fifty-one, in 1781 commanded by John Douglas Brisbane, who had been promoted to Lieutenant on 1 April 1779.[10] This *Rodney*, the second and final 'unofficial', had been purchased in the Caribbean that year.[11] and may previously have been an American customs vessel, or even a locally commissioned ship, like so many of the Royal Navy's smaller craft. She was no doubt named in honour of the commander-in-chief, in order to give physical form to Admiral Rodney's status (and seek advantage in his favours).

The master and commander of the *Rodney* sloop-brig was the son of Captain John Brisbane, who had distinguished himself in action during the on-going American War of Independence. No doubt it was Captain Brisbane's influence that won his son command of *Rodney*. Possibly the elder Brisbane was held in high esteem by Admiral Rodney but Lieutenant Brisbane was not blessed with good fortune, for

Rodney would be captured on 3 February 1782 by the French, during a vain defence of Demerara in what is today Guyana. The area was originally settled by the Dutch West India Company, which reclaimed stretches of the coast to develop sugar and cotton plantations, using slaves to harvest the crops. In the 1590s Sir Walter Raleigh had searched in vain for El Dorado, the fabled city of gold, in the region's vast jungles and, in 1781, the British – probably acting under orders from the money-hungry Admiral Rodney – regarded Demerara as such rich territory they seized it. The main aim was to prevent the Dutch from shipping Demerera's highly desirable goods to rebel American colonies and instead divert it into British hands.

The new rulers constructed a fort at the mouth of the river, Fort St George, and began laying out a settlement around it, the beginnings of Georgetown, the modern-day capital of Guyana. In early 1782, *Rodney*, the 20-gun frigate *Oronoque*, sloops *Barbuda*, 16-guns, *Sylph*, 18-guns and *Stormont*, 16-guns, together with the schooner *Henry*, 6-guns, failed to deter a French expeditionary force composed of five warships led by the 32-gun frigate *Iphigenie*. The *Oronoque* would appear not to have had a full complement, perhaps due to disease, and of the nominal guns available across the force only 75 were actually capable of being manned. French firepower amounted to 140 guns, out-gunning the British by 65 weapons. In terms of available manpower, there were 380 British sailors and marines while the French mustered 1,500 soldiers and matelots.[12]

The story of this obscure moment in British naval history can be found in the 'Lieutenant's Log' of Tudor Tucker, at forty-years old a rather elderly Lieutenant, from the loyalist side of a family whose rebel scions included the first Treasurer of the USA, also named Tudor Tucker. Lt Tudor Tucker RN joined *Rodney* at the end of July 1781. By mid-August, *Rodney* was alongside in Antigua, where she went into refit and then sailed for Barbados, which she soon left. On Friday, 19 October, *Rodney* dropped anchor in the lower reaches of the Demerara river, which flows north for 230 miles from its source in the rain forests. She stayed there through the early autumn and into winter, as war clouds loomed ever more ominously on the horizon.

Wednesday, 30 January 1782 dawned fair, but a storm approached in the form of the French naval force. The *Rodney* was hailed by the *Oronoque*'s Commanding Officer, who told Lieutenant Brisbane of the enemy ships, which 'he supposed intended to attack the river at some time.'[13]

Brisbane called Lt Tucker over and 'ordered by him to go on shore and take charge of the fort …'

Not long after, it was decided it should be abandoned, with Tucker instructed to spike the guns, but before he could complete the task, he was hailed from *Rodney* and told to return to ship. An attempt to break out into the open sea was planned. The *Sylph* and *Henry* had earlier sailed out from the river to see if there was any chance of the British naval force making it, but the French were too well positioned. *Sylph* and *Henry* retreated and brought back gloomy news. There was probably a council of war where it was decided the best course of action was to surrender. On 31 January, Lieutenant Tucker's log noted that at 1 am *Rodney*

> *… weighed and made sail up the river in company with the* Oronoke [sic], Barbuda, Sylph, Stormont *and* Henry *… at 5 anchored … at 11 am a Flag of truce flew off from the* Oronoke [sic] *…*

On 2 February Lt Tucker was ordered to come on board *Oronoque* and, in the early hours, tasked with taking an offer of surrender to the French commander. Sent off in a boat under a Flag of Truce, at 8 am going on board *Iphigenie*, Tucker delivered the letter, two hours later receiving a verbal reply, then setting off back up the river. But, when he went aboard the *Oronoque*, Lt Tucker found two French officers already there, having arrived an hour before him. Subsequently, *Oronoque*'s captain and the governor of Demerara went down the river to agree final terms. Sunday, 3 February dawned fair but it was a black day for the Royal Navy as, at 10 am, Tucker was told by Brisbane that capitulation of British naval forces had been agreed, with *Rodney*'s guns to be discharged and secured.

Admiral Rodney gained revenge for the taking of Demerara by defeating a Franco-Spanish fleet at the battle of The Saintes, on 12 April 1782, so ending the enemy's dreams of conquering further British colonies in the Caribbean. Rodney deployed the tactic of cutting the enemy line that would reach its apex when used by Nelson at Trafalgar more than two decades later. But, what of *Rodney*'s Brisbane and Tucker? Their lives were but footnotes of British naval history, forgotten in the shadows of great victories like The Saintes. Neither man was destined to reach a ripe old age.

Released from captivity, Lieutenant Brisbane was put aboard one of the French warships taken as prizes at The Saintes, the captured vessels sailing for Britain in company with a large convoy of merchant ships in July 1782. By mid-September, they were off the Newfoundland Banks, hit by severe gales for three days during which the *Ville de Paris*, French flagship at The Saintes, sank with the loss of all but one sailor and *Glorieux* went down with all hands. The *Rodney*'s Lieutenant Brisbane was among those drowned. Following his release from captivity Lieutenant Tucker returned to his unspectacular career in the Navy, getting married in December 1784 and not receiving promotion to Commander until February 1796.[14] He died four years later.

The third *Rodney* of this story – the first 'official' vessel of the name – was a 74-gun third-rate ship of the line built by the private shipyard of William Barnard, on the River Thames, close to Deptford Royal Dockyard.

During an active warship construction life of some thirty-nine years, Barnard's Deptford Green Yard, established in 1780, built twenty-six warships and a dozen East Indiamen. The *Rodney* was one of eight 74-gun ships constructed by Barnard, a type for which it had a good reputation.

Among them was the legendary HMS *Orion*, which saw action in the battles of the Glorious First of June (1794) Cape St Vincent (1797) and Trafalgar (1805).

The 1,754 tons third-rate *Rodney* was ordered by the Admiralty Board on 28 May 1808,[15] for, despite the victory at Trafalgar nearly three years earlier, the French naval threat remained acute, particularly as the potential building capacity of shipyards under the sway of Napoleon remained even greater than Britain's. To retain dominance of the oceans the Royal Navy needed supremely useful 74-gunners and so private yards like Barnard did well. The amount of wood devoted to constructing a ship like the 74-gun *Rodney* would make a modern-day conservationist weep, for 3,000 full-grown oak trees were used in the hull alone.[16] Despite a heavy workload, Barnard completed *Rodney* in the remarkable time span of just 20 months. The new *Rodney* was launched on 8 December 1809, more than 17 years after Rodney the man had passed away.

The progression from humble cutter to a line-of-battle-ship, reflected the rise of the Admiral's renown, for good or ill. It was no doubt hoped the name *Rodney* would indicate a good fighting spirit, rather than reflect the more controversial aspects of Rodney's personality and reputation. After his success at The Saintes, Admiral Rodney was called home from the West Indies and dismissed from his post by a new government keen to show the country it meant to make up for the disastrous conduct of the war to retain America. When the success of The Saintes became widely known, and acclaimed throughout Britain, Rodney was given the freedom of many towns and cities, awarded the thanks of both the Commons and Lords, was made Baron Rodney of Stoke-Rodney and received the considerable pension of £2,000 a year. However, his financial difficulties pursued him into his retirement and he died on 24 May 1792, with debtors snapping at his heels.

As *Rodney* was being fitted out, rigged and also equipped with her weapons, and while her press gangs were scouring ports looking for sailors, many hundreds of miles to the south, British involvement in the Iberian Peninsula was hotting up.

Napoleon was attempting to use the Continental Blockade to shut European ports to British trade, from the Baltic to the Mediterranean. However, the British Army was not large enough to contest Napoleon's might on land across several theatres. It had become clear, despite the disastrous retreat from Corunna in January 1809, which saw the Royal Navy lift thousands of troops off the beaches – a forerunner of Dunkirk 130 years later – that Spain and Portugal still offered the best means of sapping the strength of the French Army and destroying the myth of Napoleon's invincibility.

The warships that saw service in support of Wellington's army in Spain were true practitioners of what today is referred to as littoral warfare. By dominating waters just off the shore they were able to keep land forces supplied and leapfrog enemy obstacles by taking troops up and down the coast. British warships also influenced events on land directly through bombarding enemy forts, cutting sea lines of communication to Napoleon's troops, and supporting isolated pockets of friendly forces. Transport of troops by sea, and their re-supply, was so much swifter, less dangerous and wearing, than using the often atrocious roads of the Iberian interior. Meanwhile, the Royal Navy denied the French every advantage offered by the sea and forced them into an ineradicably hostile terrain where Spanish guerillas picked at their entrails like voracious vultures.

The *Rodney* was by the early summer of 1810 at Plymouth, with orders to join the Mediterranean Fleet and, in preparation for her first voyage into a war zone, was receiving stores and also taking aboard impressed men to bring her complement up to its full strength of 700.

Among those delivered to her was eighteen-year old Joseph Bates, a young American who had already seen many adventures since first going to sea as a cabin boy in 1807. From the moment he stepped aboard, Bates found his card was marked by *Rodney*'s First Lieutenant, who had received reports of his several escape attempts. The officer glared at him and growled: 'Scoundrel.'[17]

The Commanding Officer of the *Rodney*, Captain Bolton, warned his boat's crews they would be flogged if they allowed Bates anywhere near their craft, in case he tried to escape again. The new batch of pressed men went down to dinner but a few hours later many of them, including Bates, were ascending *Rodney*'s rigging to unfurl sails. On sailing from Plymouth, *Rodney* set course down the Channel, to join the Mediterranean Fleet on its blockade station in the Gulf of Lyons, off Toulon. *Rodney* first stopped at besieged Cadiz, joining eight other British warships supporting the Spanish fleet[18] with the objective of assisting the host nation's vessels to set sail for Gibraltar where they were to be refitted, having been virtually confined to port since Trafalgar. Bates was sent to one of the Spanish ships, the *Apollo*, with 49 other sailors from the *Rodney*. After her refit at Gibraltar, *Apollo* set sail for Port Mahon, on the island of Minorca, which was once more being used by the Royal Navy as its main support base for the blockade of Toulon. Bates made another unsuccessful bid to escape, giving up and returning to the ship after finding he could not get off the island. He escaped flogging because officers in the *Apollo* were impressed that he returned voluntarily, but Bates soon rejoined *Rodney*, at Gibraltar.

In October 1810, an Anglo-Spanish force tried to take the fort at Fuengirola, which was held by Polish troops fighting for Napoleon. It was hoped this would entice the French garrison at Malaga to sally forth, enabling an attempt to recover that important port, but it all went horribly wrong, with the Poles refusing to surrender. Lord Blayney, commander of the landing force, was overjoyed to see a magnificent 74-gun British warship cresting over the horizon.

> *At this moment His Majesty's ship* Rodney, *with a Spanish line of battle ship, appeared off the coast, and I learnt that they had on board the 82d regiment, one thousand strong, which had been sent from Gibraltar to reinforce me; my anxiety to receive them was of course very great, and boats were immediately sent off to assist in landing them.*[19]

Blayney went aboard *Rodney*, to dine with her captain and discuss plans for taking the fortress. The following day *Rodney* and other warships were moored broadside on to the shoreline, so their cannons could bear on the enemy positions. Polish cannon balls were soon whistling through *Rodney*'s rigging and there was some hesitancy among her topmen, who did not go up to furl the sails quickly enough for the officers' liking. Because of such tardiness, *all* seamen were 'ordered aloft, and there remained exposed to the enemy's shot until the sails were furled.'

> *While in this condition, a single well-directed shot might have killed a score, but fortunately none were shot ...*[20]

The *Rodney*'s 32-pounder guns spoke, belching flame and smoke, but the ebb and flow of battle placed British and Spanish troops in the line of fire, so she stopped her cannonade. The British lost the initiative altogether and were hurled back, with the hapless Blayney taken prisoner. When this happened Spanish and British troops fled down to the shore. Boats brought the dead and injured out to *Rodney*, the slaughter having lasted from 2 pm to sunset; Bates and his shipmates were tasked with washing the blood out of the boats and hurling corpses over the side. Meanwhile, Blayney suffered the indignity of watching *Rodney* and the other vessels vainly bombarding the fortress in which he was now held prisoner.

> *I went on the rampart, from whence I had a full view of the shipping. The fort was still firing at the* Rodney, *and at the boats with the troops, which approached close to the shore. A few minutes would have brought them to my assistance, and they would certainly have changed the fortune of the day in my favour; but fate ordered it otherwise. While thus absorbed in my own melancholy reflections, I could not help exclaiming, as I*

> *looked on the* Rodney *and* Topaze, *there is the ship where a few days since I dined in social friendship, and there the frigate which brought me to this shore, rejoicing in the sanguine hope of serving my country; all on board then, are free, while I am doomed to pass an indefinite period in captivity, deprived of the society of all those who are dear to me in the world!*[21]

Rodney and the other warships withdrew and headed east, but a storm blew up, one vessel '... dashed to pieces on the rocks of the Island of Sardinia, and nearly every one of the crew perished.'[22] With the gale abating, *Rodney* joined the fleet off Toulon.

For a time *Rodney* was in Port Mahon, as flagship of Rear Admiral Thomas Fremantle, one of Nelson's legendary 'Band of Brothers' who fought alongside England's greatest naval hero at both Copenhagen, in 1801, and Trafalgar, in 1805. Fremantle had been made Rear Admiral in 1810 and yearned for action, having been ashore for some years. He joined the Mediterranean Fleet under the command of Admiral Sir Charles Cotton, who regarded his subordinate as a dangerous talent to be kept in check. In early 1811 Fremantle expressed fears that Minorca was weakly garrisoned by the Spanish and could easily be taken, leaving the fleet off Toulon without proper support. Cotton decided that, as his subordinate was so concerned, he may as well have command of Port Mahon, and that is how Fremantle came to transfer his flag into *Rodney* from the 110-gun *Ville de Paris.*[23] Fremantle was happy to receive an independent command and especially grateful to be away from his boss,[24] writing home from *Rodney* to his wife:

> *Cotton is incapable of governing this fleet.*[25]

Fremantle, as was the custom, took a select group of supporters into *Rodney*, including all the officers of the *Ville de Paris*, a band, plus sailors to man small boats, in all sixty people.[26] Orders soon began to fly out from *Rodney*, providing the jump-start needed to get the island's dockyard working at a higher pitch, so it could begin refitting some of the fleet's weatherworn ships.

Essential supplies were dispatched to ships on station off Toulon and when Spanish naval stores from Cadiz and Cartagena arrived, to ensure they did not fall into the hands of the encroaching French, Fremantle hammered out a deal to buy them. Of major concern was the fact that 300 of the 600-strong Minorcan garrison were French prisoners persuaded to serve in Spain's Walloon Guards. In *Rodney* Fremantle brooded on the matter and wrote to Cotton that the Walloons 'seem daily to be more disinclined to the English and I cannot too strongly impress upon you the importance of this place which can be carried by a Coup de Main.'[27] But the danger passed and Fremantle left *Rodney* in August 1811, sailing in the new 74-gun HMS *Milford* to become Britain's chief naval representative at the Neapolitan court in Sicily. Ultimately, he commanded British warships during a successful campaign in the Adriatic, after a period in home waters returning to the Mediterranean as Commander-in-Chief, but dying at Naples in 1819, aged fifty-four.

William Henry Smyth, grandfather of the founder of the Scouting movement, Lord Baden-Powell, joined *Rodney* in the summer of 1811. Prior to this Smyth achieved renown when he transferred from *Milford* to command a Spanish gunboat in defence of Cadiz.[28]. It was probably for this excellent work that on 14 December 1811 Smyth was promoted to Master's Mate. This remarkable twenty-three year old sailor, who was destined to be a noted hydrographer and an admiral, possibly used his time in *Rodney*, as she cruised off Spain throughout 1812, to collect data for charts still used by mariners as recently as 1961.

At least three of *Rodney*'s sailors had fought in HMS *Victory* at the Battle of Trafalgar. They joined *Rodney* at the beginning of August 1811, like Smyth drafted from *Milford* before the latter sailed for Sicily carrying Fremantle. It is likely they were switched for men the admiral wanted to take with him. *Rodney*'s Trafalgar trio were: Gunner's Mate John Brown, from Ireland, in his thirties; Thomas Sedgwick, from Sunderland, County Durham, in the north of England, a Quartermaster's Mate in his forties; Charles Thomas, in his mid-thirties, from Boston, America, who became a member of the *Rodney*'s Carpenter's Crew.[29] Fellow American Joseph Bates was, meanwhile, getting into trouble again, this time for hanging trousers up to dry behind *Rodney*'s maintop sail after his daily laundry. The ordinary sailors were required to present themselves in pristine smocks and trousers, but, with only three changes of clothes a week, and not enough time each day to wash and dry clothes before inspection, it was a tall order to avoid punishment for appearing in soiled garments. Therefore, Bates had the bright idea of hanging his clothes out in the breeze where they would dry in double quick time. However, the sail was furled sooner than expected, the enraged First Lieutenant demanding:

> ... *whose trowsers* [sic] *are these found hanging in the maintop?*[30]

Not wanting to see his shipmates punished, Bates owned up. Receiving a savage telling off, he narrowly avoided a beating but was put on the so-called 'black list' for six months, which involved shining brass and iron work, plus carrying out other demeaning chores on top of daily routine. It all had to be fitted into time usually spent resting off watch or sleeping.

> *There was no punishment more dreaded and disgraceful.*[31]

Two years on from leaving London, *Rodney*'s officers decided it was time to refresh her reserve water supply, as down in the deepest part of the hold were casks filled from the Thames, not yet touched.

Young Joseph Bates was there when the bungs were removed, seeing his shipmates set light to the foul air that came out with a candle and recalling, 'it would blaze up a foot high, like the burning of strong brandy.'[32]

According to Bates the water was perfectly clear, the sediment having settled a long time ago. Some of it was drawn off and poured into glass tumblers for *Rodney*'s officers to taste. One of them held his tumbler up to a lantern and pronounced it 'the purest and best of water'.[33] Bates thought it tasted good, but he couldn't help wishing he was drinking from the pure springs of Vermont or New Hampshire.

When it came to refreshing the minds of *Rodney*'s men, those that could read availed themselves of books from the ship's portable libraries, which averaged two volumes for every ten men. Reading was allowed on every day except Sunday, which was reserved for a church service starting at 11 am. Bates, a born and bred Presbyterian, saw the prayers of *Rodney*'s sailors and marines as pure hypocrisy:

> ... *how little their hearts were inclined to keep the holy law of God, when almost every other hour of the week, their tongues were employed in blaspheming his holy name; and at the same time learning and practicing the way and manner of shooting, slaying and sinking to the bottom of the ocean, all that refused to surrender ...*[34]

The most notable encounter at sea for this *Rodney* came in the middle of a gale on 15 January 1812, when a ship was spotted off Cape Sicie, in the Gulf of Lyon, and the battleship set off in pursuit. Meanwhile, two British frigates – *Apollo* and *Alcmene* – were using subterfuge to patrol close to the coast, flying French colours. Mistaking these two men 'o' war for friendly vessels, the fleeing ship sought their protective custody, only to be boarded. All this commotion alerted the French to something untoward and they ordered out a dozen of their line-of-battle ships from Toulon. With *Apollo* and *Alcmene* in the process of snaring their prize, *Rodney* stoutly hove to and barred the path of on-coming French warships, which, seeing a British battleship standing in their way, decided the situation was not worth a fight and returned to port.

With extra manpower available, and carrying the senior officer, it was *Rodney* that put a crew aboard the prize, which was sailed to Port Mahon.

Later that year a severe storm battered *Rodney* badly while on station with the fleet in the Gulf of Lyons, Bates and his shipmates fearing the worst.

> *For a while it was doubted whether any of us would ever see the rising of another sun. These huge ships would rise like mountains on the top of the coming sea, and suddenly tumble again into the trough of the same with such a dreadful crash that it seemed almost impossible they could ever rise again.*[35]

Ten ships of the fleet were badly damaged, including *Rodney*, her captain instructed to take her back to Britain for repairs.

Her men were overjoyed – going home meant they would finally receive their pay and be allowed twenty-four hours leave ashore, many dreaming of roistering and whoring in the taverns of Plymouth. Bates, on the other hand, fantasized about finally escaping servitude in the Royal Navy. However, as the *Rodney* prepared to sail for Britain from Port Mahon, fifty of her sailors, including Bates, were called forward and told to get their things together, as they were transferring into the 74-gun HMS *Swiftsure*. She had just arrived and would in all likelihood serve three years on the Mediterranean station. Bates was plunged into utter despair:

> *I was doomed to drag out a miserable existence in the British navy.*[36]

Bates remained in *Swiftsure* until the war between Britain and America, provoked in large part by the former's habit of pressing the latter's citizens into service in the Royal Navy, broke out. He became a Prisoner of War in 1812 and, after incarceration in a prison ship, then Dartmoor, eventually arrived home in the USA, on 15 June 1815. A career as a merchant service captain followed, before Joseph Bates devoted himself to carrying out God's work, taking part in the anti-slavery movement and helping to found the Seventh-day Adventist Church. He died in 1872 at the age of eighty.

By 1814 *Rodney* was flagship for Vice Admiral Sir George Martin, Commander-in-Chief Lisbon. Her commanding officer was Captain Edward Durnford King, who had distinguished himself while in command of the frigate HMS *Endymion*, encountering the Franco-Spanish Combined Fleet off Cadiz in 1805 prior to Trafalgar, but escaping destruction by pretending to signal a Royal Navy force astern of him. In November 1814 Captain King was appointed to the 74-gun *Cornwallis*, but ill health forced him to resign his command and return home. *Rodney* returned to Britain with other ships of the fleet following the abdication of Napoleon in April 1814. Thirteen years later she was renamed *Greenwich*, so her previous name could christen a new vessel. The Napoleonic-era *Rodney* (now *Greenwich*) was decommissioned and sold off in 1836, ending a career in which she experienced no pitched battles at sea, but had played her part in maintaining pressure in the Iberian Peninsula, so helping to bring the little French Emperor down.

Notes

1 Some naval officers in the Georgian Royal Navy were allowed to take their wives to sea.
2 Geoffrey Callender, *Sea Kings of Britain.*
3 Peter Trew, *Rodney and the Breaking of the Line.*
4 Royal Naval Museum, *Information Sheet No. 19, George Rodney.*
5 *The Commissioned Sea Officers of the Royal Navy 1660–1811*, edited by David Syrett, R.L. Dinardo.
6 *Complete Navy List.*
7 To this day the historic link between Saltash and George Rodney, its former MP, is marked in the town by having a pub named The Rodney. Northamptonshire, meanwhile, has The Admiral Rodney pub, at Long Buckby, marking its own links with the great man's political career. There are numerous other pubs named after Admiral Rodney dotted around England.
8 Admiral The Hon Augustus Keppel was court martialed in early 1779 due to accusations of cowardice in battle by Vice Admiral Sir Hugh Palliser. Keppel was cleared and many other senior naval officers, who were outraged that he had even been charged, refused to serve at sea.
9 *Steel's List of the Royal Navy*, January 1783.
10 *The Commissioned Sea Officers of the Royal Navy 1660–1815.*
11 David Lyon, *The Sailing Navy List.*
12 National Maritime Museum, Navy Board Lieutenant's Logs, *Rodney* 1781–1782.
13 Ibid.
14 *The Commissioned Sea Officers of the Royal Navy 1660–1815.*
15 John E. Barnard, *Building Britain's Wooden Walls.*
16 Robert J. Winklareth, *Naval Shipyards of the World, From the Age of Sail to the Present Day.*
17 *The Autobiography of Elder Joseph Bates.*
18 *The Naval Chronicle, Volume IV*, Edited by Nicholas Tracy.
19 *Lord Blayney's Narrative, Volume I, Chapter II.*
20 *The Autobiography of Elder Joseph Bates.*
21 *Lord Blayney's Narrative, Volume I, Chapter II.*
22 *The Autobiography of Elder Joseph Bates.*
23 A new three-decker built by Chatham Dockyard in the 1790s and named after the French flagship at The Saintes.
24 Ann Parry, *The Admirals Fremantle 1788–1920.*
25 Ludovic Kennedy, *Nelson and His Captains.*
26 Ann Parry, *The Admirals Fremantle 1788–1920.*
27 Ibid.
28 *Dictionary of National Biography.*
29 National Archives and also John D. Clarke, *The Men of HMS Victory at Trafalgar*, but this latter publication lists Thomas as coming from Boston in the UK.
30 *The Autobiography of Elder Joseph Bates.*
31 Ibid.
32 Ibid.
33 Ibid.
34 Ibid.
35 Ibid.
36 Ibid.

Chapter Two

AN EXECUTION AT MALTA

Steam propulsion for warships, along with breech-loading guns firing shells, possessing huge range and incredible accuracy, would eventually consign the wooden sailing ship to the dustbin of history, but not just yet. In the late 1820s the navies of the world were not sure those technological innovations were advanced enough to warrant abandoning a design of warship that had for centuries ruled the waves.

The fourth *Rodney* was therefore a 92-gun second-rate wooden wall line-of-battle ship designed by Sir Robert Seppings, Surveyor of the Navy since May 1813, and a former master-builder at Chatham. This *Rodney* was christened at Pembroke Dock in June 1833, having been on the stocks since 1827 in order to allow the weather to season her frame. She was the first British two-decker man 'o' war to carry more than 90 guns, her design being 'the culmination of the art of wooden shipbuilding'.[1] Fitted out at Plymouth, *Rodney* was sent to the Mediterranean, setting sail in September 1835 under the command of Captain Hyde Parker, who came from a distinguished naval family.

Her stated complement was 720, but *Rodney* usually carried 677 (484 adult sailors, 47 boys and 146 Royal Marines), most of her sailors coming from the south-west of England.[2]

The *Rodney*'s Commanding Officer had been a Midshipman in the 32-gun *Narcissus* as long ago as 1801. Hyde Parker lingered as a captain for twenty-eight years prior to commanding *Rodney* because, in the wake of the Napoleonic Wars, with the Navy shrunken, and so many elderly admirals clogging up the system, promotion was hard to come by, as were sea commands. Therefore, Parker was extremely grateful to be appointed to *Rodney* on 19 August 1835. A few weeks later he took her out through Plymouth Sound to the open sea. *Rodney* arrived off Barcelona on Boxing Day 1835, with orders to act as a guard ship for British interests and citizens at a time of civil war in Spain. In March 1836, *Rodney* sailed for a maintenance period at Port Mahon, returning to watch over Barcelona in mid-April. Throughout the next year or so she spent much of her time at anchor off the Catalan city, waiting for the call to action.

Staining *Rodney*'s time in the Mediterranean would be the execution of a Royal Marine named Thomas McSweeney, from County Cork, in southern Ireland. He was twenty-one years old when he joined *Rodney* in September 1835, from 79 Company, Royal Marines of the Plymouth Division. It was while *Rodney* was at anchor off Barcelona, on 16 July 1836, that a fateful incident, which led to McSweeney hanging from *Rodney*'s yardarm, took place.

The marines were hoisting the ship's pinnace inboard and Lance Serjeant James T. Allen, a twenty-four year old from Kent, noticed McSweeney was absent from the upper deck working party. Going below at around 7 pm, he found the missing marine slinging his hammock, in preparation for turning in later.

It seems there was already bad blood between the two and McSweeney was hauled before *Rodney*'s executive officer, who told him to wait nearby in the custody of a sentry until there was an opportunity for formal charges to be laid. Allen exchanged words with McSweeney who, in turn, told the Lance Serjeant he had been reported wrongly – something the NCO angrily denied. The Irish marine's own anger boiled over and he rushed Allen, pushing the NCO into the ship's waist. It was a drop of just 6 ft, but unfortunatelyAllen fell on his head. Restrained by fellow marines, McSweeney was told by *Rodney*'s Gunner:

You'll be hanged for that you blackguard.[3]

Five days later Allen died from his injuries in *Rodney*'s sickbay and was buried at sea the following morning. On 1 August Captain Hyde Parker requested a court martial for McSweeney, writing to the Commander-in-Chief of the Mediterranean Fleet, at Malta. Clapped in irons, McSweeney was transfered from *Rodney* to the frigate *Childers*, which was sailing for Malta.

McSweeney's court martial took place over two days – Friday, 25 and Monday, 27 February 1837 – aboard the ship of the line *Revenge*, at anchor in Malta harbour. He was not provided with a lawyer, conducting his own defence and proving inadequate at cross-examining witnesses. Corporal William Johnson, one of *Rodney*'s Royal Marines was asked by the court martial panel if he believed McSweeney acted with malicious intent. He replied:

I think he did.

According to Lieutenant William R. Payne, McSweeney claimed Allen often called him an 'Irish bugger' and sneered at him. Lt Payne said McSweeney protested he 'led the life of a dog'. The court adjourned until the Monday, when McSweeney presented a written statement, which he asked Judge Advocate William Henry Brown to read out. The defendant claimed it had all been a terrible accident, but did admit to being provoked by Allen, who allegedly told him.

You bogtrotter, you are in for it now.[4]

McSweeney said he hoped 'it will not be supposed that I could be so desperately wicked as to wish to take away the life of a fellow creature purely for reporting me and calling me a name ...'[5]

Lt Payne and *Rodney*'s Mate, Mr Norman, spoke as witnesses for the Irish marine, revealing they found no fault with his character or conduct. It had already been ascertained McSweeney was sober when the incident happened. However, despite such mitigation, the court martial panel was unanimously of the opinion the charge was proved and 'adjudged the Prisoner to be hanged by the neck until he is dead.'[6] With no defence lawyer, it could be considered by modern standards that McSweeney did not receive a fair trial. It has been claimed his statement was actually written by one of the ship's officers[7] – certainly his minimal and ineffective cross-examination of witnesses suggests he may have been illiterate and probably none too bright.

The sentence was not carried out until the summer, with *Rodney*, which had been under refit at Port Mahon, arriving at Malta on 5 June. She dropped anchor in the centre of Grand Harbour, a spectacular amphitheatre for the forthcoming execution, with ships of the Mediterranean Fleet arrayed all around. At 5.15 am on 8 June, McSweeney was transferred to *Rodney* from HMS *Ceylon*, where he had been incarcerated temporarily. Such was the interest among Valetta's citizenry, they left their homes in the middle of a cholera epidemic to witness the hanging. Aside from battlements and buildings around the harbour being packed with spectators, the rigging of all the assembled warships was manned. A heavy, breathless silence fell:

> *Capt. Parker's voice, as he read the sentence and warrant ... was distinctly heard at some distance by the people in the numerous boats on the water.*[8]

McSweeney stood on a platform over hammock netting, receiving absolution, the noose already snug around his neck. The end of the rope, reaved through a block dangling from the yardarm, was held at its end by marines and sailors selected from each warship in the harbour. They waited for the signal to haul him up. As was the tradition when enacting capital punishment, armed boats were sent to surround *Rodney*. They had orders to fire if sailors and marines selected for the grisly job proved reluctant to carry out sentence.

> *Upon the firing of a gun, as soon as the warrant of execution was read, they launched the wretched man into eternity, by running him quickly up to the yardarm, a height of 60 or 70 feet. His death seemed to be instantaneous; for he had lost much of his strength from his long confinement, and a dread of his horrid end ...*[9]

For half an hour McSweeney's corpse turned in the breeze. Taken down, it was transported to the chapel of San Salvador, behind the Naval Hospital. In its edition of 14 June 1837 *The Malta Government Gazette* solemnly intoned:

> *May his crime meet with mercy at the Throne of Grace.*

McSweeney's grave is at Vittoriosa Churchyard, over the years becoming a place of homage for Roman Catholic pilgrims commemorating the many so-called wrongs inflicted by the English on the Irish.

> *A cult developed and devotees started showing their respect by lighting coloured glass oil lamps ... and placing them and flowers on his tomb.*[10]

McSweeney's ghost is said to linger by the grave and possess mystical powers – a childless couple who visited were allegedly blessed with twins after praying there.

Leaving the unfortunate McSweeney incident in her wake, *Rodney* departed Malta and headed west across the Mediterranean, where, for many more months, she loitered off the coast of Spain. An incident occurred, which involved another fall, but this time, on 5 August 1838, when *Rodney* was making a transit from Sardinia to Minorca, one of her sailors plummeted from the maintop yardarm into the sea. Without stopping to think, Master's Mate F.H. Stevens leapt in to save him. A boat was lowered and both men were brought safely back aboard, Stevens' bravery later being saluted with the Humane Society Award for 1838.

The *Rodney*'s first encounter with potential war service was in the Royal Navy's campaign against Egyptian forces threatening to overthrow the Ottoman Empire. An army led by Ibrahim Pasha, the son of Mehemet Ali, who ruled Egypt, invaded Syria in 1832 and proceeded to swiftly conquer it, threatening Constantinople, the Ottoman capital, but a Russian army was landed and faced it down. Hostilities broke out again in 1839, the Turks striking back by sending an army officered by Prussians to kick the Egyptians out of Syria, but the offensive failed. The situation required a close watch by the Royal Navy's Mediterranean Fleet, to prevent threats to trade and British strategic interests, especially after many ships of the Turkish fleet joined the rebels at Alexandria in July 1839. Egypt's own fleet was composed of well-built French warships with mediocre crews, but commanded by officers from France.

Among battle-hungry British sailors, there was some hope this force might make a break for the open sea, but it remained a slim one and nothing much happened. France had, not surprisingly, decided to back the Egyptians while Russia continued to support the Turks. Anxious not to come to blows, as seemed likely at one point, the British and French agreed to assemble a 'fleet of observation' in order to give the Egyptians pause for thought and ensure Russia did not monopolise influence with the Ottoman Empire. It was feared the Russians were seeking to expand west along the coast of the Black Sea and also sought greater access to the Middle East and beyond. *Rodney* was among warships in the 'fleet of observation'. In a letter to his brother in England, Private Charles Hankinson of the Royal Marines, a veteran of 16 years service, apologized for not writing before, but explained he had hoped to be home long ago, were it not for a tedious waiting game.

> *The Turkish Fleet are still in Alexandria, but if I had my will they should soon ... perish there.*[11]

By way of compensation, Hankinson explained he had sent a letter to their mother on 1 January, mailed back via the steam frigate *Gorgon*. It is hard for us in an era of instant communication to comprehend how distant even the Mediterranean could seem in the mid-nineteenth century. Letters took months to reach home and replies were equally long coming back, so perhaps a break in communication of three years was not so exceptional, especially if Hankinson was not terribly close to his brother, as was often the case in the 1800s, when families were large and life hard.

Rodney was in early 1840 lying at anchor in Vourla Bay, Gulf of Smyrna, on the eastern coast of Turkey. News of the court martial of fellow Royal Marine Thomas McSweeney had probably made the newspapers back home and was possibly mentioned in his brother's letter to him, but Private Hankinson claimed not to know. Perhaps his purpose was not to single out someone regarded as having been the worst kind of murderer. Or, could it be that he was simply ashamed of McSweeney's fate? Besides, there had been plenty of other miscreants.

> *... you say you saw an account of a court martial held on board this ship, but as we have had five courts martial since we left Malta I cannot tell which you allude to. The first was upon a Lieutenant of the* Talavera *who was honourably acquitted, the second upon the Chief Engineer of the* Confiance *who was dismissed the Service, the third was upon a Mate of the* Gaston *who is to serve two years longer at sea before he can be promoted. The fourth was upon an seaman of the* Powerful *who was sentenced to death and the fifth upon two seamen of the* Ganges *who were acquited. You must excuse me giving you more particulars on the subject.*

Acknowledging he knew of Queen Victoria's intention to wed the German Prince Albert – they married on 10 February 1840 – Private Hankinson told his brother that *Rodney* recently acted as guard ship for the Dowager Queen Adelaide when her yacht left Malta for a cruise. There was precious little else for Private Hankinson to report.

> *You will wish to know how our time is occupied ...*

He suggested British warships were occupied with doing nothing.

> *... for a very good reason because we have nothing to do, only keeping the ships stocked with water, which is done one day in a week, and every Friday we all go to General Quarters which is customary in the Navy ...*

His brother had obviously asked about the possibility of action against the Tsar's fleet.

> *... with respect to the Russians we have not seen any of them, but in answer to your question whether I think we could thrash them. I must say (from what I hear of their navy) that I have no doubt of it.*

With the letter sealed for sending back to Britain, Private Hankinson heard good news, scrawling on its outside that other warships of the fleet had sailed for home and *Rodney* might soon follow.

He added a note about an incident involving *Rodney*'s Launch, which a few days earlier was returning '... loaded with water, when on account of the strong gale that was blowing she could not make the ship.'

> *She filled and sank with 2 officers and 20 men who were all saved. The boats of the Squadron were very smart in rendering assistance.*

The loss of the Launch delayed his letter long enough for Hankinson to scribble yet more on the outside, explaining how he had to wait until the Ship's Barge returned to get it away to a vessel headed home. Hankinson signed off:

> *We are ordered home, do not write.*

In returning to Britain, *Rodney* missed her chance to play a central role in decisive action by the Royal Navy to resolve matters between Turkey and Egypt, but she would still be there at the latest attempt to resolve the 'Eastern Question'.

After a short refit *Rodney* was commissioned back into the Royal Navy's front line order of battle on 13 May 1840, under the command of fifty-four year old Captain Robert Maunsell, the third son of the Archdeacon of Limerick,[12] who had entered the Navy as a captain's servant in February 1799. Six years on the beach ended with his appointment to *Rodney*. On Thursday, 10 September 1840, the ship was unmoored at 4.30 am, sailing from Plymouth at 8.30 am, straight into heavy weather. By late September *Rodney* was at Gibraltar, where conditions were still inclement, but she found better weather as she neared Malta.

On 13 October *Rodney* sailed for Alexandria to join the Royal Navy squadron blockading the Egyptian naval port. Shortly after, *Rodney* headed for St Jean d'Acre, part of a group intended to reinforce a British naval force already there, as the Royal Navy was liberating key fortresses along the coast of the Levant from the Pasha's troops. On Monday, 2 November, in preparation for possible action, Captain Maunsell ordered that *Rodney*'s great guns, her 32pdrs, should be exercised and two days later the ship's log recorded:

> *9 [am]. Lowered boats. Tacked, fired great guns at cask.*[13]

Arriving on 6 November, *Rodney* exchanged signals with a steam warship, discovering there had been 'a great victory obtained by the Fleet at St Jean d'Acre with little loss.'[14] The British naval campaign had culminated in the bombardment of

Acre on 3 November, with 9,000 Egyptians killed, and 3,000 taken prisoner. On 9 November *Rodney* supplied *Benbow* and other British warships with provisions and embarked Egyptian prisoners, which were to be taken to Beirut. Ten days later she was back off Alexandria in company with *Revenge, Carysfort, Medea, Cambridge* and *Vanguard*, where, finally, a little excitement unfolded, as her log recorded:

> Medea *made the signal 'Ship on Fire'.*

At 9.00 am the *Rodney*'s boats took across buckets and people to fight the blaze in *Medea*, while those left behind wondered what had caused it.

> *12.30. Boats returned here, found a shell had exploded ... killing the Bombardier ... and the Master Gunner – wounded the Surgeon, the Commander and a Boy.*

On 21 November, Captain Maunsell, who had become friendly with the Pasha during a previous spell in the Mediterranean, was sent ashore from *Rodney* to negotiate with Mehmet Ali. The eccentric, but dynamic and brave, Commodore Charles Napier followed up Maunsell's meeting with detailed negotiations and a convention was signed on 27 November, in which the Egyptians agreed to withdraw from Syria, on provision that Mehmet retained control of Egypt.

On Saturday, 28 November, with *Rodney* still cruising off Alexandria, at 10.00 am her lookouts spotted *Revenge* making the signal 'Peace with Egypt'.[15] For taking part in this campaign, which officially lasted from 10 September to 9 December, *Rodney* was able to garner the Battle Honour 'Syria 1840'. A year on she was still in the Mediterranean off Alexandria and later at Malta. She headed for Gibraltar in late November 1841, but by summer 1842 was once more at Alexandria. And so, the routine duty of maintaining Pax Britannica continued year-in year-out.

By early 1845, *Rodney* was at Portsmouth under the command of sixty-two year old Captain Edward Collier. He had seen action against pirates in the early 1800s and was a lieutenant in the 36-gun *St Fiorenzo* when she fought the 32-gun French frigate *La Psyche* to a stand-still in a brutal encounter. After service on the Canadian Lakes in the War of 1812, Collier made Post Captain in November 1814, commanding the 42-gun HMS *Princess Charlotte*. His sea commands continued until the 1820s, but there was a break until he was appointed Commanding Officer of the 36-gun frigate *Castor* in early April 1837. The *Castor* was very active in the Syrian campaign, carrying out a number of raids and, during the bombardment of Acre, Collier was wounded. Paying off the *Castor* in 1841, he was ashore for more than three years before being appointed Commanding Officer of *Rodney*[16], which was fitting out at Portsmouth, having been brought forward from reserve, where she had been since returning from the Mediterranean. In 1845 *Rodney* was to be involved in a series of sea trials by an Experimental Squadron, provoked by concern that British warship construction, and with it the quality of Royal Navy seamen, had deteriorated to a dangerous degree. When the Navy Board was merged with the Admiralty Board in 1835, Seppings, the man who had designed *Rodney* using traditional criteria established over centuries, retired to Taunton, Somerset, and was succeeded by Captain William Symonds RN, who, until that time, had only successfully designed racing yachts, together with sloops and brigs for the Navy. He was a proponent of transferring the virtues of his smaller vessels – wide beam and an underwater section triangular in form – to ships of the line. The fact that he was not a professional naval architect, and was seeking to break decades of tried and trusted ship design, indeed rules that had protected Britain from invasion for many decades, upset a lot of people, not just naval architects who felt the scientific Seppings approach (evolving ships incrementally) had been discarded unfairly. The first of Symonds' ships of the line was HMS *Vanguard*, 78-guns, launched in 1835. There followed eight sister ships and also the *Albion*, 90-guns, and *Queen*, 110-guns.[17] Critics of Symonds' design doctrine suspected his ships would roll vigorously and be unstable gun platforms, no matter how fast they were. The British custom in fighting at sea had always been to close with an opponent and then, preferably at point-blank range, use the extraordinary rate of fire achieved by highly trained gunners to shatter the hulls of enemy ships. If warships rolled excessively, gunners struggling with heavy guns and cannon balls on pitching decks would find it difficult to keep up their rate of fire. Many of their shots might well be fired into the air, at best damaging an opponent's rigging and sails, and, at worst, falling uselessly into the sea. It had always been the custom of the French and the Spanish to fire at the sails and rigging of British ships and then run away. It was therefore outrageous to some observers that Symonds' (allegedly) faster, yet more unstable, ships now threatened to inflict the same habits on the Royal Navy. What mattered in battle was the tactical ability of British seamen to squeeze the most out of even the most unfavourable sailing conditions and it was still anticipated decisive naval battles would be fought at close quarters on the open ocean. Two divergent schools of naval architecture were not the only problem cleaving the naval establishment, for, with the abandonment of widespread deployment of the press gang, the Royal Navy, which had been cut from 149,000 men in 1815 to just 19,000 by 1818, clearly did not need quite the same number of seamen. It was forced to recruit those that it did require in competition with the merchant marine. But, not only were advertisements failing to attract the right calibre of sailor, Commanding Officers themselves conspired to reinforce a terrible state of affairs. They seemed to believe tall, strapping specimens of manhood, who would look good parading on the upper decks and manning rigging, were more worthy recruits than men whose chief attribute was skill as sailors.

In 1845, *Rodney* and other ships designed under Seppings, who had died five years earlier, were matched against ships of the new era, in the aforementioned Experimental Squadron. It conducted three cruises to settle which was better and was initially commanded by none other than Rear Admiral Hyde Parker, the *Rodney*'s former captain. Aside from *Rodney* of the old school, there was *Trafalgar* and *St Vincent*, both three-deck first rates, and *Canopus*, another two-deck ship of the line. The Symonds' ships were *Queen*, a first-rate, *Vanguard*, *Albion* and *Superb*, these last three two-deckers.

In its edition of 22 March 1845, *The Times* described the Experimental Squadron cruises as a 'nautical burlesque', claiming the Admiralty was determined to fix the outcome so the Symonds' ships would prove to be better than older pattern vessels. By 15 June 1845 the Experimental Squadron was assembled at Portsmouth, each ship taking aboard stores, stowed only in the proper spaces with nothing between decks, and also with a full war complement of sailors. Each vessel would be required, at the commencement of the first cruise, to provide reports on weight of masts and rigging, dry provisions, cannon balls, guns, fresh water and ballast. The draught of each ship fore and aft was recorded. Significantly, so *The Times* of 16 June reported:

Clinometers, instruments which register the ship's rolling and pitching, are supplied to each.

On 28 June *The Times* claimed the Admiralty was tipping the scales in favour of Symonds' ships.

If we compare Rodney *with* Canopus, Vanguard *and* Superb, *we find that* Rodney *has 575 tons more displacement than* Canopus, *and 752 more than either of the others. Here, then,* Rodney *has to drag 752 tons more through the water than* Vanguard, *and 575 tons more than* Canopus [a French-built ship captured as long ago as the Battle of the Nile in August 1798] *with the same area of sails. This is surely very much against the* Rodney *in summer winds and light weather, and it would not be very surprising if, under these circumstances, the* Rodney *were left behind.*

The *Times* suggested rather than short duration cruises in home waters during the most clement part of the year, the Experimental Squadron should be sent on a six-month deployment, fully victualled. It should stay at sea in the Channel, or elsewhere off the French coast, for the entire voyage, some of it in hard winter weather, much as British ships of the line had three decades earlier. A vessel that rolled excessively in such sea states would have less time on station to keep an enemy shut up in port, for sailors would not be able to stand such conditions for too long.

The Experimental Squadron sailed from Portsmouth on 15 July, calling at Cork from 7 to 18 September and then setting course for Plymouth, which it reached on 20 September.[18] Eight days later it left Plymouth under a new commander, Rear Admiral Samuel Pym, his predecessor having fallen ill. Back at Plymouth by 10 October, the third and final experimental cruise of 1845 involved only *Rodney* and other two-deckers, of both old and new design, departing port on 21 October – Trafalgar Day – and returning to Plymouth on 3 December. The task of commanding the squadron at sea now fell to the captains of *Canopus* and the *Vanguard*, no elderly flag rank officers having survived the rigours of even short cruises. In a race involving the entire eight-strong squadron, *Rodney* rose to the challenge of showing what her design was capable of, leaving all other ships far behind, for, with all her sails set, she displayed a spectacular 27,100 square feet of canvas.

She lay over, held by the wind. Great seas pounded her, but she shook them off, shivered and plunged ahead ...[19]

On hearing of *Rodney*'s exploits, Rear Admiral Pym was moved to observe in his official report that she 'beat the whole fleet.' Aboard *Rodney*, there was one young sailor for whom the October 21 toast to the 'Immortal Memory' of Nelson meant a great deal, for he was a blood relative of the legend: Thirteen-year old the Hon. Maurice Horatio Nelson, was one of *Rodney*'s midshipmen during the Experimental Squadron cruises. During his time in *Rodney*, Midshipman Nelson witnessed discipline doled out to sailors every bit as prone to wayward behaviour as those his illustrious forebear commanded with such humanity. During the first Experimental Squadron cruise, Nelson noted in his 'Midshipman's Log' that 22 August 1845 began at 7 am with the ship's sailors and marines assembled to witness punishment of 'John Grady AB with 24 lashes for drunkenness, Roberts AB with 36 lashes for also.'[20] The seeming inability of latter day Royal Navy sailors, whose seamanship skills had been questioned so keenly by *The Times*, to handle their work without blundering would not have improved the temper of *Rodney*'s Captain Collier, who was on the afternoon of 5 October (during the second cruise) forced to lower boats to pick up Able Seaman John Berry who had fallen overboard. As *Rodney* sailed down the Channel with the other squadron ships on 25 October there was another mishap, as Midshipman Nelson noted:

> *Richard Potter AB fell overboard from foreyard. Let go life buoy, saved man, lowered boat, picked up life buoy.*

On 28 October hammocks airing on the upper deck were lost overboard with 'one in number to be charged against the wages of William Moffat AB'[21], the hapless sailor who failed to secure them properly.

A sailor was killed in an accident aboard a few days later, Midshipman Nelson noting on 31 October: 'Committed body of John Drake AB to the Deep.' As she headed back to Plymouth at the end of November, two more of *Rodney*'s sailors were punished for indiscipline: 'James Hayes with 48 lashes and Henry Rooke with 24 lashes.'[22] Returning to Portsmouth, where she was to go into refit, on 2 January 1846 *Rodney*'s sailors shifted over to the hulk *Rattler* but a care-taker crew was left in the ship even after she went into dock. Unfortunately some of her sailors gave in to the temptation of strong drink, even though they were duty men, on 3 January Midshipman Nelson noting:

> *0.30 AM. Sent guard to relieve those in HMS* Rodney, *found guard drunk and corporal of guard fallen into dock. Sent to hospital.*

By the end of the month, all *Rodney*'s consumable supplies had been taken to storerooms in the dockyard. As it was feared the Devil might make work for idle hands, her men were employed bringing the ship of the line *Bellerophon* forward from reserve, making her fit for service in just three days. Fitting a ship for active service involved a mind-boggling amount of work, from arranging miles of rigging, to guns hoisted inboard and installed in their appropriate decks, with ammunition enough for a battle. The effort included yards being hoisted and sails hung, anchors and their chains brought aboard and fitted, together with supplies needed for the ship's complement to endure months at sea. By such efforts *Rodney*'s men convinced a dubious public that the modern sailor could at least aspire to equal his renowned forebears. After her refit at Portsmouth, *Rodney* embarked on further experimental cruises, this time with a 'Squadron of Evolution'. However, such experimental cruises proved very little for all the uproar they caused and Symonds began to fall out of favour with the Admiralty Board. Captains of warships involved were able to counteract any deficiencies in design and so ships more or less all performed the same. The Admiralty might not openly admit its dismay, and the skill of ship captains might disguise deficiencies, but the only true test would be war and perhaps the Admiralty preferred to rely on rules of ship design that beat Napoleon after all. A number of of Symonds' ships were altered in build to adhere to the old principles; those already in commission were in many cases modified to reflect the virtues of Seppings' work.[23] Faced with such a lack of confidence, Symonds resigned as Surveyor of the Navy in 1847. Meanwhile, *Rodney* had sailed for the

Mediterranean towards the end of 1846, still under the command of Collier, who also brought her back to British waters, paying the vessel off at Portsmouth on 8 March 1849. The *Rodney*, by then some sixteen-years old, was refitted and would within a few years fire her guns in anger for the first time. For the mettle of her men would be tested both afloat in the Black Sea and also in trenches before the Russian bastion of Sevastopol.

Notes

1 Lawrence Phillips, Vice-President, The Society for Nautical Research, in his chapter on Pembroke Yard published in the *Pembrokeshire County History Vol IV.*
2 Jack Snowden, *The Crime and Punishment of Thomas McSweeney.*
3 Ibid.
4 Ibid.
5 Ibid.
6 Ibid.
7 Ibid.
8 *The Malta Government Gazette*, 14 June 1837.
9 Ibid.
10 *The Times*, 2 November 1992.
11 National Maritime Museum, AGC/5/24, Letter by Hankinson, Charles, Private, Royal Marines, 1840.
12 Peter Davis, of Zeist in the Netherlands, runs an excellent web site on the Victorian RN, on which can be found biographical details of Robert Maunsell and other officers. See Sources.
13 National Maritime Museum, LOG/N/R/1, *Log of Her Majesty's Ship* Rodney *1840–42.*
14 Ibid.
15 Ibid.
16 Collier's biography can also be found on the web site run by Peter Davis. See Sources.
17 *Line of Battle.*
18 Series of reports from *The Times* concerning the voyages of the Experimental Squadron, as carried by the web site run by Peter Davis. See Sources.
19 C.R. Benstead, *HMS Rodney.*
20 National Maritime Museum, Midshipman's Log, Hon M.H. Nelson, HMS *Rodney* 92 guns 1845–1846.
21 Ibid.
22 Ibid.
23 *Line of Battle.*

Chapter Three

SO MANY BRAVE FELLOWS

Having started the decade with flag-showing and trooping duties, on one voyage taking several hundred soldiers to South Africa, in early 1853 *Rodney* was preparing to set sail for the Mediterranean. Joining her was a young clergyman, keen to broaden his horizons and do something more meaningful with his life. At 2 pm on 10 February, twenty-five year old Rev. Robert Hinds went aboard *Rodney*, sleeping onboard a ship for the first time in his life that night. In the morning, he went ashore to buy furniture for his cabin and *Rodney* sailed from Spithead at 8 am on 12 October, right into a severe storm that lasted all day. The bad weather continued as *Rodney* struggled across the Bay of Biscay but, by 17 February, she was in sight of the coast of Portugal and soon off Cape St Vincent. On 19 February, *Rodney* went through the Straits of Gibraltar, finally finding more favourable weather, the Rev. Hinds painting a lyrical picture in his diary, but it didn't last long:

> *Gloriously fine morning. Wind changed and now blowing right on our stern. A lofty range of mountains covered with snow in sight on the coast of Barbary, some of them above 6,000 feet above the level of the sea, going about 11½ knots an hour. About 4 o' clock came on to blow hard. At night it rose to a perfect gale. Became sea-sick for the first time. Went to bed soon after 6 o'clock but couldn't sleep for the rolling of the ship and the noise of things tumbling up and down. About 12 o'clock the hawse plugs had been washed out, and the sea came rushing in torrents. It was truly awful. Got up about half past 12 when the cry for all hands on deck was raised, rushed out of my cabin half dressed and escaped with difficulty to the bread store room, the only dry place in the ship.*[1]

Rodney experienced difficulty with steering, there was five feet of water in the hold and now it was all hands to the pumps. The Rev. Hinds went to bed again as the crisis passed, getting little sleep, the gale blowing into the next day. He provided a delicate description of throwing up:

> *Got up about 10 o'clock. Drank some porter and ate a little biscuit but was soon obliged to part with them.*

The weather improved, the ship got herself back into good order and by 28 February was at Malta. The Rev. Hinds did lots of sightseeing, also visiting a hospital to carry out pastoral duties, but most of all he enjoyed being on dry land.

There was by late April pressure for the Royal Navy's Mediterranean Fleet to send some of its ships to shore up the Turks against Russia, in a row over who had custody of religious sites in the Holy Land, itself a symptom of underlying tensions rather than a cause. The *Rodney* stayed at Malta until 8 June, setting sail for the Aegean at 7 am, the only ship not towed out of harbour, a real tribute to her sailors' seamanship.

Russia invaded the Danubian principalities of Moldavia and Wallachia in late July 1853 and there was concern that the Russians meant to launch an attack on

Constantinople. To counter Russia, the British, Ottomans and French assembled a joint fleet in Besika Bay, opposite Tenedos, just outside the Dardanelles. The British contingent was made up of seven ships of the line, including *Rodney*, and eight frigates. *Rodney* was under the command of Captain Charles Graham, a brother of the First Lord of the Admiralty, Sir James Graham. The Ottoman contribution was two battleships, four frigates and one corvette, while the French sent nine ships of the line. On 21 August Rev. Hinds wrote:

> *Saw a comet tonight, it appeared to be moving rapidly towards the verge of the horizon ... Does it portend something, and, if so, what?*

The Ottomans declared war in early October and for *Rodney* it could only mean action was not far off. She would be at the forefront of whatever transpired, for the Royal Navy was 'the main executor of Britain's foreign policy.'[2]

Three days after the Anglo-French naval force reached Constantinople, it emerged France and Britain had agreed an alliance with the Ottoman Empire, guaranteeing its security from further Russian aggression. It was anticipated blockades would be enforced in the Black Sea and Baltic, together with destruction of the enemy's fleets and bombardment of coastal forts, the Royal Navy functioning much as it had in the Napoleonic Wars. Britain's aim was to ensure the Russian Bear remained caged, with even more limited access to the open oceans and also no territorial expansion that might threaten India. Meanwhile, in *Rodney*, the Rev. Hinds celebrated his 26th birthday on 1 December, two days later a Turkish war steamer arriving with news of a terrible naval defeat at Sinope on 30 November. This dreadful reverse for the Allies needed a response.

Rodney was the first ship of the squadron to enter the Black Sea and behind her came *Britannia*, squadron flagship, with other ships of the line following on, namely *Albion*, *Vengeance*, *Sans Pareil*, *Agamemnon*, *Bellerophon*, *London*, *Queen* and *Trafalgar*. In mid-January 1854, the Russians were told any of their ships found at sea would be treated as hostile. Meanwhile, the Anglo-French fleet headed for Kavarna, a port approximately forty miles north-east of Varna. Following a declaration of war by Britain and France on 27 and 28 March, the first shots to be fired in anger by Allied warships came on 22 April, courtesy of nine vessels sent to stir things up at Odessa. Next, French and British steam warships tested the defences of Sevastopol, keeping their distance in glorious weather, with only a slight breeze to trouble them.

The Allies hoped the Russians would sally forth and do battle, on 29 April the Rev. Hinds noting:

> *Began to blow a little early this morning, and by daylight it had risen to half a gale. We all paraded before the walls of Sevastopol this morning with colours flying and every demonstration likely to tempt them out.*

In harbour were ten sail of the line, four steamers, three frigates and four corvettes, all counted by scouting ships, but the enemy remained reluctant to come out. May Day offered more beautiful weather, with the Allied ships hove to, small boats flitting from vessel to vessel either under sail or rowed by robust sailors. The Rev. Hinds observed 'the Crimea is in sight with its lofty mountains covered with snow', reflecting on the undertones that made this idyllic Black Sea scene so different from back home:

> *There the arts of peace and industry flow . . . here nothing but how to bring the enemy to action, and the shortest way of annihilating them, is thought of.*

In the meantime, rehearsals for the drama of war kept everyone sharp, disturbing the beauty sleep of *Rodney*'s Rev. Hinds. It was about 11 pm and he had just turned in when, suddenly, the drums beat out the call to Quarters. Everywhere throughout the ship sailors and marines tumbled out of hammocks, clearing the decks for action with utmost speed and efficiency so that, should the enemy fleet show itself, *Rodney* would give the Russian warships a pummeling.

Under pressure from the Austrians and a Turkish army, the Tsar's troops withdrew from the Danube and the Allies decided the best means of bringing down the Russian Bear was an attack on Sevastopol, both Allied armies and naval forces mounting a combined assault. By 1 July, *Rodney* and others were back at Kavarna, where a tragic incident marred a picnic on 7 July. The pleasant torpor of the picnickers was interrupted by 'loud cries for the doctor',[3] *Rodney*'s assistant surgeon running off to see what all the fuss was about. Soon, someone came back up with dreadful news. A young midshipman in the picnic party had accidentally shot a sailor crewing the boat that brought them ashore.

> [the bullet] *entered a little to the right . . . below the navel. We instantly packed up everything and made for the ship with all speed.*[4]

The unfortunate man was rowed back to the ship, but little could be done and, at noon, on 10 July, he died. But 'the fatal deed' was only the latest unsettling incident to afflict *Rodney*. Around the same time one of her sailors fell from aloft and, while he was deflected off some part of the ship, fell into the sea unconscious and disappeared, the man he brought down miraculously escaped with just cuts and bruises, bouncing off a boat on the upper deck.

The Allied commanders decided a reconnaissance of the Crimean coast should be conducted, to assess likely landing places. On 21 July, the British warships, accompanied by some French vessels, departed Kavarna, setting course for Sevastopol. The wind died away in the evening, with boats being lowered to take the ships in tow, but it soon picked up again and five days later, *Rodney* went close to Sevastopol, in an attempt to assess the strength of enemy batteries, for a landing close to the city was the favoured option. Her chaplain scrutinised the enemy citadel.

> *Towards evening when the sun shone full upon the place I had the best view of the shipping and harbour that has been yet afforded; we were tolerably close in and with the aid of telescopes were able to make out the number of guns on the several batteries commanding the main entrance . . .*

Sevastopol was protected by ten coastal batteries containing nearly 550 guns and, with an Allied assault plainly not far off, a further eighty guns were added. The 530 guns of the Russian naval vessels in the port would also come into play, either in a sally forth (unlikely) or anchored as additional batteries. Many in the Allied camp thought the forthcoming campaign would be a short one, with Sevastopol taken in a couple of weeks. Well-to-do citizens of Sevastopol came out to picnic on the coast, making a day out of watching British warships shuttling back and forth. The Allied scouting group sent a steam war vessel forward to present a calling card, the *Fury* firing an impudent rocket.

Rodney changed course during the night of 26 July and went to examine Balaclava Bay, to the south of Sevastopol. It looked quite inviting, the Rev Hinds' attention attracted by the Monastery of St. George, some five miles to the west of Balaclava itself. He noted on 27 July:

> *The land rises very abruptly from the water's edge ... there is a convent surrounded by beautiful gardens on the slope of the hill towards the water, and also a few houses, very clean looking.*

Further back from the shore, on high land, a Russian signal post sent signals down the coast, reporting the presence of an Allied warship.

Returning to Kavarna, on 31 July the body of the *Rodney* sailor brought down by his falling shipmate was discovered washed up on a nearby beach.[5] The Rev. Hinds ventured the poor man must have struck one of the lower gun ports, for the corpse 'presented a very shocking appearance, one side of the head was completely driven in, and one leg broken.'

With increasing numbers of British, French and Turkish troops waiting ashore, the unsuitability of that stretch of coast as a place to encamp thousands of men was becoming all too apparent. The French troops brought with them cholera and the squalid conditions of the camps were a breeding ground for its spread to warships. On 10 August, just three days after the Reverend Hinds noted the arrival of 6,000 French troops in the hills above, he recorded particularly grim news:

> *The dreaded disease cholera broke out in the ship this morning; it had been raging among the French ships to an alarming extent for some time.*

On 12 August the commander-in-chief of the British naval forces, Vice Admiral Sir James Whitley Dundas, took his ships to sea, in a bid to halt the march of cholera, but it failed and casualties still mounted. Four of *Rodney*'s men were claimed in one day and by 17 August seven had died. On 19 August a letter from the Commanding Officer of another British warship to *Rodney*'s Captain Graham revealed 105 men had expired due to cholera in the fleet flagship, *Britannia*; *Albion* had lost sixty; *Trafalgar* thirty-three.[6] The Royal Navy, with its traditional fanatical pursuit of cleanliness, could not tolerate this state of affairs and engaged in a campaign of eradication, which eventually succeeded, but not until death had enjoyed a rich harvest. For around a week after the British fleet returned to anchor at Kavarna, day and night there were boatloads of dead being taken away to be buried at sea. In all 302 British sailors and marines were claimed by cholera, some 130 of them from *Britannia* alone. The French lost close to 300 of their men to the disease.

The waiting for action was now at an end, the Allies unleashing their amphibious expedition of war against the Russians, the Rev. Hinds writing on 7 September:

> *Weighed this morning under canvas and are proceeding on our way to attack Sevastopol.*

The French embarked 24,000 soldiers and artillery, along with some cavalry; the British 22,000 infantry and the Light Brigade of cavalry; the Turks took 5,000 troops.[7] The British carried their troops in merchant transports, with a few in naval vessels, while the French and Turks stuffed their warships. The Allied fleets combined on 8 September but soon parted company, the French heading off towards Sevastopol, for another look at enemy defences. En route to the Crimea, Allied commanders constantly reviewed options for landing spots, ultimately choosing Calamita Bay. The town of Eupatoria was a dozen miles north of Calamita Bay and would also be seized. Soon *Rodney* was off the chosen landing beach and, on 14 September, the day after Eupatoria's surrender, troops began to disembark. The landings commenced in fair weather, but a heavy swell rolled in and made it impractical to continue, disembarkation of British troops and supplies not being completed until 18 September.

The drain on *Rodney*'s manpower by requirements ashore would characterize the forthcoming campaign. In a memorandum of 17 September 1854, Vice Admiral Dundas instructed that forty Royal Marines from *Rodney*, including a captain, two sergeants, one corporal and a drummer, as well as thirty-five privates, should go ashore 'for service at Eupatoria'.[8]

Meanwhile, Allied warships kept pace with the armies during their march along the coast of the Crimea, preserving their logistical lifeline and offering a means of escape if the worst case transpired. The guns of warships could also be brought to bear on the enemy's army during any battles. However, while the men in the ships witnessed the battle of the Alma, they made no significant contribution to its outcome. The Russians were shy of attacking during the landings, for fear of the naval guns. They preferred to place their army on the commanding heights above the river Alma, out of reach of floating firepower, forcing the Allied troops to attack uphill. The warships witnessed the 20 September clash, the Rev Hinds noting on that day:

> *One of those heavy Black Sea fogs with which we are so well acquainted came on this morning soon after breakfast and of course nothing whatsoever could be seen …*

At 10 am the fog cleared and *Rodney*'s men saw the armies rousing themselves.

> *… large bodies of infantry were seen moving along the beach towards the high ground occupied by the enemy.*[9]

Battle was not joined until after lunch, the troop formations having taken the entire morning to get into their starting positions, particularly the British, who were rather slow. Aside from *Rodney* and other Allied warships, spectators included civilians from Sevastopol, sitting on specially constructed stands overlooking the battlefield. From his vantage point on *Rodney*'s upper deck, the Rev. Hinds saw smoke erupting from artillery guns on both sides, then Russian and Allied infantry formations clashing. The day went in favour of the Allies, but at heavy cost. On 21 September, *Rodney*'s captain returned from a meeting in the *Britannia*, bringing news of the British casualties – 500 killed and 600 wounded. The *Rodney*'s men helped clear up the dreadful debris of war, with boats from each ship going in to evacuate the wounded to a troop transport that had been converted into a makeshift floating hospital. The Rev. Hinds reflected:

> *… it must be a very melancholy sight to see so many brave fellows laid low in so short a time!*[10]

Two days later the boats finally finished bringing out the wounded, with *Rodney's* returning officers and men telling of horrors they had witnessed:

> *... and the descriptions they give of the wounded and the amputations ... are something truly appalling.*[11]

The Allied naval force continued to hope the Russian fleet would emerge to do battle, enabling eradication of the principal threat to the supply lines of Allied land forces. During the battle of the Alma, the Allied warships could have sailed south to Sevastopol in an attempt to force the harbour, but naval commanders were unwilling to leave the armies without support. As the Allied armies resumed their march south, on 23 September, the Russians sank five of their ships of the line and two frigates in the harbour channel, thereby preventing Allied vessels from forcing their way into Sevastopol.

Clearly there was not going to be any fleet action at sea, so Allied commanders further denuded warships of men and now guns, which were sorely needed ashore, where cholera still thinned the ranks.

On 26 September Balaclava was taken, becoming the principal supply base for the British and, on 1 October, orders came to *Rodney* for some of her guns to be landed immediately. One hundred-and twenty men and officers, together with five 32-pdrs, were sent over to the *Sans Pareil* and taken into the port. *Rodney* was soon some 260 men short and would be sorely in need of their skills; for it was proposed the fleets should bombard Russian forts guarding the entrance to Sevastopol harbour. It was a mad plan, for it exposed the warships to extreme danger for little hope of a decisive result. The British fleet that bombarded Sevastopol on 17 October consisted of thirteen ships of the line (eight sail and five steam screw) and thirty-eight other vessels. The winds were light, the sailing ships relying upon steam-powered sloops and frigates lashed to their disengaged sides. Such was *Rodney*'s plight before the fury of the Russian guns:

> *Already short-handed through cholera, she had landed several of her guns and her best gunlayers to help the army, but the men left on board were well disciplined and she had excellent officers.*[12]

The ships fired on Fort Constantine and the Telegraph battery, the former being *Rodney*'s target, on the northern side of the harbour mouth, but the Russians managed to catch the French and British vessels in an effective crossfire.

At 2.10 pm *Rodney* fired her first gun, having been delayed due to so many ships jockeying for position. In the meantime, as the Reverend Hinds later revealed, *Rodney* endured the ministrations of Russian gunners.

> *For a long time before we opened fire shot and shells struck and damaged our hull and rigging, but fortunately no accident received to life and limb. We continued to pour in our fire whenever we could bring our guns to bear, but I fear from our great distance off we did not effect much destruction among the forts as we could have wished.*

The *Rodney* tried to provide covering fire for the inshore squadron, especially HMS *Agamemnon*, which was receiving a severe battering. However, *Rodney* ran aground on a shoal, her sailors not actually noticing in the cacophony of her guns thundering and shot hitting the hull. The Rev. Hinds described the moment:

> *About 4 o'clock we touched the ground while endeavouring to get closer in order to take off the heavy fire under which the* Agamemnon *was suffering. The Admiral (Lyons)* [Rear Admiral Sir Edmund Lyons, the deputy C-in-C of the British naval forces] *noticing this, sent up the signal 'well done* Rodney*' . . . The fire we managed to keep up was wonderful considering how few men we had on board at the time . . . things began to look very black with us. The enemy had got our range . . . the ship was on fire in three or four different places.*

The chaplain was nearly overcome by smoke while tending to wounded in the Orlop Deck. However, despite increasingly dreadful conditions, *Rodney* kept up her fire and, by running guns from her disengaged side forward, lessened the weight in her stern. She was extracted from her predicament by the steam warships *Lynx* and the *Spiteful*, which put across a tow. 'I came up about eight o'clock in the evening and had something to eat,' related *Rodney's* chaplain.

> *I was very tired and had a severe headache, having been at my quarters since half past one o'clock. All the time we were down below we could distinctly hear the heavy shots as they struck against our side. In the evening I went aboard the* Spiteful *to bury two poor men who had been killed during the day, one by accident at their own gun, and the other by a shot from the enemy. It is truly wonderful how we escaped with as little loss of life and limb. We had only two wounded . . . The Admiral could hardly believe the Captain in hearing his report of casualties next day, and asked if we were sure no men were suffering.*

Rodney was badly damaged but not as much as other vessels. For all their efforts the British ships did little damage to the Russian forts.

Such was the need for skilled gunners and extra infantry, increasing numbers of *Rodney*'s sailors ended up in trenches around the besieged Russian naval city. On 28 October 1854 it was noted by military chiefs that *Rodney* had by then sent ashore six 32-pdr guns with the men to man them and they were now part of a Naval Brigade of 3,316 officers, sailors and marines.[13] Twenty-five more men were contributed from each ship of the line and by 20 October the Naval Brigade had suffered 12 killed and 53 wounded. A total of 2,400 sailors and 2,000 marines, plus 65 officers and 50 shipwrights, were ultimately contributed by the Royal Navy to the effort ashore, with 140 guns landed. Sailors and marines were accustomed to making up for inadequacies in Army artillery and infantry, but, initially, the British Army commander in the Crimea, Lord Raglan, suggested sailors should be used as orderlies in the rear areas, to free soldiers for the front. Such was the impact of disease and attrition suffered, the Navy's men inevitably ended up in the thick of the action. The Naval Brigade fought at the Battle of Inkerman on 5 November 1854 and British sailors and marines would win four Victoria Crosses during the Crimean War. Among sailors from *Rodney* serving ashore in the Naval Brigade was twenty-seven year old William Hall, an Able Seaman from Canada who was the son of liberated American slaves. He had previously been to sea in merchant ships but in 1852 enlisted in the Royal Navy at Liverpool. Hall proved to be a brave fighter, receiving medals from both the British and Turkish military. After leaving *Rodney*,

Hall would achieve lasting renown while serving in HMS *Shannon*, winning the Victoria Cross by manning one of the ship's guns at the siege of Lucknow, during the Indian Mutiny.

On 14 November a great storm inflicted damage around the fleet, including a narrow escape for *Rodney*:

> *Our ships were in great danger, the* Marengo, *84, having drifted within half-pistol shot of the* Britannia's *hawse. A Turkish ship of the line cut her masts away, and was close to the* London, *and the wreck of her masts athwart the cables of the* Rodney.[14]

The gale lasted about 24 hours and the sea 'got up fearfully',[15] while at Eupatoria a number of transport ships were lost.

On 21 November, the Rev. Hinds reported *Rodney*'s Captain Graham was invalided home, the ship to be commanded by Captain King of the *Leander*. Ashore there were more casualties among *Rodney*'s men, but sometimes news was slow in coming.

> *On the 9th of this month a fine young officer, a mate belonging to this ship, was killed in the trenches on shore. His name was Karslake and is much lamented.*[16]

In late December Admiral Dundas resigned, the perception being he had failed through playing second fiddle to the armies. Dundas had been in the Navy since 1799 and, prior to his appointment as a Rear Admiral, was a Post Captain for thirty-four years. He was a kindly gentleman, not decisive enough for war command, while his successor, Lyons, was energetic and dynamic, although also of advanced years.

With the spring, a new campaigning season could open and the siege of Sevastopol sucked in even more men from the warships. On 13 April 1855 *Rodney* landed a further four officers and 200 men to reinforce the Naval Brigade at the request of Lord Raglan. Despite this hemorrhaging of manpower to the fight ashore, it was decided the navies should again bombard Russian defences, with *Rodney* among ships told to prepare for this new bombardment, which began on 9 April and lasted for several days[17]. The reasoning behind robbing *Rodney* of even more skilled gunners before such a task was that she would only be bringing one side of guns to bear; therefore crews from weapons that might otherwise be silent may as well bolster the effort on land. Admiral Lyons felt this was not the right way to do things – he preferred attacking Kerch, to cut the enemy's supply lines, hopefully starving the Russians into submission. On 3 April 1855 Lyons informed the Secretary of the Admiralty of the forthcoming bombardment – the dispatch was received on 17 April, the Admiral explaining the British squadron would be spearheaded by six line-of-battle ships, including *Rodney*. But he did not hold out much hope of success other than forcing the Russians to man their seaward-facing defences, so relieving pressure on Allied land armies. The Admiralty's response to hearing that he had sent ashore a further 200 seamen and officers from *Rodney* was to remind Lyons that his first duty was manning the vessels properly. When in May 1855 Lyons sailed in *Royal Albert* to lead a strike against Kerch, he left behind *Queen*, *London*, *Rodney*, *Inflexible* and *Spiteful* off Sevastopol to maintain the seaward flank. Meanwhile, the killing and maiming on land continued, with no decisive result, while at sea the glory of nature lulled everyone into a sense of peace, as *Rodney*'s chaplain noted:

> *Mayday. What a lovely morning! A nice light breeze so soft yet so cleansing coming in from the westward and the sea which yesterday was rolling in and breaking madly upon the beach is now as smooth and unruffled as heart could desire. Everything around seemed to rejoice in the beauty of this morning sun; even the singing of birds on the shore, especially the soaring lark, can be heard on board the ship; whilst the report of the guns, which we can see are being fired at Sevastopol, does not reach us to interrupt.*

On 18 June, the 40th anniversary of the Battle of Waterloo, some of *Rodney*'s men shed blood alongside the troops of the old foe, the auspicious day deliberately chosen by Allied land commanders for a big offensive, symbolizing how far the former enemies had travelled from that bloody Belgian battlefield. In *Rodney*, off the Katcha, the Rev. Hinds recorded another failure:

> *... this great sacrifice of life failed to gain for us the objective we had in view. The ships hovered about the mouth of the harbour but they did not go in and attack.*

Several of *Rodney*'s sailors were killed, and a number injured, during attempts to storm Russian forts, the British suffering around 1,500 casualties. The whole campaign seemed a catastrophe and people wondered what the generals would do to retrieve the situation, having laid siege to Sevastopol for nine months with no sign of its defences cracking. On 29 June, the Rev Hinds recorded that Lord Raglan had died, increasing the sense of gloom and yearning for peace.

> *May the war and the horrors that accompany it soon terminate, and may God grant that we, and those few that have survived of the original expedition, be released to return to our homes.*

On 22 July there was another outbreak of cholera, Rev. Hinds hoping it would be an isolated incident, but there was more sad news to report, this time from ashore.

> *We lost a young marine officer on the heights of Balaklava* [sic] *the day before yesterday ...* [He] *had been through the whole campaign. He fell a victim to fever, suffering an attack of diahorea.*

In mid-August the Allies conducted a savage bombardment but attacks on the Redan and the Malakoff forts, the principal strongpoints in the Russian defences, still faltered. It would not be long until Russian endurance was at an end. The French finally took the Malakoff on 8 September, the British failing to seize the Redan fort during the same assault. However, the Russians, feeling their position doomed, withdrew from the Redan, which the British discovered evacuated on the night of 8 September. At 5.30 am on 9 September, two of the other forts in the southern defences of Sevastopol were blown up, while, at 7 am, the last Russian crossed a bridge to take refuge in northern fortifications. Those of their warships that remained afloat in the harbour were destroyed by the Russians, as were the docks. On 10 September, *Rodney*'s chaplain went ashore with a naval medical officer to take a close look at Sevastopol, investigating what remained of Russian fortifications destroyed the previous day.

> *The stinking hot smell of powder was particularly offensive. An immense number of dead bodies of Russians, who had perished in the explosion, lay mangled around in every horrible variety of form. It was a shocking sight.*

There was burning debris as well as human body parts scattered in every direction. Later, men from the British warships picked through the devastation around the forts, town and dockyard 'most of them [bringing] back some little trophy or other.'[18]

Some of the vessels in the harbour were still on fire, the Russians were busy bolstering the north side of the city, where, it appeared, they planned to make a final stand. On 17 September a telegraphic communication was sent from the new First Lord, Sir Charles Wood, to Rear Admiral Lyons, instructing the latter that, provided the generals did not object, he could re-embark the Naval Brigade sailors in their ships. He was also instructed to send *Rodney*, *Niger*, *Wasp*, *London* and *Albion* to Malta.

On 6 October the Rev. Hinds recorded his ship's release from duty off Sevastopol, which had finally surrendered at the end of September, *Rodney* receiving a sentimental send-off as she set sail for Constantinople. Passing under the fleet flagship's stern, *Rodney* was 'greeted by three lusty cheers from that ship's company, her band at the same time striking up "Should old [sic] Acquaintance".'

The light breeze bore *Rodney* away at a stately four knots and five days later she reached Constantinople, but was soon on her way again. By 20 October she was passing Cape Matapan, and reached Malta on the 24th. *Rodney* received orders for home, the Rev. Hinds celebrating his twenty-eighth birthday at sea on 'a nice mild autumn day'. However, the ship hit bad weather that lasted for days, making it difficult for her to make enough headway, on 13 January *Rodney*'s chaplain recording the misery and frustration of the passage:

> *We are no nearer Spithead today than we were this day* [last] *week. I question very much whether we have held our own. Today the motion is so great and so disagreeable that there is to be no divine service.*

The following day he called on the Almighty to intervene.

> *But oh! Such a night...it was next to impossible to sleep; I, however, managed to induce ... God to extend his influence.*

His prayers were partially answered, the wind dropping but the sea remained very lively. However, on 15 January the Rev. Hinds noted gladly:

> *Hurrah! A fine fair breeze has sprung up, and our head is once more turned in the right direction.*

Following her return, *Rodney* was one of the stars in a Fleet Review held to mark the triumph of Allied arms over Russia. She then sailed to Chatham to be rebuilt around a steam engine and was launched again in January 1860. During the Crimean War, *Rodney* displaced 2,626 tons, but now was 2,770 tons. She discarded twenty of her guns to accommodate the steam engines. Sent to the China Station, *Rodney* oversaw consolidation of British trading influence in the Far East. In autumn 1868 there were attacks on Christian missionaries in China, so *Rodney*, acting as flagship of Vice Admiral Sir Henry Keppel, was sent up the Yangtze to Nanking with a squadron of small vessels, to exact guarantees from Chinese authorities that protection would be provided. *Rodney*'s sailors were in a landing party under her Commanding Officer, Captain Algernon Heneage. The *Rodney* had prior to this seized a gunboat called the *Tien Chi*, which was held hostage to gain leverage on the Chinese. In January 1869 *Rodney*'s sailors and marines were in another landing party, sent to punish piratical villages on the River Han. Men belonging to these communities had attacked the gunboat *Cockchafer*, resulting in eleven British sailors being wounded. *Rodney* was in refit at Hong Kong, so the flagship's men were sent up river in another vessel to exact revenge. Several villages were burned and 88 villagers were killed or wounded, while the British landing party suffered five wounded in skirmishes. The *Rodney*, by then the last British wooden battleship in sea-going commission, was relieved as flagship and sailed for home, paying off at Portsmouth in late April 1870. She was sold out of the Navy in 1884[19], so ending an active and globe-girdling fighting life of fifty-one years.

The next *Rodney* was one of six Admiral Class ships, the majority of them named after notable flag officers from Britain's glorious naval past. An all-steel vessel, she was built at Chatham and launched in October 1884, with a displacement of 10,300 tons and complement of 430. The last battleship to incorporate a figurehead,[20] her cruising speed was just over eight knots. A forerunner of the Admirals, HMS *Captain*, capsized because of her low freeboard and high topweight, but *Rodney* and her sisters – the first class of modern battleships built to a similar design – sensibly had less top-weight. It cost £665,963 to build this *Rodney*, which had a beam of 68 ft and draught of more than 27 ft. Her principal weapons were four 13.5-inch breech-loading guns, although the Admiral Class had no standardised armament.[21] For example, the first in the class, HMS *Collingwood*, had four 12-inch guns. Such variation occurred because the Admiralty was feeling its way towards a standard for breech-loading big guns. Muzzle-loaded weapons were prone to being accidentally double-loaded, one such incident in 1879 leading to a gun exploding in HMS *Thunderer*. This could not occur with breech-loaded weapons, for the simple reason that it was far easier to check for double-loading. Opening a breech revealed light at the far end, or blackness, indicating whether or not something was already up the spout. Aside from that, breech-loading guns were far easier to load, the late Victorian *Rodney* being able to fire a 13.5-inch shell every two minutes. There was great debate at the time as to the best calibre of weapon and length of the barrel needed to take advantage of slow-burning powder, which gave greater range and velocity (and therefore penetrative power). With barrels 36 ft-long, and capable of firing a shell weighing 1,250 lbs, which could penetrate armour 27-inches thick at a range of 3,000 ft,[22] *Rodney*'s main guns could, theoretically, destroy any ship afloat. However, design flaws in the mountings threatened to nullify this awesome power, for the big guns were mounted in 'armoured cylinders called barbettes'[23] open to the sky, and therefore the elements as well as bullets and shrapnel. Later barbette vessels were provided with hoods, which gave protection to the guns' mechanisms and the men operating them. Although reckoned to be good sea boats[24], because the Admirals had a low freeboard the main armament had to be mounted high up, in *Rodney*'s case 20 ft above the water. Despite this, in rough seas the 13.5-inch guns could not be operated. Both *Rodney* and sister ship *Howe* experienced problems with 'the increased frequency at which the decks were swept by waves'[25] due to their increase in dimensions over the *Collingwood*. They were five feet longer and six inches broader in the beam, caused by the need to accommodate the weight of bigger guns. This, in turn, meant *Rodney* and *Howe* sat deeper in the water than *Collingwood* by 18-inches. The maximum thickness of the *Rodney*'s own belt armour was 18-inches, tapering to eight inches, backed with 20-inches of teak, but because the ship was lower in the water than designers had envisaged, this belt was often submerged. The navies of the late Victorian era were most concerned about swarms of torpedo boats and therefore *Rodney* also packed a considerable secondary punch, in the form of six 6-inch guns, plus 6-pdr guns and 3-pdr weapons, whose job it was to eliminate the torpedo boat menace. On the debit side the storm of shell plumes and spray kicked up by the battleship's own smaller calibre guns would in any action make it difficult for aimers and layers of 13.5-inch guns to see enemy capital ships, while the huge amount of smoke added to their blindness. Only the reality of war would prove whether or not *Rodney* might be a killer or a victim, but at least the navies of potential enemies were also struggling to perfect steel battleship design. It is clear the old arguments between the Seppings' and Symonds' schools, which resulted in the previous *Rodney*'s participation in experimental squadron cruises, paled in comparison to challenges faced by warship designers in the 1880s. Sail power, and the conflict between revolving gun platforms and masts, was at least consigned to history. This *Rodney* only retained a mast for lookouts and gunnery spotters, for she was also an all steam ship, with bunkers that could accommodate 1,200 tons of coal. Her engines were capable of 7,500 hp and would, at a stretch, propel the ship to just over 17 knots.

Such was the delay in manufacturing her main armament, *Rodney* did not actually enter service until the summer of 1888. Commissioned on 20 June, she was assigned to the Home Fleet as flagship but, by May 1890, was in the Channel Fleet, staying there until May 1894 when she sailed for the Mediterranean, under the command of Captain J.H. Rainier. In keeping with Victorian naval style, she sported buff funnels, a black hull and a white-painted superstructure, which, combined with immaculate, gleaming brasswork, was clearly meant to dazzle enemies into submission.

As a sentinel of Pax Britannica, *Rodney* put men ashore at Crete in early 1897, when Greece came to the aid of Greeks still living under Ottoman rule. The great powers of France, Russia, Austro-Hungary and Britain, did not want war to break out between Greece and Turkey, fearing it could spread across the Balkans and imperil the peace of Europe. On 13 February, a multi-national flotilla set sail from Navarino, the British contingent consisting of the battleships *Revenge* and *Barfleur* as well as *Rodney*.[26] The Allied warships, with an admiral from each contributing nation embarked – Britain, France, Russia, Italy and Austria all sent ships – anchored off the Cretan shore intent on keeping the warring factions apart. On the same day the international flotilla left Navarino, a Greek warship called *Misoulis* fired on a Turkish troop transport, the *Fuad*, carrying arms and ammunition to reinforce besieged Turks at Canae. This ship had also embarked troops for transportation down the coast, so the Greeks decided to try and stop her. The Commanding Officer of one British warship went aboard *Misoulis* to protest against Greek actions, warning that a similar incident would result in the Royal Navy using force.[27] Meanwhile, Christian insurgents ashore were bombarding Canae and the Turks were threatening to land reinforcements if the Greeks sent troops to Crete. The great powers, although united in the international squadron, were jockeying for position on the wider diplomatic stage: the Germans resolutely pro-Turkey; the British adopting a neutral position, feeling Crete should probably be united with Greece, but not via military force.

The British might identify with the cause of Greek freedom, for which they had fought at Navarino in 1827, but seventy years later valuable trade was at risk, for the Turks imported an annual average of £8,000,000 worth of British goods.[28] In the House of Commons, MPs were keen to know if British warships would take action independent of the other nations. The following day, 15 February, the Greeks put soldiers ashore, not far from Canae, to support the insurgents, but without interference from *Rodney* or any other Allied warship. However, the multi-national flotilla had landed detachments at Canae and Heraklion, 100 men from each ship, who placed themselves between the two sides at those key locations and elsewhere. Meanwhile, Greek warships were warned off and threatened with the use of the force if they attempted to support their troops with bombardments. A declaration of union with Greece inflamed the situation on the island, while in Britain pro-Greek MPs attempted to turn the tide against the Turks, by making claims of atrocities. They perhaps hoped news of such horrors would force the multi-national fleet to weigh in on the Hellenic side. In the House of Commons, an MP asked Foreign Under-Secretary Lord Curzon if it was true several Christians had been roasted alive in bakers' ovens during disturbances in Canae. Curzon said no evidence had been found. Curzon indicated patience was running out, but gave only a vague response to claims that Allied warships had carried out a bombardment.

> *Our information is not to the effect that there has been any attack up, or bombardment of, Greek forces in Crete. The insurgents outside Canae, in spite of the injunctions from the Admirals, renewed their attacks on the town yesterday.*[29]

There had indeed been a bombardment, on 21 February, with *Rodney* among warships lobbing shells at insurgents advancing from Akrotiri against Canae, an event lasting all of five minutes and causing no casualties. It was the first, and last, time the late Victorian-era *Rodney*'s guns were fired in anger.

In the Reichstag, Berlin, on February 22, it was claimed a German warship, the *Kaiserin Augusta*, which had arrived off Canea alongside *Rodney*, put ashore 50 men, and then joined in the cannonade alongside the British, Russian and Austrian warships.[30] The next time a German warship encountered a vessel named HMS *Rodney*, some forty-four years later, it would not be on friendly terms. The bombardment hardened the attitude of the rebels and outraged the Greeks. In Athens there was 'great excitement against Europeans'[31] and wild threats of an action by the Hellenic Army against Turkish forces in the Balkans. In early March, with insurgents besieging a Turkish garrison at Candanos, another international landing force, under the command of *Rodney*'s Captain Rainier, again including sailors from the battleship, was put ashore to lift the siege. Together with Turkish troops, the Allied sailors escorted muslim civilians to the coast, harassed all the way by Christian insurgents. The same month a blockade was instituted to try and contain the situation. Athens ordered an attack in Thessaly, but Turkish units under the command of German officers defeated ill-prepared Greek troops. Eventually Greece and Turkey withdrew their troops from Crete and it became an international protectorate until 1913. It was finally united with Greece after the First Balkan War.

Following her adventures in the eastern Mediterranean, *Rodney* was brought home to service in 'Special Reserve'. As one of the oldest of the Royal Navy's 'first-class' battleships, she was sent to Queensferry on the Firth of Forth. Her Commanding Officer, Captain Gerald W. Russell, who had last seen active service supporting the Army in the Egyptian War of 1882, was given responsibility for coastguard duties, *Rodney*'s district stretching from just south of the Firth of Forth, all the way around the top of Scotland to Cape Wrath. *Rodney*'s shortfall in Royal Navy sailors was made up with officers and ratings from the coastguard service. For example, as there were no midshipmen under training to handle small boats, grizzled old senior coastguardsmen undertook that duty. Sometimes there was friction between the young ordinary ratings of *Rodney* and the coastguardsmen. In one incident, a youngster loudly cursed the coastguard officers in the ship and found himself hurled into the sea by a grey-bearded veteran.[32] The bread and butter of *Rodney*'s time on this station was rescuing mariners in distress and retrieving vessels run aground. There was great emphasis on the bullshine so typical of the Victorian Navy. A senior officer might have nothing better to do at Queensferry than get into a boat handled by a coastguardsman to investigate how smart the ship was looking.

> *Possibly he has been round the ship in his gig, to see that the paint is smooth and perfect, the boats hung square, the brasswork glittering in an orthodox manner; and if there is any failure, someone is going to hear about it.*[33]

On 8 November 1906, *Rodney* was placed on the disposal list, finally being sold off for scrap in 1909 to Wards of Morecombe in the north-west of England, as part of Admiral Fisher's mass culling of the Royal Navy's obsolete warships. She fetched the princely sum of £21,350, representing a loss of more than £640,000 to the British taxpayer. However, without such experiments in naval architecture, ugly and flawed though they may have been, the march of technological progress would not have led to the next two *Rodneys*, which represented the apex of British capital ship design.

Notes

1 National Maritime Museum, JOD/65, Hinds, Rev. Robert, chaplain of HMS *Rodney*, diary, Black Sea and Crimea, 1853-56. The Hawse was the portion of a ship's bow where there were holes through which passed cables. Hawse plugs were used to prevent water from entering the ship.
2 Trevor Royle, *Crimea, The Great Crimean War 1854–1856.*
3 National Maritime Museum, Hinds, Rev Robert.
4 Ibid.
5 Ibid.
6 Ibid.
7 Trevor Royle, *Crimea, The Great Crimean War 1854–1856.*
8 *Russian War, 1854 Baltic And Black Sea* official correspondence, edited by D. Bonner-Smith and Captain A.C. Dewar, Navy Records Society, 1943.
9 National Maritime Museum, Hinds, Rev. Robert.
10 Ibid.
11 Ibid.
12 Frank C. Bowen, *Wooden Walls in Action.*

13 *Russian War, 1854 Baltic And Black Sea* official correspondence, edited by D. Bonner-Smith and Captain A.C. Dewar, Navy Records Society, 1943.
14 Ibid. Dundas writing from *Britannia*, off the Katcha, giving an account of the great storm.
15 Ibid.
16 National Maritime Museum, Hinds, Rev. Robert.
17 *Russian War, 1855 Black Sea Official Correspondence,* edited by Captain A.C. Dewar, 1945.
18 National Maritime Museum, Hinds, Rev Robert.
19 Note attached to National Maritime Museum, *Abstract of Log of Her Majesty's Ship* Rodney.
20 *Royal Navy Day-by-Day.*
21 Richard Humble, *Before Dreadnought.*
22 David Hunter, *Periscope,* July 1980.
23 Richard Humble, *Before Dreadnought.*
24 David Hunter, *Periscope,* July 1980.
25 D.K. Brown, *Warrior To Dreadnought.*
26 NMM, RAI/309, Journal of HMS *Rodney,* Captain J.H. Rainier, 1895–97.
27 *Western Evening Herald,* 15 February 1897.
28 *Western Evening Herald,* 22 February, 1897.
29 Ibid.
30 *Western Evening Herald,* 23 February 1897.
31 *International Herald Tribune,* 24 February 1897.
32 *Navy & Army Illustrated,* 4 March 1899.
33 Ibid.

Chapter Four

THE SHIP THAT NEVER WAS

It was a headlong dash to destiny on a fine, late May day, as ships of the Royal Navy's Battle Cruiser Fleet raced south at full speed. They made sharp targets against the bright western horizon for gunners in German battlecruisers racing north out of a gloomy east at an equally reckless rate. At 4.00 pm on 31 May 1916 a large section of HMS *Lion*'s Q turret roof was blown off, falling with a blood-chilling clang onto the upper deck. With fires raging, the ship was only saved by a dying Royal Marine officer, Major Francis Harvey, both his legs blown off, issuing orders to flood an ammunition magazine. But, despite this action, which won Harvey a posthumous Victoria Cross, nearly half an hour later, after a clutch of smouldering cordite charges ignited, flames shot down into shell handling and magazine spaces and, after incinerating seventy men, vented out of the top of Q turret. While *Lion* survived this calamity, the battlecruiser *Indefatigable*, bringing up the rear, shuddered to three heavy hits from German big guns and exploded. Momentum driving her shattered hull forward, she rolled over to port and under the waves, entombing 1,017 men. Only two of *Indefatigable*'s sailors lived to tell the tale. At 4.26 pm HMS *Queen Mary* was rent asunder by deep penetrating shells, 1,266 sailors and marines dying as she also exploded. The stern of the destroyed battlecruiser stayed for a moment above the waves, screws still turning, wretched survivors clinging on before it too slid under. In the early evening, as heavy-weight battleships of the Royal Navy's immensely powerful Grand Fleet came into action, forming a six-mile crescent of firepower across the northern horizon, the Germans scored more lucky hits, finding HMS *Invincible* and delivering blows that blew her apart. *Invincible* sank in 30 seconds, broken in two by a massive explosion in the magazine serving her P and Q turrets, both ends of the slain ship poking above the surface of the water. Inside were 1,021 dead. And so, on a single fateful day in the North Sea, three British battlecruisers were blown apart, killing 3,304 sailors and marines. Prior to that day the Royal Navy had been riding high on battlecruiser victories. At Heligoland Bight, on 28 August 1914, and off the Falkland Islands, on 8 December the same year, German warships could not escape their high-speed and large calibre guns, the Kaiser's fleet paying a heavy price in blood and iron. But the Royal Navy failed to understand the lessons of a clash at Dogger Bank, on 24 January 1915, where *Lion* had previously nearly blown up, due to deep penetrating German shells.

The danger uppermost in First Sea Lord Admiral John Fisher's mind when HMS *Invincible*, the world's first battlecruiser, was conceived some years earlier was of enemy cruisers preying on shipping lanes and killing the economy of the British Isles. The new ships would be deployed to the far corners of the empire, hence two of them being named after, and funded by, Australia and New Zealand. The battlecruisers would range the oceans and destroy enemy ships wherever they appeared. However, events at the battle of Jutland in summer 1916 decisively exposed battlecruisers as fatally flawed. They were large, carried big guns and were fast. They were also too thinly armoured to fight battleships or even enemy battlecruisers. Despite the loss of *Queen Mary*, *Indefatigable* and *Invincible* at Jutland, the Royal Navy did not want to acknowledge battlecruisers were only fit for the scrap heap. The glamour, the irresistible allure of the concept – speed and cruising endurance allied with those big guns – remained and so, despite serious doubts, a new *Rodney* was begun, laid down at Fairfield's shipyard in Scotland, on 9 October 1916.

Battlecruiser *Rodney* was the product of British desire to improve still further the extremely formidable Queen Elizabeth Class fast battleship design. In early 1915, with the Queen Elizabeths, including the legendary *Warspite*, just entering service[1], the Director of Naval Construction, Sir Eustace Tennyson-d'Eyncourt, was asked by the Admiralty to begin designing a class of even more formidable warships, which would, hopefully, incorporate the virtues of battleships and battlecruisers: fast, heavily-armed but well armoured. The selected design should also overcome the problem of heavy war loads in ammunition, fuel and supplies making capital ships so low in the water that their secondary armaments were awash and therefore rendered useless.[2] Water taken inboard also tended to make warships heavier and more ungainly.

Between autumn 1915 and early 1916, with the Western Front bogging down into the sort of trench warfare so grimly familiar to sailors and marines of the Crimean War-era *Rodney*, a series of designs using various balances of speed, armour and guns were considered. Meanwhile, the spectre of big battlecruisers able to outrun and outgun the next *Rodney* loomed across the North Sea, where Germany was building the impressive Mackensen Class, which promised to be very fast indeed and well armed. In April 1916 the design for *Hood* and *Rodney* plus two sisters, *Anson* and *Howe*, was confirmed. The new Admiral Class battlecruisers were to be 860 ft-long, with a displacement in excess of 36,000 tons. They were to be armed with 15-inch guns and capable of more than 30 knots.

What had doomed the battlecruisers at Jutland was inadequate armour, sloppy ammunition handling practices and old, unstable cordite[3]

Post-Jutland, aside from increased armour protection, the new *Rodney*'s gun mountings were made more robust. Ironically, after all the effort to ensure her upperworks were not awash, the modifications meant *Rodney* would be a 'wet' ship, with portions of her upper works submerged at high speed. In the summer of 1916 construction of other classes of battlecruiser was also well under way in Britain, on the building slips or nearing completion, but the modifications delayed *Rodney*'s construction. In the end, pressure for cutbacks, as an economically exhausted country struggled to maintain the war effort, killed off what would have been the next HMS *Rodney*. There were those who said further investment in so many battle-cruisers was asking for trouble. Also, having failed to break the British blockade at Jutland, Germany slowed construction of the Mackensens and instead invested resources in building U-boats, which were to be used in a savage war of attrition against trade. There was no longer the same urgency for a counter-weight to new German battlecruisers, so *Rodney*'s construction was halted on 9 March 1917, with the contract cancelled altogether in October 1918. The same fate befell two of her three sisters – *Anson* and *Howe* – but the ship most advanced had been launched in late August 1918 and was completed in the spring of 1920. Two decades later HMS *Hood* would, like the ill-fated battlecruisers of Jutland, explode with huge loss of life when German shells ripped into her. In a strange twist of fate, the next ship to bear the name *Rodney* would be constructed despite post-war economies and, in May 1941, avenge *Hood*. But that tale comes later.

The *Rodney* that would be *Hood*'s avenger was a product of tough times and the naval officer who conducted hard bargaining to bring her into existence knew all too well battlecruisers were a dangerous breed. Ernle Chatfield was the captain of HMS *Lion* at Jutland, where his vessel was flagship of Vice Admiral Sir David Beatty, commander of the Battle Cruiser Fleet. Legend has it that, after the *Indefatigable* and *Queen Mary* exploded, Beatty turned to Chatfield and exclaimed:

There seems to be something wrong with our bloody ships today!

Chatfield gave no reaction – the truth of what Beatty said was self-evident and needed no response, for at the time of the outburst *Lion*'s captain was contemplating a mushroom cloud of smoke 1,000 ft high where *Queen Mary* had been. It signified the deaths of many friends. Joining the Royal Navy at the age of thirteen, Chatfield was the son of a naval officer, a gunner by trade and one of Admiral Fisher's young bucks. In 1912 he was given command of the cruiser *Southampton*, under construction on the Clyde, but appointed captain of *Lion* in early 1913.[4] As flag captain of the hard-charging, some would say reckless, Admiral Beatty, Chatfield saw a lot of action, not only at Heligoland Bight but also Dogger Bank, where, of course, his 'big cat' had used up one of her lives.[5] When Beatty was made commander of the Grand Fleet post-Jutland, he took Chatfield with him, to be his flag captain and chief of staff.[6] Knighted in spring 1919, Chatfield's fortunes remained hitched to Beatty's star as the latter climbed to become First Sea Lord. It was in his capacity as Assistant Chief of the Naval Staff that Rear Admiral Chatfield found himself tasked with conducting negotiations leading to the construction of the next *Rodney*.

A new naval arms race had started before the blood on the battlefields of the First World War was even dry. Now the main rival for the Royal Navy's crown as ruler of the Seven Seas was the United States Navy, rather than the Kaiser's fleet, which had scuttled itself at Scapa Flow after surrendering. At the close of the conflict, the Royal Navy had thirty-three dreadnoughts and super-dreadnoughts, plus nine battlecruisers and three light battlecruisers, with *Hood* approaching completion. Ten of the dreadnoughts and four battlecruisers had 12-inch guns, being hopelessly out-gunned by newer capital ships of other navies, particularly those of Japan and the USA.[7]

Some people saw the build-up of navies as the cause of war even though 'arms races were the symptom, not the cause, of national rivalries.'[8] Opposition to even bigger capital ships being built at potentially ruinous expense, grew around the world. In America, the Navy Department wanted to build more, but Congress was not keen. The Senate was inclined to back a bigger, stronger Navy but pacifist leanings of the population at large could not be ignored. During the war it had been the clear intention of President Woodrow Wilson that the USA should become an active champion of democracy across the globe, which would inevitably require a powerful navy. This was obviously a direct challenge to the Royal Navy. The US President's intention made the British realize they must stay ahead of the game, or at least bargain for naval parity, but the USA would not enter negotiations without Britain tearing up its military alliance with Japan. The Americans and Japanese were squaring up to each other in the Pacific, with one faction in Japan, led by Prime

Minister Hara Kei, keen for compromise, but militarists were determined to build up the army and navy, despite the crippling cost. There were many Japanese who believed it was time to fulfil their manifest destiny as the dominant race in Asia. Looking at European colonies with covetous eyes, they were wary of growing American influence. With the British willing to abandon the treaty with Japan and Hara Kei signalling he was ready to talk, the Americans suggested a conference on naval limitation in Washington D.C., scheduled to begin in November 1921. It did not get off to a good start: Hara Kei was assassinated at a railway station in Tokyo and Japan's position became less conciliatory. The British delegation was led by seventy-three year old Arthur Balfour, who had been Prime Minister at the turn of the century, First Lord of the Admiralty during the war and also Foreign Minister. Admiral Beatty, as First Sea Lord, was at Balfour's side and Rear Admiral Chatfield was also there, in an advisory capacity.

Beatty retained faith in the Navy's battleships as the first line of defence and felt, with the Americans and Japanese so committed to maintaining a strong naval presence in the Pacific, Britain had no choice but to invest in new capital ships that would be equally powerful. He was, like Chatfield, aware the lessons of Jutland must be incorporated into whatever vessels were built, if any, following the Washington conference. Some naval experts were suggesting that a lot more ships, but of only 10,000 tons displacement – in other words hordes of heavy cruisers – would be a better investment than big, lumbering battlewagons.

The American Secretary of State, Charles Evans Hughes, proposed a ten-year battleship building holiday and it was agreed the UK, USA and Japan would accept ratios of 5-5-3 in capital ships respectively.

Chatfield was left in charge of advising the British delegation in January 1922, when Beatty went home to fight the Royal Navy's case against a savage round of defence cuts. At the Washington Conference the British initially hoped to limit gun calibres to a 15-inch maximum but this proved impossible, as the Japanese would not give up their two newly commissioned 16-inch battleships, *Mutsu* and *Nagato*. The *Nagato* was 33,800 tons, armed with eight 16-inch guns and laid down in 1916, with *Mutsu* following in 1917. The Americans were also determined to retain battleships with 16-inch guns. In 1916, Congress had authorized ten battleships and six battlecruisers, with four Colorado Class battleships each of 32,500 tons displacement and armed with eight 16-inch guns laid down between 1917 and 1920.

For their part, the British had conceived a class of 'battlecruisers', designated the G3 design. Calling them battlecruisers was similar to today's Royal Navy describing its new Daring Class as destroyers, when the reality is they are cruisers – a political and emotive label rather than something that reflects design reality. The G3s were to be armed with 16-inch guns – five turrets mounting two heavy guns each or four turrets, each with three guns. Another option envisioned giving the G3s 18-inch guns. The G3 battlecruisers would be hugely expensive, but were ordered anyway at the end of 1921, with the promise of four huge battleships to come in 1922. This sparked a conflict between the British Treasury and Navy, also provoking pacifist protests. Both the Americans and Japanese had rather hoped the British would be satisfied with their ten relatively modern 15-inch gun battleships, of the Queen Elizabeth and Royal Sovereign classes, as they outgunned many older vessels in both the USN and IJN. But Chatfield believed the RN's 15-inch-armed battleships were not a sufficient safety margin and saw his chance to discard the costly – and unrealistic – G3s, but still get new capital ships.

With Admiralty concurrence, I at once asked Mr Balfour to demand our right to build two new 16-inch ships. A long debate took place over this, but eventually it was agreed to.[9]

However, Chatfield was concerned that, with such large guns, there would not be enough tonnage left over to provide adequate armour. The American proposal of 32,500 tons displacement was not enough to carry 16-inch guns and provide proper protection, so Chatfield pushed for 35,000 tons.

I was determined not to build British ships that were unsuitable, after our lessons of Jutland; ships that would be unbalanced, owing to so much weight being put into guns, that they would have too little protective armour, as had been the case in our battlecruisers; ships that a lucky shot could blow up, with their crews.[10]

The Admiralty helped Chatfield by sending a telegram stating that, if other nations were to have some ships with 16-inch guns, then so must Britain. Chatfield told Balfour the tonnage MUST be 35,000 tons.

... after two weeks' discussion a 35,000 ton standard displacement was agreed to by the powers concerned.[11]

This was without taking into account the ships' oil and water. Balfour, suitably fired up by Chatfield, argued vociferously for the higher tonnage and a clause allowing it to be without oil and water was a key concession, as it 'put an additional 2,500 tons in the bag to cover 16-inch guns'[12], enabling it to be 'spent' on armour protection. The naval limitation treaty was signed on 6 February 1922, setting parameters within which the leading navies were meant to operate. The UK was allowed 580,450 tons in capital ships, the USA 500,450 tons, the Japanese 221,170 tons, while the French were permitted the same, and Italy limited to 182,800 tons[13]. The other leading European naval powers had basically been relegated to the second division. Ultimately American and British navies would draw down to 500,000 tons worth of capital ships each while Japan would rise to 300,000 tons. Japan retained its two 16-inch battleships while America kept *Colorado, West Virginia* and *Maryland*.

Britain was allowed twenty-two capital ships, composed of eighteen battleships and four battlecruisers but to achieve the limits twenty-one Royal Navy battleships and battlecruisers were scrapped; the most powerful battle fleet the world had ever seen was no more. Absorbing this blow, the British were concerned the ten-year holiday would lead to skill fade. The workforces that had built the dreadnoughts would simply dissipate and yards become derelict. Even worse, only limited reconstruction of existing battleships or battlecruisers was permitted. On the positive side, no European navy could come close to Britain's and the Royal Navy lost only obsolete ships worn out by war. The mindset at the time was that future wars could be avoided in the talking shop of the League of Nations, where everybody could be good pals, their discussions finding a solution to disagreements between states. Chatfield noted disconsolately:

That being so, why build new navies and waste money?[14]

He also reflected: 'Weapons were not a defence against war, they were on the contrary said to be the cause of war...'[15] Chatfield conceded it was reasonable in the wake of a terrible global conflict that navies should be limited in the short-term. However, human nature being what it was, he feared major war would come again and the Royal Navy should not be weakened too much. Beatty was well pleased with the results of the Washington conference and it was soon known the two new 16-inch gun battleships were to be called *Rodney* and *Nelson*, celebrating two famous fighting admirals. The warship construction picture other than these battleships was, however, rather bleak, with only five new 8-inch gun heavy cruisers allowed along with conversion of battlecruiser hulls to carriers. For all his pragmatism, Chatfield mournfully noted that the Washington Treaty gave the government a good excuse to cut a swathe through the Royal Navy.

On top of the Washington Treaty's ten-year battleship building break, the British in 1919 had also introduced a ten-year holiday from investment across the whole Armed Forces. In mid-August 1919, the Government of the day, which included Winston Churchill as Secretary for War, declared:

> *It should be assumed ... that the British Empire will not be engaged in any great war during the next ten years, and that no expeditionary force is required for this purpose.*[16]

The Treasury was not keen on an end to this 'holiday', as it meant from 1929, effective checks on defence spending were off. Therefore, the Government decided it should be renewed every year, in effect putting the Armed Forces on ten years' notice for war forever. *Rodney* and *Nelson* would be the only new battleships built for a very long time, possibly the last of their breed in the British navy.

Notes

1 For more on the remarkable fighting life of HMS *Warspite*, see the first book in this series, by the same author.
2 HMS *Hood* Association, *H.M.S.* Hood *Design Background.*
3 Ibid.
4 T.A. Heathcote, *The British Admirals of the Fleet.*
5 The battlecruisers *Lion* and *Tiger* were known affectionately as 'The Big Cats' and here we are referring to the former.
6 T.A. Heathcote, *The British Admirals of the Fleet.*
7 H.P. Wilmott, *Battleship.*
8 Ibid.
9 Chatfield, *It Might Happen Again.*
10 Ibid.
11 Ibid.
12 Ibid.
13 Willmott, *Battleship.*
14 Chatfield, *It Might Happen Again.*
15 Ibid.
16 Quoted by Gordon Corrigan in *Blood, Sweat and Arrogance.*

Chapter Five

DAWN OF THE OLYMPIANS

Dozens of dockyard workers and their foremen, wearing flat caps and rough overcoats against a cold, damp day, peered over the side of the towering hull at a sea of top hats and bowlers sprinkled with ladies in their fur.

Appliances of the local Fire Brigade were arrayed on either side, for there was a risk the friction of *Rodney*'s launch might ignite grease and animal fat smeared on the slipway to ease the ship's passage to water.[1]

That same day, beyond the broad mouth of the Mersey and across a chilly sea, the last British troops were being withdrawn from the new Irish Republic. Earlier in the year Egypt ceased being a British protectorate, while in India, an activist named Ghandi agitated for an end to the Raj. The very empire *Rodney* was being created to secure, and which had been established largely due to the power of the Royal Navy, was unravelling. However, on that cold December day in Birkenhead, the gigantic battleship seemed to prove British sea power still reigned supreme, despite those far away events and claims that warplanes were now more lethal. In uncertain times it was easier to believe in the awesome majesty of a steel-hulled battleship, held together with rivets hammered home by the honest labour of thousands of men, than puny paper and glue biplanes with their fragile wires and struts. However, two impudent biplanes from a nearby airfield circled overhead, like vultures at the feast. Time would tell, but, on 17 December 1925, nagging doubts about the battleship's supremacy were surely dispelled by the sheer spectacle of the launch.

A bottle of Imperial Burgundy, suspended by red, white and blue ribbons from the bows, was hurled by Her Royal Highness, the Princess Mary, Viscountess Lascelles, at the battleship. However, it did not shatter and, instead, rebounded.

> *Recapturing it, she took a second throw, only to see the bottle carried away in the strong breeze, completely missing the ship. The third throw was well delivered with both hands, striking the stem squarely, and amid a cracking of glass and the bubble of escaping wine the ship was named.*[2]

The Princess uttered the time-honoured blessing:

> *I name this ship* Rodney. *God bless her, and all who sail in her.*

Rather than a chisel parting the last, symbolic, restraining wire, a button was pressed, which lit a bulb somewhere under the hull, signalling to waiting yardies that the final impediments should be knocked away. Sliding down the building slip, the gigantic bows gathered pace away from the platform on which dignitaries stood. To either side of *Rodney* an estimated 20,000 people cheered, as piles of wooden debris under the keel splintered, the hull hurtling ever faster, bunting fluttering as she hit the water with a massive splash. Drag chains ensured *Rodney*'s entrance into her natural element was blessed with at least a modicum of grace. A Union Jack flew proud from the jackstaff on the battleship's prow, while tall-funnelled tugs gathered below, all watched by crowds of onlookers at the water's edge. The miniscule vessels nudged the 20,000 tons hull towards a dock where *Rodney* would be completed.

The design for *Rodney* and sister ship *Nelson* was approved on 6 February 1922, the invitation to tender for construction issued on 16 October. The following month it was decided Cammell Laird at Birkenhead, on the Mersey, should build one, while Armstrongs, on the Tyne, would construct the other. Established in the 1820s, Cammell Laird did not build its first Royal Navy battleship until the beginning of the twentieth century, but rapidly established a record for good work, in 1913 completing the dreadnought HMS *Audacious*, and during the First World War building cruisers as well as destroyers. Having suffered cancellation of *Howe*, sister ship of *Rodney* battlecruiser-that-never-was, in the closing months of the war, Cammell Laird was awarded a contract to build the light cruiser *Capetown*, completing her in the year battleship *Rodney* was begun. While the official order for the ships was not placed until New Year's Day 1923, a vessel known as Number 904 – the future *Rodney* – was laid down at Birkenhead on 28 December 1922, the same day as *Nelson* on the Tyne. The workers who built *Rodney* swarmed 'like ants about her gaunt projecting ribs, clothing them with sinews of steel'[3], the battleship taking shape from the bottom up, on a massive steel keel plate, which was itself laid upon wooden blocks sturdy enough to support her gigantic proportions.

Admiral Chatfield, who had been appointed to the Navy Board in April 1925, gave a speech at the post-launch lunch, in his capacity as Controller of the Navy, the man in charge of warship construction. He later confessed to an off-the-cuff approach. The Admiral suspected that, as Cammell Laird knew he hated giving speeches, they deliberately neglected to tell him in advance.

> *... sitting down at the table, I saw my name on the menu, as having to make the principal speech before a very large and distinguished gathering.*[4]

But it was more than appropriate Chatfield spoke, as he played such a key role in bringing into being *Rodney* and *Nelson*, the latter launched three months earlier, although he left no record of what he said in two volumes of autobiography. But, perhaps Chatfield preferred to blot the lunch out, as it was the platform for a war of words between shipbuilding industry and Admiralty.

Mr William Lionel Hichens, chairman of Cammell Laird since 1910, used his speech to hit out at several groups of people. Two of the principal targets of his tongue-lashing were sitting there before him: the gentlemen of the press and Mr W. C. Bridgeman, First Lord of the Admiralty. Remarking how the 'mysterious laws of the Admiralty' forbade him from saying too much about technical details, Mr Hichens ridiculed coverage of *Rodney*'s construction. The battleship had yet to receive her armament and Hichens had evidently become weary of endless articles suggesting she would be a paper tiger; a big hull but, due to endless economies in the defence budget, possibly without proper armament.

'Why were the Admiralty so mysterious?' he asked, sarcastically.

> *Could it be that they were anxious to obscure the fact that they had nothing to hide, or was it that, goaded by the urge towards economy fostered by all the tiresome committees and sub-committees appointed in recent times, they were placing dummy guns and papier mache armaments?*[5]

Mr Hichens also addressed dilemmas facing the shipbuilding industry, which was suffering from a lack of warship construction work. With more than a touch of irony he told his fellow diners he might 'descend upon the misfortunes of the shipbuilding trade, and seize upon the presence of the First Lord as an opportunity to urge upon him an ambitious and extensive Admiralty programme [of warship construction] . . .

> . . . *but* [Mr Hichens declared] *he would not because for one thing the First Lord was actually alive as anyone to the sad state in which shipbuilding found itself at the present time, and for another, he would never be party to suggesting to the Admiralty that they should build ships which were not required.*[6]

It seemed the world, and in particular the rising global power, America, was foretelling the death of British industry, but Mr Hichens remarked there was still life in the old dog yet:

> *I have not the least apprehension that we shall not recover from the depression which exists to-day, but we have to be allowed to work out our own salvation in our own way.*[7]

The First Lord of the Admiralty then rose to his feet and gave an ill-tempered speech, remarking rather sourly that he was aware *Nelson* and *Rodney* were already being described as the 'cherry tree class' because 'they had been cut down by Washington.'[8] The First Lord said that he had become 'rather tired of receiving lectures in the House of Commons' from MPs who claimed he was failing in his duty to the Navy and the Nation. In fact, his duty was to 'combine economy with efficiency' but 'he would never let economy hinder the Royal Navy's efficiency.'[9] And, finally, there was a brief speech from Lord Derby, a former War Minister during the First World War, recently returned from the post of British Ambassador to the French Republic, who was a local landowner and community leader. He declared that, if accounts connected with the building of the *Rodney* could be examined 'it would probably be found that Cammell Laird took on the contract for the ship less for profit than for the purposes of giving work to the employees.'[10] Such sentiments, naturally, reflected hard times for the British shipbuilding industry, for having experienced a post-war boom both to replace shipping lost and meet resurgent world trade, the tonnage produced had slumped from 2,055,624 tons in 1920 to just 1,538,042 tons in 1921.[11] The drastic reduction in Admiralty orders following the Washington Treaty compounded matters but, in December 1925, there was much work still to be done on *Rodney*. The first British battleship to be launched with her boilers already installed[12], in subsequent months, she took on a further 15,000 tons in weight, principally composed of guns, armour and machinery. All the fittings were carefully scrutinized by Cammell Laird, for *Rodney*'s entire design was dictated by the need to save weight and remain within the Washington Treaty restrictions, although other nations cheated, keeping the exact displacement of their suspiciously heavily-armed and well-armoured capital ships secret. The British played by the rules of the game: A discarded version of *Rodney*'s design envisaged one of her three turrets behind the bridge tower, but this would have contravened the weight limit. The *Rodney*'s eventual displacement was 33,900 tons, 1,100 tons short of the Washington Treaty limit, but some 400 tons more than *Nelson*.[13] At full load *Rodney* would displace 40,000 tons. *Rodney* was 710 ft long, with a beam of 106 ft and a mean draught of 30 ft. With the main armament of nine 16-inch guns in three turrets at the front – known, going aft, as A, B and X – and all the superstructure and machinery at the back, the length had been reduced, successfully saving weight that could be spent on protection. The vulnerable core of the ship was protected by a heavily armoured citadel, also known as 'the armoured box'[14], which was itself within the hull plating. The armour was arranged at an angle to deflect shells but *Rodney*'s armoured belt was only 13 ft wide in the vertical, considered by some naval experts too narrow, leading to fears that heavy shells could penetrate if they hit the ship under the water line. To protect the machinery of the 16-inch guns, and associated magazines and shell handling rooms, as well as other key areas, such as gunnery control positions, the *Rodney*'s armour belt was 14-inches at its thickest.[15] The armour was only an inch thinner over the 6-inch ammunition magazines and engine spaces, while on the turret faces it was 16-inches thick, with nine inches on the back, between eleven and nine inches on their sides and seven-and-a-quarter inches of protection overhead. There was 15 inches of armour around the barbettes, obviously intended to stop penetration of one of the most critical areas of the ship. The armour on the upper deck was six-and-a-half inches thick. The armoured deck over the magazines was more than 6-inches thick, something that would eventually save the ship from disaster in time of war. *Rodney* also had to be strong enough to withstand hits from torpedoes. Whereas other ships had external bulges – the idea being the torpedo would expend its explosive energy on hitting the bulge rather than penetrate the hull – *Rodney's* torpedo defences were incorporated into her hull. They took the form of an outer layer of air-filled compartments with a water-filled inner one. A serious problem previous battleship designs suffered from was funnel smoke obscuring the principal gunnery controller's vision. In *Rodney* and *Nelson*, the funnel was well astern of a tower 'said to be almost indestructible by gunfire'[16] which contained the control position for the guns. The funnel was also well away from magazines, avoiding the possibility of plunging shellfire penetrating to the very heart of the ship, causing a catastrophic detonation. The eight-sided (octagonal) tower, which was known colloquially as 'the Octopoidal' (or even 'the Octopedal'), not only provided facilities for gunnery control, but also torpedo controllers, a bridge for any embarked admiral, plus bridges for signalling and navigation, together with accommodation and offices.

It was an inconvenience no heavy armament could fire directly astern, and one of the three 16-inch turrets was unable to fire directly ahead, but *Rodney* could easily manoeuvre to open arcs of fire, ensuring all nine main guns were brought to bear. Nevertheless, some naval purists, offended by *Nelson* and *Rodney's* brutal modernism, voiced serious misgivings about the main armament's inability to fire astern[17]. They felt the ability of eight of twelve 6-inch guns to fire astern and ahead hardly made up for perceived flaws in main armament.

It was neatly summed up by the renowned *Jane's Fighting Ships*, which in the 1940s observed of *Rodney* and her sister that their design was 'peculiar, in that it is governed more by constructional than tactical principles.'[18] One of *Rodney*'s officers, however, regarded her as the fruit of a brilliant mind. He claimed D'Eyncourt had produced in *Nelson* and *Rodney* the 'most powerful and invulnerable fighting units that human ingenuity has yet been able to contrive.'

The same officer felt *Rodney* inspired a mixture of dread and awe.

> *I challenge any one who claims to possess what I am pleased to term a soul, to stand on* Rodney's *fo'c'sle and contemplate the stark grey mass of turret and gun that stretches away before him – I challenge him to stand there by himself and not feel a definite tingle of pride and fear.*[19]

While admitting the new battleships were 'an outrage upon convention' the officer admired *Rodney*'s peculiar, yet somehow inspiring, 'cold austerity', and 'suggestion of inhuman power'. For him, *Rodney* exerted a grim fascination.

It numbs your brain. Yet you exult. If, that is, you have a soul.[20]

Other officers who served in *Rodney* did not enjoy such a mystical conversion, one very junior member of her ship's company, aware of her pedigree as a shortened version of the G3 design, remarking:

They were vastly different from the First World War battleships ... Instead of re-designing from scratch, in order to get them into service quickly, the Admiralty just chopped off the stern ... and so they came out with this peculiar shape. Very odd ships.[21]

Prior to the G3s being cancelled, in excess of £500,000[22] was expended creating 16-inch and 6-inch guns, together with their mountings, so it was indeed fortunate they could be used in *Rodney* and *Nelson*.[23]

A single 16-inch gun was 103 tons in weight and 62 ft long, each turret weighing 1,500 tons. The pre-dreadnought battleships of the Renown Class constructed in the 1890s – state-of-the-art formidable warships of the late Victorian era – could manage a *combined* broadside (four 10-inch guns and ten 6-inch guns) totalling 2,500 lbs, which was 452 lbs in excess of a *single* shell from *Rodney*. Each 16-inch shell was 2,048 lbs in weight[24] and travelled at 2,670 feet per second – nearly 14 nautical miles in 30 seconds, or a nautical mile every 2.27 seconds. A 16-inch gun in *Rodney* could fire between 180 and 200 shells before needing to be replaced and was capable of 40 degrees maximum elevation, giving it a maximum range of 35,000 yards (22 miles). It was reckoned a shell from *Rodney*'s main armament could penetrate 14-inches of armour, potentially enabling the ship to destroy any vessel in existence. *Rodney*'s 16-inch guns combined a high velocity with a lighter shell but were not thought to have the same penetrative ability as the eight 15-inch weapons mounted in the Queen Elizabeth Class. These combined a low velocity with a heavy shell. However, in total, a nine-gun broadside by *Rodney* was heavier compared with any one of the Queen Elizabeths.[25] Bearing in mind D'Eyncourt's vain efforts to ensure secondary armament in *Hood* was clear of the sea, *Rodney* was, by contrast, a distinct success, with a high freeboard. The secondary armament was innovative too, being mounted in turrets on the upper deck, whereas previously, even in the Royal Sovereigns, completed just over a decade earlier, 6-inch guns were mounted within the hull, battery-fashion. Aside from keeping secondary armament clear of the water, it was also possible *Rodney*'s designer realized a quicker rate of fire might be achieved, if the 6-inch weapons benefited from mechanical loading.

The 6-inch shell weighed 100 lbs, which was supposed to be the limit a man could lift and load with a reasonable degree of speed. By the time they built the post-World War One constructions they had come to the conclusion that the 6-inch should be power worked and in turrets.[26]

Although the 6-inch guns were supposed to fire up to eight rounds a minute they only managed half that rate in the 1920s and 1930s[27] but, during the Second World War, six rounds was achieved. The 6-inch guns could also double as Anti-Aircraft armament. In reality this role fell primarily to half a dozen 4.7-inch AA guns and lots of smaller calibre weapons. The *Rodney* had two 24.5-inch torpedo tubes fitted, one either side of the bows below the waterline. The largest diameter torpedoes in any Royal Navy warship, they were specially shortened, enabling them to be moved around the ship more easily. Provided with enriched air propulsion, they carried a warhead packed with 743 lbs of explosives.

The *Rodney*'s first Commanding Officer arrived on 20 May 1927, Captain H.K. Kitson, whose objective was to get her ready for trials, with a nucleus crew working alongside contractors. *Rodney* was to be a Plymouth-based warship, and therefore sailors from the Devonport Division headed north to prepare her for sea. On a Saturday morning, 13 August 1927, a largely completed *Rodney* left the construction yard to take centre-stage in the Mersey, under the gaze of thousands of onlookers, before heading down river to the Irish Sea. The battleship set course for waters off Plymouth, conducting speed trials on the Admiralty's measured mile, in Whitsand Bay, between 29 August and 7 September[28] The *Rodney*'s power was provided by eight Admiralty three-drum boilers, which were fired by oil, and her machinery was geared turbines, turning two shafts. The contractors and nucleus crew gradually wound up her speed, on 30 August going from 13 knots to 18 knots and on 1 September managing 21 knots. The following day she achieved nearly 23 knots and on 7 September *Rodney* reached 23.8 knots.[29]

Carrying 4,000 tons of fuel oil, and running at top speed, she burned up 16 tons an hour.[30] Her cruising speed would be 12 knots, with a range of 16,500 miles. Even the super-dreadnought HMS *Warspite* managed 25 knots during sea trials at the beginning of the First World War, while Japan's 16-inch gun *Nagato* had a top speed of 26.5 knots (but only a range of 5,500 miles at 16 knots). However, the US Navy's *Colorado*, the other type of 16-inch gun battleship *Rodney* was built to counter, could barely manage 21 knots, with a range of only 8,000 miles at ten knots. The British Empire, with colonies and protectorates strung across the globe, needed a heavy hitter with range and, bearing in mind the amount of armour *Rodney* carried, 23 knots was about the best that could be hoped for. Still, *Rodney* was regarded by many as woefully under-powered for a modern battleship, especially with her displacement and broad beam. She steered badly, was slow to answer the helm, despite the fact that the rudder could be swung over in 30 seconds.[31] She possessed erratic steering astern. The propellers had to work very hard to move *Rodney* through the water, one Commanding Officer considering he needed 10 knots underway before he could get the ship under control – she took a while to build a head of steam and this was not helped by boilers being removed to shorten the design. Preliminary gunnery trials took place in mid-September, after which the battleship headed north, in order for Cammel Laird to complete fitting out and rectify faults. This took nearly two months, during which her nucleus crew went home to Devonport, returning to Birkenhead in early November 1927. The hand-over ceremony duly took place on 9 November, the battleship signed into the care of the Navy. By 12 November *Rodney* was off Plymouth, but did not sail into her homeport, for she was destined to undergo further defect rectification work at Portsmouth. On 6 December, *Rodney* finally went alongside in Devonport for the first time since her completion. Entering the Sound at around 3.00 pm, she was greeted by tugs waiting to shepherd her along the deep water channel, and, most crucially, ease her passage through the potentially treacherous Devil's Narrows, the slim neck of water between the Sound and the Hamoaze.[32] A tow was put across as a precaution, *Rodney* successfully negotiating the route. Her arrival was long awaited in the city of Plymouth, for there had not been a brand new battleship commissioned into the fleet at Devonport for some years, but she did not receive quite the reception anticipated.

> *Unfortunately, the time of her arrival was uncertain, so that only a comparatively small number of people, who happened to be on the Hoe, at Mount Wise, or at other points along the water front, saw the great ship . . .*[33]

Rodney was, however, welcomed by the Commander-in-Chief, Plymouth, Vice Admiral Sir Rudolph Bentinck, who sent greetings from a signal station at Admiralty House, Mount Wise, as *Rodney* entered the Hamoaze.

For those witnessing her passing, *Rodney* 'presented an imposing spectacle, with her long deck, on which nine 16-inch guns are mounted, and her tremendous tower.'[34] Once in the upper reaches of the Hamoaze, *Rodney* berthed at No7 wharf in Devonport's North Yard to await the sailors and marines who would make up her full complement on commissioning into the Atlantic Fleet the following day. A *Rodney* sailor recalled one of her new arrivals claimed an interesting history:

> *. . . the ship's cat of the* Tiger *was transferred to the* Rodney *when the ship first commissioned. The cat had its own hammock, kit-bag and service certificate. He* [the sailor] *remembered reading the certificate and seeing an entry that the cat had been charged with 'Indecently assaulting Minnie'* [another cat] *for which 'crime' he was ordered 'to be castrated'!*[35]

The local *Western Evening Herald* reported the estimated total cost of the *Rodney* up until the end of the current financial year as £6,085,884, not including armament and ordnance, which would ultimately add another £500,000. From 13 December to 27 December, a Christmas break was granted to those of the ship's officers and men yet to take leave. There was plenty of work in the meantime, with embarkation of food supplies, torpedoes, shells and many other items that make up the cargo of war carried by a fighting ship. *Rodney* would be ready to play her part as a front line warship as soon as Christmas was over.

As the year came to a close, *Rodney* embarked on intensive gunnery trials, which uncovered a series of problems, not least the necessity to fire the central gun in each trio separately from the others. If all the guns were fired, in triple salvoes, severe damage to *Rodney* could result. The resulting restrictions reduced the rate of fire. It had been anticipated at one salvo every 50 seconds, but the need to fire in alternate salvoes – the centre guns in one turret and outer two guns in the others – delivered an actual rate of one every 65 seconds.

There were also concerns about X turret guns being fired on the extreme aft bearing. According to Oscar Parkes, in his pre-war *Ships of the Royal Navies*, the A, B and X turrets had arcs of fire, respectively, of 298, 330 and 250 degrees.

As Controller of the Navy, Admiral Chatfield attended the gunnery trials and, having seen so much action in the First World War, was not afraid of putting himself in the firing line:

> *So we trained the after turret right-aft, and elevated one gun to its extreme elevation, so that its muzzle was not more than a few feet from the bridge.*[36]

Chatfield and the two other 'test dummies' waited for the explosive moment.

> *The shock of the full charge was very severe and gave a feeling of one's chest being crushed, but actually the result, on those present was very slight.*

However, the bridge superstructure was very badly beaten up in some places and modifications were introduced to mitigate against potential harm. The triple-mountings were a radical step for the Royal Navy, an attempt to achieve decisive firepower, but at the same time save weight, by having fewer turrets. It was the first time that many guns had been housed in a single turret in a British warship and, according to Royal Marine Subaltern James Moulton, they proved troublesome:

> *They didn't work at first and we had a lot of technical experts, gunnery officers, torpedo officers and so on ... the first year of that commission was unsuccessful and unhappy.*[37]

Making the whole process work, was of course no easy matter. The shells – each one 5' 7-inches tall and weighing around a ton – were taken from their bins in the turret's shell room, deep within the ship, which carried two hundred 16-inch shells per gun, and put into a hoist to be taken up 60 ft to the gunhouse. The men in *Rodney*'s shell handling rooms wore cotton overalls and rubber shoes to ensure that nothing could cause a spark. Both shells and charges were sent up in the vertical position, the hoists totally enclosed and flash-tight. They were only exposed when taken out of the hoists to be put into the breech of the gun. A ramrod then pushed home the shell and its charge, the latter containing a quarter of a ton of cordite (contained within three silk bags). The hydraulically-operated breech was closed, locked and, finally, the gun was ready to fire. And so, from the deafening sound of muzzle-loaded guns in the Victorian-era *Rodney*'s gun decks at Sevastopol, packed with humanity, we have now progressed to a situation where the gunners are cogs in a complex machine. They only see dials passing on instructions of where to turn the turret, what angle to elevate the guns. Battleship *Rodney*'s gunners do not even see what they shoot at.

> *The few men in the turret hear little but the noise of their own machinery, the clang and crash of the hoist, the roar of the air blast clearing the bore of burning gases. A sharp crack comes to them from a world that is riven with the thunder of the guns they fire.*[38]

The men in the turrets do not even fire them, for that job belongs to the gunnery officer in his control position, although the guns can devolve to local command and control if need be. If their own ship is hit with a hammer blow, the gunners might not know what has happened until waters rush in to claim them or *Rodney* explodes. Only five per cent of a battleship crew actually saw the action during a battle: the rest held their nerve and listened to the thunder beyond their metal universe. However, to those in the unfortunate vessel they were firing at, the sight of *Rodney*'s big guns unleashing hell was no doubt a bowel-loosening, knee-trembling experience; the flame and great clouds of smoke; the roar of on-coming death, ripping the sky apart as a shell made its passage with the unnerving sound of an express train. The blast from *Rodney*'s guns could break windows five miles away and, as the shock wave moved through the ship, any crockery, personal ornaments, furniture or even doors not secured (or removed prior to the shoot) were likely to be smashed.

The two new battleships acquired more than just one nickname. While 'The Cherry Trees' might have been an early label, the more enduring nickname for *Rodney* was 'The Rodbox'. However, to many the new battleship's silhouette, with its short quarterdeck and long forecastle divided by the beefy Octopoidal, resembled a gigantic boot. As a result, *Rodney* and *Nelson* were also nicknamed 'The Pair of Boots'. There was no doubt they presented a radical silhouette compared to battleships which had gone before them. They appeared alien and other-worldly. A naval officer who served in *Rodney* during the 1930s referred to them as 'Olympian'[39], remarking with more than a hint of affection:

> *... like Zeus, or a fat policeman, they carry that air of accepted predominance which says: 'I am here. You're quite safe now. Pray don't worry.'*[40]

It took 1,314 men to sail and fight *Rodney*, but with an admiral and his staff embarked the number rose to 1,361.[41] The electricity generated by the ship could light a small town, which of course *Rodney* was and, as such, possessed half a dozen telephone exchanges. The well-equipped sickbay had an x-ray machine and *Rodney* even contained a chapel – the oak panelled church of St Christopher, the patron saint of travellers – which was commissioned on 28 April 1928, by the Bishop of Plymouth and Chaplain of the Fleet. To provide home comforts, including cigarettes, sweets, newspapers and books, *Rodney* had a Book Stall. Feeding the ship's sailors and marines was by the central messing system in which galleys cooked all the food, which was then taken to various messes while still hot. Some 2,400 eggs were fried every day for breakfast and hundreds of loaves – 1,500 lbs of bread – baked daily. The catering mod cons included a bacon slicer and a machine for peeling potatoes but, as one officer remarked, onions still had to be peeled and chopped by hand, resulting in tearful sailors. Were the ship to have a beef dinner, it would involve consuming an entire oxen 'less skin and offal'[42] plus three quarters of a ton of potatoes. A mere six pence (modern money equivalent) was spent each day, per sailor, and yet *Rodney*'s men were certainly well nourished in the early years of the battleship's career, at a time when many people beyond the Navy struggled to even put scraps on the table. While others starved during the global economic depression, *Rodney*'s typical daily menu was a relative feast:

> *Breakfast: Sausage and egg.*
> *Dinner: Soup, beef and kidney pies, boiled potatoes, cabbage, jam tart.*
> *Tea* [3 pm]*: Buns.*
> *Supper: Liver and bacon.*

Or

> *Breakfast: Bacon and tomatoes.*
> *Dinner: Soup, roast beef, roast potatoes, marrowfat peas, apples.*
> *Tea: Jam and butter.*
> *Supper: Steak and chips.*[43]

Among the young men tucking into such hearty meals during *Rodney*'s first commission was young Royal Marine officer James Moulton, who would go on to find fame as a commando forces leader in the Second World War.

In late 1928 Moulton belonged to one of the fleet's largest detachments of ship marines, numbering 117 riflemen, plus NCOs, a RM Warrant Officer Gunner, two Subalterns and one Captain RMs. Joining *Rodney*, from the battleship *Revenge*, on 5 January 1928, was eighteen-year old Midshipman Frank Roddam Twiss, who would one day be a distinguished Admiral. *Rodney* immediately impressed the future flag officer.

> *The size of the gunroom & the ventilation of our chest flats and the general smartness of a new ship was the most prominent point I noticed. In fact the ship seemed three times as large as the* Revenge ... *After supper in the gunroom I turned in, but the noise of electric motors and fans seemed at first so loud that I slept very little.*[44]

Whereas *Rodney* of the 1850s could land her own main armament to bolster artillery at the siege of Sevastopol, this was obviously not possible with 16-inch guns. Therefore, the 1920s battleship had her own field guns and, to ensure they could contribute fruitfully to any land campaign, *Rodney*'s men were sent to practice hauling and manning the weapons at Devonport's Gunnery School. Similarly, continuing the same tradition, refining the ship's ability to project power ashore, some of *Rodney*'s sailors were sent for machine gun practice, including Midshipman Twiss. He was also required to learn the art of shooting down aircraft. Along with other young sailors, he entered a simulator, which was 'a large tower like a turret.'

> *Here there was a special arrangement of mirrors, which could be turned and moved, thus making the reflection of a model aeroplane move across a painted sky ...*

The ship took aboard ammunition on 2 February and sailed the next day, not forgetting to hoist the captain's car inboard before leaving.

Rodney headed for Portland, where she was to carry out a series of trials with her revolutionary torpedo armament that bordered on the farcical. This wasn't surprising, with a new type of torpedo that would remain unique to *Rodney* and *Nelson* in the British fleet. *Rodney* was accompanied by the destroyer *Vanoc* on her first firing, the latter tasked with retrieving the test torpedoes, which were suitably trimmed to float. Midshipman Twiss noted:

> *About 10.00 or later we fired one torpedo from the port tube which was found alright, but as the* Vanoc *was about to hoist it inboard, a rope, I believe, parted and the torpedo got underneath the destroyer and sunk.* [sic] *All efforts to retrieve the torpedo having failed, we returned to harbour about 12.30.*

Undeterred, torpedo trials continued, with Twiss noting of one errant weapon on 12 February:

> *... it was reported that the track of the torpedo was seen to turn through 180 degrees ... and as a result had gone by our own stern.*

The torpedo was eventually recovered and another fired from the port tube, appearing to sink close to the ship. However, just as divers were preparing to retrieve it, a signal was received: it had not sunk after all, a recovery had been successfully completed by another vessel. The torpedo was eventually delivered back to the ship, although, mysteriously, minus its engine. This later arrived wrapped in brown paper. On 26 February the ship carried out more torpedo firings, in nearby West Bay, but then bad weather set in, keeping *Rodney* in port. On

1 March, the wearisome torpedo trials resumed, this time witnessed by Midshipman Twiss from the battleship's bridge:

> *The first one, however, ran with his nose above water, having first described a neat circle* [but] *he settled down in the right bearing and was all the easier to pick up.*

By early April, *Rodney* was Devonport bound, but only after a diversion to waters off the Isle of Wight where she first encountered her sister ship at sea. The *Nelson* was leading a showpiece exercise with the battleships *Iron Duke, Marlborough, Benbow* and *Emperor of India*. The king of Afghanistan was aboard *Nelson*, by then flagship of the Atlantic Fleet, with many senior Royal Navy officers also embarked. Returning to Devonport on 4 April, *Rodney* at month's end received a new Commanding Officer in the shape of Captain Loftus Tottenham, and a number of other replacements. Subaltern Moulton welcomed a change in *Rodney*'s ruling regime, from technocrats to people who were, in his opinion, more efficient man-managers. He recalled, with more than a tinge of sarcasm:

> *By* [a] *remarkable thing they replaced these experts with real leaders. The* [new] *Captain was a very meticulous chap who, if you got through a forenoon watch with nothing going wrong, you felt proud ... the difference was we were a happy ship and not only that, our guns worked and our torpedoes ran. It is a lesson that I have never forgotten the value of: leaders had to be efficient at their technical jobs but they also had to inspire people to follow them.*

Ahead for *Rodney* lay the Atlantic Fleet's 'Summer Cruise' to the anchorage at Invergordon in Scotland. Warships between the world wars had a regular cycle of cruises as fixed as the seasons of the year. The Spring Cruise would see the Atlantic Fleet sail for the Mediterranean where it found calmer waters for exercises, with perhaps a foray to the Caribbean as an alternative. Aside from deploying to Invergordon, the Summer Cruise encompassed pleasant visits to British seaside towns and also foreign shores, such as to Norway or some other Scandinavian port of call, showing the flag and forging closer bonds with friends abroad. After summer leave, *Rodney*'s sailors and marines could expect to set sail again at the beginning of September, on the Autumn Cruise, to carry out further Atlantic Fleet exercises, heading once more for Invergordon. But this was *Rodney*'s first run through the inter-war cycle and, leaving Devonport on 30 April, she led other battleships out past the Hoe, later meeting *Nelson* off Portsmouth along with more units of the fleet. While *Rodney* and *Nelson* had different home ports, at sea they were united in the 2nd Battle Squadron, forming the vanguard for the trip north. On the night of 2 May, *Rodney* got a taste of being 'attacked', Midshipman Twiss managing to secure a ringside seat.

> Nelson *and* Rodney *were in line ahead with navigation lights only. Two attacks were made on us by destroyers with no lights. The first was by two destroyers very close, on opposite course to us on the port side. We picked them up with searchlights and followed them as they passed at a very short distance. The second attack was by two destroyers on the starboard side. We picked these up with searchlights and they put up a smoke screen, later disappearing.*

There were mock air attacks the following day and all the way up through the North Sea *Rodney* and other capital ships were harassed. On arriving at Invergordon, Twiss was among those who went ashore to play golf, but such leisure pursuits were brief, for the ships soon sailed for an intensive series of exercises. During a 'Blue Fleet' versus 'Red Fleet' battle exercise on 24 May, 'about 11.00 [am] a report came to *Rodney* from one of the destroyers that enemy aircraft were in sight,' recalled Midshipman Twiss.

> *High-Angle parties closed up but this proved to be a false alarm. Reports of the enemy's movements began coming in fast and suddenly at 12.15 eight torpedo planes made an attack on us ... Only one* [practice] *torpedo was fired at us and by altering course and due to the inaccuracy of the torpedo we were not hit.*

At 6.00 pm the same day a further seven torpedo planes attacked, but *Rodney* was regarded as valiantly fighting them off. After yet more exercises, *Rodney* headed for her maiden call at the fleet anchorage of Scapa Flow, in the Orkneys, arriving on 4 June. *Rodney*'s men found that at Scapa there were no trees, nor grass but brown moss only, and not much green at all to be seen – although there were some sparse clumps of heather and a few determined sheep somehow finding sustenance. Ashore, there was a golf course and sports pitches to divert men from the bleakness and a hut masquerading as a canteen.

There was more torpedo firing at Portland in late June and early July followed by further fleet exercises, *Rodney* acting as flagship of the 'Red Fleet', which included the battlecruiser *Renown*, training cruiser *Adventure* and four destroyers with a 'convoy' to protect. 'Red Fleet' was based on Portsmouth while the enemy 'Blue Fleet' operated from Falmouth and consisted of *Benbow*, flagship, with *Marlborough*, *Emperor of India*, *Repulse*, destroyers and a 'convoy' of drifters. A 'Yellow Fleet', based on Paignton, was composed of three cruisers, with *Snapdragon* as flagship. During the course of 'hostilities' Yellow came in on the side of Blue, so *Renown* was ordered on 4 July to 'bombard' Paignton – but the Blue Fleet coasted over the horizon and '*Rodney* left the convoy and joined in a general action. We had 'B' & 'X' turrets put out of action ...'[45] The ships afterwards headed for Torbay, where, on 6 July, a sailing regatta was held. On the evening of 10 July, a searchlight display was given, with all naval vessels lit up. The fleet dispersed the following morning, *Rodney* heading back to Portland for torpedo trials, which were as unfortunate as the earlier set, on 16 July Midshipman Twiss noting:

> *The first torpedo went astray at the start & after circling 'round set off on a wrong course, later disappearing altogether.*

During magnetic signature trials on 17 July in West Bay an aircraft, sent up with a photographer aboard to take some portraits of the battleship, crashed into the sea, but fortunately its three occupants, one of whom was injured, were pulled out of the water by the destroyer *Tara*. After a courtesy visit to Seaton, where *Rodney*'s cricket team drew with the locals, the battleship finally headed back to her home port where she would spend around a fortnight before sailing again. For *Rodney* was assigned to be Royal Guardship at Cowes Week, on 11 August King George V and Queen Mary coming aboard, attending a service in the ship's chapel and taking the salute of a march past from the quarterdeck. His Majesty expressed satisfaction at the ship's high standard. The Royal Yacht sailed at 7.00 am on 12 August, *Rodney* an hour later setting course for Devonport, where she would be the star attraction of a new charity event. Navy Weeks at the three main naval bases of Devonport,

Portsmouth and Chatham, were a response to the dire economic situation. In the pre-Welfare State Britain of the late 1920s there was real hardship among ex-sailors, and the many widows and orphans of those from the Naval Service killed in the recent war. The reduced size of the Navy restricted the money raised by serving officers and men, who anyway had to support their own families on modest salaries. Therefore, a fund-raising show for the public aimed to fill the gap. The first Navy Week at Devonport ran from a Tuesday to Saturday, with people coming from as far away as South Wales, the Midlands and Bristol to see *Rodney* and other ships. A special train was even laid on, originally to have been composed of four coaches but soon extended to six. While it had been announced no photography would be allowed in the dockyard, on some days 1,000 cameras had to be left at the gates. Aside from *Rodney*, the *Hood*, *Iron Duke* and *Lion* were also on show, alongside the cruiser *Devonshire* and aircraft carrier *Glorious*, plus three submarines. More than 67,000 people went through the dockyard gates and such was its success it was felt Navy Week might become an annual event.

Towards the end of September 1928 *Rodney* headed north, for some attention to her hull, going into Liverpool's capacious Gladstone Dock because there was no room at Birkenhead. *Rodney* next set sail for the usual routine of exercises at Invergordon, which did nothing to lift the gloom of Subaltern Moulton, who was finding life as a battleship Royal Marine far removed from the hard soldiering he desired.

> *The marines were a pretty frustrating outfit.* [They] *had a vintage period, shall we say in Victorian days, but with expansion of* [the} *Royal Navy to meet the German menace, they became more and more just ship marines ... Their primary war-like duty was manning their share of the armament of the fleet. In the* Rodney *we had one 16-inch turret and two 6-inch turrets ... I, as a subaltern, had charge of one of the 6-inch turrets.*

Moulton had been on a gunnery course at Whale Island in Portsmouth where marines were taught on 15-inch gun turrets and 6-inch battery guns, the latter operated by hand, all of which hardly prepared the young officer for service in *Rodney*.

> *There was a great deal of frustration and certainly you could run into a bad patch of having nothing worthwhile to do ... There was no real distinctive job for the Royal Marines. You had a military training plus naval gunnery but I don't think it fundamentally made much sense ... One had to keep watch in harbour, which always fell on the junior officer and it was a dull and onerous job and it was leading nowhere.*

For a young, ambitious officer, with dreams of battlefield glory, it was simply soul destroying, especially when Moulton had to keep his marines occupied with activities more suited to butlers, acting as servants to officers. The Royal Marines were also responsible for the cleanliness of the Wardroom flats – the decks onto which the officers' cabins opened out. Brass polishing every morning was a high priority. Moulton recalled that his men were frequently employed 'in maintenance duties, in cleaning the ship, and in ceremonials. . .that's how they spent most of their time.'

Even when the *Rodney*'s Royal Marines were allowed to do something with their infantry training, during exercises at Invergordon, it was woefully unrealistic. The detachment would play at landing troops in pulling cutters, a tactic used at the Gallipoli landings in 1915, with heavy casualties. Moulton regarded rowing ashore as 'hopelessly vulnerable'. It was easy to see what the result in real life was likely to be:

> *... while we were pulling ashore our cutters, the Fleet Air Arm fighters came and 'shot' us up. We were actually sitting ducks.*

Once on land Moulton's platoon deployed as four sections – two Lewis gun and two rifle – plus an HQ section.

> *You couldn't get much beyond that. You çouldn't have transport. We used to pull handcarts about. Well, I won't sneer at handcarts too much. Later on I saw them used with some effect in Diego Suarez* [during the second world war] *in the first hours of the landing.*[46]

It was difficult to keep Royal Marines fit for marching when they were in the warships. An attempt was made at least to rectify this, and also give the ship's marines some feeling of proper infantry action. Each summer *Rodney*'s detachment and those from other ships marched from Devonport up to Wilsworthy Camp on Dartmoor, for annual battalion-sized manoeuvres.

At the beginning of 1929, the Atlantic Fleet, including *Rodney* and *Nelson*, sailed for the Mediterranean, embarking on a series of exercises that would ultimately take them to Malta. After joining the Mediterranean Fleet for a mock war off the fortress island, there were further exercises, involving British aircraft carriers, in the western Med, before the Atlantic Fleet set course for home. While *Rodney*'s sailors enjoyed some shore leave with their families in Plymouth, at Portsmouth, in early April 1929, Vice Admiral Chatfield took command of the Atlantic Fleet, hoisting his flag in HMS *Nelson*, which shortly thereafter sailed north in company with *Rodney* and other ships for the usual exercises based on Invergordon. A fleet assembly at Torquay in early July was a pleasant interlude and *Rodney*'s Midshipman Twiss took full advantage, managing a spot of tennis at the Devon holiday resort's Palace Hotel and a swim in the same establishment's pool. The day after his sporting activities ashore, a crisis erupted – on 9 July two British submarines collided in the Irish Sea and help was urgently needed. '...a sudden signal from the C-in-C told us to prepare to proceed forthwith to the position of a sunken submarine,' reported Midshipman Twiss.

> *All boats were hoisted and steam was raised, when we were told to wait. At 16.30, however, we were ordered to proceed and we unmoored and proceeded at 12 knots for a position off Milford Haven. Very little was known of the accident except that submarine* H47 *had been in collision with submarine* L12 *and the former had sunk in 55 fathoms. The destroyer* Vivien *had preceeded us, having gone on at full speed and all the other ships in the vicinity were being rushed to the spot while salvage lighters and diving apparatus were being sent at full speed.*

Clearly, there was still hope some of the submariners might be saved, for at 8.00 pm *Rodney* was signalled to arrive over the sunken submarine's position by 8.00 am.

> *We then went on to full speed.*

A signal to the ship revealed *L12* had struck *H47* at a right angle, ahead of the conning tower, on the port side.

> H47 *had sunk instantly with doors open, only the captain and one rating being saved. There had been casualties in the* L12, *several being* [chlorine] *gas poisoning.*

In fact, three of *H47*'s sailors had been lucky enough to jump clear but another 19 were trapped inside the stricken boat, on the seabed.

To emphasise the urgency, on the night of 9 July *Rodney* received yet another signal, ordering her to be at Milford Haven as soon as possible, so she went to 22 knots. *Rodney* arrived at 6.15 am, anchoring two miles from Pembroke Dock. The destroyer *Tilbury* came alongside and rescue gear was hoisted aboard the battleship, including a huge German deep diving apparatus called 'The Iron Man's Suit'. Also brought aboard *Rodney* were underwater lights, diving pumps, cables, even a decompression chamber and also a Professor Hill, who was a diving diseases specialist. However, the ship did not immediately weigh anchor, as the weather was considered too bad for diving and the exact position of the submarine was not yet known. After the stricken boat was located all hope of saving the crew soon evaporated, with efforts to first supply air and then to actually salvage the submarine officially abandoned. An L Class boat had dived close to *H47* but there was no response when attempts were made to communicate via an underwater telephone. 'It is certain that her men are dead,' *The Times* mournfully noted.

In his journal Midshipman Twiss described the events of Thursday, 11 July:

> *We sailed from Milford Haven at 17.30 flying the flag of R.A.S.* [Rear Admiral Submarines] *and set course for the position of H47. We arrived there at 21.20 and at sunset a memorial service was held over the spot where H47 sank, a seaman guard 100 strong firing 3 volleys ... After this we set course for Portsmouth, but soon entered a dense fog, which forced us to proceed at 8 knots throughout the night.*

Back at Devonport by the end of July, *Rodney* once more entered the familiar cycle of summer leave and participation in Navy Week followed by autumn exercises off Invergordon, setting sail and joining the rest of the Atlantic Fleet to 'battle' north. During Navy Week, while *Rodney* again was the centre of attraction, the battleship *Ramilies* was equally impressive, displayed in a floating drydock, with members of the public allowed to actually walk underneath her. This second Navy Week, which attracted more than 87,000 visitors, raised £5,000 for naval charities.

In late September, *Rodney* suffered severe machinery defects that forced her into drydock at Portsmouth, for urgent repairs that took more than two months to complete. Before the year was out, she received a new Commanding Officer, in the shape of Captain Andrew Browne Cunningham – known as A.B.C. – a Scottish First World War destroyer veteran who was later to win renown, during the Second World War. But commanding a fleet in war lay a decade in the future and the battleship he took charge of on 15 December 1929 was a daunting enough prospect for the forty-six year old Captain, who admitted:

> *To one who had never commanded anything larger than a small cruiser the* Rodney *appeared enormous.*[47]

He fretted about handling such an unconventional capital ship in confined waters, what with a stem so remote from her bridge and having already acquired a reputation for being slow to answer her propellers. Oliver Warner, one of Cunningham's biographers, has given the opinion that *Rodney* 'could have been a tough proposition for anyone who had spent so much of his sea time in destroyers.'[48] However, the Admiralty must have had faith in Cunningham, or it would not have given him command of one of the world's most powerful warships. While *Rodney*'s new CO may have been worried about how he might handle her, the ship's sailors were more than a little anxious about how he would deal with them. One young officer later confessed: '... we were all rather apprehensive as he had a reputation as a tiger ...'[49] Cunningham's rule would contribute towards *Rodney* gaining a reputation for being host to Bolshevik subversion, the vessel being unfairly branded 'The Red Ship'.

Notes

1 W. Gordon Campbell, *HMS Rodney – The Story of a Battleship.*
2 *Western Evening Herald*, 18 December 1925.
3 C.R. Benstead, *HMS Rodney.*
4 Chatfield, *It Might Happen Again.*
5 *Western Evening Herald*, 18 December 1925.
6 Ibid.
7 Ibid.
8 When American general and first US President George Washington was six-years old one of his favourite pursuits was hacking at things with a little hatchet. He killed his father's prized cherry tree by attacking it with his axe, although young George did not actually chop the tree down; hence the allusion to Washington (in this case the Washington Treaty) 'chopping down' *Rodney* and *Nelson* from 'full-size' battleships is slightly off the mark. However, everyone got the joke.
9 *Western Evening Herald*, 18 December 1925.
10 Ibid.
11 Ian Collard, *Cammell Laird.*
12 W. Gordon Campbell, *HMS* Rodney *– The Story of a Battleship.*
13 Oscar Parkes, *Ships of the Royal Navies.*
14 C.R. Benstead, *HMS* Rodney *at Sea.*
15 D.K. Brown, *The Grand Fleet.*
16 Talbot-Booth, *The Royal Navy.*
17 Oscar Parkes, *Ships of the Royal Navies.*
18 *Jane's Fighting Ships of World War II.*
19 C.R. Benstead, *HMS Rodney at Sea.*
20 Ibid.
21 Palmer, IWM Sound Archive.
22 Oscar Parkes, *Ships of the Royal Navies.*
23 In the G3 design there were to be sixteen 6-inch guns in twin mountings. The Furious Class battlecruisers of the First World War mounted a single 18-inch gun, so the 16-inch weapons of *Rodney* were not the biggest ever in a British capital ship.
24 D.K. Brown, *The Grand Fleet.*
25 R.A. Burt, *British Battleships 1919–1939.*
26 Moulton, IWM Sound Archive.
27 D.K. Brown, *The Grand Fleet.*
28 John A. Roberts, *Ship's Monthly*, March 1971.
29 Ibid.
30 *Jane's Fighting Ships of World War II.*
31 Ian Collard, *Cammell Laird.*

32 While Devonport Naval Base is often said to stand on the Devon banks of the Tamar, the Hamoaze is the broad stretch of water created by the confluence of the Tamar and the smaller rivers Tavy and Lynher, which then flow together into the Sound, via the Devil's Narrows, after passing the dockyard and naval base at Devonport.
33 *Western Morning News*, 7 December 1927.
34 Ibid.
35 Taken from a document called *The 'Invergordon Mutineer' in Plymouth*, held in the Naval Studies Department of Plymouth City Library, and all about the visit of Plymothian RN seaman, and Invergordon Mutiny, agitator Leonard Wincott.
36 Chatfield, *It Might Happen Again.*
37 Moulton, IWM Sound Archive.
38 C.R. Benstead, *HMS* Rodney *at Sea.*
39 Ibid.
40 Ibid.
41 *Jane's Fighting Ships of World War II.*
42 C.R. Benstead, *HMS Rodney.*
43 Ibid.
44 Twiss, Royal Naval Museum.
45 Ibid.
46 In 1942, Moulton play a key role in commanding Operation Ironclad, which saw an amphibious assault on the port of Diego Suarez and occupation of Madagascar, a Vichy French territory. It aimed to prevent the Japanese from using the island to increase their domination of the Indian Ocean.
47 Cunningham, *A Sailor's Odyssey.*
48 Warner, Cunningham of Hyndhope.
49 Quoted by Pack, in *Cunningham the Commander.*

Chapter Six

THE RED SHIP

On 16 December 1925, the day before *Rodney*'s launch on the Mersey, the Admiralty issued a statement to be read to ships' companies and posted on noticeboards in both vessels and shore establishments. It was keen to counter a 'communist propaganda' pamphlet.

> *The leaflet hints that the recent reduction in pay of new entries is a step towards the reduction of existing rates. This is untrue and has no foundation in fact.*[1]

The pamphlet also allegedly claimed officers' daily food allowance alone was equivalent to the daily pay of a lower deck rating. The Admiralty explained that officers received the same victualling allowance as ratings.

> *The writers of these leaflets are not really interested in the pay or welfare of the lower deck. Their aim is to cause discontent so as to facilitate their real object, which is to introduce by revolutionary violence a form of government similar to that which brought nothing but bloodshed, misery, and starvation to Russia. These people know that they can never achieve their object so long as the services remain loyal to their trust; hence, they are using every endeavour to undermine that loyalty.*[2]

Loyalty was not necessarily universal among sailors who found themselves in a Service with which some had little affinity. Prior to the Spithead mutiny of the 1790s, Quota Acts forced local authorities to send their criminals and agitators to the Navy for war service. This clearing of jails and alternative sentencing by magistrates brought into the Navy many men who, unlike those swept up by the Press Gangs in Britain's ports, had no familiarity with the sea, were generally more truculent and might also be well enough educated to absorb writings on the 'The Rights of Man'.

A similar situation arose in the economically depressed Britain of the 1920s and early 1930s. There was no need for the press gang or an emptying of prisons, for there were very few other jobs available offering reasonable pay, good food and accommodation, with a bit of travel and a purpose in life thrown in. New recruits arrived at Devonport Barracks at a time when the Navy was hard-pushed to man even those few ships economic restrictions allowed it to keep in service. Converging with this was the continuing rise of the technocratic officer. In late 1929 *Rodney*'s new Commanding Officer found poor man management persisted and partly blamed it on the 'big ship' mentality.

> *Big ship time is said to be necessary to us all. I have never found it to be so. What I do know is that any captain will tell you that the best officers to be found in big ships have come from submarines or destroyers. It is my experience here.*

Cunningham felt destroyers were better disciplined, their officers more in touch with their men.[3]

> *The skipper of a destroyer gets soaked to the skin on the bridge just the same as any sailor, but his opposite number* [in a battleship] *walks dry-skinned from his luxurious cabin where he has been sitting aloof from all goings on, to an equally luxurious bridge.*[4]

But, while he was keenly aware of the problem, Cunningham was new to big ship command and, truth to tell, probably unaware his own tough managerial style was not always understood by members of the Lower Deck who found themselves joining up more out of economic necessity than a love for Navy life. Under Cunningham's command few could argue *Rodney* was not an 'efficient ship'.[5] To some, who probably knew only the world of the Wardroom, *Rodney* was even a happy ship.

On 31 December 1929, *Rodney* exited dry-dock at Portsmouth and embarked on machinery trials, in preparation for a deployment to the Mediterranean. The *Rodney*'s Commander – Executive Officer, or second-in-command – was Robert L. Burnett, described by Cunningham as 'a man with a good hold and an excellent way with the men.'[6] Like his boss he would see a fair bit of action in the Second World War. During his time in *Rodney*, Burnett was noted for being an effervescent ball of energy, keen on arranging entertainment for the men, and with more than a touch of the panto dame about him, as Cunningham would soon discover. The presence of rather too many chiefs and not enough Indians continued to niggle Cunningham, for, while he agreed the battleship was a particularly complex machine, he felt Lieutenant Commanders and Lieutenants were doing jobs more properly undertaken by a Midshipman or Petty Officer. In addition to lacking opportunities for responsibility, there was consequently not a lot of experience to be had in watch-keeping at sea either for the junior officers.

By late 1929 the Atlantic Fleet comprised the battleships *Nelson* (flagship of Vice Admiral Chatfield as Commander-in-Chief), *Rodney*, *Barham* and *Malaya*, with the battlecruisers *Renown*, *Repulse* and *Tiger*. Aircraft carriers *Argus* and *Furious* were assigned, along with cruisers *Frobisher*, *Vindictive*, *Comus* and *Canterbury*. The cruiser *Centaur* was in charge of two destroyer flotillas, while *Empress of India* and *Marlborough* were both training ships for boy sailors. At the beginning of 1930, *Rodney* was with other ships of the fleet trapped at Portland by a gale, which they rode out at anchor. *Rodney* was given the honour of leading the fleet to sea but was slow to get under way and Chatfield flashed a sharp signal to an embarrassed Cunningham, informing him *Nelson* would lead the fleet out instead. Coming from destroyers, Cunningham had failed to appreciate that piling on revolutions in shallow water meant energy was dissipated, churning up the seabed rather than making the battleship answer her helm. Conducting battle exercises on the way south, the fleet called at Gibraltar, where a lunch party hosted by Captain Cunningham provided Commander Burnett with an opportunity for cheeky cross-dressing. For, when there proved to be rather too many men, the Commander dressed as a female guest, allegedly getting away with it, despite being 'podgy' and blessed with an 'eternal red faced grin'.[7] By February 1930, *Rodney* was at Algiers, where a befuddled French pilot came aboard.

> *He was suffering from what might be called a heavy hangover. It was clear that the unorthodox arrangement of the* Rodney's *bridge so far aft quite confused him, so he most willingly concurred in our going in stern first through the breakwater, fully believing that it was our normal method of procedure*[8]

Returning from the Mediterranean, Cunningham mulled over a remark by a senior officer of his acquaintance who, after receiving a tour of *Rodney*, advised him: '... on no account allow yourself to become entangled in the technicalities of this great ship.' Cunningham decided to have no time for troublesome machinery and that extended to people supposed to ensure its efficient operation. One of *Rodney*'s young torpedo officers, Stuart Paton, was more than once in hot water when his weapons did not work properly. Cunningham also especially hated seeing sailors in grimy overalls – the working rig of the torpedo department. However, Paton found the captain would explode but then, once the storm subsided, might see humour in a situation caused by perennially temperamental machinery. Cunningham liked to tell Paton, with a twinkle in his eye:

> *Mind you don't do it again!*[9]

Despite his captain's mercurial nature, Paton was sure he would have 'walked barefoot through Hell for such a man.'[10]

Most troublesome of all were *Rodney*'s 16-inch guns, with their revolutionary and temperamental triple mountings, which must have provoked many a gunnery officer into sending a silent prayer skyward.

The Gunnery Officer during Cunningham's reign was Lieutenant Commander Geoffrey Oliver, who definitely saw both sides of *Rodney*'s CO, having awaited his arrival with some trepidation.

> *He had a formidable reputation in the Service as a martinet, and well-meaning friends condoled with me on what they told me I would be in for.*[11]

Oliver discovered Cunningham went at everything with an 'intense spirit of attack' in order to drive people to excel, convinced what he wished to see done was always achievable. It invariably was, with Cunningham's eye for detail, whether it was improper uniform or an unpolished brass nut, totally unyielding. Offences provoked a stern rebuke and Lt Cdr Oliver experienced Cunningham's peppery nature when called upon to explain why the 16-inch guns had experienced an embarrassing malfunction. Cunningham asked crisply: 'In what capacity are you appointed here?'

'Your gunnery officer sir,' replied Lt Cdr Oliver.

> *Go away then ... Make your toys work. And don't waste my time with excuses.*[12]

To his officers at least, Cunningham could not help but reveal that behind the ferocity 'there was the kindest heart imaginable.' One of them remarked:

> *I think it was these two 'opposites', laced with an almost boyish sense of humour, that captivated and bound us to him.*[13]

By late March 1930, *Rodney* was at Devonport, paying off at the end of her first commission, the majority of her complement swiftly dispersing. However, on 16 April 1930, ratings from the Devonport Barracks were paraded in two groups of around 300 and marched down to her.

> [They] *Tramped over the cobbles. They edged round the basin, across the caissons. They stumbled over the railway lines. They picked a careful path among the litter of industry ... And along the ample frontage of berths number 6 and 7, where HMS* Rodney *lay, serene and grey in sunshine, they came to a halt.*[14]

The ship was commissioned back into service, sailors streaming aboard. They collected their hammocks and were led by remaining old hands to see where they would live and work. *Rodney* was a collection of neighbourhoods, defined by the various messes, which were composed depending on rank and job.

A big ship like that with a big crew, you only knew the immediate people you work with, your messmates and a few pals. It is like small town, a lot of people you don't know at all.[15]

In the evening, when sailors went ashore to explore the pubs of Union Street, the black ribbon bands of their hats proudly displayed the name of their ship: HMS *Rodney*. That, at least, gave them a corporate identity.

Vice Admiral Chatfield hoisted his flag as Commander-in-Chief Atlantic Fleet in *Rodney* at Spithead on 28 April 1930 and, in company with the *Renown* and *Barham*, she headed east past the Nab to rendezvous with Chatham warships, before setting course for Invergordon, with the usual battle exercises on the way.

Chatfield left *Rodney* on 8 May, heading south by train on the first leg of a journey to assume command of the Mediterranean Fleet.

Rodney gave her big guns a thorough work-out, Lt Cdr Oliver and Capt Cunningham keen to see the battleship's first full charge 16-inch shoot under their stewardship proceed perfectly. The former was wary of the latter's anger if things did not go smoothly, while Cunningham had yet to preside over the firing of anything bigger than the 6-inch main armament of a cruiser. Something as mechanically complex as *Rodney*'s 16-inch guns would always be prone to the occasional problem. The tension in the gunnery control position was palpable as the turrets swung and the great barrels elevated, in order to hit a target 20,000 yards away. Lt Cdr Oliver leaned over the voicepipe and told the bridge:

Ready to open fire.

The sailor on the other end reported this to Cunningham, followed by a pause before Oliver was advised: 'Captain wants to speak to you, Sir.'

There was another pause before Cunningham's voice came over the voicepipe: 'That you, Guns?'

'Yes, Sir,' replied Oliver, with more than a little trepidation, but he heard Cunningham exclaim:

Lift up your heart![16]

By the end of May, *Rodney* and the rest of the fleet were at Scapa Flow, where they met *Nelson*, carrying the new Commander-in-Chief, Admiral Sir Michael Hodges. There were rowing and pulling regattas, punctuated by hard-fought tug-of-war battles between ships, in which *Rodney*'s Royal Marine team invariably triumphed. After Scapa, *Rodney* headed west around Cape Wrath and across a short stretch of the Irish Sea to Portrush, on the Ulster coast. Having hosted just two HM Ships in two years, the good citizens of the pleasant little seaside resort were overjoyed to be honoured with *Rodney*'s presence, a civic delegation rowing out as soon as the battleship hove into view. The dignitaries were ushered to Cunningham's day cabin where they overwhelmed him with tributes to his magnificent ship. A volcano of praise erupted from the ebuliant Mr R.B. Adams, J.P., Chairman of Portrush Urban Council. As they sipped cocktails, the Captain and his officers listened with 'genuine astonishment and considerable gratification to Mr. Adams' opinion of us . . .'[17]

However, if there is one thing a warship cannot abide it is riding at anchor in shallow waters during a spell of rough weather, and over the next few days the battleship experienced just that. Adams was displeased to be told that if the weather did not abate, *Rodney* might have to leave without any of her people setting foot ashore to participate in a specially arranged 'Navy Week'. He did not understand how Royal Navy sailors could not handle a little bit of inclement weather. The long, slow Atlantic swell made recovering boats treacherous and damage had already been caused to at least one. It was also tricky to transfer people. Life in *Rodney* herself was most uncomfortable. Having a cup of tea in the wardroom was almost impossible, like trying to take a sip while sitting on a seesaw. Most dangerous of all, was the prospect of *Rodney*'s anchors dragging and the ship going aground. A local newspaper, dismayed by *Rodney*'s inactivity, reported, with barely suppressed incredulity, that 120 of her sailors were actually seasick.[18] When advised *Rodney* might set sail within the next few hours, a mortified Mr Adams dispatched a letter in which he told Captain Cunningham: 'The disappointment of the people of Portrush, should you depart . . . would be too great for words of mine to express.'[19] However, the weather improved and the battleship stayed, much to the delight of Portrush, which now welcomed *Rodney*'s sailors with open arms. *The Belfast News-Letter* published a photo essay showing the great and good of Portrush with Captain Cunningham and also Royal Marines on parade. There were images of visitors being shown around the ship and Cunningham ashore cutting a tape to declare 'Portrush Shopping Week' open. *The Belfast News-Letter* reported there was glorious sunshine – a bright blue sky and a calm sea. It was the perfect setting for 'the most powerful battleship in the world.'[20] At the 'Shopping Week' opening *Rodney*'s CO was accompanied by Cdr Burnett and two junior officers, while the ship's band contributed a merry soundtrack for festivities. No one could take their eyes off the magnificent *Rodney.*

> *. . . the huge crowd that assembled were always able to see the giant battleship not far away. She was a potent advertisement for the Empire.*[21]

Local politicians, mindful of the Depression, were pushing patriotism as the answer to economic ills and Captain Cunningham felt obliged to lend his support to the cause, telling the crowd:

> *We are the servants of the Empire, and it is our job, in peace or war, to keep open and police the long sea routes along which the Empire trade passes. In my profession we do not know much about business, but I do not think that there was ever a time when it was more necessary for the Empire to work together and tide over our present difficulties.*[22]

However, *Rodney*'s fearsome captain was not yet released from ribbon cutting. A street in a new housing development was to be opened and named in honour of the ship, with Mr Adams inspired enough to remark:

> *In the years to come boys from this very street may some day go into the British Navy.*[23]

Cunningham used silver scissors to cut the tape, declaring it a great honour to have a street named after HMS *Rodney*. He said she was one of the two most powerful battleships in the world and it was likely none of her size would be built in the future. Captain Cunningham promised it would be entered into the ship's log that on 11 June, a street in Portrush was named *Rodney*.

As a symbol of the bond between the battleship and Portrush a black Persian kitten was presented to Cunningham. Christened Rodney, the kitten took to life at sea, proving fearless, stalking seagulls along precipitous parts of the ship, twice being saved from drowning in the sea.

Then, one day, he was missed.

A battleship is a big place for a small kitten to go missing, so it was thought Rodney might well turn up after a few days. However ...

Weeks passed and still he did not return.

It was with great sadness the battleship's log recorded him 'missing, believed drowned.'[24]

Following a defence diplomacy visit to Iceland, to help celebrate 1,000 years of the Icelandic Parliament, *Rodney* headed for an Atlantic Fleet assembly at Falmouth, and the annual sailing and pulling regatta. She made a covert diversion to the Scillies, for Cunningham could not bear to lose to another ship, so for a few days his sailors trained hard in order to beat all comers. At Falmouth they achieved mixed results, despite the secret training sessions. After a post-regatta call at Lyme Regis, where the local council arranged a dance and a sailing competition as highlights of a four-day friendship visit, *Rodney*'s summer cruise of 1930 ended at Devonport on 22 July, a Tuesday. The ship had sailed 4,000 miles in three months and she came back alongside at 4 pm, having waited three hours for the afternoon tide to provide enough deep water to take the channel through the Sound and Devil's Narrows. *Rodney* was berthed at Devonport's coaling wharf, which was not the most popular place for an oil-fired battleship that prided herself on smartness, for, when the wind blew, it sprinkled her with coal dust. Ahead lay another Navy Week, in early August, with 90,000 people coming to Devonport to see how the Senior Service worked.

After the traditional autumn cruise north to Invergordon with the rest of the Atlantic Fleet, *Rodney*'s destination was a refit at Portsmouth Dockyard. Captain Cunningham, ever mindful of the warning not to become overwhelmed by his ship's technology, was no admirer of a decision by a previous senior officer to take it easy with *Rodney* for fear of breakdowns in her complex and cutting edge equipment. This easy-going attitude inevitably trickled down to become a mindset he had little time for. For example, prior to *Rodney* entering dry-dock at Portsmouth for deep maintenance it was customary to take three days disembarking ammunition. This length of time was not acceptable to Cunningham and, as *Rodney* approached Portsmouth, Lt Cdr Oliver was called to the Captain's day cabin for some surprising instructions. As Oliver entered, Cunningham looked up from his desk, unleashing the greeting:

Ah, here comes that bloody Gunnery Officer![25]

The Captain told Oliver he intended dropping anchor at Spithead that afternoon, with ammunition lighters coming alongside at dawn. All ammunition would have to be disembarked immediately, in order for the ship to dock. The Gunnery Officer's limp protestations that this would take some doing were 'swept aside in a withering torrent'.[26] Cunningham instructed Oliver to tell Cdr Burnett he was to supply any additional manpower needed to achieve the de-ammunitioning on schedule. Burnett, aware he would catch flak from Cunningham if the ship did not look pristine on entering harbour, was 'nearly in tears';[27] men usually engaged in making *Rodney* smart, and looking smart themselves on the upper deck, would be ordered to 'lift derricks, rig whips, etc., ... instead of beautifying the ship for her arrival in harbour.'[28] It set up the most terrible conflict in Cdr Burnett's mind – between getting messy work done on time, yet still making the ship smart enough not to anger the CO. That was perhaps Cunningham's intention.

> *As the anchors went down turrets swung round, derricks reared up and hordes of previously hidden men in overalls ... set about preparations for de-ammunitioning.*[29]

Oliver duly reported the ship was ready to disgorge her shells, a steely look in the Captain's eye indicating the evolution would have to be completed to schedule.

> *We were up at five next morning. All went according to plan, and it was well before midnight that the last hoists went over the side.*[30]

Cunningham's spell as CO of *Rodney* came to an end in December 1930, as sea time was a rare commodity with so few ships in commission. He had to make way for other ambitious officers eager to climb up the promotion ladder. Commanding a battleship like *Rodney* was a make or break job: succeed, and progress to flag rank was almost guaranteed, while those making a hash of it would never command another ship, their careers effectively over.

As far as their Lords of the Admiralty were concerned, Cunningham had done well and, in July 1931, took up his next appointment, as Commodore in command of Chatham Barracks, having spent the intervening period recovering from surgery to correct a long-standing ailment.

In *Rodney*, there are indications that, while officers came to love him, despite his inclination to cut people off at the knees – earning him the nickname 'Cuts' – some ratings hated Cunningham. They were inevitably so much more distant from the god-like captain of a battleship than they might have been in destroyers. They probably did not appreciate the nuances of Cunningham's leadership technique.

Indeed, officers as a group were considered to be in a different world from the Lower Deck with whom they had very little contact. One of *Rodney*'s sailors later remarked:

> *The relationship was practically non-existent unless they gave you an order. There was no fraternization. They were Wardroom and you were Lower Deck and that was that.*[31]

Ordinary sailors possibly saw only Cunningham the martinet. If the regime prior to his was more interested in technical matters than tough man management, the shock to the system may have been severe. The presence of the kind of bolshie lower deckers only a hard hand could control, combined with a return to softer management after Cunningham left, with Cdr Burnett also departing, may have made a dangerous combination. It might explain why things came to a head, during the notorious Invergordon Mutiny. Nineteen-year-old Ordinary Seaman Edward Harris, the son of Cirencester publicans, was one of *Rodney*'s most junior sailors, having joined the Navy in the late 1920s because he didn't fancy being a farm labourer. He was in no doubt Cunningham's strict regime fomented rebellion.

> *Under* [Cunningham's] *command the ship became rather mutinous ... Right through my service in the Navy he was the only officer that I'd heard booed down the gangway when he left the ship. I wouldn't say there was discussions about a mutiny but there was a lot of unrest in the ship. It wasn't a happy ship.*

Harris further reflected:

> *Under Cunningham, it was a very efficient ship, yes, but the discipline was rather harsh. Punishments that you would have got on the* Rodney *were perhaps double what you would have got on other ships for the same crime. I think this is what got the ship's company's backs up. Certain ships had these strict officers who were totally different to the normal run of officers and Cunningham was one.*[32]

Lieutenant Commander George Campbell Ross joined *Rodney* on 5 June 1931, as deputy Marine Engineering Officer, and witnessed the chain of events leading to mutiny. Ross discovered that his boss, the Chief Engineer Commander, was nicknamed Ginger, 'on account of a fringe of ginger curly hair framing a bald head ... a tough character.'

> *Of medium height and broad shouldered, he was immensely strong. It was alleged that he had once won a wrestling contest with a large bear in a circus in Cornwall.*[33]

The Chief Engineer Cdr's capacity for pink gin was allegedly 'prodigious' and he always insisted on drinking out of the same glass.

Asked why, Ginger replied:

> *Because I dislike the taste of dishcloths.*

The Commanding Officer of *Rodney* by this time was Captain Roger Bellairs, whom Ross had previously encountered while serving in the cruiser HMS *Effingham*. The Commander was now Richard Schwerdt 'a short, tubby man with a red complexion and a blue scar on his face where he had been hit by a coal bag when he was a midshipman during coaling operations in the First World War.' Ten months on from Cunningham's reign, Ross believed *Rodney* was a well-trained, happy ship.

The annual Navy Days loomed and also in August the ship's company were given leave in two watches, but the blue touch paper that would lead to mutiny had already been lit and was smouldering away. At the beginning of August the findings of the May Committee, which had been convened to consider economies in the pay burden of the Armed Forces, were leaked to the press. The Royal Navy's sailors were astonished; junior officers and ratings would have their pay reduced by 25 per cent and unemployment payments would be cut. However, these were only recommendations, so everyone waited to see if the Board of Admiralty would resist them, anticipating a stiff fight on their behalf.

The *Rodney*, in company with *Warspite*, sailed from Plymouth on Tuesday, 8 September, intending to arrive at Invergordon four days later, after fleet exercises in the North Sea. *Rodney* was joined off Portsmouth by *Hood*, *Repulse*, *Valiant* and *Malaya*, also picking up cruisers from Chatham. *Nelson* stayed at Portsmouth, as the Commander-in-Chief was in hospital at Gosport. Command of the fleet devolved to Rear Admiral Wilfred Tomkinson, with his flag in *Hood*. For three days, as it progressed through the North Sea, the ships stayed at Action Stations. 'We encountered very rough weather and this gave the officers and men no time to think about pay cuts,' recalled Lt Cdr Ross.

There were 100 officers in the Wardroom and an amusing event occurred during our voyage to Invergordon. During a lull in the exercise, the ratings were piped to dinner and we, in the Wardroom, sat down to a well-earned meal. A long dining table seating about 40 officers was laid with a white table cloth on which were the cruets, sauce bottles, water jugs and the silver. Soup had just been served when the ship gave a huge roll. Someone had forgotten to lock the two middle parts of the table together with the consequence that one end slid across the deck, the heavy jugs and silver descended through the large gap, dragging the table cloth down with all our soup plates, knives, forks and glasses. We were left sitting on our chairs 'round two bare pieces of table underneath which was the most awful mess of soup, cutlery, sauces, plates and so on. On Friday 11 September, a signal from the Admiralty was posted on the notice boards. It said that owing to the financial crisis facing the country, the pay of officers and ratings would be cut; an Admiralty Fleet Order giving details of the cuts was on its way. More information came to us over the BBC when we learned that the cuts in pay were to take effect from October 1st. The A.F.O. did not reach Hood *until Saturday afternoon. It had apparently, been wrongly sent to* Nelson*, which was still at Portsmouth ... However, we learnt enough when we read the newspapers, which came onboard at Invergordon and were shocked to learn that the Board of Admiralty had accepted all the recommendations of the Navy Committee without apparently obtaining the views of the fleet. They were completely out of touch with the feelings of the lower deck; a despicable bunch of sods, was our immediate, undisciplinary, feeling about them.*

Junior ratings like *Rodney*'s Edward Harris, having joined in 1925 or later, were already on a reduced rate of pay, but now those who had benefited from the post-1919 pay rise were to have their salaries reduced to the 1925 level. Officers would suffer an 11 per cent cut. The Army and RAF escaped such drastic measures altogether. Leading seamen and senior ratings in *Rodney* who had recently signed on for a further ten years were particularly bitter; they were committed to another decade in the Navy potentially with a lot less money. It was all part of the nation's tightening of the belt in the midst of the Depression, but, on top of all the other hardships associated with life in the Service, such as months on end separated from families, it was a very heavy blow.

On the ship's arrival at Invergordon, sailors in the Engineering Department, wary of the acid-tongued Ginger, came to see Lt Cdr Ross in private.

They all had the same story to tell; disaster faced them, they were up to their limits in Hire Purchase payments and mortgages. Some even expressed sympathy for the financial dilemma in which I must also be placed.

In *Rodney's* lower deck, there was a feeling of foreboding, described by one ordinary sailor as a climate of suspicion:

When you was onboard ship the atmosphere didn't seem to be right. It was tense and everyone was looking at each other, like you was spying on each other. You could cut the air with a knife, it was that thick.[34]

The crunch would come on the Tuesday, when ships of the Atlantic Fleet were ordered to set sail for gunnery exercises. As the deputy head of the Engineering Department it was the responsibility of Lt Cdr Ross to issue orders for the Stokers to go below and raise steam. On the Monday morning Chief Petty Officer Jennings, the Regulating Chief Stoker, approached Lt Cdr Ross. As a Regulator – one of the ship's policemen – Jennings was responsible for the welfare, work schedules and discipline of 250 stokers, so he had his finger on the pulse. The stokers respected him, so when Jennings told Lt Cdr Ross there was 'an ugly spirit about the Mess Decks,' it was a reliable indication of trouble to come. Jennings added:

> *Last night I was awakened by music from a gramophone and then heard strange voices saying to our men in their hammocks, 'Don't forget. When you are ordered to go below, you refuse to go'.*

Lt Cdr Ross went to see Cdr Schwerdt, who told the captain it might be an opportune moment to nip the discontent in the bud, by assembling the ship's company on the forecastle to remind them where their duty lay.

> *Captain Roger Bellairs was a shy man and a poor speaker, a surprising weakness in a gunnery officer. His words failed to carry ...*[35]

Climbing down from his bunk at 5.30 am on Tuesday morning, Lt Cdr Ross was about to have a wash when Ginger entered his cabin looking harassed. The flustered looking engineering Commander told his deputy: 'The hands have been piped to turn to on the Upper Deck to prepare for sea and no one is moving.'

'I expected this after the events of last night,' confessed Lt Cdr Ross. 'And I am afraid that our chaps in the Engine-room department will also refuse duty. I have already arranged to go below to see what I can do.'

Ginger told him: 'Phone me in my cabin and let me know what is happening as soon as possible, I must inform the Captain.'

In his mess Ordinary Seaman Harris was in the thick of the mutiny, and, like the rest of his messmates, ignored the call to hands.

> *No one took any notice and we just slept on and eventually people did get up ... If any ship had put to sea from Invergordon that morning, the mutiny was a flop. We were the last ship to go into harbour and anchor, therefore we were the first ship to come out. All eyes were on the* Rodney, *because if the* Rodney *put to sea the whole fleet would have had to go ... I think there was a committee and it was generally known what was required to be done and volunteers carried out their duties, such as bringing food up from the galleys ... It wasn't a fight between the lower deck and the officers, it was just purely over the pay.*[36]

Ordinary Seaman T.R. Hiscox, born and brought up near Devonport Dockyard, came from a long line of Royal Navy sailors.

Having received his training in the old hulk *Impregnable* at Plymouth, he first went to sea in the *Emperor of India*, which had recently been transferred to the Chileans. While still at Devonport, preparing to sail for her new homeland, a bloody mutiny broke out in the former British battleship, allegedly inspired by communist agitators. Nor were British vessels immune, for in early January 1931 there was a mutiny aboard the Devonport submarine depot ship *Lucia*. Subsequently, ratings in *Lucia* were sentenced to hard labour or dismissed from the Service, while her captain and two officers were retired and put on half pay. The West Country seemed to be a breeding ground for mutineers and Hiscox certainly had no love for officers or the hard naval discipline he found in *Rodney*.

> *Well, she wasn't all that happy ... She wasn't as relaxed as other ships. I had a brother who was a cook on the* Repulse. *I used to go across and see him. You could tell the difference once you stepped onboard. There was no shouting 'get up there and get moving'. Well, I dunno, we had some bright ones* [officers] *onboard ship. The captain, no one cared much for him. Well, as boy, I never got in touch with them ... the messdeck officers were alright ... but the Master at Arms and all that, seemed a bit tight ... I won't say they wasn't liked but I didn't get on with them. I had one or two days down in the cells myself.*

Boy Seaman J.H. Sampson worked on a farm after leaving school, but got the sack and joined the Navy in 1930, so his mother would have one less mouth to feed at home. He enjoyed life at sea but also found *Rodney's* regime a little harsh. Boy Seamen were kept apart from the other sailors and banned from talking to them, except when working on the upper deck.

> *It was the second day aboard and we were in our mess, the mess next to the Ordinary Seamen, when one of the Ordinary Seamen came to the bulkhead door and asked if anyone from Somerset was there. I replied and he said: 'Do you get the local rag?' which was the* Somerset Gazette *and I said: 'Yes, my mother sends it on every week.' And he said: 'Let me have a look at it, when you get it.' No sooner had I said yes than I got a terrific thump alongside the ear. 'Twas the Petty Officer in charge of our mess. That gives you some idea of the discipline. We were told we weren't to talk or mix with the Ordinary Seamen and that was my punishment.*

On the Monday night, after arriving at Invergordon, an experienced stoker approached Sampson and his fellow boy seamen.

> *He told us that when the Petty Officer came 'round in the morning, to call us, not to get out of our hammocks. If the Petty Officer forced us, we had to warn him to look in the Ordinary Seamens' mess and he would find two or three stokers there waiting for him. We thought it great fun because we never liked the idea of getting up at five o'clock in the morning anyway ... The Petty Officer came around and called us and two or three told him where to go. They also told him that there was a mutiny. Apparently he didn't know, and he left.*

Ordinary Seaman Hiscox was surprised to be stirred by something different to the customary bugle call.

> *We woke up in the morning to the sounds of music ... how the hell they got the piano up on the top deck that time of the morning, God only knows, but he* [the piano] *was there and everybody was there, and you could see all the ships and everyone was making noise and singing.*

A senior rating made an attempt to preserve some form of routine by instructing Hiscox and other junior ratings to swab out the bridge, but there were no more orders and people just milled around. Although the sailors 'downed tools', much of the routine of the ship ran as normal, for it was a very British sort of mutiny. On the first day everyone stopped for afternoon tea. Main meals were provided on time throughout. The rum ration was still distributed and duty picket boats ran from ship-to-ship, only manned by midshipmen rather than ratings. On the upper deck, at least, resistance offered by *Rodney*'s mutineers to any attempt at weighing anchor was passive.

> *They wanted to slip the buoy and move out, but a lot of the lads put their feet and their arms through the links of the cable up on the foc'sle, more or less defying the officers to move the capstan a couple inches, thereby causing serious injury if they had tried it.*[37]

When Warrant Engineer Officer Tonkyns rang his cabin, Lt Cdr Ross asked where he was and what was going on. Tonkyns had managed to get into the engine room just before the mutineers shut and sealed heavy armoured hatches on the upper deck. Lt Cdr Ross said he would endeavour to get down there to see him. On his way, Ross met a Chief Stoker who told him stokers detailed to raise steam had refused. Lt Cdr Ross told him to round up Engineering Department senior ratings so steam could be raised without them. Spotting three senior rates, Lt Cdr Ross told them to accompany him, but one of them warned that men on the upper deck were in an ugly mood and would probably resist any move to open access hatches.

But Lt Cdr Ross was determined to get into the engine room, deciding risks would have to be taken.

> *There was only one alternative left and that was to go up to the boat deck and descend by the metal rungs built into the engine-room ventilation trunks – a very draughty route. Mr Tonkyns was delighted to see some friendly faces when we had completed our long descent.*

Two senior rates were asked to climb up the ventilation trunks with orders for others to follow them back down. Finally, with enough men assembled to begin the job, Lt Cdr Ross explained the objective:

> *We have been ordered to raise steam and have the main turbines ready by eight o'clock. Organise yourselves in three watches; those already down here, let's get moving. Should the men up top change their minds, we shall not have wasted any time and the ship can go to sea as planned.*

Lt Cdr Ross was also anxious about the crucial life support systems of the ship, namely: the auxiliary machinery, which backed up any failure in the main plant; electric generators that supplied light and power; evaporating and distilling plants, which created fresh water; supply of power to pumps in the fire main.

> *And what about the refrigerating machinery which kept the meat and vegetables compartments cool, to feed 1,500 men? Fortunately, the men agreed to keep all essential services running ... By this time it was clear that we were not going to sea, so steam was shut down. It was 11.30 when I went on to the upper deck and walked towards the forecastle. It was crowded with men, some of them singing, as they had brought a piano from the recreation room below. I could see that it was a place to be avoided, so I went down to the wardroom for a much-needed drink. It had been an anxious morning.*

Commander Schwerdt was in there with some other officers and asked what was happening in the Engineering Department. Lt Cdr Ross assured him 'essential services' would be kept running. Ross gave the opinion that very little else could happen until the Admiralty vowed to fight the proposed pay cuts. This prompted Cdr Schwerdt to follow in the disastrous footsteps of the captain. 'I am going to address the Ship's Company and put sense in their bloody heads,' he exclaimed. The order 'Clear Lower Deck! All hands to muster on the forecastle' was piped throughout the ship. 'Five minutes later, together with a few other officers, I followed him along the upper deck,' recalled Ross.

> *This little squat man looked pathetic, as he stood on a table, his complexion redder than usual.* [He said:] *'I am appealing to you all not to take matters into your own hands. You must go back to work and not behave like bloody fools.' The men let out guffaws of laughter and told him not to use rude words. It was a disaster and I think he knew it.*

One of the ordinary seamen listening to this unfortunate speech was Charles Cloake, who had joined the Navy in 1924, at the age of sixteen, to avoid the dole. Like other sailors, he took a dim view of Schwerdt's so-called words of wisdom on pay cuts.

> *We had this lecture on economics. He told us about the state of the country's finances* [as if to say] *the Government wouldn't have imposed these pay cuts unless it was absolutely necessary. So a rating asked him what percentage of his pay would he sacrifice? And he didn't answer. He got down ... and went away.*[38]

After lunch an attempt was made to get the men working, by piping them to turn to, but, again, only the senior rates responded. Lt Cdr Ross decided, rather than confront them, it might be best to give the ratings time to cool down and relax by awarding them a rest period. However, at 6.00 pm a Chief Engine Room Artificer named Smyth and two other senior ratings came to see Lt Cdr Ross with disturbing news.

> *They had overheard some speeches in the Recreation Space where some seamen had voted to prevent Chief and Petty Officers from working. There had also been a motion to land all Chief and Petty officers ashore but this had been lost on a show of hands.*

Again, not wishing to provoke the mutineers, but keen to make an effort as required by naval discipline to get the ship moving and, if possible, to sea, Lt Cdr Ross and senior ratings agreed they should go to work, but avoid confrontation. In the meantime, Rear Admiral Tomkinson was trying to find out the state of play in the ships of the fleet, sending an officer to gather facts.

'What is going on in the *Rodney*?' demanded the Admiral's emissary, adding a disapproving comment about 'sailors on the forecastle singing ...'

The *Rodney*'s officers explained junior ratings were refusing to allow the ship to go to sea until the Admiralty restored their pay.

'That is mutinous,' the Admiral's man stated. 'We've got no trouble in *Hood*. All is quiet.'

One of *Rodney*'s officers snapped:

'Balls! All your sailors are on deck, cheering our men on.'

'Well the Admiral wants a full report on everything that occurred in *Rodney* and all the other ships at Invergordon.'[39]

Having witnessed this exchange, Lt Cdr Ross privately reflected perhaps officers in other ships would later not tell the truth, in order to avoid ruining their careers.

On Wednesday morning the mutineers exerted heavy pressure on the Stokers not to get up steam. During a meeting on the forecastle they were told to tell their Petty Officers and Chief Petty Officers not to do any work after 9 am. Lt Cdr Ross subsequently gave orders for everyone to cease work and stay in their messes, with instructions that only auxiliary machinery should be kept running to supply 'essential services'. However, it was pointed out by a senior rate that water filters would have to be cleaned, or they might clog up, preventing essential ingress for the boilers. In a clever attempt to crack the solidarity of the mutiny, Ross suggested it should be explained to one of the ringleaders, Leading Stoker Lee, that someone had to carry out this essential work or the ship might be at risk.

> *He was a vociferous speaker at the forecastle meetings and was due to address the men again in the afternoon. Lee was also arranging the routine for running the ship's boats and the attached drifter. Lee went down to the engine-room ... Within five minutes, five men appeared, threatening Lee with their fists if he did not get out immediately. Somewhat surprisingly, he tried to argue with them ...*

Lee was advised by a senior rate it might be wise to back off. Later, Lt Cdr Ross encountered Lee on the upper deck, remarking: 'I hear that you did not get on with the job of cleaning the filters.' Lee replied: 'I could not, Sir. I was threatened. It was impossible. Sorry, Sir.' A large crowd of stokers gathered and they apologized for not going below to help Lee work on the filters, but explained the Seamen were threatening them. Lt Cdr Ross understood the difficult position they were in. 'Please try to be sensible,' he told the stokers. 'Violence won't get you anywhere.'

The stokers told him they did not object to the senior rates working, but Seamen nearby overheard this and decided to intervene. One of them pushed his way into the huddle of stokers surrounding Lt Cdr Ross and shouted: 'Don't listen to him!' Ross later recalled:

> *I looked him in the face. I had never seen him before but he looked crazy. I walked away. I learnt there had been another unpleasant episode in the engine-room, just after Lee had been told to leave. Leading Stoker Magee, a pleasant little Irishman, went below to put in the Main propelling machinery turning gear. In a couple of minutes he was up again, visibly shaking.*[40]

Magee told Lt Cdr Ross he was terrified and did not dare go below again. That afternoon Ross met with his senior rates in the Engineers Workshop, ordering them to assume normal working routine. 'If anyone tries to interfere with your work,' he told them, '... take his name and ask him to see me.' For all their threats the seamen did not attempt to interfere with the Engineering Department senior rates. By now, the Admiralty, which had been paralysed by news of mutiny, finally did something to defuse the situation, sending a conciliatory Admiralty Fleet Order through by signal, which read:

> *The Board of Admiralty is fully alive to the fact that among certain classes of ratings special hardship will result from the reduction of pay ordered by H.M. Government. It is therefore directed that ships of the Atlantic Fleet are to proceed to their home ports forthwith to enable personal investigation to be made by a Board of Enquiry and*

representatives of the Admiralty with a view to necessary alleviation being made. Any further refusals of individuals to carry out orders will be dealt with under the Naval Discipline Acts. This signal is to be promulgated to the fleet forthwith.

The captain decided to gather *Rodney*'s men on the forecastle and read the signal out. Once again, according to Boy Seaman J.H. Sampson, Bellairs made a poor impression on the men, who regarded him as 'rather on the weak side.'

He got up on the 16-inch gun turret and pleaded with the men to return to their duties and at the end of his speech he asked for one favour. Could he have his messenger boy back for duty? The crew left it up to the messenger boy and I believe, I am not absolutely sure, he went back as the captain's messenger.

Satisfied they had achieved their main objective, the sailors returned to work and ships raised steam. As *Rodney* headed south, Lt Cdr Ross was asked to write up a report on the mutiny.

Ginger toned down my report; I do not believe that he really appreciated the ticklish situations in which I had been placed. Our Captain summarized all the information sent to him by his officers and forwarded it to the Commander-in-Chief. He was an honest man and told the truth – unlike other Captains who allegedly watered down their stories of the mutiny. Thus Rodney *became known as* The Red Ship.

The alternative nickname 'Moscow Rodney' also supposedly reflected communist agitation in her lower deck. But Ordinary Seaman Charles Cloake believed it was all 'an exaggeration'.

She wasn't like that at all.

It was all due to hysteria stirred up by newspapers, including those in *Rodney*'s home port.

They gave the impression that there had been violence and people were in cells and it simply wasn't true.

There was a real fear that, once in port, there would be a mass walk-off from the *Rodney* and other ships, with protest marches through Plymouth centre. A major intelligence effort was immediately mounted to try and head this off and winkle out troublemakers. *Rodney*'s Charles Cloake encountered a friend who was part of the covert intelligence-gathering operation.

[He was] *an old messmate of mine who had left the Navy. I met him ashore in a pub and he was in naval uniform and I was curious. He told me then that he was in the police and he had been put back into uniform to try and find people who were trying to stir up trouble, civilians.*

For *Rodney*'s Lt Cdr Ross, the aftermath of the mutiny was a sad time.

We landed the few ringleaders at Devonport. I hoped that they would receive only minor punishments. They were sent under armed guard to the Barracks, given harsh drilling on the parade ground and finally discharged from the Navy. Several officers' careers were cut short but the major blame undoubtedly lay with the Board of Admiralty. Unlike other mutinies of the past, the sailors were not against the officers. I must confess that I had much sympathy for the men. The Admiralty went a long way towards restoring the cuts in pay; they had no alternative if they wanted to keep a Navy. In those early 'thirties' the country was facing a financial crisis, the aftermath of the American depression. The Invergordon Mutiny brought us off the gold standard and caused a sharp drop in the value of Pound Sterling. In the eyes of the world, a powerful Royal Navy, such as we then possessed, established us in a position of influence. A mutiny was inconceivable. It need never have happened.

At the end of September the Government announced pay cuts across the Armed Forces, in teachers' pay and also the police. Cuts in Royal Navy pay would be limited to ten per cent, with the exception of senior commissioned officers, Lieutenant Commander and above, who still had their salaries reduced by eleven per cent.

For the Wardroom as a whole it meant fewer courses on the menu, less expensive wines and rationing of cigarettes. Weddings were postponed, cars garaged and wives unable to follow their husbands' ship from port to port.[41] For senior and junior sailors of the lower deck with family burdens, the choices were said to be more stark. Wives had to chose between prostitution and menial jobs, such as scrubbing floors. In Chatham, Commodore Cunningham viewed events at Invergordon with dismay, criticising officers for being out of touch with their men. In his autobiography, published nearly thirty years later, he betrayed no awareness that his hard regime in *Rodney* may ultimately have led to her being dubbed 'The Red Ship'. His successor as Commanding Officer in *Rodney*, Bellairs, was judged to have failed utterly, and was not given another sea command after seeing out his time to the end of the ship's second commission on 12 April 1932.

Notes

1 Quoted in the *Western Evening Herald*, 17 December 1925.
2 Ibid.
3 Oliver Warner, *Cunningham of Hyndhope.*
4 Ibid.
5 Ibid.
6 Cunningham, *A Sailor's Odyssey.*
7 S.W.C. Pack, *Cunningham The Commander.*
8 Cunningham, *A Sailor's Odyssey.*
9 Oliver Warner, *Cunningham of Hyndhope.*
10 Quoted in Warner's book.
11 Ibid.
12 Exchange recorded *Cunningham The Commander.*
13 Quoted by Warner, in *Cunningham of Hyndhope.*
14 C.R. Benstead, *HMS Rodney at Sea.*
15 Cloake, IWM Sound Archive.
16 Recounted by Warner in *Cunningham of Hyndhope.*
17 C.R. Benstead, *HMS Rodney at Sea.*
18 Ibid.
19 Ibid.
20 *The Belfast News-Letter*, 16 June 1930, a clipping kept by Cunningham and deposited with his papers at the National Maritime Museum, Greenwich. See Sources.
21 Ibid.
22 Ibid.
23 Ibid.
24 C.R. Benstead, *HMS Rodney at Sea.*
25 Warner, *Cunningham of Hyndhope.*
26 Ibid.

27 Ibid.
28 Ibid.
29 Ibid.
30 Ibid.
31 Cloake, IWM Sound Archive.
32 Edward Harris, IWM Sound Archive.
33 Ross, IWM Department of Documents.
34 Hiscox, IWM Sound Archive.
35 Ross, IWM Department of Documents.
36 Harris, IWM Sound Archive.
37 J.H. Sampson, IWM Sound Archive.
38 Cloake, IWM Sound Archive.
39 Exchange related by Ross, IWM.
40 Ross, IWM Department of Documents.
41 C.R. Benstead, *HMS Rodney at Sea.*

Chapter Seven

SEND FRIED EGG TO ADMIRAL

The *Rodney*'s new Commanding Officer was legendary in the Royal Navy for charging the entire German fleet in his destroyer at the Battle of Jutland.

On that fateful day in the North Sea, Lieutenant Commander John Tovey led a charmed life, for although HMS *Onslow* was hit amidships by a shell from an enemy cruiser, as the British ship was about to fire torpedoes, she continued to float and fight. On seeing the main High Sea Fleet steaming hard out of the mist, Tovey turned his ship to make a solo attack run. Firing her last two torpedoes, *Onslow* swung away and escaped amid shell splashes as the Germans tried in vain to hit her. Like Cunningham, Tovey spent a lot of time in destroyers, but prior to taking over *Rodney* in April 1932 held a shore appointment. The sheer scale of the battleship, and her reputation for being an awkward customer, initially caused him anxiety too.

> *Tovey admitted to feeling some trepidation when he first looked out of the* Rodney's *bridge windows over the three massive turrets and saw the jackstaff in the dim distance, but he enjoyed the challenge of mastering such an unwieldy monster that was so reluctant to turn off the wind.*[1]

Tovey's biggest challenge, however, was handling men, rather than the vessel, for, in the wake of Invergordon, *Rodney* was not a happy ship. Morale remained very low.

> *... we were unjustly considered to be the 'Bolshie' ship because we had told the truth.*[2]

The battleship's sailors needed someone they could relate to, but with authority and the ability to impose discipline without resorting to overly harsh measures.

Forty-six year old Tovey was just such a man who, in his dealings with junior officers and ratings, 'had an uncanny ability to assess their potential and their limitations and to get the best out of them, steadying the wayward and putting heart into the diffident and discouraged.'[3]

After getting to know him, Lt Cdr Ross described Tovey as 'a great little man, a born leader.' Although a committed Christian, Tovey did not expect his men to be perfect – he knew sailors were prone to falling from grace through drink and women – but he loathed laziness, lying and disloyalty.

> *Men found it easy to talk to him, and he would always listen to and respect the views of his juniors and encourage them to accept responsibility and show initiative.*[4]

But Tovey was not the only key appointment to *Rodney*, for Cdr Schwerdt was removed from the ship and replaced with Cdr Geoffrey Cooke[5] who, Lt Cdr Ross noted, had an immediate impact on morale:

> *Cooke appeared to be more tolerant and understanding – which is what we badly needed. A good Commander has more effect on the morale of a ship than the Captain.*[6]

There was also a new Commander-in-Chief in the shape of sixty-year old Admiral Sir John Kelly, considered a real sailor's sailor, with an affinity for the lower deck. Brought out of retirement to command the Royal Navy's key striking force, he renamed it the Home Fleet, giving it a fresh start following the mutiny. With *Rodney* one of two ultra-modern battleships in the Royal Navy, indeed one of the most powerful warships on the face of the planet, it was important her complement felt valued and exuded a sense of pride. Therefore, Admiral Kelly made a great effort to boost the spirits of the ship, coming aboard for a special inspection at Rosyth. He climbed onto a table to speak to one thousand sailors assembled on *Rodney*'s forecastle.

> *He was a big man with a rugged complexion, a deeply lined face, blue eyes and inspired a feeling that here was a man one could trust. 'As you can see I am no oil painting,' were his opening remarks. This convulsed us all with laughter and won us over. After he had explained the crisis through which the country was then passing, we felt we could do anything for him.*[7]

Some senior officers thought Kelly a bit too eager to make friends with the Lower Deck, but there was no doubting his extraordinary charisma, allied with an iron will to ensure the Home Fleet achieved full, cohesive, fighting efficiency. While he made sure ordinary sailors gained their self-respect, Admiral Kelly also warned them in no uncertain terms that disobedience of, and disrespect to, officers would be severely dealt with. He re-introduced the Divisional System, which had been used to great effect in Nelson's day.[8]

To keep warships on their toes while at anchor it was not unknown for flag officers to try and flummox everyone, by suddenly asking for a specific seamanship task to be carried out. There was great competition among the ships not to be the last to complete such 'Monday evolutions', as they were called.

They might normally be asked to 'Lay out bower anchor' or 'send marine band ashore', with most of the ship's company arrayed on the upper deck, waiting to spring into action, depending on which task was requested. However, not long after assuming command of the Fleet, Admiral Kelly decided to shake things up a little, with a rather unusual 'evolution' signalled from HMS *Nelson*.

> *SEND FRIED EGG TO ADMIRAL ON BOARD FLAGSHIP*

Nelson, meanwhile, was tasked with sending a poached egg to *Rodney*. The *Nelson* appeared to beat *Rodney* to the draw, but with a rubbery-looking egg that seemed to have been fried rather than poached. One of *Rodney*'s officers remarked: 'We are prepared to swear it. They had sent us one left over from breakfast.'[9]

Tovey and Kelly did not always see eye to eye, but that was perhaps because they shared certain characteristics. The former often told the latter exactly what he thought about a particular issue when other officers might have been more diplomatic and kept quiet. Admiral Kelly wrote in a confidential report on the *Rodney*'s Commanding Officer:

> *Captain Tovey shares one characteristic with me. In myself I call it tenacity of purpose; in Captain Tovey I can only describe it as sheer bloody obstinacy.*[10]

However, Tovey won the unstinting admiration and respect of his men.

> *His impact was magical, and the* Rodney *quickly became a happy and efficient ship. He demanded the highest standard of every department and stressed their interdependence; no one was allowed to feel unimportant.*[11]

In late 1932, Lt Cdr Ross received a letter from the Engineer in Chief of the Navy suggesting he should become Assistant Naval Attaché at the British Embassy in Berlin, as he was one of the few German speakers in the Royal Navy. As his wife had already given up following *Rodney* around, and was living with her parents in Berlin, Lt Cdr Ross felt it an ideal appointment. However, the Foreign Office considered Ross might be compromised, by having a German-born wife through whom undue pressure might be exerted. Therefore, he was subsequently offered the post of Assistant Naval Attaché in Tokyo. Receiving confirmation of his new appointment, Ross was officially promoted Commander, on 10 January 1933 handing over to his successor and leaving *Rodney*.

> *I had served eighteen months in the ship and it had not been an easy life. A few months earlier, I would have been happy to go, but now I was saying goodbye to a number of fine friends ... I had learnt the virtues of patience, tolerance and, above all, the significance of discipline. It helped me in the years to come.*

Londoner Robert Craddock was an orphan who came to *Rodney* at the age of sixteen, in August 1932, finding his Spartan messdeck contained several tables, with metal bars overhead to swing hammocks from at night. The boy seamen were roused to begin their working day at 5.30 am, and, after stowing hammocks, scrubbed the upper deck. If there was to be a visit by a VIP, such as the King, *Rodney*'s decks would be 'holy-stoned' – rubbed almost white with a piece of stone, which removed the upper layer of grime. Cleaning the paintwork and renewing it was also part of the daily routine, as was polishing brasswork. Breakfast was at 6 am, with the nominated 'cook of the mess' going to collect the food in a container and bringing it back to the messroom. Regulars on the menu included fish and chips, corned beef, stew, and there was still soup with dinner everyday. A weevil coming out of bread or biscuits was not an uncommon sight, but this didn't deter hungry youngsters and they would still send back for more.

'Weevils couldn't be helped,' recalled Craddock. Complaints about food were, however, forthcoming when sailors thought the chefs had a case to answer.

> *On one occasion they gave us a tin of sardines between two, and there was a complaint about this. The captain got the chefs to make Cornish pasties to make up for it. You could always complain about your food and the chefs took notice.*

Prayers were said every day after breakfast and then the boy seamen dispersed to their various duties. For Craddock that might include looking after the lifeboats; cleaning them and making sure the sails were in good order, as well as checking their food supplies were dry and first aid kits were present and correct. There was, of course, a regular routine of exercises, such as 'away lifeboat' and 'man overboard'. Craddock discovered that Wednesday was 'make and mend day', which nominally gave a sailor the opportunity 'to sort out any buttons off your shirts or your trousers.'[12] To this end he was given a sewing kit called a 'Housewife'. The reality was, of course, that 'make and mend' was a half-day off, the most popular pursuit being a snooze on the upper deck. One long service rating so engaged, catching up on his sleep, mouth wide open, suffered the misfortune of a seagull dive-bombing him. In revenge, the sailor went down to his messdeck, got some bread and smothered it in mustard. Returning to the upper deck, he threw it over the side and watched as a couple of seagulls swooped down and gobbled it up. 'It choked the beggars,' was the salty observation of *Rodney*'s Robert Craddock. In the evening, if not on duty, sailors like young Craddock gathered around their mess deck tables and played a hand of cards, draughts or even Mah Jong. Such was the rhythm of life for *Rodney*'s youngest sailors in the mid-1930s.

In early 1934, *Rodney* headed across the Atlantic for a visit to the West Indies. Originally the trip had been awarded to *Nelson*, but she ran aground on the Hamilton Banks in the Solent. The Commander-in-Chief, Admiral William Boyle, transferred his flag to *Rodney*, which had waited in vain in Cawsand Bay for the flagship to appear over the horizon, before heading for Portland to embark the admiral. *Rodney* hit very bad weather after calling at the Azores.

> *... so many boats smashed in ... it was terrible ... we weren't allowed on deck for about three days.*[13]

Once through the storm, *Rodney* assumed a settled daily routine, which, under Admiral Boyle, a keen royalist, included the ship's company singing 'Land of Hope and Glory'. *Rodney* called at Barbados, Dominica, St Kitts, Grenada, and from there sailed for Stavanger, before heading for Molde, another Norwegian port. Finally setting course for home, *Rodney* visited Fleetwood on the Lancashire coast, where her sailors and marines were accorded the honour of free travel on the trams and buses.

Midshipman Frank Morgan joined *Rodney* at Number 7 Wharf, in Devonport's North Yard, on 21 November 1934, along with another midshipman named Peter Hill-Norton, the latter a future Admiral of the Fleet.

Morgan spent two days looking around the ship, becoming acquainted with his new home. Following three weeks Christmas leave at home, he rejoined the ship on 1 January 1935. Ammunitioning followed, Morgan receiving responsibility for a lighter and supervising embarkation of 247 16-inch shells. One of his shipmates described the challenge involved:

> *How do you handle 16-inch shells out of the lighter onto the deck and down into the shell rooms, the magazines? You had no cranes onboard. We had to rig a wooden derrick which would have been 20 ft long, with an arrangement of tackles to hoist the ammunition onto the deck and down.*[14]

On 15 January the ship, since the end of August 1934 under the command of Captain Wilfred Custance, sailed from Devonport for a spring cruise to the West Indies, *Rodney* following on behind *Valiant* and *Barham*, rendezvousing with the Commander-in-Chief Home Fleet on 16 January 1935, in the English Channel. Midshipman Morgan noted *Rodney* immediately 'went to divisions in gas-masks, and after prayer we exercised "Action".' In the evening the midshipmen did physical exercise and then witnessed a night encounter exercise, with searchlights and star shells criss-crossing the sky. The crash and thunder of full-scale gunnery exercises soon followed.

The ship dropped anchor at Grenada around 5 pm on 1 February, *Rodney* later visiting Trinidad, St Lucia, Dominica and St Kitts. By early March she was heading back across the Atlantic, by the sixth of the month reaching Fayal in the Azores, which was a welcome end to an intensive series of exercises. By 17 March, *Rodney* was at Gibraltar, having endured yet another spell of combat training.

On 16 July 1935, there was a Silver Jubilee Review for King George V, with *Rodney* present in the Solent alongside her sister ship and other powerful units, including battleship *Valiant* and the *Hood*, as well as vessels of the Mediterranean Fleet. There was no doubt in the minds of commentators that *Rodney* and *Nelson* were the most formidable vessels on display.

They are the most powerful fighting ships in existence, with nine 16-inch guns as the main armament and unequalled powers of resistance to gun or torpedo attack.[15]

After a brief spell at Devonport following the Review, *Rodney* set sail again for the Solent, for she was once again Guard Ship at Cowes Week and, as such, blessed with the traditional visit from the King and Queen.

Rupert Hardwell was one of five marines arrayed on the top of a 16-inch gun turret as King George V and Queen Mary came aboard.

I was with three other buglers and we sounded the salute as we usually did on such special occasions.

Marine Hardwell, born in 1915 when his father was away fighting on the Western Front, was brought up yards from the Royal Marines barracks at Stonehouse, in Plymouth, and it seemed only natural for him to go into the Corps. Joining up at the age of fourteen, as a bugle boy and drummer, he earned the nickname 'Sticks'. At the age of seventeen he was sent from Stonehouse to train as a ship's marine at Deal, passing out in the King's Troop. His first vessel was the cruiser *Danae*, seeing service in the West Indies. He transferred into the *Rodney* in January 1934 after *Danae* returned for a refit at Devonport. Having missed the turmoil of Invergordon, by the time Marine Hardwell got to *Rodney*, the atmosphere aboard was much improved. '*Rodney* was a very good ship and everyone seemed to get on,' he recalled.

I was Captain of the Gangway for quite a while, after being in the general working party to start with. It ended up I was a clerk to the Captain of Marines and his Lieutenant. I enjoyed life at sea and especially the opportunity for sports. I played water polo for the Rodney *against teams from other ships.*

Promoted to Corporal in spring 1936, Rupert Hardwell possibly did not find his subsequent period ashore, as a clerk in Stonehouse, terribly enthralling, for in April he was discharged from the Royal Marines and joined the local police force. The curse of inactivity losing *Rodney* good men, to either other military units or civvy street, was a recurring theme, for life as a ship's marine continued to feature rather too much ceremonial and bullshine and not enough soldiering.

The canvas against which *Rodney* played out her life in the 1930s was daubed with increasingly dark colours even though there were efforts to limit naval power. The London Naval Conference of January to April 1930 attempted to restrict British, American, Japanese, French and Italian fleets until 1936. The British were allowed to build 146,000 tons of heavy cruisers, the Americans 180,000 tons and

Japanese 108,400 tons. Construction limits for light cruisers were also agreed: Britain (192,200 tons), America (143,500 tons), Japan (100,450 tons). Another attempt at naval limitation was made at the World Disarmament Conference, held in Geneva 1932/34, but the coming to power of Hitler in Germany and Japan's blatant arms build up for a concerted campaign of conquest in Asia, quickly exposed it as a vain enterprise. German naval forces had been secretly breaching internationally agreed tonnage limits for some years. For example, fast, heavy cruisers, or 'pocket battleships', built in the late 1920s and early 1930s were specially designed for commerce raiding voyages and conclusively violated their official statistics.

In March 1935, the Nazi regime officially discarded its arms limitation obligations under the Treaty of Versailles, which had imposed stiff conditions on Germany after the First World War. Even prior to Germany abandoning the Versailles limitations, two battlecruisers were on order, as well as dozens of submarines.

Britain was keen to constrict German naval expansion in the wake of the collapse of Versailles restrictions and the Nazis were surprisingly responsive. In 1935 the Anglo-German Naval Treaty allowed the Kriegsmarine to reach 35 per cent of the strength of the Royal Navy. A second Anglo-German naval agreement in 1937 would be similarly ineffective. The 1935/36 London Naval Conference, involving Britain, America, Japan, Italy and France, was a last gasp attempt to limit navies, which achieved nothing significant. In March 1936 German troops re-occupied the Rhineland without Britain and France doing anything to stop it. The Spanish Civil War began in July 1936, when fascist troops led by General Francisco Franco rebelled against the socialist Republican national government. By November the fascists had Madrid under siege and occupied much of southern Spain. Soon Italy and Germany were supporting the fascist cause via both land and air forces, with a less overt contribution from naval units. The Russians came in on the Republican side and socialist volunteers flocked to the colours in the legendary International Brigades.

The Royal Navy had been ready for trouble for some time, with a deployment of the Home Fleet to Gibraltar in early 1936 rather than a cruise to the Caribbean.

After a programme of exercises in the Atlantic and western Mediterranean, *Rodney*, by now under the command of Captain J. Whitworth, returned home to give her complement leave before she returned again to Gibraltar, to stay there as guardship until the middle of July, by which time fighting in Spain had erupted.

British tourists were trapped in Madrid, and in resorts on the north-east and north-west coast of Spain. Also stranded were British citizens living and working in Spain and there were many thousands of other foreign nationals at risk from the fighting. Between July and October 1936 more than thirty warships of the Mediterranean Fleet had evacuated 6,000 refugees belonging to fifty-five countries, a third of them British.

Following Navy Week, and visits to British ports, in early October, after unloading her ammunition at Devonport, *Rodney* sailed for Portsmouth and her annual refit. Rejoining the Home Fleet, she deployed in early 1937 to Gibraltar for exercises in the Mediterranean and Atlantic. Relations between the British and German navies remained cordial and, when the pocket battleships *Graf Spee* and *Deutschland* called at Algeciras, across the bay, there were visits between the ships of the Home Fleet and those of Hitler's navy. By April *Rodney* was back in home waters and, following exercises in the Channel, headed for the Thames estuary, dropping anchor with other ships of the Home Fleet off Southend, sailors from *Rodney* and *Nelson* travelling to London for the coronation of King George VI on 12 May. The Home Fleet had set sail from the Thames, on 14 May, assembling at Spithead for a Coronation Review, alongside the Mediterranean Fleet and foreign warships. *Nelson* was flagship, her retinue composed of *Rodney, Royal Oak, Resolution, Ramillies, Royal Sovereign* and *Revenge*. On the afternoon of 20 May, the King and Queen Elizabeth boarded the Royal Yacht *Victoria & Albert*, the Board of Admiralty embarked in the yacht *Enchantress*, to review assembled warships. France had sent the *Dunkerque*, of 26,500 tons, which had only recently completed sea trials and bore striking similarities to *Rodney* and *Nelson*, with all her main guns – eight 13-inch guns in two turrets – situated forward. Germany sent the *Graf Spee*, the US Navy the 28,000 tons pre-First World War dreadnought *New York*. Japan sent the nine-year old heavy (13,300 tons) cruiser *Ashigara*, armed with ten 7.9-inch guns. Aboard *Ashigara* was Cdr Ross, one-time *Rodney* engineering officer, assigned as naval review liaison officer following his stint as Assistant Naval Attaché in Tokyo. Russia contributed the 26,000 tons *Marat*, a battleship with a dozen 12-inch guns. To many the gathering of warships from so many nations in the Solent proved the brotherhood of the sea could rise above the disheartening politics of the time. However, a cruel fate lay ahead for some ships that were there. In the summer of 1940 *Dunkerque* would be heavily damaged by the gunfire of British warships that she was peacefully at anchor alongside in 1937. Desperate to prevent the French fleet from being turned against it, Britain was forced to attack Mers-El-Kebir and other Vichy naval bases, *Dunkerque* being among those ships subjected to Royal Navy bombardment. She later made it to Toulon, but when the Germans tried to take her over in late 1942 she was scuttled. The *Graf Spee* too was scuttled, choosing self-destruction little more than two years on from the Coronation Review, becoming trapped on the River Plate by a hunting force of British cruisers after a raiding sortie into the South Atlantic. In late September 1941 *Marat* would be sunk at her moorings, in Kronstadt Naval Base, by German Stuka dive-bombers, but even then her guns would continue to fire in defence of Leningrad. As for *Ashigara*, she would help sink the Royal Navy cruiser *Exeter* during the Battle of the Java Sea just over five years on from the Review. In June 1945, the British would gain revenge, the submarine *Trenchant* sinking *Ashigara* in the Bangka Strait.

However, in those fading halcyon days, when war was not necessarily a certainty, the peacetime naval routine carried on. In July 1937 *Rodney* made a very successful friendship visit to Norway, as flagship of Commander-in-Chief, Home Fleet, Admiral Sir Roger Backhouse.

It was recorded in the letters of *Rodney*'s Midshipman D.C. Woolf, who had previously visited Oslo in the cruiser *Frobisher*, when he made friends who now gathered on the shores of the fjord to welcome the British battleship:

> *On Monday 21st, I, being up at 4 o'clock, did not turn in again, as, with the sun out and sailing up the Oslofjord was such a beautiful sight that I remained on deck until we reached Oslo. It really was something unforgettably lovely, the scenery some of the finest I have yet seen. I think I must have missed this part in our visit in* Frobisher. *About 8 o'clock* [a.m.] *we passed ... where Mrs Shyberg lives, and there they all were waving frantically and me, with one eye on the Admiral's bridge, tentatively and inconspicuously waved back. It caused me much amusement, as Mr Shyberg kept*

on dipping his Norwegian Flag from their mast in the garden. Of course, as is the International custom, the wretched signalman in Rodney *had to answer and was consequently dipping our ensign up and down. This amused them highly, Mrs Shyberg thinking it was through me that they were doing it, not knowing the custom. We anchored in Oslo about 8.30 amidst 21 gun salutes to the King* [of Norway] *and all the official stuff one has to do on these occasions.*[16]

Midshipman Woolf changed some money and went ashore that afternoon, having arranged to meet someone towards whom he seems to have had an unrequited romantic inclination. Woolf wrote that he headed 'to Astrid's flat, where I found her awaiting me for tea. We talked and talked and gradually all her English began to come back. She really is the most charming girl ...'

However, Astrid was married to Arne, who came home around 6 pm, after which they all went to dinner. Such ship visits to friendly foreign ports also involved quite a bit of pomp and ceremony, as Midshipman Woolf noted.

Friday was a panic day as King, Queen [of Norway] *decided to inspect the ship – colossal panic, clean collar, frock coat and sword, dirty white gloves. King comes on board, 21 guns and then another 7, as he is an Admiral in our Navy ... Panic over and King and Queen go and have lunch with Admiral.*

On the Saturday, Midshipman Woolf showed Astrid, her father and two British friends around *Rodney*, the tour concluding with English Tea at 4 pm. Before his guests departed, Woolf took them down to the ship's canteen where a special purchase was made.

Astrid is mad about Cadburys chocolate so the men folk had to smuggle a whole lot ashore [in their pockets] *for her as it is impossible to get in Norway.*

The *Rodney*'s visit to Oslo was approaching its end and a big farewell dance was held aboard ship, to which Arne, Astrid and her mother and father came. There were between 350 and 400 guests, including the King and Queen of Norway, members of their court and various ambassadors, Midshipman Woolf relating:

Most of the senior officers had to dance with the Queen!, who is a very active woman, and simply loves to be surrounded by uniforms.

He reported Astrid was taken away for several dances by another officer, named Batten, while Arne propped up the bar. '... as for me, I leave you to guess,' wrote Woolf.

I made a grab for the most marvellous looking blonde and kept her until 'God Save the King' at 2.30. Perfectly wonderful girl and what's more spoke English.

Officers were also allowed to invite special guests aboard ship the following night, to bid a more personal farewell. Midshipman Woolf later escorted Arne and Astrid ashore.

I really think they were very, very sorry to say goodbye to 'Mrs' 'Rodney' *as Astrid called the ship, and she said that she did not understand how it was possible for us to become so friendly in so short a time ... I said goodbye at the quay and I need hardly mention that I don't think I have ever been so sorry to leave a place.*

The *Rodney* would sail in Scandinavian waters again during those last months of peace, but in war she would see the coast of Norway, running the gauntlet of Luftwaffe bombers determined to sink her.

Notes

1 Taken from a tribute to Admiral Tovey written by the unidentified author 'RWP'. See Sources for web site where this can be viewed in full.
2 Ross, IWM Department of Documents.
3 Tribute to Tovey by 'RWP'.
4 Ibid.
5 For more on Cooke, see Rodney's People appendix.
6 Ross, IWM.
7 Ibid.
8 The sub-division of a ship's company into groups, with a lieutenant and senior rating in charge of looking after the motivation, discipline and welfare of the sailors under their charge. It enabled them to nip problems in the bud and make the men feel that their interests were being looked after. The theory was that the officers would be unable to avoid dealing with their men on a face-to-face basis, getting to know the worries of the lower deck. With the onset of very big ship's companies and rise of the technocrat, the more intimate and easier to run divisional interface had suffered as departments based on trade and/or technical specialistation (or lack of it) had asserted themselves, and a gulf opened between wardroom and lower deck. In the 21st Century RN, like that of the 1930s suffering from lack of resources, there is also a renewed emphasis on the divisional system.
9 C.R. Benstead, *HMS Rodney at Sea.*
10 Quoted in tribute to Tovey by 'RWP'.
11 Ibid.
12 Craddock, IWM Sound Archive.
13 Ibid.
14 Palmer, IWM Sound Archive
15 An article entitled *The King's Ships Under Review* by Francis E. McMurtrie, in the Official Programme of the Silver Jubilee Review.
16 Woolf, IWM Department of Documents.

Chapter Eight

CAPTAIN OF THE GATE

During the Munich Crisis of autumn 1938, despite the overwhelming desire of politicians and population at large to avoid conflict at all costs, the Royal Navy was on a war footing. Indeed, tension in *Rodney* at the time of Munich was far greater than in early September 1939, when war finally did break out. With the ship deep in refit, *Rodney*'s men possibly had more time to sit around listening to radio news broadcasts and reading newspapers. *Nelson* and other Home Fleet warships were initially at Invergordon, sailing for the war anchorage at Scapa Flow in late September, just as Chamberlain was arriving at Munich for a second round of talks with Hitler, but *Rodney* was still confined to dock. By now under the command of Captain Neville Syfret, *Rodney* entered refit at the end of July 1938, one of her ratings later recalling that at the time of Munich, she

... was in Portsmouth Dockyard underneath the one ton crane and they had taken the top of B turret off to change the guns.[1]

Dockyard workers redoubled efforts to get *Rodney* back in service, as one sailor saw when drafted to the battleship during the crisis:

There was talk of war ... and they soon whipped those guns back in.[2]

There was no more foreboding sign that conflict might actually come, than Able Seaman gunner Richard Hughes receiving a 'Pierhead Jump'[3] to the battleship's steam-powered drifter, which was bound for Scapa Flow to run errands for the big ships and help protect the anchorage via anti-submarine patrols. Another of *Rodney*'s Welsh ratings, Hughes was a war baby, born in December 1917, around two months after his father was killed in action on the Western Front. A keen sportsman with a fondness for fell running, he felt his horizons stretched beyond working as a chemist's assistant in an aluminium works and, shortly after his seventeenth birthday, joined the Navy. Serving in the battleships *Barham* and *Royal Sovereign* in home waters and the cruiser *Dorsetshire* in the Far East, he returned home in June 1937, receiving his draft to *Rodney* in late August.

His initial Action Station was the 16-inch shell handling room of B-turret, where he worked the grab, which placed the shell in the hoist. Not surprisingly for a lad who spent much of his youth gazing out to sea from the hills of the Conway Valley, Hughes was glad to be re-assigned to the 2pdr pom-pom on the upper deck, where he could see what was happening. The thought of war in 1938 was not something that unduly perturbed him.

I suppose like all young braves I said 'c'mon let's have go ...'[4]

Having grabbed his kitbag and jumped aboard the drifter with some of his *Rodney* shipmates, Hughes was well on the way to Scapa when the crisis came off the boil and the vessel was called back to Portsmouth.

The more informal life of a drifter crew appealed to Hughes, but he lost his billet in her after dislocating his hip playing football for *Rodney* against a Portsmouth-based air-defence searchlight regiment. After a ten-day spell in hospital he was back aboard the battleship, as the behind-schedule refit moved towards its conclusion in November.

Lieutenant Commander John Boord was appointed as *Rodney*'s Gunnery Officer in the summer of 1938, joining her during post-refit sea trials. Having previously served in the First World War era HMS *Royal Sovereign*, Lt Cdr Boord was mightily impressed, most notably with the fact that *Rodney* had 'lots of mahogany, lots of brass, nice teak decks ... a beautiful ship and plenty of open space on the decks for'ard but not aft.' Following completion of further sea trials, *Rodney* headed back to Devonport, sailing into Plymouth Sound with her silhouette changed due to the addition of a launch catapult for a Swordfish floatplane on her X turret. *Rodney* had also received radar.[5] In early January 1939, she became flagship of Rear Admiral Lancelot Holland, Flag Officer 2nd Battle Squadron and,[6] after exercises in the western Mediterranean with the French Navy, made another friendship visit to Madeira. More exercises, based on Gibraltar, followed before *Rodney* returned to British waters where, in late March, she was guardship at Dover for a state visit by the French president Albert Lebrun, *Rodney* firing a 21-gun salute to the training vessel *Cote d'Azur*, as the latter entered harbour. Meanwhile, the Germans were putting into action a plan to annex Danzig and the Polish Corridor. However, the British and French issued a statement threatening military action and the Nazis backed down, for their military was not yet ready for war with Europe's major powers. In early April newspapers were full of reports about the Italian fascist regime's annexation of Albania. That month the Nazis announced they were discarding the Anglo-German Naval Treaty. Who could now doubt that Germany was intent on war with Britain? Chatfield, by then Minister for Co-ordination of Defence, battling to squeeze more money out of the Treasury to build up the Armed Forces, felt moved to observe of Britain's lack of readiness:

> *This country in 1939 possessed* none *newer than the* 'Nelson' *and* 'Rodney', *whose keels were laid in 1923, sixteen years before the bell rang.*[7]

On 28 April 1939 Ordinary Seaman James McLean was drafted to *Rodney* from the HMS *Defiance* engineering school – three old wooden wall ships moored on the Cornish side of the Hamoaze. As he was taken across to the dockyard steps in a small diesel-powered boat, McLean gazed at the daunting bulk of the battleship. The last time the young Scot had seen her from the same angle was a month earlier, when *Rodney* had just returned from her duties as guard ship for the French state visit, a remark by an old salt putting the fear of God in him.

> *An old timer said: 'That's HMS* Rodney *... for Heaven's sake don't ever get drafted to her, it's 100 per cent Pusser* [strict Naval routine] *and just like being in barracks'.*

As luck would have it, here he was, just a few weeks later, walking along the wharf towards the dreaded ship. McLean had joined the Navy during the Munich Crisis, receiving his initial training at Devonport's *HMS Drake* barracks before going to *Defiance*. Within days of joining *Rodney*, McLean was at sea, the ship heading for intensive operational work-up exercises at Portland with *Nelson* and other ships of the Home Fleet, including the brand new carrier *Ark Royal* and First World War-era battlecruiser *Repulse*.

A former member of the battlecruiser's ship's company was another of *Rodney*'s April 1939 new boys. Peter Wells-Cole, from Lincolnshire, joined the battleship as a twenty-year old Sub Lieutenant, finding the ship's Commanding Officer [Syfret] 'tall, distinguished, austere and very silent'. Sub Lt Wells-Cole had entered Dartmouth in 1932, was sent to a training cruiser in 1935/36, then spent two years in *Repulse* out in the Mediterranean, returning home to take his Sub Lieutenant's courses and then receiving his appointment to *Rodney*.

> *I had wanted to join the Navy for as long as I could remember. One of my uncles enjoyed a long career in the Navy, but my family were in the past yeoman farmers, not sailors, while my father and great grandfather were doctors, as was my elder brother.*

To give the Home Fleet a break from warfare training, weekend leave was granted in Weymouth, meaning that, in addition to many thousands of holidaymakers, there were several thousand sailors packed into the resort. As he was not yet twenty-one, McLean was forbidden from remaining ashore after 8 pm. However, his first 'run ashore' as a member of a ship's company still turned out to be memorable, but for all the wrong reasons.

> *With two of my pals I was walking near a park and saw hundreds of sailors throwing garden seats, plants, bushes, pots and anything else they could get hold of into the main road. Visitors were running in all directions to get away from the trouble. Shortly afterwards two policemen arrived on bikes and started blowing their whistles, but it was like trying to stop an elephant stampede. What caused the riot was the local council putting up large notices saying 'DOGS & SAILORS NOT ALLOWED IN THIS PARK'. What an insult!*

The *Rodney* and other ships left harbour in disgrace.

> *The town's mayor had been to see the Commander-in-Chief in the* Nelson *to ask him to take the Fleet away.*[8]

Also new to the *Rodney* was George Daniel Montauban Thomas, yet another Welsh rating, who left school in 1932 in the depths of the Depression and went out to Kenya to work with his dad, a farm butchery manager. In late 1935, having successfully applied to join the Navy, he came back from Kenya.

Initially in destroyers, Thomas was a First Class stoker after ten months service, joining the cruiser *Neptune*, based in Simonstown. Back at Devonport by 1938, he was a Petty Officer mechanician before he had even done three years service. Aware that he was very young for his rank, Thomas was glad his thinning hair made him look older, but the absence of long service and good conduct badges on his sleeve – one earned for each period of five years service – was a give-away. On arriving in *Rodney*, he pretended he'd lost them in a darts match.

The Germans signed their 'Pact of Steel' military alliance with Italy in May, and by late June, with Germany's desire for territorial expansion clearly not sated – even after devouring Czechoslovakia – *Rodney* was at Devonport giving a curtailed summer leave to her sailors and marines. At the end of July, *Rodney* left Plymouth and, as she slid between the Hoe pier and Drake's Island, relatives of her sailors and marines were gathered on the foreshore in their hundreds to say farewell, the women waving handkerchiefs and stifling tears. However, as *Rodney* set course for Portsmouth 'there were not many who took the possibilities of war very seriously, and even fewer still who talked about war that night.'[9] At Spithead *Rodney* embarked the Commander-in-Chief, Admiral Sir Charles Forbes, becoming Home Fleet flagship, as *Nelson* was in dock.

> Nelson *was very much better maintained than* Rodney *was. There was great competition between the two ships but the* Nelson *always seemed to be getting a refit and afterwards it was to be* Rodney's *turn and a crisis occurred and the* Rodney *seldom got the proper refits that she was entitled to.*[10]

Rodney led the fleet north to Invergordon where, in early August, Admiral Forbes switched his flag to *Nelson*. Men as well as ships were being prepared for war, with ratings, including Ordinary Seaman McLean, sent ashore to improve fitness.

> *So, off we marched with the ship's band playing away, mile after mile along the road to the west. Some kept falling out, both going and coming back, and next day there was a crowd outside the ship's sickbay with blistered feet and for days afterwards ratings could be seen hobbling along.*

Exercises continued until, on 11 August, the Home Fleet received special orders to sail for Scapa Flow, in order to be ready for hostilities, *Rodney* being the first Royal Navy capital ship into the fleet anchorage. Over the next few days more and more ships arrived, bringing Britain's foremost striking force up to full strength. In late August, *Rodney* suffered severe rudder problems and was sent to Rosyth for rectification. Although possessing a dry dock big enough to accommodate *Rodney*, Rosyth was not in peacetime a fully operational dockyard, and so was short of workers.

> *There were no dockyard mateys but there was somebody who worked the pump on the drydock and the ship's company, together with a very skeleton* [crew of] *dockyard personnel dry-docked the ship. The ship's company were put to scraping the ship's bottom and repainting the anti-fouling* [paint] *which continued throughout the day and night for two days. This was unprecedented: no sailor had ever been expected to scrape the bottom and paint the anti-fouling. It had always been done by dockyard mateys.*[11]

Remarkably, she was out of dock by 28 August and by the next day back at Scapa Flow. With crustaceans and weeds cleaned off her bottom, two knots had been added to *Rodney*'s speed.[12] Such was the scale of the ship's company's achievement the Admiralty sent a signal of congratulations. The Home Fleet left Scapa on the afternoon of 31 August 1939, the Germans invading Poland the following day, sending in more than a million soldiers. When war was declared on 3 September, after Germany failed to heed demands from France and Britain to withdraw, the Home Fleet was about 300 miles south of Iceland. The signal to *Rodney* from the Admiralty at 11 am (Noon German time) said: 'Total Germany.'

Midshipman Charles Fetherston-Dilke was on the bridge.

> *Total Germany was the code word for 'commence hostilities against Germany' and there was comparative calm on the bridge, no one burst into tears or had to go to the loo . . . I suppose because it was expected. We had been through the Munich thing, so it*

didn't come as a hammer blow. I wouldn't say there was any sort of emotion on the bridge or in the ship because we were all prepared for it. We had got a good ship ... we were well trained. There was no gung-ho about it at all [just] *acceptance. That is what you are paid for ... what you are here for. That is what the Navy does when the shooting starts.*[13]

A radio speech by the Prime Minister, speaking from 10 Downing Street, was relayed over the tannoy system. The sailors and marines heard Neville Chamberlain conclude by telling them:

... it is evil things that we shall be fighting against, brute force, bad faith, injustice, oppression and persecution. And against them I am certain that the right will prevail.

Afterwards there was silence throughout the ship. Many of *Rodney*'s men were no doubt contemplating the awful possibility of air raids on Plymouth, surely a prime target for the Luftwaffe?

The man appointed First Lord of the Admiralty on the outbreak of war, Winston Churchill, saw *Rodney* and *Nelson* as the country's principal bulwark against invasion. They were the most potent weapons to wield against the enemy's battle fleet until King George V Class ships were commissioned and fully worked up for combat. Indeed, in some vital respects, Churchill obviously believed the new battleships should be more like *Rodney* and her sister. In August 1936, just a few months before the first of the KGVs were laid down, he said they should have been given 16-inch guns and not the 14-inch weapons they were actually designed around. In naval warfare, said Churchill:

The answer is a big punch.

Having been First Lord in the early years of the First World War, he knew maximum killing power was necessary:

If you can get through the armour, it is worth [sic] *while doing something inside with the explosion.*[14]

Rodney in the Second World War would vindicate Churchill's faith in the 16-inch gun, while his fears for the 14-inch would prove well founded.

If the material condition of the Royal Navy, as a whole, on the outbreak of war was in some respects precarious, at least the men were ready for the fight.

However, all sane and reasonable men hoped fervently it would be short and they could soon be with their families again. Lt Cdr Boord recalled the ship's company of *Rodney* were no exception to this rule, but Admiral Forbes soon deflated their high hopes of a swift return home.

One was not certain if the war would be over in a fortnight or how long. However, the Commander-in-Chief was quite certain [about] *what was going to happen and he addressed all the big ships at Scapa in early September, assuring them that the war was likely to be just as long as World War One.*[15]

At the outset *Nelson*, *Rodney* and other units were spread across the most likely Atlantic breakout gaps for commerce raiders, between Greenland, Iceland, Britain and Norway. They were unaware the German pocket battleships *Graf Spee* and the *Deutschland* had already made it into the hunting ground. The Kriegsmarine's

U-boats were also already in war positions and on 3 September the liner *Athenia* became the first ship sunk by a German submarine, going down west of Rockall. A major Admiralty concern was the vulnerability of Scapa Flow to both air and submarine attack. There was a view that it was too far north for the Luftwaffe. However, intriguing signs in the sky were spotted one fine evening. Admiral Forbes was enjoying some fresh air by walking up and down the starboard side of *Rodney*'s quarterdeck, while Lt Cdr Boord paced up and down the port side with some other officers, one of whom was the Fleet Gunnery Officer.

> *... we saw high in the sky a vapour trail. Well, I had never seen one before, and nor had the Fleet Gunnery Officer and we wondered what it was. The Fleet Gunnery Officer went to the Admiral and drew his attention to it. After looking at it some time Admiral Forbes sent a signal to the fleet to go to anti-gas stations ... Well, we went to anti-gas stations all perfectly well, realizing that if it had been gas it would have dispersed by the time it got down to us.*[16]

On the Admiral's orders, *Rodney* was moved over to the flagship buoy, to which was connected a telephone line linking Scapa with the mainland system. A staff officer rang the air station at Wick and asked if anyone there could shed some light on what the trail was.

> *The following day the Air Ministry came through on the telephone to say that at certain conditions of speed, height and temperature, it was possible for high speed aircraft to leave a vapour trail. It indicated they were above a certain height, which was well above the ceiling of any fighter aircraft in our possession. It turned out this was a daily event. It was a German photographic machine coming to photograph the ships in harbour, to see what our movements were. We could see this thing every night, but we couldn't take any action ...*[17]

Plainly, the Luftwaffe could reach Scapa and now, whenever *Rodney* was there, her air-defence armament was closed up for action, as was the case in all other warships. By mid-September principal units of the Home Fleet had shifted their main operating base to Loch Ewe on the west coast of Scotland until Scapa could be better defended. It was far from ideal, being not well protected and further away from the key breakout points into the Atlantic. The Clyde would also serve as a major fleet base.

Aboard HMS *Rodney*, as wartime cruising practices took precedence, there was less obsession with everything being pristine in appearance, the dress code of her sailors and marines also becoming more relaxed. Prior to the war, ratings would frequently find themselves running around on the upper deck or ashore with rifles on their shoulders and also dropping to do dozens of press-ups. It was all part of a bid to fight the innate threat to fitness posed by life in a warship. However, after hostilities began, in the short term at least, there was no time for such pursuits. The ship was closed up at Action Stations for long periods and, within minutes of war being declared, all deadlights and portholes were closed, hatches shut and no lights allowed to show. Even smoking on the upper deck was banned. The loss of the Devonport-based carrier HMS *Courageous* to a U-boat on 17 September emphatically demonstrated it was a serious, shooting war. A number of *Rodney*'s sailors had served in *Courageous* and lost many friends. The wisdom of closing and clipping water-tight doors at Action Stations was something everyone now treated as a necessity they would gladly live with, rather than an unnecessary irritation.

But the morale in *Rodney* was good, as Leading Seaman Len Walters noted:

I think all the members of the Rodney *will agree it was a fine ship to be on. It was a big ship and there was plenty to do and plenty of space. Everyone knew their job.*

Born at Trediga, South Wales in 1921, Len Walters, who had joined *Rodney* during the Munich Crisis, was glad of the strict discipline he endured during basic training.

I don't think anyone likes to be pushed around and told to go here, there and everywhere, and when you went for a shower you were inspected to make sure you had showered properly and cleaned your teeth properly and you were kicked out of bed in the morning early ... It was discipline, which is lacking today. It was that discipline which carried the Navy through in wartime.

It meant that when Actions Stations were called people moved promptly to their positions, knowing exactly what their duties were. Len Walters preferred officers to be strict but fair and straight talking, rather than easy-going. Walters himself gained insight into the art of command when promoted to Leading Seaman in *Rodney*, at the tender age of nineteen. The mess he was put in charge of was home to armourers, ordnance artificers and others who worked in 16-inch and 6-inch turrets, all of them with a minimum of fifteen years service, compared with young Len's mere twenty-four months.

Fortunately, I got on well with them and they were no trouble at all. It was one of the finest messes in the ship. They were all three-badge able seaman who did not have to be told what to do ...

However, one of Walters' new messmates decided to test his mettle.

... you join mess at lunch time and I took my lunch and sat down at the ship's side, at the table. I was half way through the meal and I realized someone was standing behind me and I turned around and said: 'Yes, do you want me?' And he said: 'You're in my seat.'

Walters told the veteran he would have to wait until after he had finished his lunch.

If I had given in to him that would have been the end of me as a person in charge of the mess. After that everything went smoothly, lovely.

Joining the *Rodney* on 20 September after a long journey north from Chatham was Arthur 'Mick' Kavanagh, a seventeen-year old Dubliner who had tried to join the Royal Navy in October 1938 but was turned down until background checks could establish he was not an IRA infiltrator. 'It was a bit daft really, especially as my uncle had enjoyed a long career in the Royal Navy, but I suppose they had to make sure,' he recalled more than six decades later.

So I got a job, making lead soldiers and then I went back again and this time they said OK and within a couple of weeks I was on my way down to Devonport, as a Boy Seaman. I was only 16.

Home on leave in Ireland, Kavanagh was recalled on 1 September 1939.

By the time I got back to Devonport everyone else had been drafted to their various ships and shore establishments, so I had to sit on my own and listen to the declaration of war broadcast in a vast, empty drill shed. On the Monday they sent me to Chatham, a Petty Officer taking me down to the Plymouth railway station. Carrying my kitbag and suitcase, I had to make my own way to Chatham.

On reaching *Rodney* a fortnight or so later, Ordinary Seaman Kavanagh found he was among his fellow countrymen.

There was a fair few aboard. If memory serves me right there were 109 Irishmen aboard Rodney. *You soon found someone who would clue you in on what was going on. I found it was easy so long as you did what you were told. My Action Station was on top of the Octopoidal, as trainer for the port rangefinder on the torpedoes. It was quite easy and I didn't suffer much from sea sickness, except for feeling a bit groggy.*

To keep track of German warships the Royal Navy stationed submarines on picket duty in the Heligoland Bight but on 24 September one of these boats, HMS *Spearfish*, was detected and damaged by an enemy depth-charge attack, somehow evading destruction, but unable to dive after managing an emergency surface. Receiving her distress call, the Home Fleet, already on a foray into the North Sea, in which it hoped to tempt out the Kriegsmarine's principal units for a showdown, was diverted to provide cover for *Spearfish* as she limped home.

By 26 September the British warships were around 150 miles off the Norwegian coast when German Dornier flying boats were detected attempting to shadow them. The cruisers *Aurora* and *Sheffield* shepherded *Spearfish*, while *Nelson*, *Hood*, *Rodney* and *Ark Royal* were at a distance, providing heavy-duty back-up. *Ark Royal* launched Skua fighters, one of the Dorniers was shot down, but sighting reports had reached Germany and bombers were ordered to attack the Home Fleet. This would be *Rodney*'s first action, the enemy aerial assault beginning around 2.30 pm. Following accepted practice of the time – aircraft carriers were unproven as air-defence platforms at that stage in the war – *Ark Royal*'s fighters were struck down into the carrier's hangar, instead of being sent aloft on Combat Air Patrol.The Home Fleet would rely upon the anti-aircraft weapons of its ships. This doctrine was deeply frustrating for those in *Ark Royal* keen to prove the lethality and utility of aircraft. The episode has been described in terms less than flattering to *Rodney* and her ilk.

… Ark Royal *staggered along in the wake of the cumbersome* Nelson *and* Rodney, *which could only make eighteen knots. To use a potential battle winner* [Ark Royal] *as a floating anti-aircraft battery for the protection of the battleships seemed to them* [the air enthusiasts] *the height of big-gun stupidity.*[18]

Four Junkers Ju88 bombers appeared from the south-east, at around 6,000 ft and unloaded their cargos, surrounding *Rodney* and other British warships with gigantic splashes and hitting *Hood* with a bomb that bounced off. A fifth Ju88 dived straight for *Ark Royal*, one of its bombs hitting the water just 30 yards from the carrier's port bow. The shock wave, combined with the carrier's evasive action, caused the *Ark* to list heavily and soot shot out of her funnel. This gave the German bomber pilot the impression he had mortally wounded the carrier. The Nazi propaganda machine wasted no time in claiming *Ark Royal* sunk, much to the astonishment of *Rodney*'s sailors and marines.

That evening the whole ship's company were greatly amused to hear Lord Haw Haw roaring out: 'Where is the Ark Royal*?' over the wireless. We could see her quite clearly from the port holes at the time ...*[19]

A German reconnaissance flight on 12 October spotted the Home Fleet was in Scapa Flow and ripe for attack. After sunset, however, under cover of darkness, and against the prying eyes of the Luftwaffe, *Rodney* and rest of the fleet left for Loch Ewe. The old battleship HMS *Royal Oak*, which had been detached to patrol waters between the Orkneys and Shetland, remained at Scapa to act as anti-aircraft guardship for Kirkwall. Unfortunately, the Germans had spotted a gap in the eastern sea defences and while a blockship had been sent north to plug the gap, it had foundered on the way. *U-47*, under the command of Gunther Prien, was sent to exploit this vulnerability, putting three torpedoes into *Royal Oak* in the early hours of 14 October, the old British battleship turning turtle and taking 800 men with her. In the aftermath of this disaster, there was a profound sense of shock in *Rodney*, especially among those who had at one time served in the *Royal Oak*.

Royal Marine Jack C. Austin joined *Rodney* in November 1939, having originally tried to enter the Royal Navy as a stoker. At the recruiting office in Whitehall, a chief petty officer assessed that the sturdily built youngster would make a good marine. 'Seeing a Royal Marine in Dress uniform had me hooked,' Jack recalled. During training Austin broke his ankle, which put him back several weeks and into a new squad but, in retrospect, it was stroke of luck rather than misfortune.

It so happens that my original squad was divided, half going to the battlecruiser Repulse. *You know how they met their end.*[20]

Life in *Rodney* during the latter part of 1939 was not exactly exciting as far as Marine Austin was concerned, the ship spending too much time in harbour for his liking:

Some said we would be unable to go to sea, being high and dry on the tin cans thrown over the side.

A rather big 'tin can' of some interest to young officers in *Rodney*, including eighteen-year old Midshipman Fetherston-Dilke, was the salvaged German battle-cruiser *Derflinger*, which had traded heavy hits with British dreadnoughts at Jutland, and was now lying nearby, bottom up. As Fetherston-Dilke clambered over the *Derflinger*'s hull, he reflected on the nature of the enemy his generation faced.

We reckoned that they were as good as us, probably in things like gunnery and damage control. They were not underestimated [and we felt that we only] *had an advantage in that we had 16-inch guns and they didn't. They hadn't got anything as big as the* Rodney *at that stage.*

Other sailors at Scapa indulged in more bizarre diversions than inspecting *Derflinger*.

A stoker, very aware that he hadn't seen a girl for months, decided that a sheep would do instead and this resulted in a sort of situation where he couldn't extricate himself, if that is the right word, and he had to be taken to hospital. So, after that, whenever any ship's boat or anything passed HMS Rodney *everybody leaned over the side and baa'd. HMS* Nelson, *who looked like HMS* Rodney, *had the flagship flag and they finally sent a signal saying that 'ships passing HMS* Nelson *are no longer to baa ...'*[21]

To provide idle hands with better distractions than a spot of bestiality, there were patrols at sea. On 23 November the Home Fleet, including *Rodney*, had just returned to the Clyde when an urgent signal reporting a German surface raider was received from the Armed Merchant Cruiser *Rawalpindi*, a well known former P&O liner. The whole fleet put to sea, with some ships heading for *Rawalpindi*'s last reported position. The battlecruisers *Scharnhorst* and *Gneisenau* had made short work of her, but the Germans evaded the Home Fleet, deciding to withdraw rather than fight. As German cryptographers had cracked British naval codes, they knew the Royal Navy was on the hunt. Dreadful weather ensured the German warships managed to slip past *Rodney* and *Nelson*, which had been positioned 60 miles off the Norwegian coast in the hope of blocking the raiders route home. Heading for the Clyde again, *Rodney* hit problems. 'Soon after ending our patrol and setting course for home waters, *Rodney* suddenly found that her rudder would not answer the helm,' recalls Lt Cdr Peter Staveley, who was a midshipman in the battleship at the time.

> *The steering system was thoroughly checked and I well remember the Engineer Commander arriving on the bridge to report the result to the Captain. He said that there was no fault on the system and so the damage must be external.*[22]

On reaching the Clyde, divers were sent over the side, discovering the rudder had indeed sustained serious damage and *Rodney* would have to be sent south for major repairs.

> *Having twin screws we steered by main engines while on passage but we occasionally took a sheer to port or starboard, which kept our escorting destroyers on their toes. On arrival at Liverpool early in December we went into the Gladstone graving dock and when the dock was dry we found that the rudder was scarcely recognisable. The frame was severely buckled and all the filling had disappeared. The explanation probably lies in the defective state of German torpedoes at that time. In spite of successes, as in the case of* Royal Oak, *there were many failures. Besides depth keeping problems, the contact pistols fitted into the warheads were being manufactured with a defect in them and as a result many torpedoes, which hit their targets failed to explode. It seems likely that a U-boat had fired a salvo of torpedoes at* Rodney *and that one of them had hit her rudder.*[23]

An incident recorded by German war records illustrates how fortunate *Rodney* was on an earlier occasion. At 10.00 am on 30 October, while prowling to the west of the Orkneys, *U-56*, commanded by Lieutenant Wilhelm Zahn, popped up to periscope depth for a scan of the surface and saw not only *Rodney* but other key units of the Home Fleet, including *Nelson*. The German submarine had managed to penetrate the protective cordon of destroyers and was in an ideal position to create havoc. Zahn could hardly believe his luck:

> *Three battleships were headed towards me head-on, making an attack difficult if not impossible. Suddenly they turned through an angle of twenty to thirty degrees, thereby placing* U56 *in an ideal firing position.*[24]

Rodney was leading the British formation and Zahn decided to let her pass through his field of vision in favour of attacking the next in line, *Nelson*.

> *An ideal set-up, the fan of torpedoes sped away smoothly, as on a practice shoot.*[25]

The German submarine went deep and Zahn listened on *U-56*'s hydrophones for explosions signifying success. What he heard was the clang of two torpedoes actually hitting *Nelson* but failing to explode. The third missed and ran its course before exploding, bringing down the attention of depth-charging British destroyers. *U-56* later surfaced to send a wireless transmission on the encounter to naval HQ in Germany, listing *Rodney* among three big juicy targets.

> *THREE TORPEDOES FIRED STOP DUDS.*[26]

Doubly fortunate for *Rodney* and the rest of the Home Fleet was that Zahn, feeling dejected after such an abject failure, waited until the evening to send his signal. The German Commander-in-Chief, Admiral Karl Donitz, could have sent the nearby *U-58* in to mount another attack had he been blessed with Zahn's report earlier.

Just over a month later, as *Rodney* headed south for the Mersey, the Home Fleet returned to Loch Ewe where disaster struck on 4 December, for, while German torpedoes might have been prone to failure, mines laid by them were all too effective, *Nelson* striking one.

The below water damage was serious, with fifty of her ratings injured, and the fleet flagship required major repairs. A month later, after thorough mine-sweeping of Loch Ewe and its approaches, *Nelson*, with temporary repairs in place, set sail for Portsmouth where she remained for six months.

The *Rodney* had meanwhile docked down at Liverpool on 9 December, her repairs taking only twenty days, no doubt accelerated by the need to get the battleship back to sea as soon as possible. Winston Churchill saw the loss of both the Royal Navy's principal battleships as a disaster of epic proportions, for it made Britain immensely vulnerable. As First Lord, Churchill typically interested himself in the minutiae of both naval administration and operational matters, even extending to recommending where individual ships should be based. During late 1939, shortly before going to France to visit his opposite number, he dictated a minute to the Chief and Deputy Chief of the Naval Staff, which stated the North Sea should be dominated by the Royal Navy to prevent raids like those inflicted by German surface ships in the First World War, and, of course, to deter invasion. Churchill was keenly aware Rosyth was vulnerable to air attack, but believed it still might have to suffice for certain periods. He wrote on 29 October 1939:

> Nelson *and* Rodney, *'The Captains of the Gate' must take their stations at Rosyth and fight it out there when not at sea.*[27]

The day after Churchill's 'Captains of the Gate' note, the First Sea Lord, Admiral Sir Dudley Pound, visited Admiral Forbes, to convey Churchill's thoughts on the importance of *Rodney* and *Nelson* dominating the North Sea. On Christmas Day 1939 Churchill wrote a minute to his staff asking:

> *How is* Rodney *getting on and when can we expect her?*[28]

Four days later *Rodney* was undocked and on 30 December due to depart Liverpool. During *Rodney*'s time in Liverpool, junior rating Arthur Kavanagh stayed ashore with an aunt and later recalled how the ship became a victim of the criminal underworld.

> *We were taking aboard provisions and someone parked a lorry in among all the others that were being loaded with our stores at Bootle and then drove it away, destined for the black market rather than the ship.*

Some teenage sailors were not allowed ashore in Liverpool at night, including seventeen-year old Ted Russ, who joined the Navy in 1937.

> *There was a funfair nearby which was very attractive to us and after dark we used to sneak ashore anyway and enjoy ourselves.*

Russ had ended up in the Navy because he was considered too short for the Army and they told him to go away, so he tried the Senior Service. After training and assignment to the Devonport Division he was drafted to the cruiser HMS *Cornwall* before going to the *Royal Oak.*

> *I didn't like the* Royal Oak *much as she was an old ship and anyway, when she was sunk I was doubly grateful for being sent to the* Rodney.

Among a new draft of sailors to the ship in late 1939 was E.L. Brown, a nineteen-year old Royal Naval Volunteer Reserve junior rating who kept a pocket diary.

The young sailor was breaking the rules, as sailors were told not to keep private diaries, in case they were captured and the enemy could glean intelligence from them. However, because some of them did break the rules, we are left with insights into the ordinary drama of *Rodney* at war that would otherwise have been lost. On New Year's Day 1940, at Greenock, *Rodney* once more became flagship of the Home Fleet and for the next two months operated out of the Clyde, on 4 January setting sail in company with the battlecruiser HMS *Repulse.*

For junior ratings in *Rodney*, such as E.L. Brown, the anticipated high drama of war in a battleship soon settled down into a dull routine, where the enemy was elusive and he was never sure what was happening in the world at large, or even where the ship was headed. As his diary entries for early 1940 reveal, having a wash or a good meal could sometimes be the highlight of his day.

5 January:

> *Still going north, on our way to guard A.M.Cs* [Armed Merchant Cruisers]. *Might be going to Halifax, Canada. Went to bed 8.30 pm. Had a bath.*[29]

6 January:

> *Change direction going East now going West. Roast pork for dinner. Went to bed 9 pm – felt miserable ...*

On the same day he also observed:

> *Aeroplane seen in distance ... after getting ready for air-raid found to be our own plane.*

On 9 January there was a submarine alert, but this barely rated a mention in the teenage sailor's lovesick diary entry, which did, however, reveal *Rodney*'s recent repairs might not have been effective:

> *Wrote to Phyl* [girl friend]. *Love her more than ever. Steering goes wrong.*

By 10 January *Rodney* was heading south for the Clyde:

> *Played Monopoly in the morning. Slept in the afternoon. Went over Boom at 2.15 pm. Dropped anchor at Greenock 5.15 pm. Went to bed 9 pm.*

Not even bothering to note what his job was in the ship, E.L. Brown's attention was at least excited by news of trouble in another ship, his diary noting rather tantalizingly on 14 January 1940:

> *HMS* Repulse *crew mutinied, refused to work.*

But his life in *Rodney* carried on as normal:

> *Went church. Went ashore in the evening.*

Bad weather closed in during January, making everyone in *Rodney* feel miserable and while other ships were in action, she seemed destined never to meet the enemy again. The Clyde suffered an air raid on 16 January, but this could not prevent E.L. Brown's trip to the cinema in Greenock, so at least shore leave was forthcoming, but sometimes the fog was so bad the battleship's sailors had to spend the night in a Sailors' Rest ashore. On the morning of 27 January *Rodney* sailed in company with *Repulse,* destined to protect a convoy from surface raiders, but encountering the 'worst storm in years,'[30] E.L. Brown's diary entry for 28 January recording:

> *Weather getting worse. Sea very heavy. Continual lookout for mines and subs. Terrible storm. Sea terrific.*

The seas stayed rough for the next two days, with all watertight doors closed, E.L. Brown noting on 30 January:

> *Sea much calmer. Air raids in Orkneys. Went to pictures onboard, saw* Hound of Baskervilles, *turned back for Greenock.*

The ship dropped anchor off Greenock on the afternoon of 31 January and nine days later *Rodney*'s sailors and marines were assembled on the upper deck to cheer in a vessel carrying soldiers of the 1st Canadian Division, the first Dominion troops to reach the mother country.

When *Rodney* was at Loch Ewe, her midshipmen were tasked with deterring U-boat attack by taking it in turn to command the battleship's drifter, on boom duty. The sailors loved it, as they could get away from battleship routine and wear less formal uniforms, adopting a piratical air. The drifter had been fitted with a 3pdr gun in its bows and depth charges in the stern. 'They had an anti-submarine net there and you had to patrol that, because, if a submarine tried to get in, the net was so arranged it would ignite a flare on it,' recalled Midshipman Fetherston-Dilke.

> *In fact one night the flare did ignite and we set off and I dropped a depth charge in the middle of the channel, which didn't go off. I was told by the captain, who was a Sub Lieutenant, to set a depth of 250 feet, which I duly did, but of course there wasn't 250 foot of water so there was a lot of nail biting going on. At half past five the next morning there was the most thunderous explosion ... but we didn't sink any submarines.*

Royal Marine William Alexander, from Ulster, arrived aboard *Rodney* on 1 February, having enlisted in March 1939, less than a fortnight after his seventeenth birthday.

There was to be no conscription in Northern Ireland because the authorities were still worried about IRA infiltration, but he was bored with his job driving the pony and cart of a clergyman back home and could see a war was coming. Another seventeen-year old joining *Rodney* in early 1940 was Gordon Smerdon, a Devonport native whose father was a Chief Petty Officer Writer before working in the dockyard. Schooled by the Navy since the age of eleven, joining the aircraft carrier *Courageous* as a Boy Seaman in his home city he helped to operate a 4.7-inch anti-aircraft gun. On 17 September 1939, when *Courageous* was torpedoed by *U-29*, south-west of Ireland, Smerdon found himself in company with a so-called 'pensioner', one of the middle-aged First World War veterans called back to service. Wearing both a red dressing gown and a non-regulation moustache, the 'pensioner' looked rather like a cinema matinee idol. He handed Smerdon his money belt, as he knew he wouldn't need it where he was going. Saying goodbye to the man in the red dressing gown, the youngster put a pair of brand new shoes he didn't want to lose, and the money belt, around his neck and jumped into the sea. Losing both shoes and the money belt, Smerdon found himself clinging to one end of an oar, with another sailor on the other end. Seeing a group of survivors not far off, Smerdon decided not to swim over to them, as his father, who had survived similar situations in the First World War, had warned him panic could grip such groups. Picked up by the destroyer *Impulsive*, Smerdon was by the next day back at the family home in Devonport. In January 1940, he received his draft to the *Rodney*. 'At the time I was delighted to go, 'cause I was getting a little bit itchy feet,' he recalled. Smerdon soon found he had developed an acute fear of confined spaces.

> *For my Action Station they put me right down the bottom of the ship into the magazine and I think I got a little bit claustrophobic ... You more or less had to go in a hole in the deck and crawl through, like a porthole, and you were battened in.*[31]

The teenager went to see the Petty Officer in charge of his section and explained his problem.

> *I told him my last ship was the* Courageous *and 'I don't think I could stand this down here' and he immediately changed it ... He was a wonderful chap, actually.*

On 18 February all leave was stopped and *Rodney* was put at one hour's notice to sail, as the German fleet was reported out, the Home Fleet eventually sailing from the Clyde the following afternoon. Admiral Forbes fully expected to meet the enemy and, despite battling rough seas, *Rodney* and *Hood* held gun practice to ready themselves for the fight ahead. At 6 am on 21 February, *Rodney* was called to Action Stations, the weather continuing to deteriorate. However, there was no dramatic clash and, on 22 February, E.L. Brown provided his usual mix of the mundane and tantalising:

> *Nothing unusual during morning. 30 Depth Charges dropped on sub. All lost. Went to bed early.*

The following day *Rodney* was called to Action Stations at 7 am, once again preparing to confront German surface raiders. However, the steering problem resurfaced and the fleet flagship was forced to turn back for the Clyde, leaving her escorting destroyers, cruisers and *Hood* to carry on. The weather was glorious on arriving back at Greenock and on 27 February, *Rodney* received a visit from King George VI and Queen Elizabeth, who were on a morale boosting tour of Scotland's warship construction yards. E.L. Brown noted:

> *King and Queen coming aboard. Arrived about 4ish. Becoming ill, wrote a rotten letter to Phyl. Wrote back and apologized.*

On 28 February, the young sailor's temperature was still rising and the next day he was admitted to the sickbay with German Measles, not being discharged until 6 March. On 7 March *Rodney* welcomed aboard Winston Churchill for a voyage north to Scapa, the First Lord plainly keen to see for himself that at least one of his 'Captains of the Gate' was fighting fit. The ship set sail at 2 pm on 8 March, providing E.L. Brown with something a little more interesting than usual to record:

> *Saw W. Churchill walking about ship smoking cigar. 16-inch shoot in afternoon, also pom-pom guns. German aircraft dropped bombs and mines. Arrived in Scapa about 4 pm. Expecting German aircraft. W.C. left ship 5 pm.*

The *Rodney*'s anti-aircraft gun crews were closed up for action and, as if to remind them the threat to life came from under the sea too, her men witnessed a grisly reminder of the cost of war recorded by E.L. Brown:

> *HMS* Royal Oak *victims occasionally coming to the surface. Poor devils.*

Air raids were by now frequent and on 16 March *Rodney* experienced a close shave, E.L. Brown reporting:

> *Picked up planes about 8 pm First one came over, heard bomb falling. Saw it miss our ship by 10 yds. Next bomb hit* Norfolk. *Killed 2 and many injured. All the fleet opened fire and all shore batteries 'round about. Planes kept coming over, firing tracer bullets, as were we. Noise terrific. Coming down Octopoidal heard* [bomb] *so dropped to the deck and got under cover. Bomb hit water. Raiders dropped incendiary bombs on shore causing many heath fires. Raid lasted 1½ hours – our guns brought down 1 plane 3 miles from ship. Noise terrific. Wherever you looked you saw guns going and tracer bullets.*

On 19 March at 2.10 pm *Rodney* put to sea in company with *Valiant, Warspite, Repulse, Renown,* cruisers and destroyers, E.L. Brown conveying the RN's determination in his diary: '... we are going to attack German convoy.'

In superb weather, the Home Fleet continued its sweep, destroyers coming alongside *Rodney* to refuel on the move, a speed of 10 knots maintained during the tricky manoeuvre. A sailor serving in the destroyer *Firedrake*, a member of the Home Fleet's Eighth Flotilla, memorably described the process of taking oil from *Rodney* 'through a flexible pipe [suspended beneath wires strung between the ships] as a suckling takes its sustenance from the sow.'[32]

Flags on other wires were used to estimate distance between ships – too close and they would be inexorably sucked in towards each other for a disastrous collision. Among those standing by on the upper deck was Leading Seaman Walters:

> *... in rough seas some of the wires used to part and the Bosun's Party would have them onboard and resplice them together and have them back out as quickly as possible in case required again.*

There was plenty of cursing all around when the wires snapped, *Firedrake*'s sailor reporting:

> *The language used during the operation had ... something of a porcine quality also.*[33]

By evening on 23 March, a gale was in the offing, the temperature dropping dramatically the further north the fleet sailed. By 24 March the temperature was near freezing and, amid snowstorms, *Rodney* sighted Iceland and kept going north. On 25 March E.L. Brown noted:

> *Damn fed up ... Saw Greenland in the night. Damn cold. Wearing two of everything.*

The following day the fleet captured a German merchant ship and turned around to head for Scapa, where ordeal by Luftwaffe air raid continued into early April, sapping morale. On 2 April, E.L. Brown recorded another close encounter with German bombers:

> *Sitting in mess playing chess with Scotty when Air Raid Warning Yellow sounded. Thinking it was practice, carried on with game ... later heard guns going and then Air Raid Red sounded off. Picking up gas mask, rushed like Hell for flag deck. There I saw guns going, puffs in the sky. Tracer bullets were being fired, a terrible din all 'round. Lasted about an hour.*

On 5 April:

> *Air raid while we were at breakfast. Beautiful day. Damn fed up with this.*

The happy situation of near misses, but no hits would not last much longer, however, and the *Rodney* would soon receive her first battle scar, a wound that could so easily have proved fatal.

Notes

1 Williams, IWM Sound Archive.
2 Walters, IWM Sound Archive.
3 Naval slang for a short-notice draft to a ship, almost as if the man in question was leaping off the pier and onto the vessel as she cast off. Sometimes this might literally be the case.
4 Hughes, IWM Sound Archive.
5 The *Rodney* was the first British battleship to receive air-warning radar, capable of detecting enemy aircraft. The cruiser *Sheffield* was also fitted with radar. The potential of this powerful invention was demonstrated in September 1937, when air-to-surface vessel radar successfully detected *Rodney* and the carrier *Courageous* at sea from a distance of five miles. In September 1939, both *Rodney* and *Sheffield* used radar to detect enemy aircraft.
6 Neil McCart, *Rodney and Nelson.*
7 Chatfield, *It Might Happen Again.*
8 Jim McLean, in letter to author.
9 Kenneth Thompson, *HMS Rodney at War.*
10 John Boord, IWM Sound Archive.
11 Ibid.
12 Kenneth Thompson, *HMS Rodney at War.*
13 Fetherston-Dilke, IWM Sound Archive.
14 Winston Churchill, *The World Crisis.*
15 John Boord, IWM Sound Archive.
16 Ibid.
17 Ibid.

18 Kenneth Poolman, *Ark Royal.*
19 Kenneth Thompson, *HMS Rodney at War.*
20 HMS *Repulse* was sunk on 10 December, off Malaya, with the King George V Class battleship HMS *Prince of Wales*, by Japanese aircraft operating from Indo-China.
21 Walton, IWM Sound Archive.
22 Staveley, IWM Department of Documents.
23 Ibid. In correspondence with the author of this book in November 2007, Lt Cdr Staveley put forward a different sequence of events to further explain *Rodney*'s rudder problems in late 1939: 'In his memoirs, Admiral Donitz reports the *U-56* fired three torpedoes at HMS *Nelson* on 30 October 1939. The torpedoes did not explode, although the sound of their impact on *Nelson*'s hull was heard.' Lt Cdr Staveley pointed out that sister ships *Nelson* and *Rodney* were 'from the beginning of the war until the end of November always in company with each other.' He added: 'It seems likely that the date of the report was a month out and that *U-56* attacked on 30 November and not 30 October, and that the attack was made on *Rodney* and not *Nelson*. This would fit in quite well with *Rodney*'s subsequent movements, entering the Gladstone graving dock at Liverpool in early December.'
24 Cajus Bekker, *Hitler's Naval War.*
25 Ibid.
26 Ibid.
27 Quoted by Roy Jenkins in *Churchill.*
28 Ibid.
29 E.L. Brown, IWM Department of Documents.
30 Ibid.
31 Smerdon, IWM Sound Archive.
32 A.D. Divine, *Destroyer's War.*
33 Ibid.

Chapter Nine

THE BOMB

With no decisive move by German land forces in the West following the conquest of Poland, at sea Norway was becoming the focus for both sides.

In the First World War the blockade imposed by British naval forces had played a major part in starving Germany into surrender and by conquering Norway, Hitler hoped to ensure that this time around the vice stayed open. There were already signs history was being repeated, for, by early 1940, the Royal Navy's hold on the oceans was already so strong the Germans were asking Russia for grain and oil. In February 1940, they even transferred one of their cruisers, the *Lutzow*, while still under construction, to the Red Navy as payment for supplies.

Therefore, the Germans were planning to establish U-boat and air bases in Norway, to loosen the blockade and strike at Britain's lifeline of merchant shipping convoys. Occupation of Norway was also needed in order to safeguard passage of vital iron ore from Sweden. The Baltic was usually frozen in deep winter and ice-free Narvik was the only port via which the iron ore – needed to manufacture armaments – could be transported. German vessels carrying the iron ore had already been using Norwegian territorial waters to evade Allied warships. The British and French therefore planned a joint operation to mine the Norwegian littoral and force the iron ore ships into international waters, where they would be legally boarded. *Rodney*'s Petty Officer George Thomas and other sailors were among those roped in at very short notice to provide the boarding parties and prize crews for captured iron ore ships.

> *I was sent to HMS* Afridi *a Tribal Class destroyer ... The usual thing, just take a toothbrush and a pair of socks and that's it. We expected to be* [away] *for a couple of weeks.*

There were intensive board and seizure exercises, teams of sailors rowing across to ships and then climbing up, weapons at the ready. They all knew their rifle drill but, as Thomas admitted, 'none of us were trained in side arms as such,' and there were serious concerns the sailors would accidentally shoot each other.

The Allies planned to forestall any German counter-measures by seizing not only Narvik but also Trondheim, Bergen and Stavanger. However they hesitated to violate the territorial integrity of a neutral country and this gave the Nazis their opportunity. When the Germans made their decisive move, in early April, the Royal Navy was under the misapprehension that the increase in activity at enemy ports was a precursor for a mass breakout into the Atlantic by surface raiders.

On 5 April Royal Navy mine-laying ships deployed to Norwegian waters with a covering force composed of the modernized 15-inch gun battlecruiser HMS *Renown* and four destroyers, including *Afridi*. The mine-laying was to be finished on 8 April, but, with news of the invasion, plans for board and seizure operations were immediately abandoned. By 7 April enough reports from reconnaissance aircraft of suspicious activity in German ports were coming through for Admiral Forbes in HMS *Rodney* to order the Home Fleet – the Flagship, *Valiant* and *Repulse*, plus cruisers *Sheffield* and *Penelope*, together with 10 destroyers[1] – to be at one hour's notice to sail. At 5.27 pm, Forbes issued an order from *Rodney* for the Home Fleet to raise steam and, at 8.15 pm, its main units left Scapa Flow and Rosyth while the German invasion, involving almost the entire Kriegsmarine, was well and truly under way. The Norwegians, who had not been in a major war for a century, were caught completely unawares, finding it very difficult to believe they were actually being invaded. While the other British units stayed off southern Norway, *Renown* was ordered north on a search and destroy mission against surface raiders. Although Forbes later claimed that by late in the day on 8 April he knew an invasion was in progress, some historians have asked why he kept *Rodney* and other Home Fleet units so far out to sea they could not effectively intercept enemy troop transports. Fragmented signals from the destroyer HMS *Glowworm*, which lost an unequal contest with the heavy cruiser *Hipper*, may have reinforced in Forbes' mind a major breakout of surface raiders was under way. After hearing of the *Glowworm* action, sailors in *Rodney* certainly believed a clash with the German fleet was imminent.[2] In the afternoon and early evening the Admiralty signalled *Rodney* that heavy ships and destroyers had sailed through the Belt, into the Kattegat and headed north. Therefore Forbes turned south but detached *Repulse* and *Penelope* to cover the northern threat and back up *Renown*. Between 8.30 am and 9.15 am on 9 April, *Renown*, ordered closer in to the Vestfjord by a direct Admiralty signal, in bad weather sighted and engaged the German battlecruisers *Gneisenau* and *Scharnhorst*, which had just escorted 10 troop-carrying destroyers to Narvik. Next, a report from a scouting aircraft indicated a battlecruiser, a pair of cruisers and destroyers – in fact *Hipper* and four destroyers – were heading out to sea, west and away from the Norwegian coast. In reality they were wasting time before going in to Trondheim. Still worried about the possibility of a mass breakout into the Atlantic, Forbes ordered *Rodney* onto a N/W course to intercept these ships.

On 9 April a Sunderland flying boat looking for the enemy was shot down and so, short of scouting assets, *Rodney*'s Walrus amphibian aircraft was catapulted to try and find the German surface fleet. Admiral Forbes briefed the aircrew himself, stressing it was urgent he discovered if the ships were part of an invasion force or surface raiders. Because the sea state was poor – too rough for *Rodney* to recover the aircraft – Admiral Forbes told the pilot to conserve fuel and abandon the search with enough left to make Norway. Forbes told the aircrew they would only be temporarily interned, as the Scandinavian country would surely be on the Allied side within 24 hours. The first round of air attacks against the Home Fleet came not long after 9 am, when the British warships were around 70 miles to the west of Bergen. There was then a lull until around 12.30 pm, when the Luftwaffe began a series of assaults by Heinkel 111s, Ju88s and Ju87 Stuka dive-bombers, lasting three hours, during which an estimated 300 bombs were dropped. The sea was rough, the weather cold and *Rodney* rolled uncomfortably. Huge columns of water rose in the air around the ships, the bombing proving spectacular but ineffective, unless a ship stopped moving. *Rodney*'s sailors expected the RAF's fighter planes to provide cover, but it was a forlorn hope; the ships would have to rely on their own weapons. Loudspeakers conveyed the sound of battle, together with a vivid description given by an officer located on the upper deck. For sailors and marines deep within *Rodney*, the difference between incoming and out-going fire was not easy to discern.

The firing of the 2pdr pom-pom – the so-called 'Chicago Piano' – was a bad sign, for it was a close-in air-defence weapon and could only signify the enemy were uncomfortably close to the ship.

At his action station on the upper deck E.L. Brown was idly watching the cruiser *Devonshire* being bombed ineffectually when, at around 3.30 pm, a German aircraft suddenly swooped down directly over the *Rodney*'s bows, a tannoy broadcast from the Air Defence Position blaring out:

> *Single aircraft starboard bow.*[3]

The raider dropped four bombs and E.L. Brown took cover.

> *I heard machine gun bullets above. Looking up, saw German twin-engined plane power-diving the last bomb. I heard whining down, so threw myself flat on deck. Heard bomb hit ship. Next thing ... ship's on fire and huge flames and smoke billowing out.*

The Royal Marine officer in command of X turret caught sight of a blurry shape hurtling past and thought it looked as big as an Austin Seven car.[4] It missed the Octopoidal, although sailors in the Air Defence Position threw themselves to the deck.[5] Junior rating James McLean was also on the upper deck, exposed to the force of the explosion.

> *With two other ratings, I was leaning over the low bulkhead, just chatting away. I heard an ear penetrating swish and my hair was sucked out from underneath my duffel coat hood whilst the skin on my face was pulled taut.*

Lt Cdr Boord thought the attack 'very well executed', as the bomber managed 'to dive on the ship from right ahead where in fact none of our anti-aircraft guns would bear ...'

> *... and it landed on the boat deck and we were extremely fortunate because it was a big bomb, and on the boat deck was the 4.7-inch anti-aircraft battery and each gun, three each side, had one armoured ready-use locker and two unarmoured ready-use lockers.*

Had the bomb hit one of the unarmoured ready-use lockers, an enormous explosion could have been triggered but, as Lt Cdr Boord recounted, luck was with the battleship.

> [the bomb] *fortunately landed on the corner of the P1, the forward port gun armoured ready-use locker ... the front portion of the bomb hit the corner of this locker and it must have caused a radial crack, because, when we found the bomb down below, the detonator in the head had gone off but the explosive was in a different compartment.*

That latter portion of the bomb nearly killed two midshipmen in the Gun-Room and, aside from demolishing various items of furniture, also smashed rifles belonging to the Royal Marines detachment stacked in racks in an adjoining passage. Lt Cdr Boord recalled the midshipmen would have been much safer had they earlier remained exposed to enemy fire.

> *The Torpedo Officer and I were on the lower bridge and we each had a doggy, a young midshipman, and they didn't look very happy. We sent them down to the Gun-Room to read a book because they were quite useless ... and they went and sat at the Gun-Room table and it was through the gunroom table that the bomb went.*

During the bombing lull Leading Seaman R. Tamblin, the ship's electrical welder, made his way forward to the Shipwright Workshop. As a member of the After Damage Control Party, during the attacks he had been standing by in the enclosed Tiller Flat and now, with the Action Stations bugle call blaring over the tannoy, rushed back through the ship. The After Damage Control Party felt 'a very slight shudder' and the telephone in their compartment rang, instructing them to investigate and put out a small fire, following a bomb hit on the boat deck abreast the funnel on the port side. As they emerged from the Tiller Flat the Chief Petty Officer in charge of the party told Tamblin and an Able Seaman to go up a deck through a hatch above and assess the extent of the damage.

> *We found a state of chaos in the Midshipmen's Mess; the small fire was soon extinguished and, as I recall, there was one casualty there, with damage to his nose.*[6]

One of the midshipmen was found trapped under the furniture and was swiftly pulled to safety or he might otherwise have succumbed to noxious fumes. The front portion of the bomb had, in fact, crashed into workshops used by the engineering room and ordnance artificers, hit a four-inch thick armoured deck, 'punched a large hole'[7] in it, then 'ricocheted upwards to an armoured bulkhead, hit the deck above and dropped to the deck again.'[8] On the other side of the bulkhead, Royal Marine Jack Austin was working in a cordite handling room for the P2 6-inch gun.

> *I was sitting on the armoured deck with my two mates, and fellow Royal Marines, Les Peach and Bert Lavers. We had our backs to the bulkhead one second and the next we were picking ourselves up several feet away. It was the one day in my life I felt panic. All I could see was bags of cordite out of their cases and large Catherine Wheels of flame coming through the badly bent bulkhead. It was the sergeant shouting 'STILL!' that snapped me out of it ... The only means of communication was by voice pipe to the turret, and they had no idea what had happened. We asked them to send a damage control team down. I can't say I became battle-hardened instantly, but I was always in control of myself, except for a few butterflies in the tummy, but once the action started I was O.K.*

A Royal Marine crewing the 6-inch gun above the cordite handling space knew he'd narrowly escaped death, no matter what the officers said.

> *The bomb hit the ship 12 feet from my 6-inch gun turret ... The incredible response to this major incident was a message over the intercom from the ship's Commander that we had possibly been hit by a small incendiary bomb.*[9]

In reality, *Rodney* had been hit by a 1,100 lbs armour-piercing bomb,[10] and the most serious threat to the battleship came from a hatch being left open. Leading Seaman Len Walters, who was in a 6-inch shell handling room saw how disaster so nearly happened. He recalled that *Rodney*'s Warrant Officer Gunner 'before the bomb dropped told me to open the armoured hatch enough for him to get out.'

> *I worked the chains to open the hatch and, as he clambered up the ladder he told me to leave the hatch open, as he would be back soon. While he was away, we were hit by the bomb ... Had it exploded, the* Rodney *could well have been another* Hood*, as the open hatch invited the flash to possibly reach the Shell Room and the Magazine below. It*

doesn't bear thinking about what might have happened. However, our Magic Genie was working overtime that day and we were safe. Not so the Warrant Officer Gunner, as he was caught in the fire along with two midshipmen, plus a dozen other lads who were injured. I never did see the Warrant Officer Gunner again, nor hear of any questions as to why he was away from his Action Station.[11]

Mick Kavanagh had been detailed off as a runner, taking messages on bits of paper around the ship for the admiral's staff. It was a job usually done by teenage sailors, who ran in their bare feet to avoid slipping on the decks. His most vivid memory of the Norwegian campaign was being seasick frequently. When the bomb hit, a somewhat green-looking Kavanagh was told to grab some weighted canvas bags containing secret documents and stand by to hurl them, rather than the contents of his stomach, over the side.

Ultimately, minor damage was inflicted on the internal structure by both blast and splinters. A fire was started in the galley flat, which was swiftly extinguished and the P1 6-inch gun turret was put out of action for only a short while.

... the fire filled many areas with thick smoke. At the time we had been closed up at Action Stations for long enough for someone to think about action messing. The Chefs were therefore busy cooking pasties to pass around the crew at their stations. Trays of pasties lay on the deck when the bomb hit, filling the galley with smoke and fumes; a Chef was trampling on the trays of pasties shouting 'I'm blind, I'm blind.' How many pasties were saved is not known. But it wasn't funny at the time.[12]

While the smoke, fumes and fire caused by the bomb impact inflicted at most three casualties, it was water pouring through the crack in the armoured deck that caused a further fifteen, who were far more seriously injured. Ken George, an Engine Room Artificer, was in the Number 4 Turbo Generator room and could hear little of the action except the crack of 4.7-inch AA guns and 'relatively pleasant' pom-poms.

I was not aware that an armour piercing bomb weighing half a ton had passed through three decks... The Electric Ring Main Junction Box, which housed the supply current from the No. 4 Turbo Gen was right under the dent in the boiler room flat [the Engine Room Artificer's and Ordnance Artificer's workshop]. *Water from the fire main being used to control the fire in the workshop and the adjacent compartments poured through cracks into the damaged junction box. The repair party, who were standing, received very serious burns while those who were sitting all escaped injury. At my station in the generator room I was still unaware of what was happening in the flat above. Because of the overloading I rang the switchboard to find out what was happening. I was told to 'hang on' as things needed to be sorted out!!! Looking back, after learning of the proximity of the partial open hatch, I am convinced we really did have a Guardian Angel.*[13]

Marine Bill Alexander was among those detailed to help transfer the casualties to the hospital ship *Isle of Jersey*. He later described it as one of the most unpleasant duties he had ever performed: '... the smell of burnt flesh was really dreadful.'[14] Lt Cdr Boord felt *Rodney*'s lucky escape taught some valuable lessons about sailors protecting themselves better. However, he seems to have mistakenly believed the

German bomb, rather than water pouring into the electricity junction box, caused the flash:

> *... the flash flame approached quite slowly along the corridor and all the mens' bell-bottomed trousers had blown up and they were burned around their ankles. Well, after that, it was the custom during aircraft attacks to put your socks outside your bell-bottom trousers to have some protection ... The hands and face should have been protected by anti-flash clothing.*

However, standard issue naval socks were 'rather too tight to go over bell-bottom trousers.'

> *The socks that were knitted by all the good ladies of England and sent out as charity socks were more loosely woven than the Pusser's issue socks and they were therefore popular.*

Anxious to glean some intelligence about the types of armour-piercing bombs the Germans possessed in their inventory, samples were taken of the explosive and the various parts of the weapon gathered together, so *Rodney*'s shipwrights could make a wooden template. That night, Leading Seaman Tamblin was tasked with 'welding a temporary steel patch over the hole in the armour deck to maintain the water tightness.'[15]

While he was doing this, a team led by a Leading Seaman Jimmy James – all volunteers fortified with a tot of rum – was extracting the remnants of the bomb from the ship and jettisoning them over the side.

> *A number of Royal Marines maneuvered the remains of the bomb onto a short mat, steel ladders were removed to ensure clear passage, and the load was carefully carried along the upper deck and dropped over the stern.*[16]

The truth about the 'small incendiary' was plain to those involved, including Marine Nicholl, who said of the delicate procedure:

> *When we eventually threw the remains of the bomb off the quarter deck, it did take a few of us to do so ... the bomb was 500 kilos in weight, so much for the Commander's report about a 'small incendiary'.*

Junior rating G. Conning, who had joined the *Rodney* in July 1939 from *Royal Oak*, recalled the British press gave the lucky battleship a nickname after the incident:

> *They called us the bomb bouncing battleship after that, as the press said it bounced over the side. It bounced alright, but not overboard.*[17]

There was plenty of evidence on the upper deck to show *Rodney* had been fighting for her life – it was littered with shell cases and stink of cordite hung in the air. Even though the bomb penetrated and made its mark, not many of those in the ship actually knew of *Rodney*'s hit, aside, of course, from the small percentage of sailors and marines actually able to see what happened.

To some of those looking on from destroyers in *Rodney*'s screen, the bomb looked enormous and they fully expected to see the battleship blow up or begin sinking by the stern[18], but she sailed on, apparently soaking up punishment unharmed.

But other vessels in the Home Fleet were not so lucky. HMS *Gurkha*, a Tribal Class destroyer, was one such. Her Commanding Officer changed course, so his AA weapons could be brought to bear more effectively, but by doing so *Gurkha* lost the protection of the Home Fleet's inter-locking fields of fire. The Germans saw their chance and bomber after bomber descended on *Gurkha*, blowing her stern off and stopping the ship dead in the water, to roll over and sink at around 7 pm that evening.

The day after *Rodney*'s close shave, the Royal Navy's 2nd Destroyer Flotilla, composed of five warships, was sent up the Ofotfjord to attack the German ships that had landed troops at Narvik, which the Allies were still intent on capturing, so it was important to clear out enemy shipping. In all, there were ten heavily-armed German destroyers and also some troop transport ships at Narvik, the 2nd Flotilla managing to sink two of the warships and half a dozen transports. The surviving German destroyers mauled the Royal Navy warships as they withdrew up the fjord, with two sunk and one seriously damaged. Meanwhile, the battleship *Warspite* and carrier *Furious* had joined the Home Fleet, on 12 April. *Rodney*'s junior rating E.L Brown reported a mystery aircraft: 'Heinkel bomber flies over us very slowly, at first thought it was our own, until it dropped bombs.'

Late on the evening of the same day *Rodney*'s gunnery officer was sent for by one of the Admiral's staff officers and asked if he thought it would be expedient to disconnect the safety depression gear on the 16-inch guns. It was explained to Lt Cdr Boord that the fleet flagship was about to venture up the Ofotfjord in company with a hunting pack of destroyers tasked with wiping out the remaining German warships at Narvik.

'The Safety Depression Gear is designed to prevent damage to the structure of one's own ship, and the targets likely to be encountered by *Rodney* next day were below the height of the turrets,' Lt Cdr Boord explained later.

> *A and X turrets were to be disconnected from the Safety Depression Gear, so as to engage the German ships in the fjord. I protested against this, saying that, as the* Nelson *was damaged it would be a pity to put the* Rodney *out of action as well. The problem was put to Admiral Forbes, who, being an ex-gunnery officer, agreed with me and instead of* Rodney *being sent in the* Warspite *undertook the job the next day. Well, as expected, the* Warspite *was very successful but she lifted her focsle deck and as a result, the ship was under repair . . . and that is a very good example of the stupidity of disconnecting Safety Depression Gear. In fact, I gave my opinion that B turret, which is higher than A and X, and the 6-inch battery each side of the ship of six guns would have been quite adequate. The* Rodney *could have gone in and done the job using her one turret of three 16-inch and two batteries of six-inch, however, the* Warspite *was the unlucky one.*

During the second Battle of Narvik, *Rodney* was ready to tow *Warspite* out of the Ofotfjord if she was crippled during the fighting, but fortunately was not needed. *Rodney* spent 14 April sailing up and down off the Norwegian coast in company with *Renown* and *Furious,* in almost continual daylight even at that time of year, potentially at the mercy of enemy air attack. On 15 April the Home Fleet set course for Scapa and two days later German bombers struck, but the British warships had already used up so much ammunition they were virtually defenceless, as E.L. Brown recorded in his diary:

> [the cruiser] Suffolk *bombed. No ammunition to fight back. Steamed into Scapa at 20 knots. German planes chasing us. Had to run owing to no ammunition.*

The *Suffolk* was left behind, but the following day made Scapa, her stern under water, obviously badly hit. She had suffered considerable casualties and on 21 April thirty-five of *Suffolk*'s men were buried at Lyness, all ships in the fleet flying their ensigns at half mast

Men from HMS *Rodney* were still at sea, in the destroyer *Afridi*, as she took part in an ill-fated attempt to eject the Germans from Norway. On 19 April, *Afridi* and other Allied warships landed infantry at Namsos and, as a supernumerary with no other duties aboard the British destroyer, *Rodney*'s Petty Officer Thomas helped disembark French mountain troops whom he was astonished to see had no skis. Unfortunately, Thomas was left behind with the landing party on a wooden jetty, in freezing weather, feeling he stuck out like a sore thumb. With no proper winter clothing, he was inevitably very cold. The inhabitants of Namsos had clearly fled the Luftwaffe, which was mounting an unrelenting air assault, while German troops were also closing in. Thomas feared for the worst.

> [I] *felt very vulnerable with the Germans in the hills all around us and the bombers dive- bombing us, with only a service revolver and six rounds of ammunition.*

After three days and nights at Namsos, during which he also helped disembark troop ships at night to avoid air attack, Thomas was grateful to be tasked with escorting a group of thirty-five German PoWs onto the French destroyer *Bison*, which was taking them to the Shetlands.

The PoWs were a mixture of civilians and service people who were kept on the upper deck despite the bitter weather. PO Thomas felt he was fortunate not to be needed for guard duty, so spent time in the French warship's senior rates mess and took a look at her engine rooms, which made a favourable impression, as the *Bison* was brand new. PO Thomas found *Bison*'s breakfast menu to be somewhat different from *Rodney*'s: Hard-boiled eggs and spinach. The French, for their part, were amazed when Royal Navy sailors asked for water to wash themselves while at sea.

Having discharged the PoWs into someone else's care in the Shetlands, Thomas was free to make his way back to *Rodney*. Both destroyers he had been in did not survive the Norwegian campaign: on 3 May, during efforts to evacuate troops from Namsos, *Afridi* was sunk by German dive-bombers, while attempting to save soldiers and sailors from *Bison*, an earlier victim. Forty-nine Royal Navy sailors, thirty French matelots and more than a dozen British soldiers went down with *Afridi*.

The Germans were determined not to let the Home Fleet rest, particularly now they had airfields in Norway and, at 9.30 pm on the night of 24 April, searchlights picked up an enemy aircraft over Scapa, *Rodney*'s anti-aircraft guns and those of other warships joining in with shore-based batteries. To E.L. Brown it was all 'very picturesque, searchlights and gun flashes. Noise terrific.'

Bad news from Norway reached Scapa on 2 May: British and French forces were in full retreat. Six days later Forbes was made an Admiral of the Fleet, 'the first one afloat since Nelson'[19] and *Rodney* was accorded the honour of flying the Union Jack at her masthead, the first warship to do so in war since HMS *Victory* at the Battle of Trafalgar. There were frequent air raids and on 10 May, Germany invaded the Low Countries, sweeping into France three days later, leading the Admiralty to make contingency plans for resisting invasion, including bayonet practice for E.L. Brown and other *Rodney* ratings. In London, Neville Chamberlain tendered his resignation, to be succeeded by Winston Churchill, who addressed the House of Commons for the first time as Prime Minister on 13 May, telling MPs:

> *I have nothing to offer but blood, toil, tears and sweat. We have before us an ordeal of the most grievous kind.*

On 23 May *Renown, Furious,* and sister carrier *Glorious* arrived at Scapa. The *Renown* was relieving *Repulse* to enable the latter to head for a mainland port to give her men leave. Sailors and marines in *Rodney* were not happy.

> *Men on board* [Rodney] *were showing signs of mutiny as* Repulse *has had 3 lots of leave, us only 1 in a year.*[20]

However, the duties of flagship were always onerous and, as the most valuable capital ship in the home waters, *Rodney* had to stick it out. On June 1 E.L. Brown wrote in his diary: 'Air Raid Warning Red, 3 planes beaten off. Still as bored as ever.' The previous day the Royal Navy, with assistance from a flotilla of privately-owned vessels, completed the evacuation under fire of nearly 400,000 Allied troops from Dunkirk and other French ports. It was the kind of operation for which battleships were not suited and, anyway, there were still Allied troops trapped in Norway. Four days later *Rodney* put to sea for the first time since surviving the bomb hit, engaging in a full round of gunnery exercises in the Pentland Firth. On 9 June, at noon, *Rodney* and *Renown* departed Scapa in order to cover the return of a convoy carrying Allied troops evacuated from Norway. There was a possibility of action against German surface ships, E.L. Brown remarking in his diary: 'Action again. Hooray.'

The following day *Ark Royal* joined the other ships, with Admiral Forbes intending to act decisively on a report of *Gneisenau* and *Hipper* at sea. The carrier's aircraft chased off a German scouting plane, but the same day news came through that *Glorious* had been sunk by *Scharnhorst* and *Gneisenau* on 8 June with great loss of life in the elderly British carrier. Her escorts, the destroyers *Ardent* and *Acasta*, sacrificed themselves in vain, although the latter did manage to hit *Scharnhorst* with a torpedo. By 10 June, *Hipper* and *Gneisenau* were skulking with *Scharnhorst* at Trondheim. The battleship HMS *Valiant* was attacked by Luftwaffe bombers, but the Home Fleet was still looking for the elusive showdown with the German Navy, and therefore headed for Trondheim, confident the clash would come. On 11 June E.L. Brown noted:

> *German plane tracks us. Zero hour midnight tomorrow. About 200 miles away from objective.*

On 12 June:

> *10 pm, in position outside Trondheim, Midnight. Planes from* A. Royal *to bomb German fleet there. We are to back them up. Expecting bombers and air raids. No sleep tonight, curse them.*

His diary entry for 13 June:

> *We lose 8 Skewers,* [sic] *2 destroyers collide in fog, we make for home at 7 knots. RAF let us down as usual, thus making the operation a failure. We hit German pocket battleship also ...*

Only one bomb had hit the *Scharnhorst* and caused little damage. It hardly seemed a good exchange for all those young men killed not only in the *Ark*'s aircraft but also in lost warships. The RAF had promised fighters to protect the 16 Skuas from Messerschmitts swarming over the *Scharnhorst*, but they failed to materialize, hence young Brown's curses.

Conditions for recovering Skuas in the early hours of 13 June were terrible – thick fog with only *Ark Royal's* mast poking above it, both *Rodney* and *Renown* close by, their sirens booming to prevent a collision. However, the consummate skill of the Fleet Air Arm pilots meant eight Skuas that survived the raid were able to land safely. With *Ark Royal* sent on ahead to Scapa, *Rodney* and *Renown* stayed behind to safeguard the two destroyers that had collided, the *Electra* and *Antelope*. The weather was by now glorious, but a blanket of gloom covered the British ships as they made slow progress back to Scapa. More than 1,000 men died in the *Glorious* alone, and 300 went down with *Ardent* and *Acasta*. Add them to the brave aviators, casualties in other ships and a grievous defeat on land and, as one historian has put it, the Narvik campaign was 'both a victory and a crushing defeat ...'[21]

The Kriegsmarine too had suffered serious losses, from which it would never really recover, including the ten destroyers at Narvik, representing half of its major escort ships. On 10 April, fifteen Fleet Air Arm Sea Skuas attacked and sank the cruiser *Konigsberg*, using the dive-bombing technique, making her the first large warship to be sunk by air attack in time of war. The Germans also lost the cruisers *Blucher*, to Norwegian shore-based torpedo batteries, and *Karlsruhe*, torpedoed by the submarine HMS *Truant*.

The myth of battleship invincibility, however, still pertained, as aircraft had yet to cause even serious damage to one. As *Rodney* dropped anchor at Scapa Flow on 15 June, she was still a seemingly invulnerable goliath of the seven seas.

So far as Britain was concerned the so-called Air Terror had yet to be experienced. When it was, the homes of some *Rodney* sailors and marines would be turned to rubble. The Nazis' blitzkrieg campaigns in Poland, Norway, the Low Countries and France proved the use of air power on the battlefield could be decisive and clearly also pivotal at sea. The *Rodney*'s bomb was truly a sign of things to come; she was so nearly the first battleship in naval history to be sunk by air power. Now, with the fall of Paris and surrender of France, *Rodney* was expected to fulfil her role as Captain of the Gate, in order to defeat any attempt at invasion by the triumphant Germans, who imagined they would be goose-stepping down Whitehall within weeks.

Notes

1 Macintyre, *Narvik*.
2 E.L. Brown, IWM Department of Documents.
3 Kenneth Thompson, *HMS Rodney at War*.
4 Ibid.

5 Ibid.
6 Tamblin, *The Rodney Buzz.*
7 Ibid.
8 Ibid.
9 Len Nicholl during an interview with the author.
10 Derrick Pearce writing in *The Rodney Buzz, Newsletter of the HMS Rodney Association*, 2000.
11 Len Walters, writing in *The Rodney Buzz*, 2000.
12 A recollection by Len Walters, *The Rodney Buzz*, April 1997.
13 Ken George, writing in *The Rodney Buzz*, June 2000.
14 *The Rodney Buzz*, 1998.
15 Tamblin, *The Rodney Buzz.*
16 *The Rodney Buzz.*
17 Conning, IWM Department of Documents.
18 Kenneth Thompson, *HMS Rodney at War.*
19 E.L. Brown, IWM Department of Documents.
20 Ibid.
21 Martin Stephen, *The Fighting Admirals.*

Chapter Ten

HARD CHEESE FOR HEROES

On 24 July 1940 *Nelson*, repaired and ready for action, arrived at Scapa Flow to become flagship of the Home Fleet once more, releasing *Rodney* on 23 August, so she could sail south to Rosyth. Her boilers needed re-tubing and, most importantly, it was an opportunity for her aggrieved sailors and marines to at last enjoy some leave. The need to make the ultimate sacrifice was something that came with service in a wartime Navy, but, with the Germans seemingly poised to mount an invasion, a suggestion *Rodney* might be forced to run away, in order to preserve her for fighting another day, had particularly aggravated her men. 'If we were overrun by the Germans it was planned *Rodney* would retreat to Canada,' recalled Len Nicholl.

> *That got up a lot of peoples' noses, particularly the married men. They didn't want to go and leave their families behind under German occupation. Single men like myself couldn't care less.*

However, in that long, hot summer of waiting to repel invaders, Winston Churchill remained so confident in *Rodney*'s 16-inch firepower that he continued to make himself unpopular with his admirals by insisting a battleship, or battleships, should be at Rosyth despite the increasing risk of air attack. He knew that if the German invasion flotillas ever left their ports, the truly decisive battle would be fought at sea, not in the air. It would be down to *Rodney* and her fighting consorts to destroy the Nazi invasion flotillas. There were frequent Luftwaffe raids and so the ship's air defences were kept on watch, with junior rating G. Conning finding he 'spent the long hours in the A.D.P. counting the number of railway wagons crossing the [Forth] bridge.'[1]

Rodney's sailors well knew what their job would be if the terrible day ever came. There was 'every possibility of us being used if the enemy really did try to do what Napoleon had tried to do and cross the Channel to invade our country.'[2] Leave always finished at 6.30 pm, because it was essential the ship knew where her men were every night and in good enough physical and mental condition to set sail and attack the German troop transports. The battleship was required to keep both her 180-strong Royal Marine detachment and a company of sailors ready to help repel invading troops, should the enemy catch her in port. Special Service soldiers parachuted in on two occasions to test Rosyth's defences by pretending to be German paratroopers.[3] The commander of *Rodney*'s Royal Marines believed he could have landed his force in 15 minutes and fought for 48 hours before needing resupply.

> *The summer passed with the* Rodney *standing by. As the winter approached, and the weather got colder and the seas too rough for a channel crossing, we were relieved from this rather tedious occupation.*[4]

While it is true that the 'The Few' of the RAF played their part in deterring Germany from seriously contemplating an invasion of Britain, quite how the Germans would have overcome the one true obstacle – the Royal Navy – is unclear. Probably the main objective of the Luftwaffe assault was to terrify Britain out of the war and into negotiating a peace deal, for Hitler was always more interested in invading Russia. 'The Few' made good copy for newspapers, cinema news scripts and radio broadcasts. After disasters in Norway and France, Britain needed a heroic victory that was easy to understand and dynamic. The Kriegsmarine could only muster 10 per cent of the Royal Navy's strength and half its destroyers were destroyed at Narvik.

The German Naval High Command knew what escort forces it had would be wiped out and the invasion vessels themselves cut to pieces by the vastly superior British navy. No one can deny the humiliation and defeat inflicted by the RAF on the Germans but to claim it alone saved Britain from invasion is ludicrous. It is one of the great injustices of recent history that 'The Many' of *Rodney* and the Royal Navy's other warships have never been given their due for their part in the Battle of Britain. As recently as 2006, the mere assertion by academics belonging to the UK's Joint Services academy that the Royal Navy prevented invasion aroused outrage among RAF veterans and their supporters, as if claiming some credit for ships like *Rodney* was a vicious slur on 'The Few'. It isn't, of course. The insults hurled at the Royal Navy in the letters pages of one national newspaper, by RAF veterans claiming that, more than sixty years earlier, the Navy was 'scared' of bombers and mines, were a gross distortion of reality, showing how strong the Battle of Britain myth has become. Certainly, *Rodney*'s sailors and marines showed during the Norwegian campaign they were not afraid of the Luftwaffe. If called on to sally forth against the German invasion fleet they would not have shirked their duty. Instead it was their lot to loiter at Rosyth, bored but ready, little realising the sheer existence of their battleship and her 16-inch guns – for the Germans had nothing to match them in front line commission at that point in the war – was Britain's surest safeguard.

Arriving aboard *Rodney* in the summer of 1940 were sailors who knew what it was like to have their homeland conquered by German invaders, for fifteen Frenchmen chose to serve in the battleship and carry on the fight. One of them was a twenty-one year old who had adopted the British name Frank Summers, as a wise alternative to his German-sounding original. 'Frank Summers' was an experienced mariner.

I had been in the French Merchant Marine for a few years and my first warship was a converted small trawler with a crew of nine when working as a minesweeper. I had a certificate to say I could take responsibility, could watch-keep. I took part in the evacuation from Dunkirk, which, incidentally, was my home town, and we did two trips. We took people off when the Germans were firing artillery guns onto the beaches. There were not very many Nazi planes, possibly because they were easing off, or because the bombs were not very effective in the sand. We took our first load of troops to Dover, and the next time, somehow, we found our way to Devonport, which was the first time I saw Plymouth Sound.

The following morning, after collecting their kitbags, the French sailors were marched by a squad of Royal Marines, the latter carrying rifles with fixed bayonets, to the naval barracks.

We were given the choice of joining the Free French naval forces or the Royal Navy. I judged that the RN was fully trained and organised for war and I wanted to fight back as soon as possible. I was given British nationality for the duration of the conflict and advised to change my name to an English one. However, I did not even speak English and as an Engine Room Artificer in the British navy, would I be able to carry out all the normal functions expected of me? Well, at least I passed a practical test as fitter and turner. I was made a Petty Officer immediately, on the grounds of my service in the Marine Nationale.

After a period of helping to maintain vessels at Devonport Dockyard, Summers was drafted to *Rodney*.

It was impressive to see Rodney *for the first time: so big, so powerful, and those huge turrets! Arriving on board I was taken to the Engineering Room Artificers' mess to be welcomed by Tom, the senior Chief P.O. Then, gradually, I met the other ERAs and John, who was to be my mentor for a number of weeks and look after me, showed me all that I had to know to become a working ERA. John was a splendid fellow and we became good friends. I learned enough English to manage the work. I found that* Rodney *carried a teacher who was very good, helping me to learn the language. I had my little book and pencil, even on shift, to take notes of new words or expressions.* Rodney *was slightly old-fashioned, even in 1940, but the propelling machinery gave no real trouble. Anyway, my experience in the French merchant navy had prepared me well for the work in* Rodney, *and I was left to manage on my own. I had arrived. I was one of the boys. I could relax and keep working.*

On 4 November, *Rodney* left Rosyth for Scapa, where she was tasked with providing heavy-duty cover for various convoys and deterring the surface raider *Admiral Scheer*, which had recently sunk the Armed Merchant Cruiser *Jervis Bay*. On the second day of December *Rodney*'s former Commanding Officer, John Tovey, took over from Admiral Forbes as Commander-in-Chief, Home Fleet. On 5 December, *Rodney* left Scapa to meet a convoy out of Halifax in mid-Atlantic, which had departed the Canadian port two days earlier. While there was no action with the enemy, *Rodney* 'sustained heavy weather damage and sailed to Rosyth for necessary repairs.'[5] Joining her that Christmas was Sub Lieutenant Eric Walton, an engineering officer who ended up in the Navy after a conversation on a mountain. A good friend, with whom he regularly went climbing, was a naval officer.

I liked the sound of what he did and the sort of life he led, so, when the war started, I managed to make sure my name was on the Naval and not the Army list.[6]

Leaving Rosyth on 13 January 1941 following completion of repairs, *Rodney* headed for Scapa and was soon under way again to escort another convoy from Halifax, which she was with from 12 February to 23 February, not encountering any enemy units. Jack Austin found the convoys left indelible memories.

In the latter half of 1940 to early 1941 when the U-boats were pack hunting, we British lost merchantmen daily. At one time, off Cape Race, we picked up a convoy of well over 100 ships. This was divided into three separate convoys. Rodney *constantly circled the middle convoy and that allowed our 16-inch guns to cover the forward and rear convoy against surface raiders, although some were still lost to U-boats. The biggest loss of merchant ships we suffered had nothing to do with U-boats or raiders. Starting out with about forty ships, we ran into the worst storm in forty years. We could only move at the speed of the slowest ships, which was about seven knots, and most of them were old rust buckets. I shall always remember standing in the cross-passage as Acting Corporal of the gangway, watching the pendulum swinging well past the thirty degrees mark and looking out the port or starboard doors to see the ocean racing past up to the guard rail and wondering when the ship would right herself. The waves were so huge we just had to keep heading into them. I think if we tried to come about we would have capsized. Even a week after we arrived home merchantmen were coming in, reaching port in ones and twos.*

Life at sea in the north Atlantic could test the mettle of the toughest men, not necessarily wearing them down in a single moment. George Thomas had seen hard conditions for German PoWs kept on the upper deck of the French destroyer that brought him back from Namsos, but in *Rodney* he hardly ever saw the outside. When he did it could be very cold and perilous.

In Rodney *you could be very isolated in your own department. In very cold weather it was sometimes months on end before we went up on deck because, in northern waters it was always the seamen on deck who had the winter clothing. Even when I did maintenance on the* [aircraft] *catapult, I was working with no protective clothing. In the darkness you had nothing brighter than a blue torch and just what clothes you could put on yourself to keep yourself warm.*

The ad hoc nature of naval operations ashore experienced by Rodney's Petty Officer Thomas in the Norwegian campaign was the norm, even after Winston Churchill ordered the setting up of the Combined Operations command in June 1940. In early 1941, members of *Rodney*'s complement took part in the first substantial Commando raid of the Second World War, on the Lofoten Islands in the Norwegian Arctic.[7] Operation Claymore's objectives were destruction of facilities that turned fish oil into glycerine for use in munitions, and sinking any enemy shipping found in harbour. It was spearheaded by 500 men from the Army's No. 3 and No. 4 Commandos, while the *Rodney* squad were all so-called volunteers, including Len Walters.

Ten lads were piped to muster at the Commander's office. We went along there and the Commander spoke to us and said that we had been chosen to go on a special mission and that he couldn't tell us anything about it and, as it could be a dangerous mission, he gave us the option of walking out the office and no more would be said. If we decided to stay that would be it ... we would be on the mission. Nobody made a move to go. We all looked at each other. If you're picked for something and you opt out of it then you are just putting somebody else in your place. You would feel bad if anything happened to them, thinking that, 'well, if I hadn't jumped out, it would have been me that copped it.' We weren't brought up that way ... once again, discipline was there and we all stayed. The Commander says: 'Having made up your minds I am going to turn you over to Lt Wells-Cole who will be the officer in charge.'[8]

Lieutenant Wells-Cole, by then acting second gunnery officer, stepped forward, telling the sailors he didn't know any more than the Commander, ordering them to go and get webbing equipment and steel helmets. He finished on a dramatic note:

Get yourselves ready, fully booted and spurred to be at one hour's notice.[9]

The *Rodney*'s Lofoten squad was composed of: three Able Seamen (two to be armed with rifles and one with a pistol, namely Len Walters); two Engine Room Artificers, one of them Ken George, who was also armed with a pistol; a Stoker Petty Officer; a

Warrant Officer Torpedoman/Gunner, Mr Bridle; two torpedomen/electricians and one signalman. They would receive their weapons when they joined forces with the commandos. With such a squad, any vessel found in harbour could be taken out to sea and sunk along with its cargo of fish oil. They were also to assist in demolition of fish oil tanks and supporting infrastructure ashore. The assault ships deployed for the mission were specially converted former passenger ferries known as HMS *Queen Emma* and HMS *Princess Beatrix*, each crewed by 50 Norwegian sailors. The escort force was provided by the 6th Destroyer Flotilla, consisting of the Tribal Class warships *Eskimo, Tartar, Bedouin* and *Somali* plus the *Legion.*[10]

On 28 February, at 11 pm, *Rodney*'s volunteers were piped to muster on the battleship's quarterdeck, Len Walters recalling a slightly surreal scene.

> *The Commander came up and shook hands and said goodbye to us. The Captain came up and wished us all the best and he said: 'I believe you are going to a ship over there,' and pointed into the blackness of Scapa Flow. We couldn't see a thing because everything was all blacked out. So we went down in the boat and it took us across ...*[11]

When he got on board *Queen Beatrix* Len Walters found she was packed with soldiers whom he was informed were 'suicide squads', who had been training for weeks. He noticed that they all carried the distinctive dagger that would soon be world renowned as the symbol of Commando forces.

> *I was issued with a .38 revolver and a bayonet. We sailed at midnight.*

Ahead lay a voyage of around 1,000 miles in rough weather, the ex-ferries, with shallow draughts and top heavy because of the landing craft and other gear, giving an uncomfortable ride. Despite rampant sea-sickness *Rodney*'s men still had to sharpen their skills.

> *On the way we had a bit of firing practice over the stern, just lobbing a few empty bottles over the side and firing revolvers or rifles at them.*[12]

Six hours into the voyage, the risky nature of the mission ahead was rammed home.

> *We were told that, if we wished, we could write farewell letters to our next of kin, and that these would be handed over to the ship's captain, who would post them for any of the men who failed to return. If you have ever tried writing such a letter, I assure you that it is not an easy task.*[13]

There was a pause at the Faroe Islands to give the commandos some extra training for the final stage and the task force reached the Lofotens on 3/4 March.

Len Walters had been detailed by the *Rodney*'s Commander as orderly cum bodyguard to Lt Wells-Cole. According to Walters, before leaving the ship, Lt Wells-Cole told him:

> *I don't want to see you more than six foot from wherever I am.*[14]

Wells-Cole later commented that he had been given general orders to 'demolish oil factories or sink shipping unless there was some vessel that could be steamed back to the UK, which proved not to be the case. There were no specific instructions about gathering intelligence.'

The day of the raid dawned fair and *Rodney*'s WO Bridle decided to take a walk on the upper deck before going down below for final preparations.

> *It was beautiful, the sea had not a ripple on it, and there was a slight swell. It was just light enough for me to see land, and there were some lights in sight. This told me the enemy had not expected our arrival.*[15]

WO Bridle decided it was so cold, a second heavy vest and pair of long johns were a necessity, but found after donning them he was only just able to pull his jacket on. After breakfast the soldiers and sailors climbed into their respective landing craft, which, at around 4.30 am, were lowered down. The destroyer *Legion* led the assault vessels in, and, as their landing craft ploughed on, *Rodney*'s sailors were given some Dutch courage in the form of a bottle of rum shared around. With just a little drop of spirit left in the bottom of the bottle, Lt Wells-Cole asked who the youngest was, which turned out to be Len Walters. 'There you are, have another drink,' the officer told him.

> *You will probably need it.*

Aside from the *Legion* letting rip with a probing blast of pom-pom fire to provoke a response from German shore batteries, which failed to come, there was no real attempt to stop the landing. A tricky moment occurred as the assault craft went in, for a German armed trawler, the *Krebs*, just happened to be coming out of harbour at the same time. The *Somali*'s guns made short work of this vessel, and later a boarding party recovered Enigma machine material that enabled penetration of German codes for three months.

As the landing craft prepared to hit the beach and lower ramps, their occupants saw trawlers in harbour hoisting the Norwegian flag – an act expressly forbidden by the Nazi occupiers. This show of defiance gave the raiders a timely boost of confidence but, when the first commandos went ashore at Stamsund from their landing craft, Norwegian civilians gave them 'a half-hearted Nazi salute', believing they were German troops on training exercise.[16]

Under the rules of war, any enemy shipping that looked worth sinking had to be taken out to sea under the White Ensign. However, there was a slight snag, quite literally, as Len Walters later recalled.

> *... we went to one inlet and there was a couple of ships there and we were going to take them out, put a depth charge in, set the fuse and blow them up. So, the first one, we hoisted the flag and we were told that there were bigger ships around the next inlet, so we had to get this flag down, because it was the only one we had.*[17]

It got snagged on the stays of the mast, so Walters volunteered to get it down and hauled himself up the snow and ice-covered mast to free the flag. The bigger ships were duly taken out and sunk and, in all, seven merchant vessels dispatched to the bottom during the raid. In all this hectic activity Lt Wells-Cole managed to row off in a boat to inspect one merchant ship without bothering to take Len Walters with him.

> *I thought: 'Oh he's gone without me and I am supposed to be within six foot of him.'*[18]

Fortunately, during the voyage north, Walters picked up some sheets of paper on which were typed useful Norwegian phrases. After scrutinizing them for a few seconds he called out to a local man in a rowing boat, somehow persuading him to go out to the same ship.

> *I got alongside, jumped on the gangway. Up I went and before I reached the bridge I heard a shot.*

Suspecting the enemy might have sprung an ambush, Walters ran to the bridge, weapon at the ready.

> *I heard voices and I came round the bridge to the chart house. I heard Lt Wells-Cole's voice ... I had the .38 revolver, and I swung round in front of the door ... It was a bit scary, because I didn't know where the shot had come from or who was being shot.*

He discovered Lt Wells-Cole with another British officer, but no Germans. The lock had been shot off a cabinet and the two officers were extracting papers they hoped might yield useful intelligence. Ken George was, meanwhile, helping to sabotage a fish oil factory when he came face to face with the enemy.

> *I entered an office to find a German officer burning papers in the fireplace. I ordered him to stop or I would shoot. Thank Christ he stopped.*

Warrant Officer Bridle concentrated on committing enemy shipping to the deep, his team taking a merchant vessel out of harbour followed by a landing craft in which he and his men would make good their escape. On the way they placed a depth-charge against the ship's boiler room bulkhead.

> *... we called our craft alongside, set the fuse alight, and abandoned the ship. It seemed hours before this thing went up, and in fact so long that some were saying it was a dud. Suddenly up she went and disappeared in about ten seconds; she would do no more work for Jerry.*[19]

Back ashore, Bridle's sailors assisted the commandos in blowing up fish oil tanks. A depth charge was used to destroy the first, but explosive packs brought by the commandos dealt with the rest. The commandos, who were surprised to find no proper German garrison, rounded up Gestapo agents, Luftwaffe personnel and quislings[20]. One of the fish oil plant owners turned out to be an expatriate Briton who had been refusing to co-operate with the Germans for weeks, despite being under threat of execution. He was delighted to see the commandos, eagerly helping them to destroy his fish oil tanks and processing facilities. He was even happier to be offered a ride home for a reunion with his family in the UK. By around 11.00 am the raiding party was withdrawing, along with 225 Germans PoWs and 60 captured quislings, plus 315 locals[21] who volunteered to join the free Norwegian forces, including eight young women who wanted to serve in the Red Cross. The *Rodney*'s men received a tremendous send-off, which must have left young Len Walters' head spinning.

> [there were] *girls going around kissing anybody they could get hold of. One gave me a jersey, a pullover with long sleeves. It smelled like something out of this world ... I don't know what perfume she had on it* [but] *I didn't wash it for a long, long time. It was a souvenir from Norway. I just had it in my locker onboard* [Rodney].

As the landing craft chugged out to the *Princess Beatrix*, WO Bridle turned around to look at the burning oil tanks, waiting for his final bit of work to reach fruition.

> *This was not long delayed, and as we got clear of the harbour, off it went, and the top of one big tank went sailing merrily through the air.*[22]

While the raiders were ashore, local trawlers returning to port supplied *Princess Beatrix* and *Queen Emma* with some fine specimens from their catch, *Rodney*'s sailors subsequently enjoying a feast:

> *By 12 o'clock we were sat down to a meal of fish and it was the best fish I ever tasted . . . straight out of the water into the frying pan sort of thing. It was beautiful.*[23]

As they sailed away from the scene of destruction, another two bottles of rum were dug out, which warmed *Rodney*'s men up no end on the journey back to the Orkneys. On their return to Scapa Flow, they found their ship was at sea, so went over to *Nelson* to await her return. Len Walters was unimpressed with what happened next.

> *As it was around supper time, we were piped to muster at* Nelson*'s Issue Room, and were each handed a piece of cheese and allocated to a Mess where we were kindly handed a slice of bread, and a cup of tea, as the only reward for our efforts at the Battle Front.*[24]

It appears that because the raid was successful for so little cost – although fourteen Germans were killed, the only British casualty had been a commando who shot himself in the leg – *Rodney*'s sailors didn't warrant any other reward, such as the week's leave they had been promised prior to their departure.

Notes

1 G. Conning, IWM Department of Documents.
2 Kenneth Thompson, *HMS Rodney at War.*
3 Ibid.
4 Ibid.
5 *History of HMS Rodney 1939–1948*, Admiralty ship's history/S.5775.
6 Walton, IWM Sound Archive.
7 A similar group was also assigned from HMS *Nelson.*
8 Walters, IWM Sound Archive.
9 Ibid.
10 Tim Moreman, *British Commandos 1940–46.*
11 Walters, IWM Sound Archive.
12 Ibid.
13 Len Walters, *The Rodney Buzz*, February 1989.
14 Walters, IWM Sound Archive.
15 Quoted in *HMS* Rodney *at War.*
16 Charles Messenger, *The Commandos.*
17 Walters, IWM Sound Archive.
18 Ibid.
19 Quoted in *HMS* Rodney *at War.*
20 Norwegian fascists, collaborating with the Nazis.
21 Charles Messenger, *The Commandos.*
22 Quoted in *HMS* Rodney *at War.*
23 Walters, IWM Sound Archive.
24 Len Walters, *The Rodney Buzz*, February 1989.

Chapter Eleven

THE *CHILEAN REEFER* INCIDENT

The beginning of 1941 was a desperate time for Britain, with the enemy sinking more merchant ships than could be built to replace them. Losses peaked in March, with 41 merchant vessels, totalling 243,000 tons, sunk that month by U-boats alone. There was every possibility the lifeline across the Atlantic would be cut and Britain starved into submission. On the loose were German surface raiders, making the situation so black that Winston Churchill, seeking to rouse the native pugnacity of Britons, issued a 'Battle of the Atlantic Directive'.

It ordered an intensive offensive against maritime marauders wherever they could be found. But therein lay the difficulty – finding surface raiders and U-boats in the vastness of the Atlantic was far from easy. The battlecruisers *Scharnhorst* and *Gneisenau* had set sail in late January, intent on striking deep into the North Atlantic shipping lanes, while heavy cruiser *Hipper* and pocket battleship *Scheer* were causing mayhem in the South Atlantic. Undergoing sea trials, secure in the Baltic from British attack, was an even bigger future menace: the brand new battleship *Bismarck*. Meanwhile, aboard the *Gneisenau*, in overall command of Operation Berlin, was Vice Admiral Günther Lütjens, on this occasion luck definitely riding with him, for the two German capital ships managed a successful breakout via the Denmark Strait.

On receiving intelligence reports of German heavy ships heading west out of the Baltic via the Great Belt, Admiral Tovey had at once ordered the Home Fleet to sea, his flag in *Nelson*, accompanied by *Rodney* and *Repulse*. Making for what he hoped was a good interception point, around 100 miles to the south of Iceland, Tovey soon realized he'd committed a tactical error by bringing his entire striking force with him, for when fuel ran low he had no capital ships left in reserve to take over or task with covering other potential break-out points.

Rodney, together with some cruisers and destroyers, was ordered back to Scapa to replenish her fuel. The Royal Navy at that time lacked the sort of fleet train that could have carried out a major replenishment-at-sea of capital ships, so obviating the whole process of sending key units back to home ports for oil. During the next eight weeks *Gneisenau* and *Scharnhorst*, together with the two surface raiders to the south, managed to sink forty-five ships and capture three, a total loss to Britain of 270,000 tons in shipping.

Joining *Rodney* at Scapa Flow in early March 1941 was Sub Lieutenant Eryk Sopocko, of the Polish Navy, who had escaped the clutches of the Nazis in the submarine *Orzel*. After learning English and being inducted into the Royal Navy, he and some other Polish naval officers were distributed around various British warships, or to the few naval units belonging to their country that had escaped to Britain. The Home Fleet set sail from Scapa again on 9 March, with *Rodney* tasked to provide heavy cover for convoys, both inward bound from Canada and sailing from the United Kingdom. Sub Lt Sopocko took his turn bridge watchkeeping and, scanning the convoy arrayed around him, thought it resembled a floating town.

> *HMS* Rodney *looks like a giant among dwarfs. Plumes of coal-smoke from their funnels stain the sky. The commander of a German U-boat would have no difficulty deciding which was the best target for his torpedoes.*[1]

Having been on the morning watch, Sopocko was awakened in his hammock at 3.45 pm by Royal Marine buglers calling General Quarters via the ship's tannoy. His Action Station was with the Royal Marines in X turret, where he manned a periscope, which he used to ensure the guns were laid on target properly. The *Rodney* turned to bring all her guns to bear on a suspected German raider in the mist. The Polish officer looked through the periscope at the mystery vessel, which was exchanging signals by Aldis lamp with *Rodney*. She was the old battleship HMS *Malaya*, so *Rodney*'s men were stood down.

Now the weather changed from light mist to overcast, with thick, black clouds and a miserable drizzle. Wireless distress signals from merchant ships under attack were intercepted, so *Rodney* went off to investigate at full speed, leaving *Malaya* to look after the convoy. Closed up for action through the night of 15 March, *Rodney* battled on, despite increasingly heavy seas, both wind and waves abeam of her, making it very uncomfortable going. She was too late to save any of the victims, but in the late afternoon of 16 March 'a raider distress message was received from the MV *Chilean Reefer*',[2] *Rodney* going full steam ahead towards the merchant vessel's last reported position.

The 1,831 tons *Chilean Reefer* was bound from Newcastle to Newfoundland, carrying a cargo of bacon. Originally a Danish-flagged vessel, in April 1940, following occupation of Denmark by the Nazis, she was stranded in the Far East and subsequently put under the Red Ensign at Singapore, retaining some of her original crew.[3] In March 1941, as a fast ship, capable of a top speed of 14 knots, the *Chilean Reefer* had independent sailing orders and, on picking up reports of German surface raiders attacking a convoy, decided to make good her escape. However, the ship's lookouts spotted the menacing silhouette of a large warship coming over the horizon, swiftly followed by gun flashes, and splashes began sprouting around her. It was *Gneisenau*, which poured shells from both 11-inch main and 5.9-inch secondary armament into *Chilean Reefer*. The merchant ship, using smoke, tried to evade the fall of shot, but it was no use. The *Gneisenau* opened fire at a range of 12 miles and, despite maintaining her onslaught until she closed to 1,000 yards, still could not sink the *Chilean Reefer*, the cargo vessel opening up with her single 4-inch gun and stubbornly refusing to surrender. Lütjens and the *Gneisenau*'s Captain Otto Fein began to suspect their target might be a disguised Armed Merchant Cruiser, potentially with torpedo tubes. She might also be a scouting vessel working with a British battleship or heavy cruiser.[4] The German battlecruiser therefore pulled back to continue her bombardment from a safer distance, while *Chilean Reefer*'s skipper, Captain Thomas Bell, gave the order to abandon ship, as she was on fire from end to end. Even so, the German warship continued to pour shells into her[5] and ordered a lifeboat to come alongside, intending the *Chilean Reefer*'s survivors to join other Merchant Navy men in captivity. It was at this moment *Rodney* steamed over the horizon, just as the sun was setting. The British battleship's lookouts had sighted a large ship and a blazing merchant vessel at a range of 15 miles. Through his periscope in X turret Sub Lt Sopocko saw a glow on the horizon, thinking it was the moon rising. He soon realized it was a ship ablaze, reflecting orange-red on the underside of the clouds. Turning his periscope, Sopocko tried to spot signs of the enemy.

> *Against the background of the fire I can see the tops of the waves but nothing else.*

Rodney was frustrated by rapidly fading light, combined with the blazing ship, making it extremely hard to see exactly what lurked behind her. Among the men closed up for action in a 6-inch gun turret was Marine Len Nicholl.

> *I could see the* Chilean Reefer *on fire. I also saw a little light in the sea, so I reported it and it turned out to be one of the merchant ship's lifeboats.*

The *Rodney*'s Paymaster-Lieutenant Allen recalled the moment:

> *We were probably silhouetted like a mountain against the light in the west ...*[6]

Lookouts in the German battlecruiser had watched with dread as the masts of what could only be a very large enemy ship crested over the northwest horizon. Now *Rodney* used a signal light to ask:

> *What ship?*

Vice Admiral Lütjens knew he would have to flee rather than fight. To buy time, *Gneisenau* flashed back that she was the British cruiser *Emerald*, creating enough confusion for her to escape at 32 knots, faster by far than the comparatively elderly *Rodney*. As *Gneisenau* showed the British battleship a clean pair of heels, she signalled her nearby tanker, the *Uckermark*, to also leave the scene with utmost speed.

Gneisenau departed so swiftly her rudder damaged one of the *Chilean Reefer* lifeboats.[7] Lt Wells-Cole had a clear view from one of the 6-inch gunnery director positions and 'saw the shadowy *Gneisenau* pushing off.'

The man whose judgment call it was, on whether or not to chase *Gneisenau*, was fifty-one year old Captain Frederick Hew Dalrymple-Hamilton. He had been Commanding Officer of HMS *Rodney* since November 1939, successfully bringing the ship through the Norwegian campaign and preserving his reputation as a safe pair of hands. An aristocratic Scot, born at Girvan in Ayrshire, he was a descendant of William the Conqueror and related to Queen Elizabeth. Entering the Royal Navy in 1905, he saw service in the First World War, having achieved the rank of Lieutenant by 1911. Post-war he was a Commander in the Royal Yacht *Victoria & Albert*, worked ashore in the Admiralty's plans division and then joined the cruiser HMS *Effingham* in the Far East. Promoted to Captain in December 1931, while serving ashore at the naval barracks in Devonport, Dalrymple-Hamilton next commanded a destroyer flotilla in the Mediterranean, between October 1933 and early 1936. By the time war broke out in September 1939, he was commanding Britannia Royal Naval College at Dartmouth and from there was appointed to *Rodney*, becoming a very popular Commanding Officer.

One of his young officers described him as:

> *A very fine captain, who everybody really loved. He was a wonderful man – great sense of humour, and really was a friend to all – and a very strong disciplinarian at the same time.*[8]

Jack Austin recalled an incident that summed up both Dalrymple-Hamilton's liking for good discipline and his typically dry Scottish wit.

> *The Captain was a tall, well-built, wonderful man with a great sense of humour. Aboard* Rodney *we had two marines who were cowboy mad, so much that they had wooden pistols, and played fast draws each time they saw each other. They often relieved each other as sentries. Just before midnight, one of the marines, we called him Quasi because he walked with a stoop, saw his relief leave the marine mess deck and enter the long passage. Taking two Webley revolvers from a gun cabinet, Quasi waited for his mate to step over the watertight door sill. He jammed the two guns into what he thought was his mate's belly and said: 'Stick 'em up!' But it was the wrong man. Instead, it was the skipper on his way to his cabin after dining in the Officers' Mess. Asked Captain Dalrymple-Hamilton: 'So you like playing with guns, do you?' 'Yes sir,' replied Quasi. 'Right, there are over 100 in the two cabinets, come down every night for an hour until you've cleaned the lot!' Can you imagine what Nelson would have done to the marine? I expect he would have had him hanging from the yardarm in no time.*

In March 1941, Dalrymple-Hamilton's greatest moment of glory still lay ahead, and the *Chilean Reefer* incident must have made him very dissatisfied. There was no alternative course of action. With the first of the new battleships, HMS *King George V*, only completed in December 1940, and still working up to full fighting efficiency, *Rodney* and *Nelson* remained the most experienced and powerful units the British fleet possessed. Approaching the *Chilean Reefer*, the *Rodney*'s captain therefore needed to have a cool head, as he was responsible for preserving a precious national asset and the likelihood of gaining a good result over the much faster *Gneisenau* in the dark was almost zero. Captain Dalrymple-Hamilton wisely ordered his battleship to make an effort to pick up survivors from the *Chilean Reefer*, rather than dash off in blind pursuit.

Rodney's searchlights swept the wavetops, at first finding only huge patches of burning oil, but then picked out a small boat rigged with a sail, rising on peaks and then sliding into troughs. It contained twenty-seven men, of British, Chinese and Danish nationality, including Captain Bell, the chief officer, plus two dead seamen. Taken aboard *Rodney*, the survivors explained they believed it was the *Gneisenau* that attacked their ship. Ten more of the *Chilean Reefer*'s sailors were believed to be in another lifeboat of which there was no sign. However, as *Rodney* left the scene it was spotted, like the first its position given away by a small light. The battleship turned around but found the boat empty. There was speculation that the occupants, on seeing *Rodney* sailing away, lost all hope and threw themselves over the side, preferring to drown rather than endure a long, agonizing death adrift in the Atlantic. Having sunk both lifeboats, *Rodney* finally departed, leaving behind only burning oil slicks and, somewhere in the darkness, the bobbing corpses of missing mariners. For Lt Wells-Cole the *Chilean Reefer* incident revealed the perils faced by the Merchant Navy.

> *It illustrated to us how fortunate we were in* Rodney, *a 35,000 tons battleship, compared with the poor, wretched merchant seamen. It brought home to us the reality of what they were going through.*

Paymaster-Lieutenant Allen conveyed the frustration suffusing the battleship.

> *... there was much controversy in the messes round the ship. Perhaps if we had been ten minutes earlier, or the sun had set in the east for a change, or we had been eight knots faster, or had an aircraft carrier – perhaps we might have brought her* [Gneisenau] *to action.*[9]

Eric Walton, who was down in the engineering spaces during the incident, later observed:

> *It was one of the most disheartening, sad moments of that early part of the war. The whole ship was so disconsolate. There we were loaded up with 16-inch and 6-inch* [guns] *and the loud hailer had actually announced 'there is the old bastard' or words to that effect. So, we knew she was in the sights. We just waited and, after an hour in which nothing was broadcast at all, I finally came on deck and there was a star shell in the air and we were picking up survivors ...*

Years later, when he was on the staff of Britannia Royal Naval College at Dartmouth, Walton discussed the *Chilean Reefer* incident with one of his old shipmates, who told him *Gneisenau* was in *Rodney*'s sights 'for three or four minutes at six miles ...'

> *... and this was a ship with 16-inch guns, with a range of about 22 miles and we never fired a round.*

The *Rodney*'s Gunnery Officer at the time was Lieutenant Commander William Crawford. Born in September 1907, he was the son of a New Zealand sheep farmer, his grandfather having been a captain in the East India company during the mid-1800s. Entering Dartmouth in May 1921, Crawford's sea time as a midshipman was served in the battleship *Barham*. He did his destroyer time in *Vansittart* in the late 1920s and then joined the *Warspite* before going to *Revenge*. Taking the trade of gunnery, Crawford served in *Queen Elizabeth* and a succession of other ships including *Ark Royal* and *Furious*. A veteran of Spanish Civil War patrols in the cruiser *Delhi*, Crawford joined *Rodney* in July 1940, finding her 'a very, very happy ship' and an efficient one, too, under the command of his uncle, Captain Dalrymple-Hamilton. As Gunnery Officer, up in the director position atop the ship, Lt Cdr Crawford would have enjoyed one of the clearest views of the *Gneisenau*, via his powerful optics. It would have been his job to give the open fire order. He later said of the incident:

> *In fact we got to a stage in the dusk where we saw a shadowy thing in the distance, about fifteeen, sixteen miles away ... and then she disappeared behind the smoke and we never saw her again.*[10]

According to *Rodney*'s junior rating G. Conning, the reasons for not opening fire on *Gneisenau* or her consort were perfectly understandable.

> *... as we approached dark was falling and* [there were] *rainsqualls. We could not get a range on the raider as the burning ship was blinding our range takers and she fled behind it. We had her supply ship or tender right in our sights but Captain Dalrymple-Hamilton would not fire as she* [the supply ship] *no doubt had seaman prisoners onboard ... I would say that the* Chilean Reefer *spoiled our chance of getting the raider as she was bound to attack the convoy that night.*

The dead *Chilean Reefer* seamen were laid out in the *Rodney*'s chapel, sewn inside white sailcloth as had been the tradition for casualties of war at sea for centuries. The day after the incident the weather was too bad to bury them but it looked likely to change by the following morning, when sailors and marines of *Rodney*, together with *Chilean Reefer* survivors, gathered on the quarterdeck for a solemn ceremony. Sub Lt Sopocko described the scene:

> *The ensign is at half-mast. The three bodies are brought up on stretchers covered with Union Jacks. Both priests* [Protestant and Roman Catholic] *are present. A short prayer. The bugles sound the 'Last Post'. We all salute as the bodies slide slowly into the sea.*

The bugles called 'carry on' and the sailors and marines returned to their work, the Ensign hauled back up to the top. Later, during a tannoy broadcast, the captain of the *Chilean Reefer* thanked the men of *Rodney* for all they had done. He made reference to this being his second war at sea, stressing how vital it was for the Merchant Navy and Royal Navy to work together in order to safeguard the nation. Some of the *Chilean Reefer* survivors later toured the battleship, in order to express their thanks. The merchant ship's rather mature Danish seamen visited the 6-inch gun turrets and shook hands with those who manned them, including Len Nicholl, who heard one of the Danes, possibly the merchant vessel's gunner, say:

> *If I had these guns I could have sunk the* Gneisenau.

However, although she got away, *Gneisenau*, rejoining *Scharnhorst*, was aware luck was running out and other major Royal Navy units were in the hunt, so Lütjens ordered both vessels to shape course for Brest, which they reached on 23 March. The Admiral and his staff were soon on their way to Germany, to prepare for another raiding sortie, this time in *Bismarck*, but when he next saw *Rodney* Lütjens would know he could not escape retribution.

Resuming her task of convoy protection on 24 March, *Rodney* soon sighted another suspicious vessel and demanded her identity. There was no response and the ship was ordered to heave to, but instead carried on her way, forcing *Rodney* to fire warning shots across her bows. Realising serious harm could result if she did not now respond, the ship signalled that she was the *Ville De Liege*, a Free French merchantman, and was therefore allowed to proceed. There were no further incidents; the encounters with *Gneisenau* and *Ville De Liege* being rare moments of excitement. The more usual monotony was oppressive – miles and miles of ocean inhabited only by the undulating silhouettes of merchant ships. Although the speed of convoys was normally 11 knots, some ships could only do three and they were inevitably left behind, *Rodney*'s sailors watching them fade in the battleship's wake. Meanwhile, the merchant seamen gazed with growing unease at the shrinking bulk of *Rodney* disappearing over the horizon. When raider alerts came in, *Rodney*'s sailors and marines could find themselves at Action Stations for days at a time, with two out of three 16-inch turrets closed up. Some men whiled away their time in games of whist or even Monopoly, while others chose to read books.

> *... sometimes the officers of each turret closed up would play each other at 'Jutland', using the 'phone connecting the two turrets to announce their moves.*[11]

But, for all their yearning for action, the men of *Rodney* could at least be proud of the fact that not a single vessel she escorted was lost. Arriving in waters off Nova Scotia,

Rodney found Halifax a dazzling blaze of light daubed across the horizon, so unlike blacked out Plymouth. The Canadian city also resembled a giant Aladdin's cave of goods no longer found back home. Poland's Sub Lt Sopocko thought it 'a fairyland'. By day two in port *Rodney*'s wardroom table groaned with fruit and there were green salads on the menu too, both rarities since the beginning of the war.

Rodney's sailors and marines took full advantage of the shopping ashore, loading themselves up with tea, chocolate, sugar, cheese and, of course, the ultimate currency with glamour-hungry young women they might wish to impress – silk stockings.[12]

While there were plenty of runs ashore, for all Canada's delights – the drinkers and womanizers finding their share of diversions – most of *Rodney*'s sailors and marines missed their loved ones and would rather have been on the other side of the Atlantic. There was at least mail for the ship waiting in Halifax, brought out by a cutter. The letters contained news of births, deaths and marriages, but such reports were invariably out of date and *Rodney*'s men worried about what else had happened since they were last home. Departing for the return voyage on 10 April, *Rodney* found herself lead escort ship for a troop convoy to the UK, reaching the Clyde nine days later.

As *Rodney* entered the mouth of the great Scottish river, tragedy struck, the 608 tons anti-submarine trawler HMS *Topaze* being run down by the battleship. The destroyer *Piorun*, escorting *Rodney*, managed to save only four of the former fishing vessel's twenty-five strong crew.

Far to the south of the Scottish anchorage, Plymouth was being subjected to an intensive campaign of terror bombing. The Germans had begun their air raids on the Devon port in the summer of 1940, not only dropping bombs on the city and naval facilities, but also leaving magnetic mines in the Sound. On 25 September that year, twenty-four Ju88s and HE111s, escorted by a dozen ME110 fighters, gave Plymouth a taste of what was to come during its first intensive bombing raid. Just under six months later, and four days after the *Chilean Reefer* incident, the real ordeal began for *Rodney*'s home port. The German bombers were being prepared at airfields in northern France, even as King George VI and Queen Elizabeth concluded a morale-boosting visit to the city. Shortly before midnight on 20 March, their cargoes of incendiary bombs were unloaded on Plymouth, a firestorm consuming the centuries-old heart and soul of one of the world's foremost maritime communities. Six more such raids were to follow in March and April, in which a total of 1,000 German bombers dropped around a quarter of a million incendiary and high explosive bombs, killing 1,179 civilians, wounding a further 3,209 and making Plymouth one of the most intensively bombed cities in Britain.[13]

Rodney's men, both those still in the battleship and others who belonged to her extended family, knew only too well how serious it was.

It was one thing to be subjected to Luftwaffe attack when sailing in a battleship and quite another for a family in a terraced house clustered close to Devonport Dockyard. Once the ship had dropped anchor on the Clyde, telegrams were brought aboard, telling in a few lines some tale of woe.

> *House destroyed. Staying with Mother. Come home if you can.*[14]

A number of the men were allowed leave, their homes reported demolished by bombing in not only Plymouth but also Portsmouth and Chatham. Their 48-hours leave started from arrival home, the main objective for a *Rodney* man being to find his family and make sure they were settled into new accommodation. On arrival at Plymouth's North Road railway station the sight that greeted a *Rodney* man would not be encouraging, for it was surrounded with piles of rubble where houses once stood. In some cases only a single wall of a building might be left and, as the sailor or marine trudged through the city, he would gaze in horror at piles of bricks, shattered glass, tiles and splintered scraps of wood, which had replaced streets he knew so well. Away from the devastated city centre, whole neighbourhoods were untouched, but among them were odd spots of devastation. As a result of the Blitz, many Plymothians took to living in the countryside at night, for it was after sunset the German terror raiders came. The *Rodney* sailor on leave might find his family now settled in a cottage outside the city. Len Nicholl, who was born and brought up close to the Royal Marine Barracks at Stonehouse, learned by telegram that a German bomb had destroyed his mother's home but she survived. Initially taken in by a member of the family living not far from Plymouth's main railway station, Marine Nicholl's family were eventually accommodated by a retired Royal Marine brigadier, in a large house at Princetown on Dartmoor. Marine Nicholl applied for leave to go home, but, as a single man, was told by the officer responsible for evaluating such requests:

No use you going home.

However, as a married man, the *Rodney*'s butcher was granted leave to go and make sure his wife was settling in to her new home at Torquay after being bombed out of Plymouth. Nicholl was more than happy to lend the man five pounds he needed to cover the trip, but never saw him again, as the butcher did not return to the ship.

Whether he was drafted to another vessel, or got caught up in the bombing I have no idea.

Teenage sailor Gordon Smerdon, whose mother lived close to Devonport Dockyard, managed to get leave and experienced the terror of German raids, hunkering down in a back yard Anderson Shelter shared by two families. Smerdon recalled he heard 'a thud ... then, a few seconds after, another thud.'

One bomb dropped only a stone's throw from where we lived. That was pretty frightening, very frightening. I was glad I got back onboard [Rodney] *again ... The civilian population went through hell.*

Rodney's Petty Officer George Thomas ended up experiencing an even closer encounter with death during the Plymouth Blitz, due to a rather a rash decision in the wake of his adventure ashore at Namsos.

I committed a cardinal sin in the service: I volunteered. When Italy came into the war on the side of Germany, having served in Kenya and being fluent in Swahili, I thought I would be more beneficial to the country in serving in East Africa. When I was paraded in front of the Engineering Commander, he informed me in no uncertain terms that I would be of more benefit to the RN and the country if I qualified as a mechanician.

So, in the summer of 1940, as the Battle of Britain hotted up, Petty Officer Thomas was sent to Chatham for his mechanician's course, finding he spent most of his time in bomb shelters and tunnels. In October 1940, the mechanician's course – which had moved to Chatham because there was not enough room in Devonport – moved back to Plymouth. On 20 April 1941, the day after *Rodney* returned to the Clyde, a stick of German bombs hit the barrack block where PO Thomas was living, killing 100 sailors sheltering in its basement. Escaping with minor injuries, he found himself and another Petty Officer lodged with an elderly couple at their house in Stoke, a stone's throw from the dockyard. Having failed to get him earlier, the Germans were obviously determined to make Thomas bitterly regret ever leaving *Rodney*. For, during a subsequent raid, the two sailors and their landlords were forced to take shelter in the cellar of the house.

> *There was a bloody great explosion, then darkness. There was so much dust it was unbelievable.*

The house had collapsed on top of them.

> *I had a brand new dark suit, which I had made up in Greenock in 1940 and when I salvaged it from the ruins it was white, covered with very fine plaster dust.*

But his suit wasn't the only casualty and while PO Thomas and the other lodger suffered only minor injuries, their hosts were not so lucky:

> *We got out and managed to extract the old people who, unfortunately, were both dead.*

Returning to the Devonport barracks the two sailors were sent to live afloat, in an old WW1-era monitor called the *Marshal Ney*, at anchor in the Hamoaze. It had been converted into an engineering school and now sailors were bedding down in its classrooms.

> *Devonport was very badly damaged and the whole of the centre of Plymouth was virtually flattened* [with] *little odd places standing out. I think the attitude was that if they can take it in London we can take it in Plymouth.*

The blitz of Plymouth and other naval home ports, filled sailors and marines in *Rodney* with a thirst to hit back at the enemy and they would soon get their opportunity, in one of the most legendary clashes in the history of naval warfare.

Notes

1 Sopocko, *Gentlemen, The Bismarck Has Been Sunk.*
2 HMS *Rodney*, Official History.
3 *Sea Breezes*, October 1989.
4 Edwyn Gray, *Hitler's Battleships.*
5 *Sea Breezes*, October 1989.
6 Quoted in *HMS* Rodney *at War.*
7 *Sea Breezes*, October 1989.
8 Crawford, IWM Sound Archive.
9 Kenneth Thompson, *HMS Rodney at War.*
10 Crawford, IWM Sound Archive.
11 Kenneth Thompson, *HMS Rodney at War.*
12 Ibid.
13 Gerald Wasley, *Blitz.*
14 Quoted in *HMS Rodney at War.*

Chapter Twelve

AVENGE THE *HOOD*

By May 1941, three years since the last major refit and nearly sixteen since her launch on the Mersey, *Rodney* was suffering the strain of war service. Still carrying battle scars from Norway, she was badly in need of a docking period. However, due to the continuing air threat posed by the Luftwaffe, it was most unwise for her to receive work in Devonport, Portsmouth, Liverpool or Rosyth, so *Rodney* was given orders to sail for the USA. News of a refit in America was received with mixed feelings by her sailors and marines: married men were disappointed at not being able to enjoy home leave; those without wives and children were excited at the prospect of several months in a peaceful port where girls would, hopefully, be both pretty and obliging, the booze plentiful.

Rodney was scheduled to depart the Clyde on 22 May, escorting the troopship *Britannic* to Canada. The battleship herself would carry 512 passengers[1] to Halifax, Nova Scotia, including: medical cases, among them men suffering from shellshock; naval cadets going for training in Bermuda; Canadian troops returning home; airmen destined for flight training in Canada; British sailors bound for the Falklands. *Rodney* even embarked a US Navy officer, Lieutenant Commander Joseph Wellings, Assistant Naval Attaché at the American Embassy in London, and a couple of USN senior rates. Lt Cdr Wellings was carrying important documents to America in a diplomatic pouch, which was soon stowed away 'under lock and key' with a Royal Marine sentry placed nearby.[2]

Confronted with all the strangers below decks, one of *Rodney*'s sailors remarked the Admiralty seemed to think the battleship was a luxury liner,[3] while another observed, rather acidly, they were 'in everybody's way including their own.'[4] Among the passengers was a Royal Navy officer and his midshipman son, hitching a ride at the last moment. Tommy Byers, a twenty-five year old Leading Seaman from Northern Ireland, brought the pair aboard:

> *I was then the coxswain of the* Rodney*'s 2nd picket boat. I had just completed a trip to the torpedo factory on Loch Long and was returning to the* Rodney*, which was anchored off Greenock, and passing the liner* Britannic*, when I heard someone calling out. I went alongside the* Britannic *and found out the person calling out was Captain Coppinger, Royal Navy. He asked me if he could get a trip on* Rodney *to America. I said I would take him to the* Rodney *to see the Captain. He went with me and later came down the gangway to ask me to go to* Britannic *and tell his son, a midshipman, to bring his suitcases and also himself to* Rodney*, as they were both to get a lift to America. Captain Coppinger was in command of HMS* Malaya*, which was docked in New York for repairs.*[5]

According to *Rodney*'s Lt Cdr Crawford, his ship was not only packed with extra people, but also laden with all manner of equipment and other items necessary for her refit.

> *... on the upper deck we had four thousand boiler tubes, because they had to retube some of our boilers; we had three eight-barrelled pom-pom mountings, and all their guns, stowed on top of one of the turrets ... In addition, we had in the chapel three or four cases of the Elgin Marbles, and, in our cells forward, I believe we had some of the last of the* [British reserves of] *gold crossing the Atlantic. So we were not in a state where we were expecting to meet the enemy.*

Secured to *Rodney*'s boat deck was a section of armoured plate, intended to be fitted below decks during the Boston refit, in order to repair damage caused by the Norway bomb.[6] *Rodney* was under way by 12.30 pm and soon settled down at a cruising speed of 18 knots, heading out past the north-west tip of Ireland, with *Britannic* directly astern and destroyers *Eskimo, Tartar, Somali* and *Mashona* forming a protective screen. Only now was the ship's final destination officially confirmed, Captain Dalrymple-Hamilton revealing on the tannoy that *Rodney* was scheduled to reach Halifax on 29 May, probably sailing for Boston Navy Yard the same day. Lt Cdr Wellings and the other two American sailors were immediately beset by Brits quizzing them about what diversions Boston could offer.

Rodney soon hit rough seas, forcing her to drop speed to 13 knots on 23 May. Charging too hard in such conditions invited damage to the ship. Battleships tried to maintain a high speed during a transatlantic crossing, in order to outrun any lurking U-boats, but if seas were rough enough to force *Rodney* to slow down it was highly unlikely a German submarine could carry out a successful attack.

That same day it was confirmed *Bismarck* and the heavy cruiser *Prinz Eugen* were in the Atlantic. The cruisers *Norfolk* and *Suffolk* were already trailing them, having reported sighting the German ships via an emergency signal at 7.22 pm.

At 10.45 pm, with *Rodney* some 800 miles to the south of the reported position of the enemy ships,[7] Captain Dalrymple-Hamilton – constantly up-dated with decoded wireless intercepts, as signals passed back and forth between Home Fleet commander Admiral John Tovey, the Admiralty and other vessels – told his ship's company and passengers that two major German warships were likely to attempt a breakout via the Greenland-Iceland gap. The pack ice from Greenland extended out to such a distance that there was only 60 miles between it and Iceland, but even this had been narrowed, due to British minefields. Captain Dalrymple-Hamilton scrutinised the scouting reports, judging that, as his ship's current course was taking *Rodney* generally in the right direction, there was no reason to abandon *Britannic*. Anyway, other units, much further to the north, were more likely to see action.

At 5.55 am on 24 May, *Hood* and the King George V Class battleship *Prince of Wales*, the latter with dockyard workers aboard trying to put right various defects, including faulty gun turret machinery, made a bold attacking run at the *Bismarck* and *Prinz Eugen*. The *Hood* failed to score a hit on either German ship before a shell, or shells, from *Bismarck* penetrated her, causing an explosion in a shell room or cordite magazine. Around five minutes after the action began, the 45,200 tons British battlecruiser was ripped apart. Only three sailors from her complement of 1,418 survived. *Prince of Wales* managed three hits on *Bismarck*, but suffered several in return from both German ships, including one on her bridge, which wrecked it, killing everyone except her captain, navigating officer and a senior rating. The British battleship broke contact as soon as possible, yet the Germans chose not to pursue and kill her. In *Rodney*, Lt Cdr Crawford was bridge watchkeeping when the news of *Hood*'s demise came through via signals. Initially the name of the destroyed ship was not given and 'hopes immediately went absolutely sky-high, with thinking that it was *Bismarck* sunk.'

> *And then a few seconds later it came through,* 'Hood *sunk' ... I remember calling the captain, and he came straight up onto the bridge. For a few seconds there was a great gloom, but then everybody accepted the inevitable ... and hoped that we might possibly get into action, to square the deal.*

While *Rodney*'s men were filled with a determination to avenge 'the mighty *Hood*',[13] it was tinged with trepidation. G. Conning later admitted:

> *When we heard the* Hood *had blown up we thought 'my God this* Bismarck *must be some ship.'*

But, he went on:

> *I would add that we had a great confidence in the* Rodney *against the* Bismarck.

Lt Cdr Walton was one of many in *Rodney* who lost friends in the *Hood*, being filled with great sadness as he listened to a tannoy broadcast revealing the destruction of the battlecruiser:

> *We had been alongside* Hood *a week before in Scapa Flow. We'd had a lot of interchange of personnel and suddenly to find the* Hood *was gone really set us back a lot ...*

Also among those losing chums in *Hood* was Sub Lt Sopocko who, with fellow Polish officers and British shipmates, mulled over what could have caused such a catastrophic explosion. In the aftermath of *Hood*'s sinking, *Rodney's* chapel became busier.

Dalrymple-Hamilton realised *Rodney* might now play a bigger role than anticipated and therefore put together his own war cabinet – called the Operations Committee – consisting of: Captain Coppinger; the Navigator, Lt Cdr George Gatacre, on attachment from the Royal Australian Navy; the Executive Officer, Cdr John Grindle; the US Navy's Lieutenant Cdr Wellings; *Rodney*'s Torpedo Officer, Lt Commander Roger Lewis and, from time to time, other officers. Their meeting place was *Rodney*'s chart house, where committee members could study reported positions of various ships and discuss the best course of action.

At Noon on 24 May, while about 500 miles north-west of Ireland, *Rodney* duly parted company with *Britannic*, leaving *Eskimo* to ride shotgun, as the destroyer was also bound for refit in Boston. Days of hard steaming lay ahead for the sickly *Rodney*, her worn out boilers and defective propeller shafts threatening disaster at any moment, but somehow her engineers performed miracles. One post-war naval historian remarked: 'She was to show what an invalid ship could do in an emergency.'[8] At some stages during the *Bismarck* chase *Rodney* 'exceeded her designed speed by two knots ...'[9] The ship's Lt Cdr Walton was full of admiration for the stamina of the marine engineering department. In his opinion *Rodney*'s engines 'couldn't have been much more clapped out.'

> *We worked the engines up to faster than they had ever been I think since trials, which meant pouring water on top of parts that were getting hot, just pumping sea water straight on top, to cool them down.*

It was so hot in *Rodney*'s engine rooms, people were passing out. The compromises made in order to keep her weight within the Washington Treaty restrictions caused severe problems.

> *Our boilers* [were] *originally saturated steam boilers adapted for super-heaters. They had generating tubes blanked off and super-heaters inserted, which was always a source of trouble. Compromise is never the best thing, so we always had boiler trouble ... leaking super-heater tubes.*[10]

During the *Bismarck* action these had to be mended 'on the run'[11], the leaks plugged in order to prevent *Rodney* losing power at a critical moment and becoming a sitting target for marauding German aircraft and prowling U-boats.

A member of the engine room team named 'Scouse' Nesbitt was the smallest boiler-maker, and therefore 'the only one who could get in there to plug the leaking tubes when chasing *Bismarck*. [This was] very dangerous.'[12] The boiler that needed repairs was shut down but was still, literally, steaming hot, so cold water hoses were played inside it and wet sacking wrapped around Nesbitt to protect him.

Nine Swordfish torpedo-bombers from *Victorious* launched a strike on *Bismarck*, making their attack runs around 11.30 pm on 24 May, managing one hit amidships, which did little damage but killed a German sailor, hurled against a bulkhead by the impact. To some in the Nazi capital ship this was a bad omen. Shortly afterwards, the still shadowing *Prince of Wales* and *Bismarck* engaged in a rather futile exchange of fire at extreme range. Lütjens' heavy use of wireless signals to send reports of *Hood*'s destruction aided the gathering British naval forces. The German admiral believed, even when the shadowing ships had in reality lost contact, they still knew where he was, due to use of radar. There was therefore little point in maintaining radio silence. He was wrong and British shore-based Direction Finding (D/F) stations were able to track *Bismarck*'s position with precision. However, it was still by no means easy for the RN to maintain contact. The *Norfolk* and *Suffolk*, which had used the mist, squalls and fog to hang on to the coat tails of the German battleship and heavy cruiser, first lost *Prinz Eugen* and then *Bismarck*.

As his own ship battered her way through heavy seas, the accompanying destroyers found it very hard going, but Dalrymple-Hamilton didn't want to slow down, *Rodney* signalling the commander of the 6th Destroyer Squadron, in *Somali*:

> *My speed 20 ... Follow at your best speed under weather conditions.*[13]

When they went at full tilt for too long, but made little headway in high seas, destroyers inevitably rapidly depleted their oil and were also more likely to sustain serious structural damage as they dug into waves. Therefore, at 3.30 am on 25 May, *Mashona*, *Tartar* and *Somali* slipped back, *Rodney* pressing on without them.

Men's senses had been sharpened by the anticipated battle with *Bismarck* and fatigue was suppressed, Sub Lt Sopocko taking the Morning-watch on 25 May, despite having failed to grab some sleep beforehand.

> *I did not feel tired; perhaps because I had no time to think about it.*

Rodney picked up a signal from *Suffolk*, sent at 4.01 am, confirming she'd lost radar contact with *Bismarck* and Dalrymple-Hamilton immediately convened a meeting of the Operations Committee. It was decided *Rodney* should attempt to stay where she was, well placed to prevent *Bismarck* reaching Brest.

Rodney was attempting to second-guess *Bismarck*, following a course keeping her poised to bisect the German ship's probable course. Peter Wells-Cole recalled of this phase:

> *We just plodded along, hoping we could catch her.*

Rodney slowed down to maintain her position, allowing the three destroyers to catch up by 8 am on 25 May.[14] It was of the utmost importance the battleship maintained radio silence, in order not give away her perfect interception position, but on the other hand it was essential Tovey knew where his most powerfully-armed unit was. When he read in an intercepted signal that *Repulse* had been sent off to refuel at Newfoundland, Captain Dalrymple-Hamilton correctly deduced Tovey would be even more anxious to link up with *Rodney*, so, at 9.00 am, decided to let the Home Fleet boss know where he was. As well as transmitting his ship's position, Dalrymple-Hamilton suggested he could loiter with the intention of intercepting *Bismarck* if, and when, she tried to go S/E in a bid to reach safety. He also informed Tovey he had three destroyers with him and visibility was 10 miles. It was Dalrymple-Hamilton's only wireless transmission of the entire pursuit, but it was perfectly timed, confirming for Tovey he had the firepower needed to decisively defeat *Bismarck* – God and fuel willing.

However, at 10.47 am on 25 May, Tovey ordered all ships to search north of *Bismarck*'s last confirmed position, for a serious error had been made in *King George V*, with the German battleship's position plotted wrongly. The *Rodney* had plotted the same land station signals intercept bearings as *King George V*, but came to the conclusion *Bismarck* was heading towards Brest, rather than north.[15] A specific type of chart was needed to plot radio intercepts, but *King George V*'s team had applied the right bearings to the wrong kind.

The *Rodney*'s Operations Committee was astonished to read a general signal instructing British warships to 'search accordingly' to the north, when they reckoned *Bismarck* was actually 60 miles south of where Tovey stated she was. Dalrymple-Hamilton could not imagine the order applied to his ship – if *Bismarck* really was going back to Germany via the northern route, then she was too far south and too slow to be of any use. The Operations Committee agreed it was best for *Rodney* to remain where she was. They felt sure '*Bismarck* was steaming southeastward toward Brest at 20-22 knots.'[16]

Captain Dalrymple-Hamilton predicted the Admiralty would soon correct Tovey's instructions. At 11.40 am, a signal was received direct from the Admiralty, telling *Rodney* it was probable *Bismarck* was heading for Brest or St Nazaire. At that moment she was positioned just 100 miles south of the most likely direct course *Bismarck* would take.

With propellers pushing their ship through the sea at 21 knots, *Rodney*'s men fully expected to see *Bismarck* cresting over the horizon at any moment. When this looked less likely, the 16-inch gun crews, who had been closed up just in case, were allowed to relax.

At 2.30 pm the Admiralty signalled new instructions to *Rodney*. She was no longer to head for Biscay and should instead steer N/E. *Rodney* had, however, already altered course away from Brest, sailing towards Cape Finisterre, to place herself across the route to both French and Spanish ports. The majority of the British fleet had been heading in the wrong direction for nearly four hours.

Having not encountered *Bismarck* by 4.20 pm, Captain Dalrymple-Hamilton went into a huddle with the Navigator and Executive Officer. They now decided to comply with the Admiralty's orders and sail North East at speed. It was later reckoned *Rodney* missed *Bismarck* by only 25 miles. At that range the German vessel would anyway have been just below the horizon.

> *If we had sighted her ... we would have had a private action between the* Rodney *and* Bismarck*, so we did think about what would happen and we were very dubious of the result, because we were only capable of doing 19 knots and therefore she could out-manoeuvre us and complete the whole engagement at maximum range until she'd hit us. I think, in point of fact, we wouldn't have sunk her, we'd possibly have been damaged a bit ourselves and lost the chase.*[17]

Instead, for gunners in the 16-inch and 6-inch turrets there was the usual boredom of being closed up with nothing to do, except maybe read a book or play cards. Len Walters was by now captain of the centre gun of *Rodney*'s A turret.

> *There was loads of false alarms of course. You never knew when it was going to be the proper one, so you just belted along there close up, waiting for action and then in time you fell out of Action Stations again. It is just one of those things. I don't remember the exact movements of the ship, except all I know is I was doing my job and that was it.*

Dalrymple-Hamilton, having not sighted *Bismarck* by 9 pm, ordered his ship around to head south-east, directly towards Brest, at a speed of 21 knots. At 11 pm, as dusk finally fell, *Rodney*'s men were again relaxed from Action Stations. Sub Lt Sopocko had earlier managed to get his head down, in the 16-inch shell room beneath X turret, surrounded by hundreds of tons of explosive – something that no longer troubled him. He found he slept there, head nestled on a folded coat, better than anywhere else in the ship. Now, like hundreds of other *Rodney* sailors and marines, he was able to return to his proper resting place, in Sopocko's case a hammock slung on the poop deck. However, everyone was ordered to sleep in their clothes, for the call to Action Stations would come at dawn. They must close up with speed, just in case *Bismarck* loomed out of the rising sun.

At 10.35 am on 26 May, a Catalina flying boat of the RAF signalled the position of a mystery battleship heading south-east, and *Rodney* was able to calculate it was *Bismarck*, some 110 miles to her south-west. Contact had been re-established after a gap of 31 hours, and *King George V* was 135 miles to the north[18] of the German battleship. The *Rodney* was already heading south-east towards Brest, so continued on the same course. Tovey was, meanwhile, concerned the Catalina had spotted *Rodney* rather than *Bismarck*, so signalled the Admiralty at 10.51 am:

> *Request a check that contact was not* RODNEY.

This confirmation duly came and so it seemed the chase was now entering its final phase, the German ship appearing to be headed for Cape Finisterre – still well placed for both French and Spanish ports. *Bismarck* was now fixed firmly in the sights of converging British warships, for when the Catalina lost touch, Swordfish from *Ark Royal* were able to take over the shadowing job.

However, early in the afternoon on 26 May, a Luftwaffe Focke Wulf Condor scouting aircraft managed to spot *Rodney* and her three destroyers, provoking a storm of fire from British ships, but the German aircraft got away unharmed.[19] In *Rodney*, they realized *Bismarck* would be advised of Royal Navy units hot on her heels. A signal was duly sent by German naval headquarters that afternoon, with the morale-boosting claim that the British battleship and her escorts were 200 miles behind. Feared for her 16-inch guns, the German battleship's command team knew *Rodney*'s slow top speed meant that, provided her luck held, *Bismarck* would be able to make France.[20]

Shortly after 3.00 pm, *Rodney* was sighted by lookouts in *King George V*, ahead on the port beam. They were slow off the mark, for some twenty-four minutes earlier *Rodney*'s sailors had spotted Tovey's flagship, fifteen miles distant, in the west. Tovey was keen for his old ship to join him for the kill, but was also aware she was seven knots slower than *King George V*.

Rodney at 7.11 pm felt confident enough to send a signal to *King George V*, confirming that she could hang on until morning:

> *RODNEY had 1600 tons of oil on hand at 1800. We use at present speed 23 tons per hour and 19 tons per hour at 20 knots. Clyde and Gibraltar are within my endurance if present course and speed are continued until 0800 tomorrow.*[21]

At the same moment, *Somali* and *Mashona* were leaving *Rodney* – *Tartar*, with more fuel, was staying longer, still waiting for the Polish destroyer *Piorun*[22] to turn up to take over escort duties.

Rodney had by now fallen in astern of the fleet flagship, a familiar and welcome sight to Tovey. The Admiral signalled her at 8.28 pm.

> *Accurate station keeping not necessary in order to save fuel.*

A minute later *Rodney* made a request for the younger battleship to slow down.

> KING GEORGE V*'s 22 knots is a bit faster than* RODNEY*'s and we are dropping distance.*[23]

Captain Dalrymple-Hamilton told his sailors and marines, via the tannoy, that *Ark Royal*'s Swordfish were going to attack but, if they failed to score any significant hits, *Bismarck* would probably escape. There was widespread disappointment in the ship after she intercepted Somerville's signal from *Renown* that the attack had indeed failed. Though not revealed that night, in fact Swordfish had mistakenly attacked *Sheffield*, but fortunately the cruiser expertly combed some of the torpedoes, while others exploded on hitting the sea. Seeking to make amends for this abject failure, the Swordfish of *Ark Royal* took off again, this time finding *Bismarck*, but it was uncertain if any damage had been caused. The *Sheffield*, by then closely shadowing the German battleship and, evading 15-inch shells, as *Bismarck* reacted angrily to the air assault, observed the enemy vessel had turned and was now heading NNW, away from the ports where she hoped to take refuge.

Captain Dalrymple-Hamilton addressed *Rodney*'s complement again, telling them it was believed no hits had been achieved during the second air attack. 'So be prepared for nothing to happen ...' His revelation of *Ark Royal*'s apparent failure sent many of his sailors and marines to bed in a gloomy mood, but shadowing

Swordfish were soon reporting *Bismarck* had completed two full circles, then stopped on a northerly heading, apparently dead in the water and wallowing. Her steering appeared crippled. The miracle had been achieved and it was now certain the British battleships would catch *Bismarck*. A reckoning was at hand and one of the *Rodney*'s men reflected:

> *We were glad to think, of all the British ships, that we would get the opportunity to avenge the* Hood.[24]

Some in *Rodney* no doubt reflected that it was the first anniversary of the Royal Navy's evacuation of Allied troops from the beaches of Dunkirk. Time for payback on that score, too.

Shortly before midnight, *Rodney*'s off-watch men were roused from their hammocks and bunks by the call to General Quarters. Sailors and marines struggled past each other along the battleship's passageways, a flood of humanity breaking in conflicting directions, momentarily log-jamming at hatches, then flowing through and clattering up ladders, pulling on duffel coats and anti-flash gear, steel helmets clanging against each other. Nobody pushed in this orderly hurry, but they all made haste and, once everyone was at their correct Action Station, the ship settled down into an eerie quiet, interrupted only by the whirring of machinery and dull boom of waves against metal. Telegraphists waited tensely by telephones and everyone had half an ear cocked to the hum of the tannoy speakers, expecting at any moment to hear the captain's voice.

At 2.00 am, it was revealed Admiral Tovey had decided against a night action, especially as *Bismarck*'s damage meant the fleet could catch her at dawn and have a whole day to bring about the German battleship's destruction. While Action Stations were relaxed from 2.00 am to 2.30 am[25], *Rodney*'s men remained ready for battle throughout the rest of the night, catching sleep where they could.

Normally on the upper deck, manning anti-aircraft weapons, Richard Hughes and other ratings in his department found themselves distributed throughout the ship to lend a hand where they might be more usefully employed, such as damage control teams. They would fight fire and flood plus hunt down holes and structural damage that might need shoring up by shipwrights who were masters at fashioning wooden supports and plugs. Around 5 am, a broadcast was made by the Executive Officer, instructing everyone to be fully awake and closed up. The men in *Rodney*'s exposed gunnery director positions were, in the words of the battleship's air defence officer, Lieutenant Donald Campbell, already 'cramped and numb from exposure to bitter winds and lashing rain.'

Daybreak came at 7.22 am and three minutes later Tovey had time for one more pre-battle instruction to *Rodney*:

> *If opportunity permits fire your torpedoes.*

His flagship did not possess torpedoes in her armament, but, as her former captain, he was keenly aware *Rodney* had two submerged tubes in her bows.

At 7.30 am Captain Dalrymple-Hamilton told *Rodney*'s men:

> *Just going in.*

Shortly before 8 am, lookouts in *Rodney* and *King George V* spotted masts, despite reduced visibility due to dark clouds low on the horizon. It was not *Bismarck*, but rather the cruiser *Norfolk,* coming from the south-west, steaming hard. *Norfolk* had earlier approached *Bismarck* thinking she was *Rodney* and flashed a signal. On realising it was the enemy, *Norfolk* quickly turned around and steamed away without firing. The Germans were too weary to fire anything but their 5.9-inch guns at the British cruiser, a Royal Marine officer in *Norfolk* later writing of *Bismarck* in this encounter:

> *She was rolling and pitching in the heavy seas, and water was streaming off her fo'c'sle as she lifted to each gigantic wave. She was an enormous and a splendid ship.*[26]

Rodney and *King George V* now wheeled and headed south-west, straight at the German battleship, presenting the narrowest profile. When in good range, Tovey intended both ships would turn parallel with *Bismarck,* enabling all their guns to bear. The *Rodney* – as the heaviest hitter – had already been given absolute freedom of manoeuvre by Tovey.

The light slowly improved, revealing 'a tumbled, wind-torn sea' and from his eyrie, *Rodney*'s Lieutenant Campbell saw 'a weak sun glimpsed through trailing scarves of rain causing the visibility to fluctuate between 12,000 and 30,000 yards.'

Having expected to spot *Bismarck,* Lt Campbell was disappointed to see *Dorsetshire* emerging from a rain squall.

King George V sighted *Bismarck* at 8.43 am, at a range of approximately 25,000 yards range (just over fourteen miles), with *Rodney* recording her own sighting one minute later, and five degrees off the starboard bow: in other words more or less dead ahead. Tommy Byers, the coxswain of *Rodney*'s cutter who had brought Captain Coppinger across from *Britannic,* now found himself with an unexpected front row seat. Normally stationed deep below, in a 6-inch ammunition magazine, he had been ordered to take the place of another man in the main gunnery director position. From Portaferry, Byers joined the Royal Navy at the age of 17, in 1934, to avoid a life digging up potatoes for local farmers.

Training as a gunner, his first ship was the anti-torpedo net laying vessel *Guardian,* in 1935, and, having seen service in Egyptian waters and also on the China Station, Byers was drafted to HMS *Rodney* in 1939, shortly before the outbreak of war. Now, nearly two years later, here he was, enthralled but also feeling terribly exposed, for one of the epic clashes in the history of naval warfare. The gunnery director position was on the Octopoidal, above the bridge, which, despite its importance, was a lightly armoured structure. 'The person I was to relieve was a Scotsman, named Lennox, who had taken ill,' Byers recalled.

> *I had been trained to operate the Range and Deflection Machine in the tower, and up there was also Mr Dick Ede, the person who fired the 16-inch guns. He was a Warrant Gunner, a Canadian ... We were sitting in a row: I was on the right, the trainer beside me and the man who did the firing on the left. In front of us was a Belfast man, an Able Seaman whose name I just cannot remember. He was on the Rangefinder, a very important job.*

Sitting above and behind these men was Lt Cdr Crawford, alongside a rate officer, spotting officer and a communications rating. As the man in overall charge, Lt Cdr Crawford would, as the controller of *Rodney*'s 16-inch guns, be more than a little busy.

It was *Rodney* that opened fire first, according to her Official History 'at 8.47 am, followed one minute later by *KING GEORGE V*, and then by *BISMARCK*' at 8.49 am, Lt Cdr Crawford recalling the moment he saw the enemy battleship:

> *And as the dawn broke – a pretty murky dawn – I sighted the* Bismarck *on the horizon. I reported to the bridge, that the* Bismarck *was in sight.*

The distance to target was 23,400 yards – just over thirteen miles – and, receiving instructions to open fire, Lt Cdr Crawford found he would need lots of luck and faith in his own instincts. Up in the ADP, Lt Campbell 'heard the sharp ting-ting of the warning fire bells from our main director below and, with a deafening crash A and B turrets opened fire.' As the 'dull drum-beat' of *King George V*'s 14-inch guns firing also sounded out, Lt Campbell saw 'four wicked-looking flashes on *Bismarck*, indicating that four tons of German steel were hurtling towards us.' The Germans recognised the importance of knocking out the 16-inch gun battleship swiftly. Lt Campbell saw an enemy shell land just 200 yards 'beyond our lunging stem', the second German salvo landing 300 yards behind *Rodney*'s stern, sounding like '50 express trains' as it roared overhead, the shells exploding on hitting the water with ear-splitting noise.

Twenty-year old Ernest Beeston was a range-taker in one of *Rodney*'s 6-inch guns and therefore able to see the action via his sighting port.

> *I'll never forget those whines as the first shells came over. It put the fear of God in you.*[27]

Tommy Byers found the sound of *Bismarck*'s shells passing overhead 'very frightening.'

For Lt Wells-Cole, the opening phase of the battle revealed that he could become accustomed to even the most extraordinary circumstances.

> *My Action Station was in the armoured conning tower, just abaft of the three 16-inch turrets, between the X turret and the Octopoidal. I had an extremely good view of the action and it was only when the 16-inch guns fired that one lost sight of what was going on due to all the smoke.*

The *Rodney*'s accuracy was initially not brilliant, the first two salvoes missing by a wide margin, but the British battleship's third salvo straddled *Bismarck*.

While *Bismarck*'s shooting was good, luck was on *Rodney*'s side. For, even as *Bismarck*'s third salvo carved its way through the air, the 16-inch shells that would spell doom for the pride of Hitler's navy were in flight. By now the *Rodney*'s X turret was also bringing its fire to bear and *Rodney*'s fourth salvo, of four shells, straddled *Bismarck*; there were only two shell splashes, indicating hits. The German battleship's B-turret 'gushed flame and smoke when two tons of armour-piercing high-explosive shells bored into her'[28] sending shrapnel scything across the *Bismarck*'s bridge, killing a number of men.[29] These hits, at 9.02 am, were credited with putting both *Bismarck*'s Anton and Bruno turrets out of the fight, causing raging fires in the forecastle. The *Bismarck*'s conning tower team were killed, communication with the turrets severed.[30] Bruno never fired again, but Anton would resume at around 9.27 am.[31]

King George V was by now hitting *Bismarck* regularly, too, and *Rodney* also recorded a hit on *Bismarck*'s upper deck. *Rodney*'s 6-inch secondary armament had joined in at 8.58 am. The German warship's shells were falling short and some were over, but none causing any damage. In X turret, Sub Lt Sopocko marvelled at the spectre of Royal Marine gunners, 'glistening with oil, wet with sweat, blackened with the stains of cordite smoke, their eyes seem aflame.'

> *They remember Coventry, London, Plymouth, especially the latter which is home to most of them. Justice, you still exist in this world.*[32]

Due to the rudder damage, *Bismarck* had by this point effectively lost control, one of her gunnery officers observing she 'was reacting to the combined influences of her jammed rudders, the seaway and the wind.'[33]

There was fight left in the German battleship but at 9.13 am, *Rodney* achieved 'a good straddle'[34], the enemy vessel obscured by plumes of spray, hits probably wiping out what remained of the bridge and inflicting serious damage to *Bismarck*'s conning tower. But now *Rodney*'s guns were being over-corrected, shells falling well beyond target. The British battleship launched torpedoes in an attempt to hit *Bismarck.*

For those below decks in *Rodney*, it was not clear if the thuds and clangs they heard were enemy shells or their own guns firing. Marine Jack Austin was, throughout the action, closed up by himself in 'the valve space between the shell room and [a 6-inch] turret'.

> *I counted up to ten broadsides, wondering whether they were outgoing shells or incoming.*

Teenage sailor Mick Kavanagh was down in the starboard 6-inch fire control area.

> *You didn't see nothing down there in the bottom of the ship. Our job was making sure that the weapons were lined up on target and ready to fire and then the director, he fired the guns. The ship was shaking every time she fired. In my old Action Station, in the torpedo fire control position, I remember we used to have these rubber plugs that popped out of your ears when the big guns fired, so I suppose from that point of view I was better off down below. During the* Bismarck *action you had so much to do, so much to worry about getting right, you didn't think about what might be happening to endanger your life, nor did you reflect on what we were doing to the Germans.*

At 9.23 am *Rodney* scored another 16-inch hit on *Bismarck* and two torpedoes were fired from her starboard tube between 9.22 am and 9.23 am. The British battleship would not fire another torpedo until 9.38 am, a single tinfish from the port tube. *Rodney*'s starboard tube had been put out of action, its sluice valve jammed with a torpedo just loaded.

At 9.27 am *Rodney* straddled *Bismarck* again, one of the latter's forward turrets firing a salvo, but the British battleship scored another heavy hit, behind the Geman ship's funnel. At 9.31 am, the left gun barrel of *Bismarck*'s Dora turret was blown off by one of *Rodney*'s 16-inch shells[35], and while the right-hand gun managed to fire a further two times, smoke soon forced its crew out. A 16-inch shell penetrated *Bismarck*'s armoured deck, causing carnage in the port engine room and between 9.30 am and 9.35 am *Rodney* managed to hit the *Bismarck*'s foretop fire control position.

Bismarck's Caesar turret was firing, but erratically'[36] and her last salvo came at 9.31 am.[37] The *Rodney*'s battle observer wrote that at 9.38 am *Bismarck* 'passes astern and comes up on port side distance still 2 miles.' Two minutes later he recorded:

> *Enemy on fire fore and aft.*

At least one 16-inch shell hit on *Bismarck* caused an explosion behind the Bruno turret, which blew off the armoured plating on the ship's bridge and also tore a ragged hole in the barbette, starting a fire inside, with black smoke pouring out.[38]

At 9.44 am *Rodney* turned to starboard and 'engages enemy starboard side'[39] achieving at least four hits on *Bismarck* for no reply. With *King George V* standing off at five miles, Captain Dalrymple-Hamilton ordered *Rodney* to steam ahead of *Bismarck* and begin zig-zagging, so bringing all nine 16-inch guns to bear, firing in broadsides on alternate beams.

One of *Rodney*'s 16-inch shells peeled open *Bismarck*' forecastle deck and started raging fires in the accommodation below. At around 9.49 am *Rodney*'s principal gun director system malfunctioned but the battleship switched to her back-up.

Between 9.50 am and 10.05 am, *Rodney*, *King George V*, *Devonshire* and *Norfolk* continued to inflict terrible damage on *Bismarck*.

Three torpedoes were fired from *Rodney*'s port tube between 9.51 am and 9.55 am. Two minutes later she fired another, and this one, almost in an echo of the disastrous trials of the late 1920s, was 'seen to leap out of the water two-thirds of the way across.'[40] But how effective were the valiant efforts of the men loading and firing them? The Torpedo Officer, Lt Cdr Lewis, himself later claimed:

> *... the opportunity of hitting an enemy capital ship with a torpedo from a British capital ship was never likely to arise again ... I always claimed that one of the last three torpedoes I fired, at a range of 3,000 yards by then, did hit the* Bismarck *and in several circles this has been accepted.*

According to *Rodney*'s battle observer, his ship scored a torpedo hit on the *Bismarck* at 9.58 am, although the German battleship's surviving gunnery officer, who was both unable to see what might have happened and concerned with other, more pressing, matters, later said this was doubtful. Sub Lt Sopocko claimed to have seen more than one torpedo hit at the height of the battle through his X turret periscope, at least one from a cruiser and one from *Rodney*.

> *A white streak shows on the surface of the emerald-green, brownish wave-capped sea. It disappears ... Under the bow of the* Bismarck *an explosion takes place. We also fire our torpedoes. Now a plume of smoke arises from under her* [Bismarck's] *funnel.*[41]

Observing hits on *Bismarck* from his position on the bridge, Captain Dalrymple Hamilton was in no doubt that his ship had achieved something remarkable. Ken George, in the starboard engine room, heard his Commanding Officer say over the tannoy:

> *We have made history in hitting another battleship with a torpedo.*

The *Rodney*'s battle observer recorded that at 9.59 am the *Bismarck* 'turned' to starboard and the British battleship continued to pummel her, the *Dorsetshire* joining in. The cruisers' participation was fitful because of the huge amount of shell splashes and smoke around *Bismarck*, which continued to make it difficult for them to lay their guns with accuracy. By 10.03 am there was a 'lull' in the action, with *Bismarck* 'well alight, clouds of black smoke from fire aft'[42].

Turning hard to port, at 10.07 am *Rodney* resumed her pounding of the German warship.

> BISMARCK *was now a wreck pouring high into the air a great cloud of smoke and flames.*[43]

At 10.11 am, *Rodney*'s battle observer noted:

> *Salvo from* Rodney *blows pieces off stern of* Bismarck *and sets up a fire with greyish white smoke.*

Having ceased fire, by 10.16 am *Rodney* was moving off north-west. While others might have had the bridge windows or powerful optics between them and the *Bismarck*, Marine Len Nicholl had nothing but fresh air, for, as the aimer of a 6-inch gun turret, he peered out a sighting port usually covered with a steel lid, but which was taken off during action. More than sixty years later, he gave this verdict on the battle:

> *I must be one of the few left on this Earth still alive who actually saw the* Bismarck *from the* Rodney *during the action, as a very small percentage of people in the ship had sight of her. Not even in the 16-inch turrets did the majority of them see* Bismarck. *I saw her battle flag flying when we first sighted her. Soon, she was burning and I quite clearly saw one of the 16-inch shells hit and blow the back off a turret and it flipped around. It was such a rough sea that every time* Bismarck *was pushed under the water, flames would go out, but then she would come up and the fires would start again. I was on the port side and I think the* Rodney's *6-inch guns were doing more damage than our 16-inch shells, which, being armour-piercing, were just going straight through* Bismarck. *We were so close, the joke later was that some of the lads on the upper deck could have thrown spuds at her. The 16-inch guns were depressed very low, as the range was a few thousand feet. To be quite candid it was like an exercise because, by this time, we knew that she could not fire back at us. It was not a good feeling to sit in a turret and watch her in her death throes. I could see their turrets were not firing. You could see there was no reply. I don't recall ever seeing anyone running around, not even someone in the water. At the time I cannot recall anyone in the* Rodney *that I knew expressing feelings of pity because, let's not forget, the* Bismarck *had sunk the* Hood *only a few days earlier. I had pals in the* Hood *who went down with her, in particular one lad on there, who was my Physical Training Instructor when I was a recruit: Lofty Whitehead. Of course when you look back you think 'poor so and sos', the* Bismarck's *crew didn't stand a dog's chance. Prior to the fight there was no trepidation whatsoever. I must admit the* Rodney's *gunnery was particularly good. I think throughout the whole* Bismarck *thing what was at the backs of most men's minds was that we didn't want to lose the opportunity of some good leave in Boston.*

The *Rodney*'s battle observer noted that *King George V* approached his ship on her port bow and turned on a parallel course, both battleships sailing away from *Bismarck*, the Home Fleet flagship using her Y turret to fire on the German warship. As *Rodney* departed the scene, *Bismarck* lying dead astern, the battle observer noting:

> *Enemy smoking heavily.* Rodney's *guns will not bear.*

Lt Campbell gazed across the sea at the vanquished enemy.

> *... down by her smoke-enveloped stern, blazing fore and aft, a smashed but still beautiful ship.*

Young Engine Room Artificer Charles Barton, determined to catch sight of the *Bismarck*, had, without getting permission, come up from the engine room for a look.

> *In the boiler rooms you could go up the up-takes – what you see as the funnel is actually the outer casing of the up-takes. Between the up-takes and the outer casing are ladders, one of which led to a small door that opened onto the boat deck. You weren't really supposed to do that, but I couldn't resist going up. I saw* Bismarck *on fire in the distance. It was a terrible sight.*

At 10.23 am six Swordfish from *Ark Royal* approached, but did not carry out an attack for fear of being hit by the anti-aircraft fire of British warships. This concern proved well founded, as *King George V* opened fire. The Swordfish crews were using hand signals to ask for a cease fire while they made a torpedo run, but *King George V*'s anti-aircraft gunnery officer thought they were German aircrew shaking their fists. He saw what he wanted to see and the fleet dreaded – Luftwaffe bombers seeking revenge.

At 10.27 am, *Rodney*'s battle observer noted a 'sudden red flash' visible from the *Bismarck*'s stern. This was actually a minute after *Bismarck*'s stern fell off[44] due to earlier damage from *Rodney*'s 16-inch shells, possibly indicating a massive inrush of oxygen feeding the raging fires within as she began to sink. By 10.28 am, the wrecked *Bismarck* – 'a smoking mass bows-on' – was five miles astern of *Rodney* and *King George V*. Observers in *Rodney* saw *Dorsetshire* crossing the German ship's bows as she went in to deliver the coup de grace using torpedoes, although it has been claimed scuttling charges triggered in her dying moments actually took *Bismarck* down. The *Rodney*'s men saw the *Bismarck* disappearing in a cloud of smoke, the battle observer simply noting, at 10.39 am:

> Bismarck *sank.*

Well aware of the extreme difficulties faced by the Engineering Department, in the immediate aftermath of the action Captain Dalrymple-Hamilton sent for the Chief Petty Officer Engineer, whose 'superhuman efforts' kept the ship going. However, he was unable to come to the bridge:

> *The messenger came back from the engine room without him and reported: 'The Chief's fainted, sir!'*[45]

Lt Campbell reported a sense of thankfulness in *Rodney* as she left the scene.

> *... but laced with sorrow and pity that so beautiful a ship and her gallant crew should be so brutally destroyed. Someone during the Great War coined the phrase: 'There is no hate in the front line, unless for those who put us there.' We were all young and lashed to the same bitter wheel with only two ways for getting off. Some of us were lucky ...*

In fact *Rodney* caused more damage to herself than the Germans did. Her upper works were covered in soot, rails and decking on the forecastle ripped away by the blast of 16-inch guns, while heat had blackened and cracked paint on the turrets. The muzzles of the guns themselves were naked of paint, for it had been burned off.

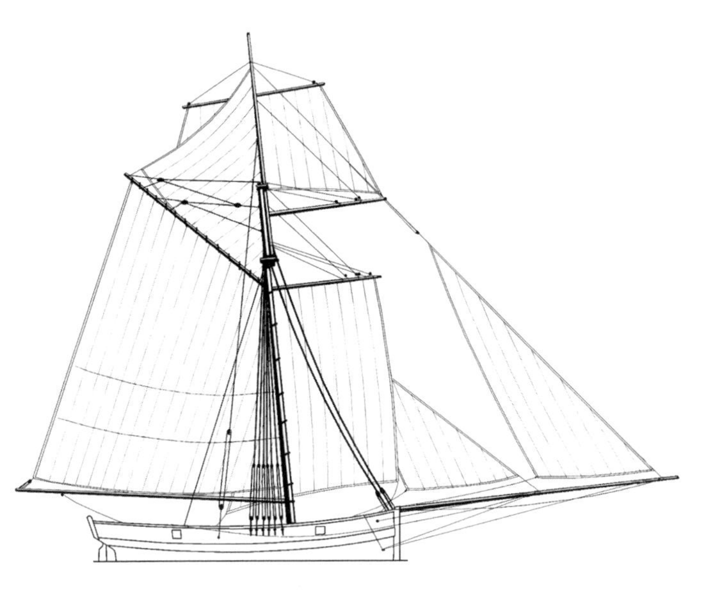

Above: The first HMS *Rodney*, a cutter of the late 1750s.

Above, right: The man the ships were named after, Admiral Sir George Brydges Rodney.

Right: The second *Rodney*, which was a 16-gun brig-sloop.

Illustrations by Dennis Andrews.

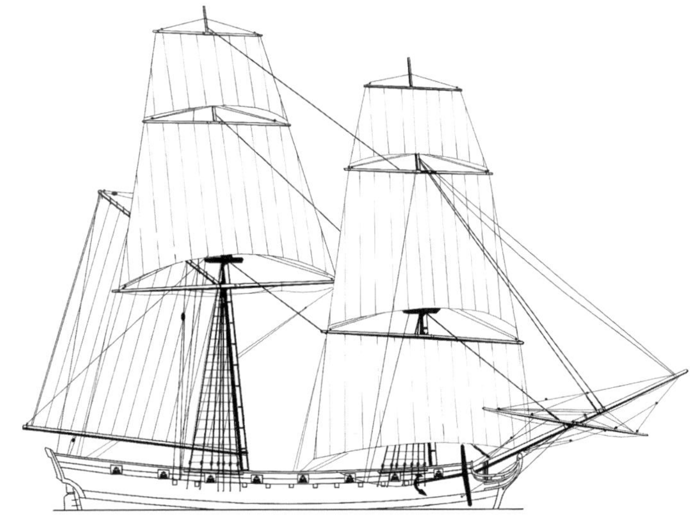

'The Continental Dockyard', a satirical cartoon by George M. Woodward, originally published in 1807. The 74-gun *Rodney* built on the Thames was part of John Bull's response to Bonaparte's shipbuilding challenge. In the cartoon a French shipwright tells an intimidating Napoleon that, as soon as a warship is built, the English capture it at sea. *Royal Naval Museum*.

Left: The Barnard-built *Rodney*, 74 guns. *Dennis Andrews.*

Right: A photograph of William Hall VC, who some years earlier served in the Crimean War-era HMS *Rodney*. *Fergusson Collection/Nova Scotia Archives and Records Management.*

A portrait of Joseph Bates, who was press-ganged into the 74-gun *Rodney*. *Dennis Andrews.*

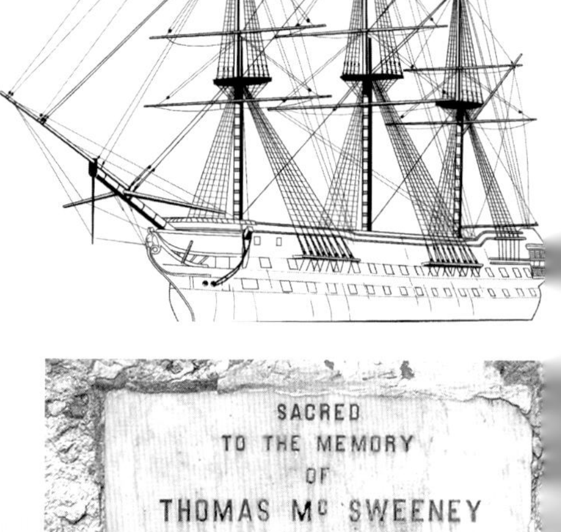

Right: A line drawing of the 92-gun *Rodney*, christened in 1833. *Dennis Andrews.*

Below, right: The engraved stone in a Malta cemetery that commemorates the death of a *Rodney* marine. *Stephen J. Borg.*

SACRED
TO THE MEMORY
OF
THOMAS Mc SWEENEY
EXECUTED ON
H. M. S. RODNEY
8TH JUNE 1837
AGED 23 YEARS.

Below: A photograph of the Victorian-era *Rodney* at anchor. *Royal Naval Museum.*

The all-steel battleship *Rodney*, in dock at Chatham and showing her high waterline, an image probably taken in the late 1890s. *Royal Naval Museum.*

The same *Rodney* in the water, with bunting flying. *Royal Naval Museum.*

A Victorian engraving of the *Rodney*'s launch at Chatham in 1884. *Royal Naval Museum.*

She was the last Royal Navy warship to mount a figurehead, seen here, and, suitably enough, it depicted Admiral Rodney himself, hand on sword. By the time *Rodney* was photographed in dock (see above) the ornate work, including figurehead, were gone. *Topham Picturepoint.*

HMS *Hood*, sister ship of the *Rodney* cancelled at the end of the First World War. *Goodman Collection.*

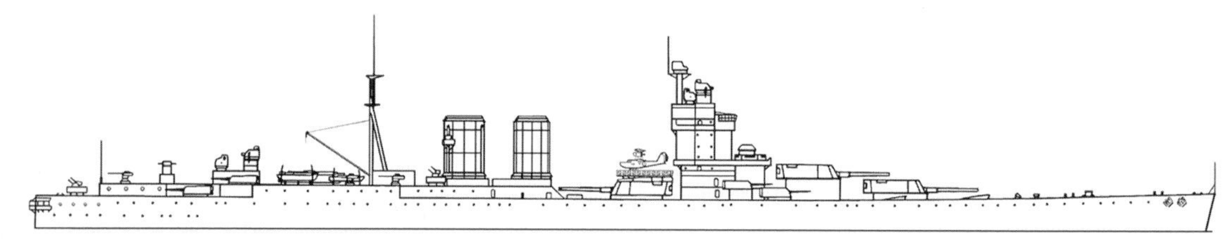

A proposed G3-design *Rodney. Dennis Andrews.*

One of *Rodney*'s 16-inch guns arrives at Cammel Laird on a railway truck. *The Times/News International.*

As *Rodney* is fitted out at Birkenhead a 16-inch gun is lifted aboard by a massive crane. *The Times/News International.*

At *Rodney*'s launch in December 1925 a dockyard official holds the bunting-festooned bottle of wine that will be smashed against the ship's bows (behind) to launch her. *Courtesy of National Museums Liverpool* (*Merseyside Maritime Museum*).

HMS *Rodney* on the Mersey, leaving her construction yard for sea trials in 1927. *Courtesy of National Museums Liverpool (Merseyside Maritime Museum).*

Battleship *Rodney* makes her way through Plymouth Sound, past the Hoe Pier (which was later destroyed by German bombs). *Goodman Collection.*

.dmiral Andrew Cunningham, who commanded *odney* in the late 1920s. *Royal Naval Museum.*

Admiral John Tovey, who was *Rodney*'s captain in the early 1930s. *Royal Naval Museum.*

odney ploughs through rough Atlantic seas as she follows in the wake of *Nelson*, circa 1934. *Hardwell Collection.*

Festooned with bunting, *Rodney* is a star attraction at the 1935 Jubilee Fleet Review. *Royal Naval Museum.*

Right: Royal Marine Rupert Hardwell, who served in the battleship during the mid-1930s. *Hardwell Collection.*

King George V and Queen Mary come aboard *Rodney* during the Fleet Review. *Nicholl Collection.*

isplaying all her power and majesty, *Rodney*'s guns are
aversed to point across the Hamoaze, as visitors swarm
n her upper deck during a Navy Week in the 1930s.
oodman Collection.

During the early days of the Second World War, 16-inch shells are hoisted aboard *Rodney*. *IWM A206*.

um issue for sailors aboard *Rodney*, August 1940. *IWM A103.*

ne of the battleship's sailors cleans the rifling inside a 16-inch gun, while another polishes the exterior casing of e gun. *IWM A1137.*

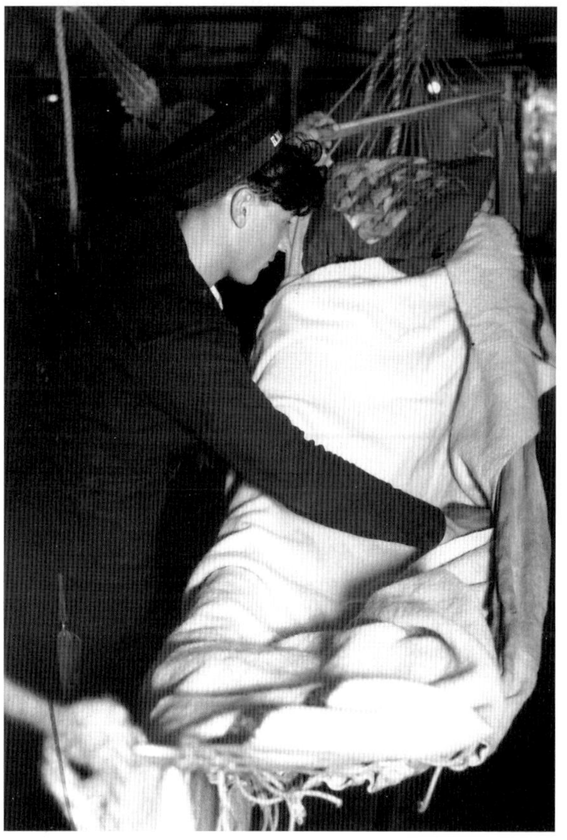

One of *Rodney*'s sailors slings his hammock. *IWM A167.*

Teenage sailor Ted Russ, who served in *Rodney* during the early days of the war. *Russ Collection*

Young Irishman Tommy Byers, who was exposed to *Bismarck*'s fire during the epic battle of May 1941. *Byers Collection.*

Rodney makes an imposing sight as she batters her way through stormy seas in March 1941. *IWM A3665.*

Above: Officers and men on *Rodney*'s compass platform inside the massive 'Octopoidal'. *IWM A145.*

Left: In August 1940, as they wait for the threatened German invasion, sailors man one of the battleship's pom-pom anti-aircraft weapons. *IWM A124.*

Rodney matelots wait in line while one of their shipmates has a haircut. *IWM A127.*

Above: A cloud of gun smoke drifts away from *Rodney* as she fires on *Bismarck*, which is clearly on fire and badl damaged (as indicated by smoke plume left hand side of image). *IWM MH15931*. Top, left: Two of *Rodney*'s engineers at work in her boiler room, somehow keeping the old battleship going. *IWM A156*. Top, right: A Roya Marine gunner works on the complex breech of a 16-inch gun in *Rodney*'s X turret. *IWM A138*.

The Crossing the Line Certificate awarded to *Rodney*'s John E. Faulkner, in June 1942. It shows Mussolini and Hitler pulling Churchill as Neptune. *Faulkner Collection*.

Be it known to all ye who enter my realm
John, E. Faulkner, L.S.
was initiated into the Solemn Mysteries of
The Ancient Order of the Oceans
on board H.M.S. "Rodney"
Be it Remembered by all ye mermaids, Whales, Sharks, Porpoises, Skates, Dolphins, Eels, Crabs, Passengers and landlubbers when ye are honoured by his presence ye shall treat him with the respect that is due to one of my Trusty Shellbacks than which no respect is greater.

The *Rodney*'s notorious 'Shagbat' (Walrus amphibia is launched. *Kavanagh Collection*.

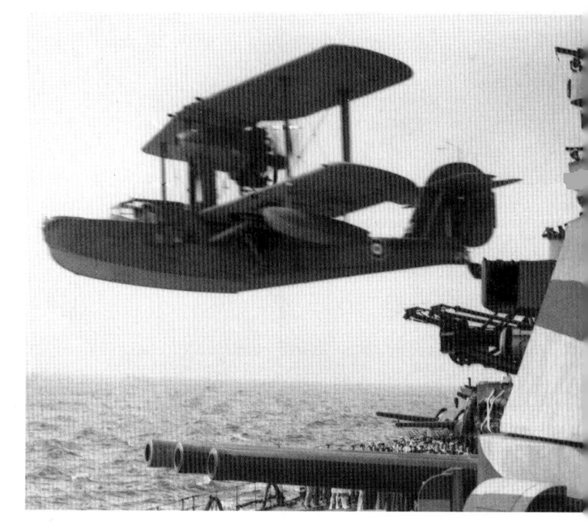

bove (clockwise from the top left): Petty Officer Bill Myers aboard the battleship in summer 1942 (*Myers* *ollection*); Admiral Bruce Fraser chats with a junior officer on *Rodney*'s Admiral's Bridge (*Maddison Collection*); MS *Eagle* sinks astern of *Rodney* during the Pedestal convoy (*Myers Collection*); a Stuka dives on *Rodney* *Maddison Collection*). Below: *Rodney* and two destroyers at Mers-El-Kebir, early 1943. *IWM A13035*.

Clockwise, from top left: The Snowden brothers, with Allan, right, and Jack, left. They met in Greenock in 1943, just prior to *Rodney* sailing for the Med and soldier Jack being posted to North Africa (*Snowden Collection*); Leading Seaman James Thoirs wears his *Rodney* hat ribbon with pride (*Mrs M. Watson*); A fresh-faced Midshipman Roger Morris (*Morris Collection*); *Rodney* fires on German troop concentrations in Normandy (*Sharp Collection*); the battleship bombards Alderney *(Morris Collection)*.

Inside the ship, decks were littered with broken glass and splintered wood. The heads suffered ruptured water pipes, flooding and urinals thrown off their mountings; the ship's longitudinal beams were cracked and had to be shored up. Bolts and rivets in plating on the hull were loosened, allowing the sea in, leading to flooding in compartments on the ship's main deck. Water mains were also ruptured.[46]

> *All electric lights were disintegrated and bulbs and sockets snapped off the leads causing live wires to be existent throughout the ship. Bulkheads, furniture, lockers and fittings were blown loose causing undue damage to permanent structures when the ship rolled.*[47]

If the after action report of one of the US Navy senior ratings is to be believed, *Bismarck* managed to hit *Rodney* with some of her secondary armament. Chief Petty Officer Miller claimed *Rodney* received four 5.9-inch hits, none of which caused serious damage. This is not corroborated by British sources and it is more likely the damage he recorded was actually caused by shell fragments. The alleged hits were: on the ADP; a 6-inch hole above the water line in the starboard side of the ship; a small hole abaft of the Octopoidal; a hit in the region of the Chief Petty Officers' mess; another 6-inch hole above the water line, wrecking three lockers belonging to senior rates.[48] The near misses that showered the ADP with shrapnel could have caused casualties on the bridge had the shells landed 20 yards further aft.[49] As it was, a near miss in the second *Bismarck* salvo fractured the hull above the armoured belt as well as showering the ADP with hot metal. Len Walters recalled that, among the damage caused to *Rodney* by her own guns, was trunking bent out of shape.

> Rodney *had 2,000 miles of wiring being held up in the bulkheads through channels and some of those channels* [were] *broken adrift, with rivets coming out, during the firing ... If they had fired a broadside they always expect a lot of repairs to be effected after that.*

During the battle, *Rodney*'s 16-inch guns fired 378 shells, her 6-inch 706. High explosive 16-inch shells were off-loaded prior to the refit, so they were all armour-piercing, which brought the benefits and problems alluded to earlier.[50] Aware of potential damage from her own guns, a fact well known from her early gunnery trials, *Rodney* had tried to adhere to the 5-gun and 4-gun pattern – salvo one, the wing guns of A and X turret (2 × 2), plus the centre of B turret; salvo two, the centre guns of A and X turrets (2 × 1) and wing guns of B turret (1 × 2). *Rodney* fired 104 salvoes of 16-inch in that fashion. Once she was well within the killing zone, and trying to inflict maximum damage in the shortest period, with no danger of enemy reply, *Rodney* fired nine broadsides, which meant all loaded guns on target firing at once. The broadsides were composed of: one eight gun salvo, three seven gun salvoes, one six gun salvo, two five gun salvoes, one three gun salvo and one two gun salvo.[51] According to Lt Cdr Wellings, X turret was the least active, due to the fact that it could not fire ahead. Technical problems caused the right hand gun of the A turret to fail completely during the action, while the left and centre guns of B turret suffered temporary faults.

These all come under the header of the usual self-inflicted bruises and scars battleships experienced in intensive combat when their big guns fired. *Rodney*, comparatively old and already badly in need of a refit prior to the action, was afloat at the battle's conclusion, could still fight and had more years of action ahead of her.

Having lasted barely more than a week on her maiden combat deployment, the brand new *Bismarck* was on the bottom of the ocean, a tomb for most of her crew and the evil ambition of a Nazi regime attempting to starve Britain into surrender via the use of surface raiders.

Notes

1 Wellings, *On His Majesty's Service.*
2 Ibid.
3 Kenneth Thompson, *HMS Rodney at War.*
4 G. Conning, IWM Department of Documents.
5 Tommy Byers, recollections in interview. See Sources.
6 Tamblin, *The Rodney Buzz,* November 2001.
7 Ludovic Kennedy, *Pursuit.*
8 Grenfell, *The Bismarck Episode.*
9 Lt Cdr Allan Baddeley, *Royal Navy.*
10 George Thomas, IWM Sound Archive.
11 Ibid.
12 Ibid.
13 Wellings, *On His Majesty's Service.*
14 Grenfell, *The Bismarck Episode.*
15 Wellings, *On His Majesty's Service.*
16 Ibid.
17 Lewis, IWM Sound Archive. In fact, as we have already seen, *Rodney* was actually being pushed to 22 knots, thanks to the heroic efforts of her engineering department.
18 Ludovic Kennedy, *Pursuit.*
19 Sopocko, *Gentlemen, The* Bismarck *Has Been Sunk.*
20 Ludovic Kennedy, *Pursuit.*
21 As with other signals quoted in this chapter, sourced in Wellings, *On His Majesty's Service.*
22 The hard-charging Captain Philip Vian's destroyer squadron was supposed to rendezvous with the two British battleships, *Piorun* taking over screening duties on *Rodney* while *Cossack, Sikh* and *Zulu* provided protection for the fleet flagship. However, on realising his ships were within striking distance of *Bismarck,* Vian decided to use his initiative and launch an attack on the German battleship during the night of 26/27 May. Despite the destroyers' valiant efforts no torpedo hits were achieved, due to high seas, but the attacks did further the process of wearing down already frazzled *Bismarck* sailors.
23 Wellings, *On His Majesty's Service.*
24 Frank Summers, in interview with the author.
25 Sopocko, *Gentlemen, The* Bismarck *Has Been Sunk.*
26 Major J.E.M. Ruffer RMs. See Sources.
27 Ernest Beeston, interview published in the *Westmoreland Gazette,* 10 May 1991.
28 Lt Donald Campbell, *An Eyewitness Account of The Sinking of The* Bismarck, an unpublished account, held by the archives of the now disbanded HMS *Rodney* Association.
29 Miroslaw Zbigniew Skwiot and Elzbieta Teresea Prusinowska, *Hunting the Bismarck.*
30 David Mearns and Rob White, *Hood and Bismarck.*
31 Miroslaw Zbigniew Skwiot and Elzbieta Teresea Prusinowska, *Hunting the Bismarck.*
32 Sopocko, *Gentlemen, The* Bismarck *Has Been Sunk.*
33 Mullenheim-Rechberg, *Battleship Bismarck.*
34 *Rodney* battle observer.
35 Mullenheim-Rechberg, *Battleship Bismarck.*
36 Wellings, *On His Majesty's Service.*
37 Mullenheim-Rechberg, *Battleship Bismarck.*
38 Miroslaw Zbigniew Skwiot and Elzbieta Teresea Prusinowska, *Hunting the Bismarck.*
39 *Rodney*'s battle observer.
40 Ibid.
41 Sopocko, *Gentlemen, The* Bismarck *Has Been Sunk.*

42 Battle observer, HMS *Rodney*.
43 *Rodney*, Official History.
44 Miroslaw Zbigniew Skwiot and Elzbieta Teresea Prusinowska, *Hunting the Bismarck*. The stern had been welded on and was poorly constructed.
45 *The Rodney Buzz*, April 1997.
46 Wellings, *On His Majesty's Service*.
47 Ibid.
48 Ibid.
49 Ibid.
50 The *Rodney*'s armour-piercing shells weighed 2,053 lbs. In addition to being heavier than 16-inch high explosive 'bullets', they were also longer, 6 ft 4-inches, against 5 ft 7-inches for the HE.
51 Wellings, *On His Majesty's Service*.

Chapter Thirteen

NO SIRENS, NO CHEERS

The Home Fleet made its way north, the battleships in company with *Cossack*, *Sikh* and *Zulu*, and by 12.30 pm *Dorsetshire* and *Maori* had caught up. Adding strength to the screening force was *Jupiter*, which arrived soon after and another nine destroyers had orders to join as soon as they could. It was of the utmost importance to protect the capital ships from U-boat and air attack, especially as the low fuel level left little spare capacity for evasive action. In *Rodney*, during the afternoon, a late breakfast of sausages, bread and butter was served to the officers, washed down with steaming hot tea. The wardroom inevitably buzzed with talk of that morning's battle, while *Rodney*'s upper deck was populated by sailors and marines hunting for souvenirs. Many found jagged pieces of shrapnel washed into the gutters after the upper deck was hosed down. The biggest souvenir collection belonged to the ship's Protestant padre, allegedly 'busy collecting while the battle was still going on.'[1] As he hunted for his own souvenirs on the upper deck, Sub Lt Sopocko was seized by the Roman Catholic chaplain, who exclaimed:

> *Didn't I say at the beginning that the* Rodney *would sink the* Bismarck*!?*[2]

The Polish officer agreed he had. Very light-headed from fatigue, already feeling the battle must have been a dream, Sub Lt Sopocko headed below and clambered into his hammock. Surfacing from a deep sleep shortly before 4.00 pm, he made his way up through the ship to the bridge, to pull a watch, finding all the windows had ultimately been broken by the blast of *Rodney*'s 16-inch guns and cleaning up was still in progress. Captain Dalrymple-Hamilton was asleep in his upright chair while Lt Cdr Crawford was pacing up and down, clearly still excited by his ship's victory. The Captain was woken up to respond to a visual signal from *Dorsetshire*, another Devonport Division ship, which had picked up eighty-five *Bismarck* survivors before reports of U-boat activity forced her to leave the scene.[3] The cruiser 'signalled her congratulations as from one West Country ship to another.'[4]

Sub Lieutenant Sopocko noted that Captain Dalrymple-Hamilton was not one to gloat over the defeat of an enemy, signalling back 'however much satisfaction he had gained from the first part of the action he was sorry it had to end as it did.'

Eager to hear reports of their key role in eliminating the *Bismarck* menace, at both 1.00 pm and 6.00 pm *Rodney*'s men gathered around tannoy speakers to hear BBC news broadcasts. They were disappointed to hear only of the part played by the Swordfish of *Victorious* and *Ark Royal*. There were but general references to the other ships of the fleet being involved. Of course, it was too early to expect detailed accounts, especially with radio silence being observed to avoid giving away the position of the Home Fleet, which was still south of Ireland. Intercepted German signals traffic continued to indicate a massive air attack was imminent but all that transpired was four Luftwaffe planes making half-hearted runs. Only two of them made a direct lunge at the battleships, the other pair of bandits deterred by flak thrown up by the destroyer screen. Then, a German aircraft came in very low over the water from ahead, the destroyers opening fire first, followed by *King George V* and, finally, *Rodney*. The bandit was surrounded by ack-ack shell splashes but escaped unscathed, ditching bombs to hasten its exit. Aboard *Rodney*, Leading Seaman Richard Hughes was in command of an anti-aircraft gun that may well have shot down another German aircraft, which now approached *Rodney* fast from astern.

> *An aircraft came in sight on our starboard quarter, a big Focker Wulf, and I was closed up on the after pom-pom,* [for by] *then of course, we had gone back to our normal action stations. I told my lookout to report to the ADP that there was an aircraft in sight. We* [initially] *didn't know whose it was or what it was ... we had a dumb period from the ADP. Obviously they couldn't recognise it ...*

Eventually, the order to open fire came through, the overcast sky dotted by a constellation of tiny fireballs, which exploded with a sharp crack, the anti-aircraft guns creating a deafening 'rat-a-tat'.[5] Hughes watched the enemy aircraft 'dip over the horizon', uncertain if it was crashing or just beating a retreat.

> *... whether* [that was because] *we hit it or not that is another thing. She didn't come back to worry us.*

The Admiralty's official history of *Rodney* is in no doubt the battleship drew Luftwaffe blood.

> *... one of the aircraft was hit by* RODNEY *and was last seen losing height as it disappeared four miles astern.*[6]

However, a hundred miles south, two of *Rodney*'s former escorts, the *Mashona* and *Tartar*, came under heavy air attack. *Mashona* was sunk, with the loss of 45 ratings and one officer. *Piorun*, still making for Plymouth, weathered half a dozen attacks by enemy aircraft, all of which she successfully fought off.

Watching the impressive bulk of *Rodney* falling and rising astern of his flagship, Admiral Tovey decided a tribute was in order for his former ship.

He had received a congratulatory visual signal from *Rodney* earlier, which finished with the opinion that the old battleship had in the *Bismarck* battle made up for 'the *Gneisenau* disappointment', an obvious reference to the *Chilean Reefer* incident. In replying, Tovey's message thanked *Rodney*'s officers and men for their tribute and speculated *Bismarck*'s sinking would have an impact far in excess of the loss of a single ship.

> *No one was more pleased than myself that the* Rodney *had the opportunity to play such an effective part in the operations.*

Tovey expressed his great satisfaction that *Rodney* and other ships of the fleet had instinctively done the right thing, without the need for 'signalled instructions'. Possibly recalling his own experience of *Rodney*'s troublesome torpedo tubes, Tovey added:

> *The hits scored with your torpedoes must have much encouraged* Bismarck's *sinking feeling and I think it is the only case of effective use of torpedoes by a capital ship.*

Tovey finished by sending congratulations to the Engine Room department for their great efforts in ensuring *Rodney* could maintain a high speed over such a long period of time 'under such difficult conditions.'[7]

After Captain Dalrymple-Hamilton read Tovey's words to *Rodney*'s ship's company via the public address system, a return message of thanks was sent, which concluded:

> *We all feel it was most fitting that the* Rodney *should have been in action for the first time under the eye of her former Captain.*[8]

The *Rodney*, with an escort provided by *Maori*, *Sikh* and the Canadian-manned destroyer *Columbia*, the latter a former US Navy lend-lease destroyer, parted company with the rest of the fleet at 5.00 pm on 28 May, with orders to head for the Clyde, *King George V* setting course for Loch Long.

The *Rodney*, her oil tanks almost dry, arrived off Greenock at 3.10 am on 29 May[9] – the day she was originally meant to reach Halifax. The battleship immediately set to replenishing her oil and victuals. Most importantly, *Rodney* took aboard ammunition to replenish magazines emptied by the *Bismarck* action. In doing so, there was an exchange that rather illustrated the profound ignorance, even at the time, of just what an amazing victory she had helped achieve and how important her role had been. 'The *Victorious* had preceded us and was received with cheers for the crippling torpedo[10] one of her aircraft had delivered,' observed *Rodney*'s Lt Cdr Campbell.

> *Making fast to the buoy, people stared at us: 'Oh – there's old* Rodbox *again; thought she was taking a fast convoy to Halifax.' No sirens, no cheers, nobody gave a damn. We sent a signal requesting immediate replenishment of ammunition. The reply was: 'What did you do with the last lot?' A bit hard don't you think?*[11]

Even worse, legend has it that, as *Rodney* sailed in, the Admiral of the Port asked Captain Dalrymple Hamilton to ensure his men lined the upper deck to cheer *Victorious* for her part in the famous victory. Dalrymple-Hamilton reportedly responded:

> *Sir, you are standing on the Quarter-deck of the ship that sank the* Bismarck.[12]

However, radio reports were finally giving a fuller account of the *Bismarck* action and there was at least a photograph of *Rodney* in the newspapers, but she never really obtained the prominence she deserved. But, as second gunnery officer Peter Wells-Cole would later remark, seeking headlines was not a priority for the battleship.

> *At the time there was a very small response to what* Rodney *did in that battle. I think it was very odd. I don't know why our part was largely ignored, but there again I don't think* Rodney *was seeking any publicity.*

Perhaps it was deliberate on the part of the Admiralty, for it would not do for the British people to know that a worn out 16-year-old battlewagon had done more damage to the *Bismarck* than the brand new *King George V*, especially when gambling on 14-inch guns for the new class of battleships had been a controversial decision. The long reach of maritime-based airpower, even ancient Swordfish torpedo bombers, was also worth emphasising as a deterrent to enemy battleships even setting sail in future. This worked, for Hitler became so paranoid about British carriers he told his fleet commanders they were not to send their surviving capital ships to sea unless they knew where the carriers were, or had sunk them prior to deployment. Certainly, during meetings with the press, the Admiralty was keen for the Commanding Officer of *Victorious* to tell his story, although less interest was shown in what Captain Dalrymple-Hamilton and the CO of *Norfolk* had to say. Due to such coverage some people realised *Rodney* at least took part in the destruction of *Bismarck*, with some of her sailors being thanked by the residents of Greenock's bars, who bought them more than a few pints of beer, with whisky chasers.[13]

A.V. Alexander, the First Lord of the Admiralty, civilian head of the Navy, visited the ship accompanied by a newsreel film crew, thanking *Rodney*'s men for their efforts. As he came aboard, he was confronted with a brand new, lovingly carved and varnished wooden tablet, hanging from the battle honours board.

BISMARCK, *1941*

Leaving the ship the following day, for he and other Polish officers had been appointed to other warships instead of going to America in *Rodney* as expected, Sub Lt Sopocko stopped by the battle honours board and, swelling with pride, gazed at its latest addition. Walking down the gangway, Sopocko and his countrymen felt they were leaving 'something very near and dear to us.'

As the motorboat chugged away from the towering *Rodney*, on her quarter-deck a large group of Royal Navy officers saluted the Poles, for whom, after all, Britain had gone to war in 1939.[14]

Battleship *Rodney* set sail for Canada on 4 June, the sea calm despite an overcast sky, expecting to reach Halifax six days later, the intention being to push her worn out engines hard again, with the hope of achieving 19 knots. Occasional zigzagging to avoid U-boats caused a two knot drop but she had plenty of fuel to manage that particular manoeuvre. Accompanied by a four-strong destroyer screen and providing protection for the Union Castle Mail Steam Ship *Windsor Castle*, the *Rodney* retained on board additional passengers, now including the future head of RAF Bomber Command, Air Vice Marshal Arthur Harris, his wife and their baby daughter. The youngster was introduced to the officers prior to lunch on the first day of the voyage, the US Navy's Lt Cdr Wellings noting:

> *Quite strange to see a 20 month old baby in the wardroom of a BB* [battleship] *during wartime – or any time.*[15]

Harris and family were given the ship's Admiral's quarters for the crossing, which, while comfortable, were at the stern of the battleship. As such, they suffered from dreadful propeller vibration, particularly as *Rodney* had to maintain a high speed to outpace U-boats. According to Harris he felt like he was permanently clog dancing.[16] The ship's rolling motion also made his wife very seasick and so the future devastator of the Third Reich had to look after the baby's needs himself; both feeding and changing nappies, with assistance from an assigned Royal Marine who acted as 'nanny'. Harris was horrified at the prospect of washing nappies. He later confessed the most disgusting ones were wrapped in newspaper and shoved out of a porthole, revealing his dirty deed to Captain Dalrymple-Hamilton, who, no doubt with a twinkle in his eye, allegedly told him:

> *Don't you know, Sir, that in wartime we're not even allowed to throw garbage overboard because submarines could follow it up!*[17]

Harris acknowledged he had heard of that warning but felt it was unlikely any German U-boat captain in the Atlantic would find a trail of nappies and realise they led to a golden opportunity to torpedo a battleship.

Typically, for an RAF officer, Harris could not help but observe, after Dalrymple-Hamilton told him the story of *Bismarck*'s destruction, that it was a single torpedo from an aircraft that had reduced the German battleship to a helpless state. He also speculated that *Rodney*'s encounter with *Bismarck* must have been 'a fairly hair-raising task for this ancient old battle wagon.'[18] During a tour of *Rodney*, Harris was shown the dent in *Rodney*'s armoured deck caused by the Norway bomb. The cheerful demeanour of the sailor who acted as his tour guide, seemed to indicate to the future RAF Bomber Command chief that the Navy had still not learned to respect the potential of airpower to sink battleships. His sour attitude towards his Navy hosts was not improved when Harris was showered with flakes of paint and cork coating, while eating dinner, due to an overhead pom-pom gun opening fire without warning. Going onto the upper deck to see what the racket was about, Harris found an RAF Whitley circling overhead, having been mistaken for a German bomber when it suddenly lunged out of low clouds. Harris was outraged at the Navy's 'no questions asked' attitude to air defence.

> *... the airman is shot at by everybody, and usually without the slightest justification.*[19]

Clearly *Rodney*'s anti-aircraft gunners were more vigilant about the threat from bombers than Harris had imagined, their justification being the dent in the ship's armoured deck.

By 6 June the destroyers had departed, intelligence reports revealing there were no U-boats in the immediate vicinity. At Halifax, *Rodney* received a far better reception than she had at home for her part in the destruction of the *Bismarck*. The ship was swamped with reporters, but *Rodney* soon sailed for Boston. On 11 June, while en route for the American port, Lt Cdr Wellings spoke to *Rodney*'s men over the tannoy system. He welcomed the fact that *Rodney* and other British warships were refitting in US yards, relieving the strain on UK dockyards and enabling the Royal Navy's men to acquaint themselves with the American people, both at work and play.

> *I am sure they will, as I do, like you and admire your courage and determination.*

Lt Cdr Wellings said *Rodney*'s time in Boston would create a mutual understanding, which would remain long after the defeat of Hitler. He finished by thanking *Rodney* for being such a good host to both himself and the USN senior ratings.

> *I was particularly fortunate to be with you in the chase and battle with the* Bismarck.[20]

At 11.00 pm on 12 June, *Rodney* came alongside in Boston Navy Yard, Lt Cdr Wellings spotting his wife and three year-old daughter waiting for him on the waterfront. The following day the Wellings family was treated to tea with the *Rodney*'s officers in the battleship, while an armed US Marine Corps security detail trooped aboard, to take custody of 'thirteen large boxes and three trunks of confidential and secret material'[21] carried across the Atlantic in a sealed storeroom. The marines escorted the top secret cargo all the way to the headquarters of US Naval Intelligence in Washington D.C.,[22] the documents no doubt detailing the growing military co-operation between Britain and 'neutral' America. When Lt Cdr Wellings finally left the ship on 14 June, all *Rodney*'s officers came to the gangway to bid him a fond farewell.

The *Rodney* did not, however, get a warm welcome from all of Boston's inhabitants, for Americans of German descent, and some with Irish roots, were far from keen on the presence of a British warship or its people.

Junior rating James McLean, who was ashore within hours of *Rodney*'s arrival, experienced the hostility first-hand.

> *The ship entered the inner basin in the dark and next morning I was eager to see what America looked like, but what struck me was huge white lettering on the side of one of the dockyard buildings, saying: 'TAKE THE WAR BACK TO ENGLAND – GOD SAVE THE KING, BECAUSE WE WON'T'. In addition, while walking in the city, we had lighted cigarette ends thrown at us out of the cars, but they were in the minority. The majority of the Boston people, most of whom were descendants of early English immigrants, were absolutely marvellous and welcomed many of the ship's company into their homes.*

Tommy Byers also found a pocket of hostility, discovering that *Rodney*'s sailors and marines sometimes had to fight to gain respect.

> *I remember going ashore the first night we were allowed with Ken Gardiner, a mate of mine, who was an Able Seaman. We went into what we thought was an American pub. You could have cut the atmosphere with a knife. As we came out we looked up at the sign over the pub: it was a German beer house. We had got the message correctly. We were not welcome in there. The Italians used to attack us also, as we passed through their area, until there was a big punch up and after that we could walk where we wanted to!*

The US Marines marked out their territory too, telling *Rodney*'s men they should stay away from a downtown bar and nightclub the Leathernecks described as 'their headquarters'[23] in Boston. However, the warning had the opposite effect, acting 'like a magnet and at the time we had some very taut[24] hands ...'

> *We had the naval heavyweight boxing champion and the Royal Navy middleweight champion boxer on board.*[25]

The *Rodney*'s men stormed into the bar, the US Marines putting up a spirited defence of their turf during a brawl rather like a scene from a John Wayne movie. The fighting spilled over onto the nightspot's stage, where one of *Rodney*'s boxers had a big bass drum smashed over his head, the remains ending up around his ankles.

> *... they sorted the American marines out anyway so we upheld the reputation of the Royal Navy in Boston at that time.*[26]

However, the abiding memory *Rodney*'s men retained of their ten-week stay in Boston was of warm hospitality and, as Len Nicholl found, some good-humoured rivalry dating back to the War of Independence.

> *We got in to Boston just before Bunker Hill Day and they gave us some stick about that being the day 'we beat you limeys' but they were only kidding. Overall we had a*

very good time and they were very hospitable. Our time there included a visit to New Bedford, which was a whaling town, on 27 July 1941. Some police met us and escorted us down there and they gave us a load of bumph on the great hurricane of 1938.

Many of the local people had roots back in Britain, or 'The Old Country', as they called it. They crowded around the bottom of the *Rodney*'s gangway, calling out for sailors or marines from such places as Liverpool or London, wherever their ancestors hailed from. Mick Kavanagh was overwhelmed with generosity, finding the Americans 'out of this world'.

We lived aboard ship but we got invited to various peoples' houses and one hotel the owner gave us free rooms if we wanted them. There was plenty of drink but no trouble that I recall.

James McLean had an encounter that could have come straight from the pages of a Hollywood script.

One night my pal and I were drinking in a bar at the Central Station. The trains don't come into the huge main hall, but stop outside and are boarded through the numerous side doors. Whilst drinking our beers, a huge black man approached and asked if it was OK to sit next to me at the bar, so I said something like 'help yourself'. There were dozens of armed soldiers all over the place because President Roosevelt was cruising on holiday in his private yacht off the coast. Eventually, this black man asked if we would like to be his guests for the night and so we agreed. He took us outside the station, called a taxi and took us into the centre of the city, which was part of the black community. In this restaurant, which was all black waiters and so on, he introduced us to the manager, saying we were his 'English' friends. We had a wonderful evening, nice meal, wine, cigars, etc., and late on he took us back to the Central Station, where we went to one of the side doors. We were stopped by a US Army Officer and challenged, so we produced our Pay Books, our naval identity books. The black man then took us out to a platform where a long train was standing and we followed him into one of the carriages. My-oh-my, what a beautiful scene it was: velvet cushions; silk curtains; telephones; drinks cabinet etc. So then the black man told us he was the personal servant to the President and had been with him for years. After a while he took us outside the station and paid for a taxi to take us back to the dockyard. I remember him saying if we had been white American sailors we would have, in the first place, probably told him to get to hell out of it. Because we were friendly and treated him as an equal he had decided to entertain us and then show us 'round the President's private train. What an experience that was.

And American hospitality seemed to know no bounds, as McLean discovered further afield.

While the ship was in dock, the American authorities arranged for every one of the ship's company to spend two weeks at an ex-army camp near the Canadian border, which comprised of a number of large huts with army beds, fully furnished plus showers and baths. Special US Army cooks provided us with lovely meals all day, and we got fresh fruits, sweets and more. In addition, ex-US Services organisations came in the evenings on a regular basis, to provide entertainment and singsongs, etc. Hence, when our names were posted on the main notice board in the ship's recreation space, it gave details of departure times and the number of the bus we were to board. There were about a dozen buses, which took us to and brought us back from the camp. It was very good of the US authorities to provide these breaks, in order that we could at least have a little relaxation, with no set routines regarding turning in at night times and getting out of bed each morning.

The stay in Boston allowed the British servicemen an opportunity to get a good look at the nation rapidly superseding Britain as the dominant power on earth. They found the standard of living of even working class Americans much higher than anyone from that social strata could expect back in the UK. Sailors from the *Rodney* who had last visited America during Prohibition were delighted to find that alcohol lubricated society once more; everyone in the States was generally much happier. Winthrop Rockefeller, the twenty-nine year old grandson of the founder of the Standard Oil Company and brother of Nelson Rockefeller, a future Vice President of the United States, even invited a group of the *Rodney*'s men to New York for four days at his expense.[27]

'Up-homers', with ordinary Americans, who were most eager to welcome them into their family homes, was a regular occurrence for *Rodney*'s sailors and marines. As is inevitable with servicemen on shore leave, particularly those who have been at war and now find themselves in a city at peace, with all the freedom and distractions so unavailable at home, there were those who got drunk, became involved in random fist fights and even tried to desert. Ashore, in a port under British jurisdiction, drunken sailors were usually extracted from trouble by a naval shore patrol and immediately hurried back to the ship, where they could sober up and face any resulting charges at the Captain's Table the following morning. However, in Boston, the city police force swiftly carted drunken brawlers away for a night in the cells, which often meant they failed to make it back aboard ship for expiration of leave at 7 am. Senior ratings and Royal Marine NCOs from *Rodney* were attached to the Boston police, helping sort out any disturbances, and on some occasions accompanying them in successful pursuit of deserters holed up with American women in distant suburbs. As the end of the refit approached, *Rodney* hosted a dance to repay the people of Boston for their hospitality, where everyone joined in the singing of a new song made popular by Vera Lynn, called 'We'll Meet Again.' There were many lumps in throats and moist eyes. A solo rendition by one of the ship's sailors of 'When the Lights of London Shine Again', also stirred emotions.

During the refit, the damage caused by the German bomb off Norway was finally remedied, with Boston's yardies replacing the cracked portion of deck with the special section of armoured plate brought over by the battleship herself. *Rodney* still possessed a part of the bomb. 'It was about the size of a dinner plate,' recalled Charles Barton.

The officers decided they wanted a piece of it mounted on a piece of wood for display in ward room. But we couldn't cut the piece off – it wore out the teeth on the saw in the workshop – so we gave up. It wasn't worth the risk of damaging the saw any further.

The refit was completed on 12 August, followed by several days of sea trials and rectification work, together with a visit to a range at Rhode Island for degaussing against magnetic mines. The ship then spent 48 hours taking on board her ammunition, which had been stored ashore in secure bunkers. At sunset on 20 August, *Rodney* set sail, the citizens of Boston lining the banks of the Mystic River to see the famous British battleship leave, one young female onlooker asking how 'a thing that shape'[28] managed to float. *Rodney* sailed out under a new Commanding Officer, in the form of Captain J.W. Rivett Carnac.

James William Rivett-Carnac, aged forty-nine, the second son of a knighted clergyman, saw action in the First World War and earned the Distinguished Service Cross, for his service as the executive officer, and gunnery officer, of the cruiser *Cleopatra*, during the British campaign to protect the Baltic States from Bolsehvik invasion. Commanding Officer of the cruiser HMS *Coventry* in the mid-1930s, between late 1936 and August 1938, Rivett-Carnac was CO of the New Zealand-crewed cruiser HMNZS *Leander* and also Commodore of the New Zealand Squadron. Returning to the UK, he served in the Admiralty and in other shore-based staff jobs until appointed to *Rodney*.[29] Meanwhile, Dalrymple Hamilton had been promoted to Rear Admiral and appointed Admiral Commanding Iceland, an important job as he was to play a major part in ensuring Royal Navy escorts for vital convoys across the Atlantic, and later to Russia, were properly supported. He would encounter *Rodney* again, more than once, maintaining a special bond with the battleship until the end of her life.

The good spirits generated by the refit in Boston were soon swallowed up by the 'drab routine of war'; the American interlude already seemed like 'Groucho Marx had burst unexpectedly into the last act of *Hamlet*.'[30] Within days of leaving Boston there was a raider alert, the German heavy cruiser *Hipper* allegedly loose in the South Atlantic. The ship went to Action Stations but the alarm came to nothing. *Rodney* set course for Bermuda and a few weeks of work-up, before heading back into the war as a fully operational fighting unit. Sailing from Tobacco Bay, she was involved in exercises and gunnery shoots, plus a secret combat exercise with the, supposedly still neutral, US Navy.

After Bermuda, which honoured the ship with a civic-sponsored dance, *Rodney* was ordered to join Force H, based out of Gibraltar, arriving at the Rock on 24 September. By the evening of the same day she was at sea again, heading for the central Mediterranean, in company with sister ship HMS *Nelson*, the current flagship of Force H, and *Ark Royal*. Still under the command of Admiral Somerville, Force H had already neutralised the Vichy French fleet, bombarded Genoa, helped bring *Bismarck* to heel for *Rodney* to destroy, and was now tasked primarily with providing escorts for convoys.

On Operation Halberd, Force H was to rendezvous with a convoy already under escort from *Prince of Wales*, cruisers and destroyers, which had set sail along with its nine fast merchant ships from Britain. Convoy WS 11X was carrying badly needed troops and supplies to the besieged island fortress of Malta, which was being pounded from the air by both the German and Italian air forces. The British clung to Malta because it was perfectly placed to act as a base of operations for naval and air forces attacking enemy convoys taking troops and supplies to North Africa. Germany's Afrika Korps threatened to take the Suez Canal, as a precursor to capturing vital oil fields in Iraq and the Arabian Peninsula. To keep the Italians and Germans guessing, the destination of the Operation Halberd convoy was said to be North Africa via the Cape. Sowing yet more confusion, from Gibraltar *Nelson* sailed out into the Atlantic, allegedly heading home to the UK, while *Rodney*, which had hoisted Admiral Somerville's flag but did not have him aboard, headed east with *Ark Royal* for the Straits of Gibraltar. Having, hopefully, succeeded in deceiving spies based across Gibraltar Bay in Spain that there was no major concentration of naval power to escort a convoy, early on the morning of 25 September, well out of sight of land, *Nelson* changed course to make a rendezvous with *Prince of Wales* and convoy WS 11X. Coming through the Straits, those sailing in the merchant ships and escort vessels were now informed of their real destination. Knowing they would face intense air and sea attack, it appeared to many the current protection force was rather weak. However, up ahead was an imposing sight, which immediately boosted their confidence: *Rodney, Ark Royal,* the cruiser *Hermione,* with attendant destroyers. An anti-aircraft gunner manning a weapon on top of the Y turret of *Prince of Wales* remarked it was 'a sight I shall always remember ...'

> *It was a breath-taking display of warships.*[31]

Further attempts at deception were made, with *Ark Royal, Nelson, Hermione* and escorts sailing close to the North African coast, while *Rodney* and *Prince of Wales,* with their cruisers and destroyers, took the convoy on a dog-leg, north-east and then south-east. Concentrating again on the morning of 27 September, the warships settled into position around, and among, the merchant vessels. The big ships – cruisers and battleships – were there to provide AA cover and also tackle the Italian fleet if it dared to come out. The main function of *Ark Royal*'s fighters was putting out a long-distance air-defence picket, hopefully preventing the majority of German and Italian aircraft from reaching the convoy.

The following day, Italian scout planes spotted elements of the convoy off Spain's Balearic Islands and both submarines and fast attack craft were soon lying in wait off the island of Pantelleria, close to the Tunisian coast. Meanwhile, the Italian battle fleet was at sea, the strength of the British escort force not correctly reported to Admiral Angelo Iachino, who flew his flag in the brand new battleship *Littorio,* with the battlewagon *Vittorio Veneto,* three heavy cruisers, two light cruisers and fourteen destroyers in support. Axis forces hoped to hit the convoy as it passed through the narrow gap between Sicily and North Africa, the notorious Narrows, within easy reach of airfields where Italian and German aircraft were based. There was also less room to hide from attack craft and submarines. Although German planes harried the convoy in the morning, intensive air attacks by big, three-engined Italian torpedo bombers started in earnest during the afternoon, under fine Indian summer skies, with calm seas, a light breeze and just a few distant, dark thunder-clouds. Len Nicholl recalled that an officer in *Rodney* correctly predicted the pattern of events.

> *We had a Commander aboard, who had done a lot of time in the Mediterranean, had been bombed, and he assured us the Italians would bomb us in the afternoon and it turned out to be quite true. They also had a go in the evening but not very much in the morning.*

The *Ark Royal*'s Fulmar fighters intercepted some of the attackers at low level, while others were tackled at high altitude, as they dropped bombs with great inaccuracy. The extremely brave Italian torpedo-bomber pilots – flying below the upper decks of the ships – did manage to penetrate the Fulmar screen, although their success rate, at least against the Halberd convoy, was pathetic.

It was like watching a movie, such was the general lack of fear of being hit by the Italians.[32] Mick Kavanagh was one of those who enjoyed the show.

> *I saw a few air attacks, stood there looking at them, like a fool, watching the aircraft coming in. You don't really think of things like your own mortality, when you are as young as I was back then.*

One of *Rodney*'s officers described the Italians as attacking 'with great courage, considering the large target they presented, and they met with tremendous fire.'

> *Everywhere you could see them falling into the drink.*[33]

Deep below decks, in the machinery spaces, the men of the engineering department possibly found it more stressful weathering the enemy attacks than those who could see how ineffectual they actually were.

'You knew how close the enemy was getting by what guns were firing,' explained Charles Barton.

> *First of all you heard the 4.7-inch and the 6-inch guns and then the pom-poms, which would open up on one side of the ship or other. Down in the engine room you would look at each other, waiting for the bomb to hit, wondering if this was it. But, then the pom-poms on the other side of the ship would open up. With a great sense of relief you realised the enemy had passed overhead and you had not heard or felt any explosion.*

Three Italian torpedo-bombers targetted *Nelson*, which sustained a telling hit on her port bow, ripping open her hull and letting in thousands of tons of water. During the enemy assault on 27 September, air gunners in both *Rodney* and *Prince of Wales* concentrated on a particular enemy torpedo-bomber, which was rather too closely pursued by one of *Ark Royal*'s Fulmar fighters. The latter was swiftly shot down, but fortunately its aircrew was plucked from the sea by an RN destroyer. There was jubilation at this 'kill' by the *Rodney*'s gunners, including Len Nicholl and his fellow marines in one of the 6-inch gun turrets.

> *We cheered, only to realize it was one of our own.*

James McLean spotted a victim of *Rodney*'s excellent, if misguided, air defence gunnery.

> *I clearly remember seeing this Fleet Air Arm pilot, on a rubber float, passing down the starboard side of the ship waving his fist at us.*

Meanwhile, the formidable Italian naval striking fleet had been detected by RAF reconnaissance aircraft, some 80 miles ahead of the convoy and steaming at high speed to intercept it. In response, *Rodney*, *Nelson* and *Prince of Wales*, together with *Ark Royal*, destroyers and cruisers, were sent to meet this threat. Due to her damage *Nelson* soon dropped out, ultimately retiring from the convoy the following day, damage control teams still battling to stem the flooding and with her speed reduced to less than 15 knots.

As senior ship on the scene, *Prince of Wales* ran up signal flags indicating the British force should steam at 28 knots. This caused a fair bit of amusement in the *Rodney*.

> *... because it was several knots faster than we had ever done in our prime.*[34]

Prince of Wales and *Ark Royal* raced ahead, leaving *Rodney* to huff and puff along in their wake, doing a stately 18 knots. The British carrier was intending to send her Swordfish to attack the Italian fleet. When they detected a Royal Navy counter-stroke hurtling towards them, believing they faced carriers as well as two battleships and lacking their own air support, the Italians turned around and headed for Naples. *Rodney*, *Prince of Wales* and the other RN warships pursued the enemy until darkness. Having not brought the enemy to action, they returned to the convoy, rejoining it shortly before 9 pm. Twelve Swordfish and four Fulmars had taken off, but failed to find the Italian fleet, returning to *Ark Royal*, with a number of the planes' tanks containing barely enough fuel to make a landing. *Rodney* and *Prince of Wales* soon followed the Force H flagship back to Gibraltar. In the meantime, Convoy WS 11X reached Malta on the afternoon of 28 September, having suffered only one ship loss, the *Imperial Star*.

There followed a period of inactivity for *Rodney*, which was deeply frustrating, the battleship parked at Gibraltar, which could never hope to possess the same scale of diversions as Boston.

To keep themselves occupied, sailors of the engineering department paid a visit to *Nelson* in dry dock, inspecting the massive hole in her bows and picking up a few tips on damage control.

'I had no affection for *Rodney*, because she had so many mechanical problems that needed constant attention,' confessed Charles Barton.

> *However, you did know that you were safe, because she was so well protected. That* Nelson *survived such a blow illustrated just how tough the design was.*

While *Rodney* was alongside, mailbags bulging with letters posted by the ship's sailors and marines to new friends back in Boston, somehow came back. Among them were a number of love letters as well as thankyou notes to hospitable Bostonians. Captain Rivett-Carnac felt obliged to write to newspapers in the American city conveying the ship's thanks and explaining *Rodney* had not callously forgotten all those people who had been such superb hosts. In the absence of *Nelson*, which had sailed for Britain, for more extensive work following temporary repairs in Gibraltar, *Rodney* became flagship of Force H. On 16 October, Force H deployed from Gibraltar, its task escorting *Ark Royal* and *Furious* as they ferried naval aircraft and aircrews to Malta, from where the planes would be flown on interdiction missions against enemy shipping. Two British cruisers and a pair of destroyers temporarily attached to Force H would slip into Malta at the same time. During this operation, Asdic[35] operators in the escorting destroyers detected what they thought were enemy submarines several times, but in one instance at least, the 'contact' was actually caused by mating whales. Aboard *Rodney* Admiral Somerville observed, with his customary wit:

> *It is hoped that the approach of winter will abate this nuisance by cooling the ardour of the lovesick leviathans.*[36]

Just before 2.00 am on 18 October, eleven Albacore torpedo-bombers and two Swordfish were flown off by *Ark* and *Furious*, Force H turning around and heading back to Gibraltar. Following another period of time alongside, on 30 October *Rodney* received orders to head back to the UK, leaving on 2 November. She carried back twenty-nine sailors from the destroyer *Cossack*, which had been sunk on 23 October in the Atlantic, to the west of Portugal, by *U-563*. Also aboard *Rodney* were some Italian submariner PoWs, who seemed very happy to be out of the war, while the ship's company fervently hoped they would get their first home leave in 10 months. They were to be disappointed.

Notes

1 Sopocko, *Gentlemen, The Bismarck Has Been Sunk.*
2 Ibid.
3 Only 115 of the men aboard *Bismarck* were rescued. Aside from the eighty-five in *Dorsetshire*, another twenty-five were picked up by the British destroyer *Maori*, with a further two saved by a German weather ship and three others by a German U-boat.
4 Sopocko, *Gentlemen, The Bismarck Has Been Sunk.*
5 Ibid.
6 HMS *Rodney*, Official History.
7 Quoted in Wellings, *On His Majesty's Service.*
8 Ibid. When this signal says 'in action for the first time', it means *Rodney* firing her main armament in anger for the first time.
9 Wellings, *On His Majesty's Service.*
10 While the Swordfish from *Victorious* had managed to hit *Bismarck* with one torpedo, it caused no appreciable damage to the ship. See Chapter Twelve.
11 Campbell, *An Eyewitness Account of The Sinking of The Bismarck.*
12 Seaman Oliver Scarrot, *The Rodney Buzz*, Spring 1998.
13 W. Gordon Campbell mentions the interviews with the press and the locals buying *Rodney*'s men drinks in his account of the ship's life. See Sources.
14 See People Appendix.
15 *On His Majesty's Service.*
16 *The Rodney Buzz*, July 1996.
17 Ibid.
18 Arthur Harris, *Bomber Offensive.*
19 Ibid.
20 Wellings, *On His Majesty's Service.*
21 Ibid.
22 Ibid.
23 George Thomas, IWM Sound Archive.
24 Naval slang for tough.
25 George Thomas, IWM Sound Archive.
26 Ibid.
27 Rockefeller could already see that war between America and Germany was coming, in early 1941 enlisting in the US Army as a Private. He rose to the rank of Colonel and was decorated for bravery during the Battle of Okinawa in 1945. After the war he distinguished himself in American politics, becoming a Governor of Arkansas.
28 Kenneth Thompson, *HMS Rodney at War.*
29 For more details of his career go to *http://www.unithistories.com/officers/RN_officersR.html*
30 Kenneth Thompson, *HMS Rodney at War.*
31 F.W. Bennett, quoted in *Malta Convoys.*
32 Kenneth Thompson, *HMS Rodney at War.*
33 Ibid.
34 Ibid.
35 Anti-Submarine Detection Investigation Committee, which was later known as sonar.
36 Quoted by William Jameson in *Ark Royal.*

Chapter Fourteen

WEST AFRICAN INTERLUDE

After the Japanese sent their troops to occupy Indo-China in July 1941, the writing was well and truly on the wall for war between the Empire of Japan and the Western powers. Economic sanctions by Britain, the USA and administrators of the Dutch East Indies, hardened attitudes. The British realized they must take military measures, and among the proposals was the creation of a powerful East Indies Fleet based on Singapore, which was to include both *Rodney* and *Nelson*. However, during the summer of 1941 *Rodney* was, of course, in refit at Boston and not then available for operations and nor was *Nelson*, still committed to Force H as flagship. Until those units were available, and the introduction into service of more King George V Class battleships in home waters, the Admiralty would leave protection of shipping lanes in the Pacific and Indian oceans to the US Navy. However, on 28 August 1941, with *Rodney* engaged in working up at Bermuda, the First Sea Lord, Admiral Sir Dudley Pound, formally proposed to Winston Churchill that she and *Nelson* should be sent to the Far East with a trio of elderly, unmodernised, Royal Sovereign Class battleships and a modern aircraft carrier, such as *Ark Royal*. What made this possible was the American navy playing a bigger part in Atlantic convoy escort duties, despite the USA's neutrality. The force proposed for the Far East would be slow compared with the Japanese units it was likely to face, and therefore could only protect commerce rather than seek battle; it was a deterrent rather than an offensive weapon. Churchill was displeased, as he felt a King George V Class battleship, plus a battlecruiser, preferably the modernized *Renown*, could act as both a credible deterrent to any moves by Japan against British interests in the Indian Ocean, and also form the nucleus of a striking group. The Prime Minister suggested the brand new battleship *Duke of York* could be sent, following her completion in November, working up to operational efficiency during the voyage to Singapore.[1] This idea horrified Admiral Pound, who pointed out it was best to keep *Duke of York* near a UK dockyard, in order to repair any defects. Her ship's company was also pretty raw. Pound again suggested *Rodney* and her sister ship should go East, with *Renown* and the carrier *Hermes*, ready for operations out of Singapore or Ceylon by the beginning of 1942. He also proposed, again, that the Royal Sovereign Class ships should patrol the Indian Ocean. Pound was keen to retain *Duke of York*, *King George V* and *Prince of Wales* in home waters to meet the threat of *Tirpitz*, sister to the *Bismarck*. Churchill was unimpressed. He thought the R Class were barely suitable for convoy escort work, describing them as 'floating coffins'[2] unable to survive a battle with anything bigger than a cruiser armed with 8-inch guns.

Well into October 1941, Admiral Pound argued in favour of sending *Rodney* and *Nelson*, even though the latter was by then receiving repairs to the damage caused by the Italian torpedo during the Halberd convoy, plus the R Class ships. Pound suggested such a force would be a substantial fleet in-being. To ensure victory, the Japanese would have to expose their home islands by diverting key warships to offensive operations.[3] They would be unlikely to risk such a gamble.

However, Churchill prevailed on the Admiralty to order *Prince of Wales* and battle-cruiser *Repulse* to the Far East, with plans in hand to send the brand new fleet carrier *Indomitable*, which never made it, due to damage sustained while working up in the Caribbean. On 25 October[4], five days before *Rodney* was called back to replace her, *Prince of Wales* set sail, destined with *Repulse* and four destroyers at Singapore to form Force Z. Admiral Tovey, still in command of the Home Fleet, was well aware of the marginal ability of 14-inch armed ships to handle a German battleship. Therefore, it was no surprise *Rodney* received orders for the UK, especially as *Nelson* was still out of action. On 8 November, *Rodney* reached Loch Ewe, but stayed only a matter of hours to offload her passengers and take on victuals, setting sail within hours for Iceland. During her very brief stop in Scottish waters there was a tragedy, which led to an erroneous report of Mick Kavanagh's demise.

> *There was another AB Kavanagh aboard* Rodney, *who lived not far from where I come from in Ireland. They were hauling a cable upon the forecastle and it parted, the whiplash proving lethal, as it went right through this other AB Kavanagh, killing him. We left that evening for Iceland. On a signal intercepted by one of the escorting destroyers it said they were going to bury someone at sea; saying ensigns should be at half mast for the funeral of AB Kavanagh.*

A sailor in one of the destroyers passed this information on to Mick Kavanagh's uncle, serving in another part of the Navy, informing him it was his nephew who had been killed.

> *My uncle got in touch with my mother to find out if it was true. She knew nothing of the sort. There was a lot of panic and she wrote to my divisional officer asking what was going on and asking why hadn't she been told of my death? He wrote back to her, reassuring my mother that I was not dead and it was in fact another* Rodney *sailor named Kavanagh.*

At Iceland, which had been a British base since 1940, *Rodney* operated from the Hvalfjord, which she reached on 12 November. Her function was to be on stand-by, at a few hours notice to sail, in order to intercept German surface raiders, particularly *Tirpitz*. Royal Marine gunner Len Nicholl was among those assembled on *Rodney*'s forecastle to hear the ship's one-time CO deliver justification for their presence in an anchorage, which, for them, was even more dispiriting than being at Scapa Flow. Admiral Tovey sought to explain how *Rodney*'s waiting around was not in vain, stressing that while her sailors and marines may not have enjoyed home leave for nearly a year it was a sacrifice worth making.

> *It seemed to me that Admiral Tovey had an obsession with* Rodney. *I recall he stood on a turret and explained the importance of what we were doing, but the crew was not really interested in what he had to say. Tovey told us that he knew we were looking for time at home, but he said he could not give us leave because he needed a 16-inch gun ship to watch the* Tirpitz, *in case she broke out of the Baltic.*

Tovey's faith in *Rodney* was not shared by the First Sea Lord, who regarded the KGV plus Nelson Class combination flawed, due to the comparatively slow speed of the latter, which meant that in any chase a concentration of fire power might not be achieved due to the older battleship falling too far behind.[5] However, Pound had not seen the superior punch of *Rodney* or *Nelson* compared with a KGV ship.

Tovey knew only too well how important 16-inch guns would be in any shootout with *Tirpitz*.

One *Rodney* sailor not enduring the tedium of Iceland was Able Seaman Tommy Byers who had been seconded to the Flag Staff of Force H, witnessing the end of a vessel his old battleship had frequently accompanied.

> *I became Admiral Somerville's Coxswain, piloting his launch. When* Ark Royal *was sunk on 13 November 1941, I was a Coxswain on a Motor Launch patrolling Gibraltar. We went to the scene of the sinking and stayed with the* Ark *for the night, for she was going down slowly and the crew was being taken off onto other ships. At dawn the* Ark *sank and it was a terrific sight: the roar of the water going into the funnels was tremendous. Several weeks previous to this I had pictures taken of me by the* Ark Royal's *photographers. I had seen the proofs and had ordered copies but they all went down with the ship!*

Joining *Rodney* at Iceland was Paymaster Midshipman John Wells-Cole, younger brother of *Rodney*'s deputy gunnery officer, Peter Wells-Cole.

'It was not really usual for brothers to serve in the same ship,' recalled the elder brother.

> *I think the Admiralty wrote to our parents asking if it would be a problem and they said it was okay. It wasn't a problem for him because our paths very rarely crossed.*

Wells-Cole the younger found that, as she was not then a flagship, the battleship had plenty of room.

> *A whole flat was available for the midshipmen to sling their hammocks. The Sub Lieutenant of the gunroom was a kindly New Zealander, who taught us to chant a Haka and make suitable warlike gestures and movements. He did his best to keep our mess bills under control, but as the pay of a Midshipman was five shillings per day, or £7.10 per month, some found it difficult not to be permanently in debt. We made a number of forays out into the Atlantic or northern North Sea probably as distant cover for convoy movements; and occasionally we fired our main armament or the 6-inch by way of practice. The noise, even closed up at my Action Station, somewhere low down in the ship, was devastating; a great roaring rumble which shook the whole vessel and caused its metal structure to reverberate when the 16-inch were fired, whereas the 6-inch produced an unpleasant crack of much shorter duration. Snow fell much earlier in Iceland and by November the landscape was white, but it was quite common for the ship's company of* Rodney *to be assembled on the upper deck for physical exercises while the Royal Marine band played from the top of one of the turrets. At this time, my rather sensitive skin was affected badly by salt air and spray. The ship's Medical Officer was prescribing some kind of tar-based ointment for my skin, which made it extremely difficult for me to keep a supply of clean collars, and from time to time I incurred the wrath of the Commander, who was a stickler for neatness as well as fitness.*[6]

During one of *Rodney*'s forays from the Hvalfjord, Frank Summers was sent out into the bitter elements from the steamy engine room.

> *I was told to repair the ship's whistle, at the top of the funnel. The weather was bitter, but at least the sea was not quite frozen!! In spite of wearing all the clothing I had, I was myself freezing cold. I finished the job just before passing out.*

The monotony of the Icelandic sojourn was at least relieved by a touch of glitz. The movie star Douglas Fairbanks Jnr. was at the time a junior naval officer in the battleship USS *Mississippi*, flagship of the US Navy's Atlantic Fleet. The modernised WW1-era battleship, armed with a dozen 14-inch guns, had just been sent to operate out of Iceland, which had been under American administration since July 1941 as a ploy to enable the US Navy to run convoy escorts across the Atlantic. Fairbanks found himself invited aboard *Rodney* for a meal with her officers and was given a conducted tour of the ship, visiting the Royal Marines in their messdeck and providing Len Nicholl with a taste of Hollywood humour.

> *He was very interested in our hammocks because in his ship they had bunks and in the north Atlantic people were being tossed out of them and breaking their legs. One of the lads asked what it was like being married to Joan Crawford and he replied: 'They are all the same lying down.'*

Visits from movie stars aside, the men of *Rodney* decided their time at Iceland was 'about the worst of the war, for the ship's company generally'.[7] If *Rodney* was to be sat doing nothing, they would rather it was in a UK dockyard, under refit, so they could spend time with their families.

To young Midshipman Wells-Cole such concerns were of little interest, for his main aim in life was not to fall foul of senior officers for heinous infractions such as dirty collars. He was pleasantly surprised to find the battleship's Commanding Officer much less fearsome than the Commander.

> *Captain Rivett-Carnac, on the other hand, was a charming and outwardly unassuming man. On occasions, when I was on cypher watch he would send for me to take a signal. When I arrived at his quarters he would hand me the signal and express the hope that he was not giving too much trouble. He would get his Steward to provide me with a cup of tea or some goodies.*

On 7 December, with *Rodney* still marooned at the Hvalfjord, came news of Japan's devastating blow against the US Pacific Fleet in Pearl Harbor, Hawaii.

A few days later the ship's sailors were thunderstruck to hear both *Prince of Wales* and *Repulse* had been sunk by Japanese aircraft in the Gulf of Siam, as the British capital ships made a vain attempt to prevent an invasion of Malaya.

The loss of the old battlecruiser made a deep impact on *Rodney*'s second gunnery officer, Lt Peter Wells-Cole, as he had known her so well.

> *When I heard* Repulse *had been sunk, I was very sad, particularly the circumstances, in which she and* Prince of Wales *were sent on a forlorn hopeless mission. She had been a very good ship and I certainly enjoyed my time in her before the war.*

Had the original plans for defending British interests in the Far East come to fruition it might well have been *Rodney* destroyed by the airpower of rampant Japan. Instead, as if in response to poor morale, on 22 December the battleship was ordered to leave Iceland for the marginally more attractive Scapa Flow, where she would spend Christmas and New Year. It was a voyage that provided Midshipman Wells-Cole with his first taste of real danger at sea.

> *We left Iceland in heavy weather escorted by three four-funnelled old destroyers, which had been leased from the Americans in return for bases in the West Indies. I think*

it was in the mid-afternoon, still quite light but with dusk drawing on. I was down in the cypher office, probably drinking one of those thick, sickly sweet mugs of navy cocoa – made from compressed bars, not powder – when there was the most enormous metallic reverberating clang from somewhere beneath us. The order was given to close all watertight doors and the engines slowed. Damage control parties were closed up and the Commander informed us over the ship's broadcast that a mine was suspected. I had visions of going to a watery grave in my small, sealed compartment in the bowels of the ship. However, secret books do not go down with their ships, but are put into a weighted bag for disposal separately. Accordingly doors were opened specially for me and I found myself on the upper deck clutching the weighted bag as the ship wallowed unsteadily in the fairly heavy seas, in the gathering dusk. One of the escorting destroyers, ahead of us, started flashing her signal lamps. The message was to the effect that she had lost a depth charge overboard as she rolled. The loss had only just been discovered; the charge had dropped through the water until it exploded underneath us through the compression effect! Soon we were on our way again towards Scapa.

The last leg of the journey provided a lesson in the power of the sea.

The Pentland Firth is one of the most disturbed pieces of water 'round our coast. Even Rodney *was dwarfed by the walls of water, which seemed to rise alongside us out of nowhere. They subsided just as quickly and then the great ship would be twisted through several degrees as the currents caught her. Altogether a weird place, and not one I should like to tackle in a small boat. I have absolutely no recollection of Christmas 1941. I am sure we went home. I must have caught a ferry to the mainland, and then there was that interminable war-time train journey south, or north, more often than not sitting on one's bags in the corridor of an overcrowded darkened train with blinds down at night.*

As the battleship sailed south, Churchill was proposing that *Rodney* and *Nelson* should be sent in the near future to the Far East, to join forces with new American battleships which were, like them, armed with 16-inch guns. The Prime Minister envisaged the two British battlewagons taking part in a fleet action alongside the USN's units to wrest control of the Pacific back from the Japanese.[8] In the meantime, *Rodney* left Scapa in mid-January, heading back to the dreaded Iceland, where the entry of the United States as a full-blown ally saw an increasing American naval presence. In early February *Rodney* did at least get some sea time, acting as 'enemy' battleship for US Army Air Corps aviators keen to practice their anti-shipping strike techniques. On 10 February, however, *Rodney* received instructions to sail for Liverpool, destined for a partial refit, the German air threat to the UK having declined enough for this to go ahead. The sailors and marines were overjoyed as now they could expect some decent leave time with their families.

No man knew how badly *Rodney* needed a refit more than the ship's new Engineer Commander, forty-year old Cdr Robert Parker, who had joined her at Scapa Flow on 13 January 1942. During his time in the battleship, Cdr Parker kept a concise diary of notable happenings within his world,[9] revealing he rapidly became acquainted with the poor state of not only *Rodney*'s boilers, but also steering, together with troublesome gears which, according to Engine Room Artificer Charles Barton, had rusted due to water contaminating their lubrication oil. *Rodney* spent the first five weeks of her refit at Birkenhead, the place of her birth, receiving hull repairs and replacement 16-inch guns, which were waiting for her, on railway trucks, as she went alongside in Cammell Laird's wet basin. For ERA Barton it was a return home, as his father had helped build *Rodney* back in the 1920s. Young Barton took leave of the old battleship gladly, feeling *Rodney* and *Nelson* were only in service because, at the beginning of the war, 'Britain didn't have a decent battleship.'

> Rodney *was a bit of a sweatshop. The machinery was old and kept breaking down. I recall I was at one point assigned to running the evaporators that made fresh water and didn't get any sleep at all. You would get in your hammock and then something would stop working and you'd be called out to fix it.*

The battleship was next moved over to the Gladstone Dock at Liverpool for docking down. Joining *Rodney* was a familiar face, George Thomas, now a Mechanician First Class, the equivalent of a Chief Petty Officer. Thomas was surprised to be back in 'Rodbox', as 'it wasn't usual to rejoin your ship after mechanicians course. Usually you went to another ship ...' He found *Rodney*'s men talking ceaselessly about their magnum opus.

> *It was the main topic of conversation in the ship for about a year afterwards, so I can go through the* Bismarck *action with you blow-by-blow.* [It was] *recounted ad nauseum in the mess.*

Meanwhile, Captain Rivett-Carnac flouted regulations to give Lt Peter Wells-Cole some leave.

> *I got married in March 1942 and Captain Rivett-Carnac told me confidentially that* Rodney *was going to the Eastern Fleet, something he should not have done. Because he knew I would be away for a long time, he arranged for me to go with my new wife to the Western Isles for a week's honeymoon.*

As ever, Winston Churchill kept an anxious eye on his 'captains of the gate', nagging the First Sea Lord with a note on 14 April:

> *Give me the latest dates for completion of repairs to* Nelson *and refit of* Rodney. *Has work been proceeding night and day on these two ships ...?*[10]

On Tuesday, 5 May 1942 *Rodney* sailed from Liverpool, headed for Scapa Flow, from where, three days later, she began a series of exercises in the Pentland Firth, designed to work her up to full fighting efficiency with sister ship *Nelson*, which had completed her own repairs at Rosyth in late April. Gunnery shoots were also conducted on the range at Cape Wrath. By 1 June work up was completed and the following day *Rodney* sailed for the Clyde, which she reached three days later, departing immediately with destroyers *Penn*, *Pathfinder* and *Quentin*, in company with convoy WS19. Cdr Parker noted that *Rodney*'s troublesome engines and steering were performing okay, managing 18 knots, at 121 revs on the propeller shafts. On 11 June, enjoying a spell of good weather, *Rodney* oiled *Pathfinder* and the following day, it being declared 'Hot', her men changed into tropical uniform. The weather got hotter and hotter over the next two days, with rain; very humid conditions. Like most British warships *Rodney* was built for operations in more temperate north European waters and her sailors found conditions extremely uncomfortable, including Cdr Parker who soon had an overhead fan fitted in his cabin. Many of *Rodney*'s ordinary sailors and marines preferred sleeping on her upper decks to being broiled alive in their messdecks. *Rodney* and *Nelson* were being sent to operate out of Sierra Leone as part of a big effort to turn the tide of war against the Axis in both the Middle East and Far East. At noon on 15 June, *Rodney* reached Freetown and four days later sailed on with WS 19P, composed of 24 merchant vessels, including liners carrying thousands of troops destined to fight in North Africa or Burma. *Rodney* and *Nelson*, together with five destroyers provided the escort, both battleships at the centre of the seven columns of ships, making an imposing deterrent. As the convoy hit the South East Trade Winds, on 20 June, the temperature cooled, a most welcome development. Crossing the Equator early on the morning of 22 June, *Rodney* and *Nelson* both held 'Crossing the Line' ceremonies. A pagan ritual, with its origins possibly in Viking sea-faring tradition, it is designed to induct new subjects into King Neptune's Realm. In 1942 it was a means of relaxing and temporarily putting down the burden of war, although the captain, bridge watch team and other people essential to running the ship safely remained on duty. King Neptune was played by a suitably garbed Executive Officer, while his acolytes, dressed as bears and other colourful characters, seized those who would traditionally have been dunked in a tank of seawater. However, on this occasion they were hosed down as the majority of the ship's company cheered and cat-called. Each sailor who was new to the experience was awarded a 'Crossing the Line Certificate', and in this case it had an unusual design: Winston Churchill depicted as Neptune, being towed by a subservient Hitler and Mussolini.[11]

By 26 June, off the southern Angolan coast, the weather had turned hot again, and cloudy. *Rodney* and *Nelson*, with the destroyers, turned back, leaving the convoy to the care of the cruiser HMS *Shropshire* and her escorts, which took it on to the Cape. In saying farewell, both battleships passed back through the convoy, cheered on their way by troops cramming the upper decks of the liners.

Heading for Sierra Leone, *Rodney* reached 17 knots, making solid progress, but on 27 June disaster struck, as Cdr Parker reported:

> *Bad day. Steering gear break down forenoon.*

The problems persisted, for on 28 June he reported:

> *Another bad day. Steering failed again.*

Trying each steering motor separately, but making only slow progress ironing out problems, the engineers had to work through the night. Each time there was a failure in steering, *Rodney* was forced to signal *Nelson* and escorts that she was out of control. They gave her a wide berth, *Rodney* using her propellers to steer. Entering Freetown at 4.00 pm on 1 July, *Rodney* had only 450 tons of fuel left, due to the excessive use of revs on the propellers to steer the ship. The engineering department was, meanwhile, still working on the steering gear and would remain hard at it for days, slowly cooking as they slaved away deep inside the ship. Cdr Parker gained some relief from his exertions by going ashore to play tennis at the Governor's House, on 13 July. He found Freetown a rather eccentric, tropical Little England, which even had an Anglican cathedral. Sailors and marines enjoyed 'bargaining for pineapples on the lovely bathing beach'[12], watched 'the natives playing football exceedingly well in their bare feet' or attended evensong in the cathedral. Of course, Sierra Leone was as prone to tropical diseases as any other place in Africa and the men had to be careful not to fall victim to a dreaded mosquito bite or unpleasant ailments to be found in local brothels. Giving her men a much needed break from the sapping heat of swinging at anchor in Freetown, and possibly saving them from the pox, on 16 July *Rodney* put to sea for steering trials, Cdr Parker noting:

> *Steering seems o.k.*

The following day, both *Rodney* and *Nelson* went to sea, at 6.30 am, this time quitting Freetown for good, with orders for Scapa Flow. *Rodney*'s steering motor problems soon returned, but, with a pressing need to evade the attentions of U-boats, the old battleship still managed a creditable 17.5 knots. Evidence of enemy submarines was soon apparent, as the destroyer *Pathfinder* 'picked up a boatload of survivors'[13] which came from the cargo ship *Cortona*. With *Rodney* still suffering steering problems, on 21 July, Cdr Parker wrote in his diary:

> *Sea. Fine & warm. Lots of submarines about.* Pathfinder *rammed one, possibly sunk.*[14]

The following day yet more submarine alarms were sounded and, perhaps, with the Admiralty feeling it was wise to be extra careful with a battleship suffering from steering problems, on 23 July three extra escorts arrived on the scene. Despite their age, both *Rodney* and *Nelson* remained key assets in an over-stretched service, which is why they were being recalled. In early 1942, the Royal Navy's battleship strength was composed of: four Queen Elizabeths, four Royal Sovereigns, two Nelsons, four King George Vs (commissioned, being built or completed). However, the Royal Sovereigns were pretty useless for anything except convoy escort work, while *Queen Elizabeth* and *Valiant*, although modernised, were out of action, after being sunk at their moorings in Alexandria by Italian frogmen in December 1941. *Warspite* was the most modern battleship left in the Far East following a refit at Puget Sound in the USA, while sister ship *Malaya*, unmodernised, was also not really suitable for anything except convoy work. Meanwhile, *King George V* was seriously damaged in a collision with a destroyer in the Arctic in May 1942.

Ship losses, and the fact that building more battleships was taking a back seat to construction of carriers and escort vessels, therefore made *Rodney* and *Nelson* even more important. Churchill's proposal to send them to the Far East for a decisive fleet action came to nothing, due to the necessity of keeping them in European waters. As recently as 27 May – the first anniversary of *Rodney*'s battle with *Bismarck* – Churchill, referring to himself as 'Former Naval Person', had written to President Roosevelt, urging him not to withdraw the battleship USS *Washington* from the Atlantic to reinforce the Pacific. Churchill felt this would prevent him from sending *Rodney* and *Nelson* to reinforce *Warspite* in the Indian Ocean. However, the Prime Minister's plea came to nothing and *Washington* – commissioned just over a year earlier and therefore one of the most modern battleships in the American navy – was withdrawn from the Atlantic in July 1942 and later sent to the Pacific where she saw plenty of combat.

With no possibility of a deep refit, on reaching Scapa at 11.00 pm on 26 July, *Rodney* immediately set to cleaning her boilers, while work continued to rectify her faulty steering, with an immediate request for Rosyth Dockyard to send engineers. They proved to be of little help, Cdr Parker observing in his diary on 31 July:

> *Experts arrived 12.40. No great ideas. Argue with me.*

Despite Cdr Parker's misgivings, the experts from Rosyth were allowed to work on the steering and spare parts were ordered to try and resolve the difficulties. In the meantime, *Rodney* was declared out of action. Solutions had to be found, for a forthcoming mission would require her steering to be in good repair, in order to evade torpedoes and bombs.

Notes

1 Robin Brodhurst, *Churchill's Anchor*.
2 Winston Churchill, *The Second World War*, Vol III.
3 Robin Brodhurst, *Churchill's Anchor*.
4 For more on the ill-fated Force Z, go to: *http://www.forcez-survivors.org.uk/*
5 Memorandum on global dispositions of British capital ships and aircraft carriers, from Admiral Pound to Winston Churchill, 28 August 1941. Published in the appendices of *The Second World War, Vol III.*
6 Account given in a letter to the author.
7 Kenneth Thompson, *HMS Rodney at War*.
8 Winston Churchill, *The Second World War*, Vol III.
9 Parker, RNM. See Sources.
10 Winston Churchill, *The Second World War*, Vol IV.
11 Crossing the Line Certificate given to HMS *Rodney* sailors Oliver Scarrott (RNM) and John E. Faulkner.
12 Kenneth Thompson, HMS *Rodney at War*.
13 Parker, RNM.
14 *Pathfinder* was not credited with sinking the U-boat, but later that year sank a German submarine in the Caribbean and an Italian boat in the Mediterranean. *Pathfinder* was sunk by Japanese air attack in 1945.

Chapter Fifteen

KEEP THE SHIP FIGHTING

The convoys of early summer 1942 were not a success and now Malta was close to starvation. Former *Rodney* sailor Tommy Byers, still on the Force H staff, witnessed how grim things had become, even for ships attempting to run supplies through to the besieged island, during the Operation Harpoon convoy in June.

> *We were attacked by Italian and German aircraft and only got two ships through. We were starved even aboard the flagship* Malaya, *only eight ounces of bread a day, ten baked beans each, that is, when we could get them.*

Malta remained so important because – at a time when both sides knew the decisive moment in North Africa was fast approaching – it was an increasingly effective base for submarines, destroyers, Motor Torpedo Boats and aircraft tasked with disrupting Axis supply convoys across the Mediterranean. However, a shortage of fuel oil by August 1942 imposed a severe handicap on Malta operations, while there was an alarming attrition rate among its defending air squadrons, due to aircraft lost on the ground. The retreat of Allied forces along the North African coast left it even more isolated. However, General Bernard Law Montgomery was building up for a big offensive at El Alamein, which would, hopefully, end the German threat to the Suez Canal. The Allies were also preparing a seaborne invasion of North Africa. Keeping the enemy starved of supplies and wearing down his powerful air forces would be critical to the success of the whole Allied cause. Only once dominance had been achieved in the Mediterranean could resources be found by the British to focus on liberating north-west Europe. The next Allied convoy to Malta, WS21S, would be make-or-break. Codenamed Operation Pedestal, the naval escort was commanded by Vice Admiral Sir E. Neville Syfret, with his flag in *Nelson*. On 2 August, *Rodney* set sail from Scapa Flow, destined for convoy duty in the Atlantic, but was then given instructions to join Pedestal. Cdr Parker kept a watch on her steering, on 4 August noting in his diary:

> *Met convoy – more escort – destination unknown. Steering gear OK on all three motors so far! Sea lumpy, fresh wind, slight roll, chilly. 12 knots. Big doings.*[1]

WS21S was composed of fourteen fast merchant ships and particularly important was the *Ohio*, an American-built tanker chartered by the UK, with a British crew, carrying 11,000 tons of badly needed fuel oil.

Pedestal involved the biggest ever escort for a single convoy[2] mounted by the Royal Navy. Aside from *Nelson* and *Rodney*, it included three carriers (*Eagle, Victorious* and *Indomitable*), seven cruisers (*Nigeria, Cairo, Manchester, Kenya, Sirius, Charybdis* and *Phoebe*) and close to two dozen destroyers. *Phoebe, Charybdis, Sirius* and *Cairo* were anti-aircraft ships, but the battleships, carriers and cruisers also bristled with AA weapons. However, the main air defence for the convoy was provided by fighter aircraft of the Fleet Air Arm. There were more than seventy Fulmars, Sea

Hurricanes and Martletts embarked in the carriers, while *Furious* was transporting forty-two Spitfires to Malta. Also embarked in the carriers were Albacore torpedo-bombers. A squadron of the same aircraft type was operating from Malta, along with a Swordfish from another unit. Available to provide top cover, on the final stretch from the Narrows to Malta, were 100 Spitfires and thirty-six Beaufighters of the RAF based on the island. Axis air strength, poised to hurl itself against the convoy, amounted to more than 500 Italian and German aircraft. In terms of naval forces, the Italians were likely to commit a trio of heavy cruisers, three light cruisers, a dozen destroyers, eighteen submarines and nineteen motor torpedo boats. The Germans were able to contribute three U-boats, along with four motor torpedo boats. This would be the most intensely fought convoy battle of the war in the Mediterranean.

Aboard *Rodney* incognito – for his flag did not fly from her – was Vice Admiral Sir Bruce Fraser, along for the ride in order to receive a warfare refresher course. Fraser had last seen action in 1915, when the light cruiser HMS *Minerva*, in which he was Gunnery Officer, supplied gunfire support for British troops during the ill-fated Gallipoli campaign. When the Second World War broke out he was Controller of the Navy, responsible, like Chatfield before him, for ensuring it built the right sort of ships. At the end of June 1942, Fraser took up a new appointment, as Vice Admiral, Second-in-Command of the Home Fleet, in other words Tovey's understudy. Initially flying his flag in the brand new King George V Class battleship *Anson*, Fraser soon transferred it to *Victorious*, watching from aboard her the disaster of convoy PQ17 unfold in early July 1942.[3] With a break in Arctic convoys, Admiral Tovey was quite happy for his deputy to take a ride in *Rodney* on Pedestal, especially as the purpose of it was to study how well close integration of sizeable carrier airpower in a convoy would work. There were many similarities between the Mediterranean and Barents Sea, except that in the former the enemy's airbases were even closer to the convoy track.[4] It was the avowed intention of the Admiralty to ensure the PQ17 disaster could not be repeated. In *Rodney*, Fraser was allowed use of the Admiral's Bridge, a deck in the Octopoidal above the Navigating Bridge, and with a cabin close at hand. It gave him 'a panoramic view of events'.[5]

As *Rodney* and the rest of the convoy passed the Balearic Islands on 10 August, Captain Rivett-Carnac picked up the microphone, to give an inspiring eve-of-battle speech, to psych his men up for the ordeal ahead. Throughout the battleship, sailors and marines paused in what they were doing and looked at the tannoy speakers. The Captain explained that the battleships and aircraft carriers were going to escort the convoy to 'within a night's steaming of Malta.'

> *... after which the convoy must be protected by cruisers and destroyers and fighters from Malta.*[6]

He revealed *Furious* was due to fly off fighters to reinforce Malta's squadrons the following day and that these planes would help protect the convoy on the last, and most hazardous, phase of its journey. The Captain did not hide the fact that a tough time lay ahead, during 11, 12 and 13 August.

> *Tomorrow, Tuesday, we must be on the look-out for high-level bombing attacks, possibly torpedo-bombing attacks in the evening as we move eastwards, and of course the usual submarines. But Wednesday is the big day, and possibly Thursday also. We*

> *shall be within a hundred miles of both Sardinia and Sicily, so must be prepared for torpedo-bomber, dive-bomber, and high-level bomber attacks ...*

He explained *Nelson* and *Rodney* would be sailing 'fine on each quarter', meaning they would be towards the back of the convoy; *Nelson* on the starboard quarter, *Rodney* on the port. Only the three carriers and their screen would be astern of the battleships, to provide the freedom needed for launching aircraft into the wind as and when required. Ahead and around the entire convoy would be cruisers and destroyers. Captain Rivett-Carnac continued:

> *It is our job, of course, to protect the convoy and ourselves, by our gunfire, from air attack. It is also our job to protect the convoy from attack by the whole Italian Fleet.*

However, the Captain revealed he felt it most unlikely the Italian battle fleet – believed at that time to be composed of a new battleship, three older ones, plus cruisers and destroyers – would actually come out to contest the convoy's passage if they believed there were battleships in escort. He suggested the Italians would only venture forth if *Rodney* was known to be at Freetown or in Plymouth. Captain Rivett-Carnac explained that *Rodney, Nelson* and the carriers would loiter west of Sardinia after pulling away from the convoy as it passed through the Narrows.

> *We have all been waiting for an opportunity to achieve something. As the Admiral* [Syfret] *has said, Malta looks to us for help, and every one of us must give of his best ... no ship in the world is so thoroughly capable of fighting and destroying and chewing up this mixed attack, if it comes, as the* Rodney.

Should a surface warship attack materialise, the captain invested his confidence in the proven ability of *Rodney* to hit with the first salvo, forecasting the Italian Navy would 'dislike the *Rodney*'s shells even more than the *Bismarck* did.'

He reminded them the ship had more anti-aircraft weaponry than ever, more radar and highly developed damage control methods. In reference to the over-enthusiastic gunners who claimed at least one British fighter plane during the Halberd convoy, Captain Rivett-Carnac observed drily:

> *... if it comes to air attack, last September the shooting was good and the guns' crews were like tigers: the only difficulty we had was in dragging them back by the tail if they sprang at the wrong target.*

To get them through the next few days, *Rodney*'s men must display 'sheer courage', rely on their skill, preserve calmness and also be quick to act. They would need to be 'utterly determined' and use their own initiative in the absence of specific orders.

> *If damage occurs, hold it, and keep the ship fighting.*

The Captain further explained *Rodney* would protect the flank of the convoy, taking any opportunity to sink Italian ships lurking in the vicinity of the Malta approaches. He joked that it was about time the evasive enemy were sent to a watery grave:

> *... they have been sculling around there far too long anyhow.*

Rivett-Carnac concluded:

> *In this way THE greatest West Country ship, the* Rodney, *will show again that she is as tough as she is strong, and as efficient as she is tough...*

He paused for effect.

> *That is all.*

This openness and no-nonsense approach inspired great affection in *Rodney*'s complement for their Commanding Officer – they loved humour in the face of adversity and their captain's absolute confidence in what he felt they could achieve. The tannoy went silent, the captain's voice replaced by static hum, the men in the messdecks temporarily lost in their own thoughts before a few ribald jokes snapped them out of it. In the bowels of the ship, there were signs not all was right with the steering. Cdr Parker worried that in a situation where *Rodney* was in very close proximity with other ships, and must neither slow down nor lose her position, things could all go wrong very quickly, with horrific effects. And that was without taking into account the threat posed by multiple bombing and torpedo attacks. Meanwhile, Peter Wells-Cole would be in charge of co-ordinating *Rodney*'s air defences, a heavy responsibility for a junior member of her command team.

> *For the Pedestal convoy I was up in the ADP, acting as the Air Defence Officer, which was a job the second gunnery officer was given when there was unlikely to be a surface action. I was up in the ADP for the best part of three days. I never went aft and, in fact, probably never went further down than the deck below. We were up there in the blazing sunshine, getting tanned. There wasn't all the fuss one might expect today about wearing sun cream to protect oneself, but I am lucky in not being fair skinned and therefore prone to getting burned. That was just as well, as we were fully exposed to the elements. I slept up there in my clothes, pulling on a duffle coat at night because, although during the day the weather was very good, it got pretty cold after sunset.*

Despite Rivett-Carnac's eve of Agincourt-style speech, when the first casualty among the ships came, it was a massive shock. Enemy scout planes had been sniffing around the convoy from early on the morning of 11 August, provoking a few skirmishes in the air, as well as signs of enemy submarine activity. The *Rodney* had been closed up at Action Stations since dawn and a determined assault by enemy aircraft was expected. As the middle of the day came, overhead the only groups of aircraft were Spitfires, taking off from *Furious* and heading for Malta. The enemy struck from below, in the form of four torpedoes fired by *U-73*, which had been stalking the convoy for well over an hour. The U-boat's captain, Kapitanleutnant Helmut Rosenbaum, had sighted a battleship, possibly *Rodney*, while successfully penetrating the destroyer screen, the submarine's presence hidden by an impenetrable layer of cold water the British escort ships' Asdic could not 'see' through. With specific orders to sink carriers, Rosenbaum soon had HMS *Eagle* in his sights, carrying out a text book attack and then diving deep. Aboard *Rodney*, the lunch period was coming to an end when the battleship reverberated to a series of explosions, those down in the engine rooms dismissing them as another pre-emptive depth charge attack by a British destroyer. Up in the ADP, Lt Wells-Cole heard 'thump, thump, thump, thump'.

The whole of the *Eagle*'s port side had been torn out; she was listing badly as thousands of tons of water gushed in. 'It was the most terrifying and dreadful spectacle,'[7] recalled one of *Rodney*'s men. Lt Wells-Cole and other members of the team in the ADP looked on with a mixture of horror and awe.

> *We had a good view of* Eagle *sinking, which was horrifying and unexpected. Although we expected things to happen, I suppose we could not have anticipated it all happening so quickly. It was a depressing and extraordinary sight. I had never seen such a big ship sink.*

For many, *Eagle*'s death was to remain the most chilling thing they ever saw, including Jack Austin, who was relaxing after lunch.

> *I saw four columns of water flying up her port side. At first I thought it was a stick of bombs but, seeing no aircraft, I knew it was torpedoes. The* Rodney *swung to port, making herself a smaller target; by this time the* Eagle *was astern of us and in less than 5 minutes had sunk.*

James McLean was crewing one of the *Rodney*'s starboard 4.7-inch anti-aircraft guns when a shipmate shouted:

> *Hell, the* Eagle *is turning over!*

Astern, about half-a-mile away, he saw *Eagle*'s flight-deck tipping and aircraft falling into the sea. Jack Salmon was handling ammunition on *Rodney*'s forward (port) 4.7-inch gun.

> *I could see men jumping from the flight-deck, and we saw planes, probably from the* Eagle, *landing on* Indomitable; *the pilots jumped out and the planes were ditched over the side because there was no room for them.*[8]

Len Nicholl was on the upper deck drinking his daily tot of rum

> *You did actually feel the four thuds because* Eagle *wasn't so far away. How they got so many off I do not know. There was a Royal Marine standing there beside me who had served in* Eagle *and he said, as she sank: 'They will never get anyone out of that ... she is a death trap.'*

By some miracle, the majority of the ship's company of 927 men was saved, with 163 men going down in her. From the Admiral's Bridge in *Rodney*, Vice Admiral Fraser trained his binoculars on the elderly carrier and actually spotted an old shipmate escaping death.

> *The Captain* [L.D. Mackintosh] *had been my Commander in the* Glorious; *I saw him slide down the flight-deck and on to the hawse pipe.*[9]

Mick Kavanagh was for a moment stunned by the carrier's demise, but didn't dwell on it.

> *I had just come off watch and was having a post-lunch smoke sat on a locker by our 16-inch B-turret.* The Rodney *was nearly last in line and* Eagle *was astern of us, to starboard. I thought: 'Bloody hell, all the planes are going over the side.' Everyone*

was blowing their sirens to get out of the way of it. You think: 'Blimey, that ship is gone!' but I was very young and, to be honest, afterwards, there was not much reflection on it possibly happening to me. In war you move on pretty swiftly. You have to or go mad.

William Campbell, a Scot who was a shoemaker in civilian life, had been called up into the 51st Plymouth Division of the Royal Marines, joining *Rodney* on New Year's Eve 1941. When *Eagle* was hit he was, with other marines, just sitting down to lunch in their mess. Suddenly the jokes and banter, the clink of cutlery on plates, died away as they heard four 'crumps', so unlike the usual bombs exploding. There was also no anti-aircraft fire in return.

We froze for an instant, forks poised midway between plate and mouth, then as we realized what was happening, rushed to our respective 'Action Stations', cutlery and crockery scattering to the deck as we ran ...[10]

Campbell and his fellow marines ran to see what had happened for themselves, thinking it might even be *Rodney* that had been hit. Instead, he saw *Eagle* going down.

It seemed incredible at the time that she still had way on and was steaming in a large circle as she capsized.

Snapping out of it, Campbell rushed down through the decks to his Action Station in a shell handling room below a 6-inch turret. Pulling on his anti-flash gear he told other marines who had been closed up about what he had seen, and they all waited in silence, listening to the sound of depth charges reverberating through *Rodney*'s hull, as British destroyers sought revenge. Campbell pondered how war was a cruel game of chance.

I suppose the U-boat commander would have been equally happy if he had hit HMS Rodney *or HMS* Nelson *rather than HMS* Eagle.

And so, the *Eagle*, which had survived so much during her time in the Mediterranean, was gone within a few minutes, her boilers exploding as she sped towards the seabed. After the bubbles subsided it was as if she had never been in this world, just another one of many casualties in the bloody Med.

In the aftermath of the *Eagle*'s sinking there was, to be frank, deep relief that another ship had bought it rather than *Rodney*.

The convoy left the war grave of *Eagle* in its wake, knowing a tough battle lay ahead. A record of action swirling around *Rodney* during the evening of D + 1 (11 August) and throughout D + 2 (12 August) reveals how it became increasingly ferocious.[11] Several torpedo-bombers came in at 9 pm on 11 August, one of their torpedoes just missing the stern of the anti-aircraft cruiser *Cairo* and crossing *Rodney*'s bows. Two enemy planes were shot down and then bombs started falling, sending up huge plumes of spray but achieving only a near miss – a bomb between a merchant ship and the cruiser HMS *Kenya*. At 9.20 pm, two enemy aircraft flew straight at *Rodney*, on her starboard beam, but a torpedo dropped by one failed to hit, while bombs just missed on the battleship's starboard side. Two minutes later a further two bombs exploded between *Rodney* and *Nelson*. A torpedo fired from astern of *Rodney*, on her port quarter, fortunately sped harmlessly past the battleship's bows. After more near misses with bombs, in return for one enemy plane shot down by the convoy's formidable anti-aircraft barrage, attacks ceased at 10.00 pm. *Rodney*'s Cdr Parker summed it all up:

> *... with convoy. Dawn action stations. 1400* Eagle *torpedoed – sunk. General panic ...*

The new day started in dramatic style for *Rodney*, as at 7.45 am lookouts spotted torpedo trails in the water, indicating a pair of tinfish heading straight at her. Turning towards the torpedoes, the ship presented her robust bows to the threat rather than her vulnerable stern, with its rudders and propellers. A hit on the bows could be survived with the loss of a few compartments, which could be isolated, whereas the loss of steering and propulsion would be fatal. James McLean was working on the upper deck.

> *The ship's siren suddenly gave two short blasts and I felt* Rodney *shudder as she went hard to port. Looking out to sea I saw three Italian torpedo planes coming towards us, just above sea level. We had just turned, when I saw the tracks of two torpedoes – one passing down our port side and the other one down our starboard side. During this time all our AA guns were belting away but I didn't see any of the planes hit. Later on the Admiral* [Syfret] *signalled and asked why the ship had gone out of line.*

That attempt to sink *Rodney* was a mere taster. Following a false air raid alert sparked by a shadowing aircraft, which was swiftly shot down, at 9.14 am a big formation of enemy bombers was spotted approaching from dead ahead. Two minutes later bombs began dropping all around and a destroyer took a hit.

At 9.17 am Ju88 bombers came diving out of the sun, the battleship's entire anti-aircraft armament opening fire, throwing up a curtain of hot metal. The enemy still managed to let go three sticks of bombs, which missed *Rodney* but nearly hit a merchant ship on her starboard side, the vitally important *Ohio*.

Overhead, a number of black parachutes blossomed, two of them coming down off *Rodney*'s starboard bow. They appeared to each have 'two small black canisters'[12] attached.

These Motobombas, as they were known in the Italian Air Force, were intended to break up the convoy, disrupt its inter-locking fields of AA fire and make it easier for the Axis attackers to pick off individual vessels. However, the Savoia–Marchetti bombers tasked with this disruption mission dropped them both too early and too high, so they failed to explode. While some ships, including *Rodney*, took evasive action, they were soon back on track. Up ahead an enemy bomber crashed into the sea but between 9.26 am and 9.53 am there was a lull. Suddenly a torpedo track was spotted, crossing *Rodney*'s bows from port to starboard, possibly from a submerged enemy submarine, and twenty-two minutes later another passed ahead, from starboard.

An enemy scout plane buzzed over but was pounced on by British naval fighters, *Rodney*'s men watching with satisfaction as it disappeared over the horizon burning brightly. At 10.34 am a British destroyer carried out a depth charge attack on a possible U-boat contact to port. Eleven minutes later a torpedo from an enemy submarine passed astern of the battleship, leading to a flurry of activity by depth-charging destroyers, as they shot back and forth in a desperate attempt to kill the interloper before it could claim a victim. At 12.08 pm a group of enemy aircraft was spotted, four of them coming straight at *Rodney* from the starboard bow, provoking the ship's anti-aircraft guns to open up. However, they did not attack the battleship, reserving their bombs for nearby destroyers, surrounding one with splashes. *Rodney* made a kill at 12.17 pm; an Italian bomber shot down on her port side. Twenty minutes later a loud explosion was heard and a plume of spray rose into the air behind a destroyer on the starboard wing of the screen, indicating either a wake-homing torpedo detonating prematurely or a near miss with a bomb. And then, as more than two dozen torpedo-bombers came skimming in over the waves, first the cruiser *Manchester* and then destroyers opened fire. Their props kissing the waves, weighed down with their torpedoes, some of the enemy planes came at *Rodney*, prompting her to join the barrage: the rapid rat-tat of the pom-poms, the metallic hammer of the Oerlikons, and then A and B turrets trained to port and two of the battleship's guns roared.

> *We loaded the centre guns of each turret with these special proximity fuses adapted from AA fuses to fit the 16-inch shells . . .* Rodney *opened fire at about 9 miles with the 16-inch and frightened us, our escorts and Italians. They disappeared* [behind spray, and] *whether they were hit or not, they didn't press on with the attack. People around us thought that we had been hit. No one expected to see 16-inch guns firing and when a 16-inch gun is fired, there is a hell of a noise and hell of a shock and a hell of a cloud of smoke, just as if you have been hit.*[13]

In the ADP, Lt Wells-Cole had no time to be worried about the torpedo near misses, which he was too high up to see anyway.

> *But I did see plenty of enemy torpedo-bombers. The 16-inch barrage was very effective. Our intention was not so much to shoot them down as to scare the living daylights out of their crews, although it was pretty frightening for us too when we fired ALL 16-inch guns by mistake.*

Between eighteen and twenty-four bandits had been spotted at a distance of some 18,000 yards off *Rodney*'s port bow, the 16-inch turrets training to meet the threat. Wells-Cole gave the order to 'FIRE' and, as he later recalled, 'a 16-inch broadside went on its way . . .'

> *That was unintentional as only one turret should have engaged . . .*[14]

Some of the high explosive shells were fitted with proximity fuses.

> *When we ran out of them, we fired just ordinary HE without the proximity fuses and these created a splash barrage. The idea of firing the 16-inch guns in the air-defence role was not new. Both* Nelson *and* Rodney *certainly practiced it on the way down for Pedestal. My job as Air Defence Officer was to call out where the threat was. We received information from the radar operators, which told us the sectors to look at for enemy planes coming in, such as 'bandits forty miles on the starboard bow.' The lookouts then located the enemy with the number one eyeball and then we passed down the details to the High Angle gunnery directors so they could direct the 6-inch and 4.7-inch guns. The close-range weapons – the pom-poms and Oerlikons – were warned off too.*[15]

Down in the engineering spaces they felt the big guns firing but did not hear them, unlike the lighter anti-aircraft weapons, which, due to the ship's ventilation system, could be heard quite clearly.

> *The ack-ack guns, being on top of the vents by the funnel, make a helluva noise down in the boiler rooms ...*[16]

More torpedo bombers came in, *Rodney*'s 16-inch guns again hurling death at them, this time non-exploding armour-piercing shells, sending up 200 ft plumes of spray, the idea once more being to literally knock the enemy aircraft out of the sky or, at the very least, put them off their aim.

Anti-aircraft gunner Jack Salmon recalled the moment:

> *... a 16-inch turret swung around, opened fire and seconds later I saw two terrific flashes and a cloud of smoke on the horizon, one plane spiralled away and crashed into the sea.*[17]

While at least one torpedo-bomber was downed on *Rodney*'s port beam, more tinfish were in the water, but luckily failed to strike home. And then into the melee came a Sea Hurricane hot on the tail of a torpedo-bomber; its machine gun bullets chewed up the enemy aircraft's fuselage and punctured the engines, sending it cartwheeling. Its demise roused a cheer among *Rodney*'s gunners. The planes stopped coming, the firing died away and a parachute blossomed ahead of *Rodney*, appearing to drop in from Heaven, the pilot swaying under it, splashing down, canopy collapsing. As she thundered by, *Rodney*'s bow wave pushed aside the airman, who was still struggling to cut himself free. Whether or not an enemy lived or died depended very much on where he landed and whether or not the crew of a destroyer felt inclined to pick up someone who a few moments before had been doing his best to kill them.

Short bursts of fire on the starboard side of the convoy were too far off to concern *Rodney* but it seemed submarines were again trying to penetrate the screen. A contact was picked up by a destroyer and enthusiastically depth-charged, while at 1.05 pm the *Rodney*'s port 4.7-inch long-range AA guns started firing at aircraft approaching on the port quarter. A cruiser opened up astern of *Rodney* with her full anti-aircraft armament, while off the battleship's port bow a dashing destroyer dropped a series of depth-charges. Aircraft were spotted approaching from starboard at 1.15 pm and two minutes later bombs fell astern of *Nelson*. It also appeared *Rodney* might not escape harm.

> *We are firing with everything we've got. Bombs fall across our bows, close. Two to Starboard and one to Port ahead. They fall diagonally. Port one near miss* [on a] *Merchant Ship's stern.*[18]

The battleship's upper decks were doused in spray, soaking her anti-aircraft gun crews while below there was feverish activity to ensure the guns were kept supplied with ammunition. The Fleet Air Arm men who maintained the ship's embarked Walrus seaplane had been pressed into service as part of a human chain, passing shells up to the 4.7-inch guns. Petty Officer Bill Myers recalled a tricky moment:

> *... not for us* [Rodney] *the modern fully automated push button supply, load and fire facility; every shell had to be manhandled from the magazine to the gun deck; almost*

the same as in Nelson's day, except that now the powder and the cannon ball were in the same container. Each shell weighed 75 lbs but after a few hours it felt more like 75 cwt. The chain was working like clockwork ... when someone dropped one of the shells. It bounced its way down the steel gangway to the deck below, tearing off its nose cap and exposing a fiendish array of wires etc. The first thing I noticed was that everyone seemed to have disappeared, as if some magician had just pulled off one of his spectaculars. I knew little about ammunition except that it is preferable to have the sharp end pointing away from you. The way I figured it was that, if the monster had decided to go 'bang', then it would have done so on its unimpeded journey down the steel gangway. I decided to take a look. There on the deck below, was our 18-year-old engine mechanic, Dickenson, in stately solitude with his foot firmly clamped on the shell to stop it rolling around. He looked up, saw me and said: 'What do I do now PO?' Something had to be done ... so I said: 'Just pick it up gently, lad, and bring it up here to me.' Which he did. As soon as he got to the top of the ladder he dumped the offending beast into my arms. We went on to the upper deck, heaved the shell over the side and dashed back inside where the chain was back in action.[19]

Three years earlier Bill Myers had been completing a three-year apprenticeship as an aircraft maintainer in the newly reborn Fleet Air Arm. After a Christmas break at a holiday camp on the Isle of Wight, Myers and other recently qualified apprentices received their drafts, depending on marks. A number, with just one per cent less than Myers, were sent to the carrier *Glorious*, and were all killed when the ship was sunk off Norway.

Bill Myers was sent to RNAS Hatston, the naval air station in the Orkneys, serving ships operating out of Scapa Flow. A series of shore-based postings followed and, after an Aircraft Artificer's course, Myers ended up aboard *Rodney*, joining the ship in the early summer 1942, as the senior rating in charge of looking after the Walrus. Now, during Pedestal, when he had a spare moment, Myers observed the frantic air-defence activities of *Victorious* and *Indomitable* with an expert eye.

I watched an aircraft land on and taxi to the forward lift where it was lowered into the hangar. I could imagine the action as it was moved back through the hangar being refuelled, rearmed and repaired while the pilot was debriefed, having a cup of coffee and a pee – not necessarily in that order – and by the time the aircraft reached the after lift he was ready to go again. It was possibly the most concentrated period of action in the annals of the Fleet Air Arm. Very comparable to the Battle of Britain, but with the added hazards of a moving airfield, having to fly through 'friendly' flak to reach it and flying aircraft inferior in performance to those of the enemy ... I had many friends in both ships and was well aware of the intense activity that was taking place both on the deck and in the crowded hangar below. Must admit to some embarrassment at the comparatively easy passage I was having, but at the same time must admit to being very grateful for the security provided by the Rodney's *14-inches of armour plating.*

At 1.20 pm on 12 August, more bombs fell on *Rodney*'s starboard side, with another miss on the *Ohio*; two minutes later destroyers off *Rodney*'s port bow disappeared behind bomb splashes. An enemy plane trailing smoke crashed into the sea, the parachutes of its crew floating down, some ahead of *Rodney*, some to port. A merchant ship was smoking badly following a bomb hit and listing to port. Smoke was also pouring out of a destroyer off the port bow. The attacks fell away,

Rodney cruising past a damaged merchant ship, the *Deucalion*, stopped dead in the water, boats being lowered over the side, a destroyer standing by protectively. The *Deucalion* faded in *Rodney*'s wake 'slightly down by the bows'. At 1.42 pm more submarine contacts among the destroyers saw a cascade of depth charges and three minutes later an enemy fighter plane was spotted coming in fast and very low, gaining time to penetrate the air defences through being wrongly identified as a Martlet or Sea Hurricane. It attempted to hit the carrier *Victorious* with two 100 lb bombs, but failed. As it beat a hasty retreat, the enemy plane, an Italian Mack I.2025, almost touched the surface of the water, shooting past *Rodney*'s bows, machine guns chattering.

Around 2.00 pm, the dreaded steering gremlins struck but, fortunately, Cdr Parker and his team were able to prevent complete failure and *Rodney* kept her position, at 15 knots. At 2.24 pm four enemy fighters came in low across the convoy, from *Rodney*'s port quarter, and eleven minutes later destroyers detected more submarines, first to starboard of *Rodney* and then port, responding with a series of depth charge attacks. At 4.40 pm lookouts in the destroyer *Ithuriel* spotted a periscope and the top of a conning tower – it was the Italian submarine *Cobalto*, which appeared to be moving into position to torpedo *Rodney*. The *Cobalto* had sustained serious damage during earlier depth-charging and, in seeking to evade British destroyers, over-trimmed, breaking the surface.[20] Diving again, she was depth-charged by *Ithuriel* and, out of control, broke the surface again at 5.10 pm. *Rodney*'s record of the action noted:

> *Submarine brought to surface six miles astern. Sank stern first.*[21]

Using a pair of binoculars, Jack Salmon looked on in astonishment at what happened:

> *... a small destroyer, name unknown to me, came in around our stern, going like the clappers, straightened up and then charged full ahead. She came to an abrupt stop and then slid backwards; she was crumpled in the bows but steamed away – the only thing I could imagine was that she had rammed a submarine.*

In fact, some of *Ithuriel*'s sailors made a vain attempt to board *Cobalto* and retrieve codebooks. However, the enemy boat sank before this could be accomplished, but forty-one Italian sailors were saved. In *Rodney*, a lull in the action allowed someone with a good singing voice to entertain his shipmates, including Jack Salmon, still standing by a 4.7-inch gun.

> *In my earphones I heard a voice serenading all and sundry from somewhere up in the Octopoidal. It was* Melancholy Baby, *but he had his own version, something which included the words 'alcoholic baby'.*[22]

At 6.36 pm, after a lull of an hour and 16 minutes, a formation of enemy bombers swept in, off *Rodney*'s port bow. Anti-aircraft fire rippled down the line of escorting warships as the planes got nearer and the merchant vessels also sent up a firestorm. Those with powerful optics and binoculars recognised the silhouettes first: Stukas, an aircraft type operated by both the Italians and Germans, but it was most lethal in the Luftwaffe's hands, especially in the Mediterranean. Fortunately for *Rodney*, the Stukas that plunged out of the early evening sky were Italian. While their pilots were without doubt brave, they perhaps lacked the fanaticism needed for men to take the kind of insane risks that sink ships. *Rodney*'s record of the event summed up the Italian Stuka maelstrom:

Stukas dive bombing. Everything lets rip.

The carriers, though, were the prime targets, because, once they were gone – and the convoy stripped of its close air support – the rest of the ships would be easy meat. Three bombs landed ahead of *Victorious* on her starboard side and then, at 6.42 pm a Stuka came in from directly ahead, in a shallow dive.[23] Captain Rivett-Carnac ordered *Rodney* turned hard to starboard[24], an armour-piercing bomb skipping over her X turret and landing in the sea on the port side, creating a big splash, but fortunately not exploding. Two more bombs hit the water on the port beam of the battleship, very near misses, only some 60 ft from the ship. The gallant Italian aviators paid the ultimate price for their assault on *Rodney*, as their Stuka was riddled with fire, its fate recorded rather drily that as 'cockpit cover came off and plane crashed astern.'[25] Legend has it Vice Admiral Fraser may actually have shot down this aircraft, although he modestly refused to claim credit.

Whenever an air attack was incoming, Fraser immediately exited his cabin, just below the Admiral's Bridge, accompanied by the teenage Royal Marine and Signalman who were assigned to him. On the Admiral's Bridge was a machine gun, which was crewed by this unlikely trio and, whenever the opportunity presented itself, they blasted away at passing enemy aircraft.

My Marine hadn't yet arrived and it was the little Signalman who turned his machine-gun and fired at this group of, I think, about six aircraft ... One aircraft came down almost straight at us, then swung off one side into the water. We thought we'd got it, but really you couldn't say for certain what had happened to it ...[26]

A gaggle of torpedo-bombers coming in from the battleship's starboard side also received a hot reception and five Stukas coming up astern of the convoy were deterred, dispersing without pressing home their attacks. But now, the Lutfwaffe's Stukas made their entrance, a dozen Ju87s peeling off and plunging from 9,000 ft to barely 1,000 ft[27] before pulling up, unleashing their bombs against *Indomitable*. Sailors and marines in *Rodney* saw the carrier straddled: five close to her stern and three more splashes either side. Then four more bombs fell, splashes obscuring her, but *Indomitable* was clearly hit; explosions forward and aft. The whole of the carrier was hidden by smoke, but the twinkling flashes of her anti-aircraft weapons could be seen, spitting defiance. *Indomitable* had been badly damaged, and was effectively out of action, but she stayed with the convoy, licking her wounds and counting the human cost; 50 men killed, including Albacore aircrew in the wrecked ward room, and forty-nine wounded.[28] During the Stuka attack, four of *Rodney*'s Royal Marines, manning anti-aircraft weapons on X turret, were injured by bomb fragments or possibly friendly fire. At 6.48 pm an enemy aircraft was shot down, crashing off *Rodney*'s port bow, but it was small recompense for the injuries sustained by *Indomitable*, still battling fires both fore and aft. Four minutes later enemy aircraft attacked from the battleship's starboard side but with no result and by 6.55 pm the sky was clear. At 7.00 pm, as the convoy, under escort from cruisers and destroyers, entered the Narrows, *Nelson* turned back. One minute later *Rodney* reversed course. As she did so destroyers were picking up submarine contacts and dropping depth-charges. The two battleships set course for Gibraltar in company with the carriers and escorts. At 7.05 pm a Martlett fighter crashed into the sea close to *Rodney*, having run out of fuel while providing top cover. The pilot was picked up by the destroyer *Zetland*. Having managed to prevent the enemy from sinking any of the merchant ships, shooting down forty-two aircraft and sinking at least one submarine in the process, the fleet was now receiving signals indicating Axis forces were taking full advantage of a weaker protection force. Ultimately only five out of the fourteen merchant ships that started the hazardous voyage to Malta made it, but one of them was *Ohio*. Severely damaged, she actually sank in the island's harbour, but her cargo was taken off. It fuelled naval and RAF aircraft and, most importantly, the submarines of the Royal Navy's 10th Flotilla, which continued to take a heavy toll on Axis shipping.

On the night of 12 August, aside from the crippled *Indomitable*, Vice Admiral Syfret was probably concerned about *Rodney*, for the violent evasive action she had been forced to take during the day worsened the steering problems Cdr Parker was so familiar with. In his diary, Parker summed up the day's action:

> *Big day. Bomber, Dive Bomber, Torpedo Bomber, Submarine attacks all day. In ER* [Engine Room] *from 0530–2300 ... several near misses. Steering gear bad ... left convoy ... they were attacked immediately after.*

The *Rodney*'s boiler tube problem, which dogged her pursuit of *Bismarck*, also resurfaced, reducing her top speed to 18 knots. This would slow the entire fleet down, as its pace had to match that of the slowest vessel.

As they reflected on the day's events, *Rodney*'s men were astounded by their good fortune, Len Nicholl among those amazed their ship had not suffered severe damage.

> *How* Rodney *got through unscathed was a miracle, because we had sticks of bombs dropping around us.*

The return to Gibraltar proved a sad affair, Bill Myers looking on from *Rodney* as the *Indomitable* buried her dead.

> *A typical Mediterranean evening, the sea flat calm, the sun still high in a clear blue sky and the silence was sheer bliss after the deafening clangour of the previous few days. Suddenly we could feel the ship losing speed, the flag was lowered to half-mast and our attention drawn to* Indomitable. *From the stern of the ship we could see bundles toppling into the sea as 'Indom' buried her dead. There were some 50 of them – a sight that remains vivid in my memory to this day.*

Peter Wells-Cole finally came down from the Air Defence Position at around 11.30 pm on the night of 13 August.

> *Admiral Fraser bought me a congratulatory drink in the ward room, handing me a large whisky and soda and we had a chat. I was absolutely exhausted. I'd managed very little sleep during the previous three or four days and had been sustained by soup and bully beef or cheese sandwiches.*

Rodney entered Gibraltar harbour at 6.30 pm on 14 August, still suffering problems, described by Cdr Parker as 'steering gear in a weak state – tubes in the boilers going [defective] as had happened during the convoy.'

The following day Cdr Parker led his team on a closer inspection of the superheaters and the circulator in the boilers, using the engineering workshops ashore to carry out repairs. To check out the steering problems, Cdr Parker donned a diving suit and went under *Rodney* to take a good look at the rudder. There was the suspicion enemy action had damaged it, in a similar fashion to that which occurred in 1940. Surprisingly, it was discovered to be alright.

While the engineering department was grappling with *Rodney*'s vulnerable rear end, her men were blowing off steam with a few runs ashore, availing themselves of Gib's dubious delights and encountering some hostility from long-term residents. Before he headed into town one night, Bill Myers went to take a look at *Indomitable* in dry-dock, seeing 'a hole in her side big enough to accommodate two double-decker buses.'

> *Then on to Main Street to patronise those well know watering holes –* The Trocadero, British Empire, *and the* Universal, *possibly the nearest we would ever get to the traditional drinking dens as portrayed in Hollywood's version of the Wild West. A Spanish band and Spanish girls dancing flamencos and flashing their castanets and other things.*

The entrance of ebullient matelots did not go down too well with soldiers who had been stuck in Gib for years as its resident garrison. The only invaders they fought belonged to the Royal Navy.

> *... in walks a crowd of sailors in their poncy white suits who had just come down for a quick Mediterranean cruise and were most probably on their way back home. It was an explosive atmosphere. There were no Colt 45s but everything else followed the Hollywood pattern – tables and chairs flying, a few bloody noses and then in would come the shore patrol, bang a few heads and restore order. John Wayne would have felt at home.*

At 2.00 am on 16 August, *Rodney* set sail in company with *Victorious*, the battleship's steering still not in good condition. Switching back to her No. 3 steering motor, *Rodney* somehow sailed on, feeling confident enough by 17 August to undertake the tricky evolution of re-fuelling two destroyers on the move. Two days later, however, the ship hit a gale and, predictably, the steering motors immediately started playing up, as they were being over-worked. It was clear a period in dockyard hands was necessary. The following day the situation got worse, the boilers becoming extremely temperamental, threatening to deprive the ship of power. Despite these difficulties, *Rodney* managed to reach Scapa Flow where, before leaving the ship, on 21 August, Vice Admiral Fraser sought out the battleship's Navigating Officer, Commander J.G. Forbes, on the bridge, thanking him for bringing *Rodney* back safely to home waters. Sixteen months later, as Home Fleet commander, Fraser, flying his flag in HMS *Duke of York*, would lead the force that sank the German battlecruiser *Scharnhorst* off the north Norwegian Cape. *Rodney*'s Navigator now plotted a course for Rosyth, the ship arriving in the Firth of Forth at 11.30 am on 22 August, dropping anchor above the bridge. She was soon moved into the basin and docked down in Rosyth's 3 Dock for repairs to steering, boilers and her 'many hull leaks'.[29]

It was the end of a quite incredible journey for the elderly battlewagon, her Official History recording of her part in Operation Pedestal:

> RODNEY *took her full share in repelling the attacks and, so far as could be seen in the general situation, had quite a number of successes against enemy aircraft, though she, herself, was damaged by a near miss.*

Within two months *Rodney* would be involved in a curious episode of which her Official History makes no mention, either because it was not felt worthy of note or, more likely, due to its extreme secrecy.

Notes

1 Parker, RNM.
2 RN web account of Pedestal/Peter C. Smith, *Pedestal.*
3 In early July 1942 thirty-six merchant vessels made up PQ17, heading for Murmansk and Archangel, but the convoy was ordered to scatter by the Admiralty, which wrongly believed *Tirpitz* was about to attack it. The main escort force withdrew to fight the German battleship. In the space of five days twenty of PQ17's merchant ships were lost, picked off one-by-one. It was realized that convoys should not scatter when facing such a potential threat and that close escort by aircraft carriers was crucial to combating enemy aircraft, submarines and surface raiders.
4 Humble, *Fraser of North Cape.*
5 Ibid.
6 The quotes from Rivett-Carnac's 'eve of battle' speech are all taken from *HMS Rodney at War.*
7 Description in *HMS Rodney at War.*
8 *The Rodney Buzz,* April 1997.
9 Humble, *Fraser of North Cape.*
10 W. Gordon Campbell, *HMS Rodney – The Story of a Battleship.*
11 Kenneth Thompson, *HMS Rodney at War.*
12 Quoted by McCart in *Nelson and Rodney.*
13 Hughes, IWM Sound Archive.
14 Peter Wells-Cole writing in the *The Rodney Buzz,* April 1999.
15 Peter Wells-Cole in interview with the author, July 2007.
16 Ibid.
17 Jack Salmon, *The Rodney Buzz,* April 1997.
18 Kenneth Thompson, *HMS Rodney at War.*
19 *The Memoirs of Commander William L Myers RN (Rtd).*
20 Peter C. Smith, *Pedestal.*
21 Kenneth Thompson, *HMS Rodney at War.*
22 The crooner was allegedly Peter Wells-Coles, though he does not recall serenading the ship with the song in question, but, as he freely admits, it was a long time ago and there was a lot going on.
23 Peter C. Smith, *Pedestal.*
24 Ibid.
25 Kenneth Thompson, *HMS Rodney at War.*
26 Humble, *Fraser of North Cape.*
27 Peter C. Smith, *Pedestal.*
28 Ibid.
29 Parker, RNM.

Chapter Sixteen

COUNTERFEIT *TIRPITZ*

As the tiny fishing vessel passed Cape Wrath, the aptly named jagged cliffs at the bleak north-west tip of Scotland, her crew were reminded of home. Ahead for the Norwegian exiles sailing in *Arthur* lay an attempt to 'sink' HMS *Rodney*, a rehearsal for a mission to send the sister ship of *Bismarck* to the bottom of a fjord. Since the winter of 1940 a covert ferry service, smuggling spies in and out of Norway had been run from the Shetlands, using native fishing boats that would, hopefully, not arouse the suspicions of the German occupiers and their informants.

The plan was to use one of these vessels, the aforementioned *Arthur*, to carry and launch a pair of Chariots – converted 21-inch torpedoes piloted by two frogmen – which would drop, or attach, warheads under the hull of *Tirpitz*, to be detonated by a timer, hopefully dealing her a mortal blow.

Neutralising the German battleship remained an obsession with the British, for if *Tirpitz* broke out into the Atlantic from her lair, near Trondheim, it was unlikely the Royal Navy could marshal the same maritime strength it had managed in May 1941 to pursue and destroy *Bismarck*. In March 1942, *Tirpitz* made a foray against Convoy PQ12, headed for northern Russia, and the Home Fleet sought an interception with no result: an attack by planes from *Victorious* failed, due to defective torpedoes. Germany's only battleship once more took refuge in a fjord, where she was invulnerable to attack by both surface warships and aircraft. The disaster of PQ17 in early July, when *Tirpitz* emerged from her lair for only a very brief period, remained a very painful lesson for the Royal Navy in just how serious even the threat of a single battleship on the loose remained. Without even leaving her hideaway, *Tirpitz* handed the Germans the initiative, for what remained of the Home Fleet's striking power was constricted by the need to remain ready to counter her.

The Royal Navy had to find some way of neutralising Germany's single proper battleship and regain ascendancy in home waters. The search for a solution led to *Rodney* becoming a counterfeit *Tirpitz*. Only a year earlier the men of the British battleship had spent months in northern waters, being held in reserve by Admiral Tovey to battle the German capital ship; now, in late 1942, *Rodney* was herself sitting at anchor in a bleak fjord, this time Loch Cairnbawn, giving her men nothing much to stare at except the steep, tightly wooded sides of the surrounding slopes, the occasional white croft alleviating the monotonous greens and browns. Less bleak than Scapa Flow, but offering no diversions ashore, as Rosyth or Liverpool might have, it only inspired *Rodney*'s complement to weary acceptance of yet one more stretch of boredom. Fortunately, during the recent dockyard period, many of the battleship's sailors and marines managed to enjoy a spot of home leave. The *Rodney* arrived at Rosyth on 22 August and soon moved into the basin, entering dry-dock on 25 August. Cdr Parker considered repairs to steering and boilers were an urgent matter and *Rodney* also had other serious defects, for on 26 August he noted: 'Many hull leaks.' With the battleship in dockyard hands, receiving not only urgently needed repairs but also additional close-range anti-aircraft weapons, Bill Myers was among those heading south. Arriving in his hometown of Paignton, on the south Devon coast, he met 'a charming young lady' at a dance, whom he walked home. On a headland overlooking the sea, the romance of the moment – full moon, warm breeze and a sky studded with twinkling stars – seized the young couple and they began to make love. However, their passion was interrupted by a patrolling member of the Home Guard who prodded Myers with a bayonet fixed on the end of his Lee Enfield rifle, demanding:

Don't you know that you are in a restricted area?

Trained in martial arts, Myers considered taking the rifle off the Home Guardsman, but then thought better of it. The indignant sentry pressed on:

Don't you two know that there is a war on?

The young couple burst out laughing and, after making themselves decent, walked away, Myers later recalling that, aside from his recent experiences being bombed in the Mediterranean, his companion had survived her own encounter with the Luftwaffe.

Before being evacuated to Devon the young lady in question had emerged from the shelter of a London Underground station to find that not only her house but also her whole street had been demolished during the night by a German land mine. It sure was one hell of a war.

Meanwhile, Mick Kavanagh went on leave to Dublin, catching the ferry from Glasgow to Belfast, not having been home to see his mum since 1939, when he proudly wore his Royal Navy uniform. Three years later, with the pro-Nazi IRA active in Ireland, he went back in civvies. While at home he bought a new pair of shoes and decided to wear them in on the return trip.

But the ferry on the journey back was held up by fog, so I had them on for much longer than intended and they started to hurt me a lot. The result was one of my big toes went septic and I ended up in the Rodney's *sickbay for three weeks. They gave me some injections. It gave me jaundice.*

For French matelot Frank Summers, there was of course no home leave, but he did at least have a pen pal.

Naturally, with my homeland occupied by the Nazis, I received few letters. However, there was a 'Marianne de Guerre'; a young lady with a good knowledge of French who wrote to me as part of her war effort for the Allied cause. But, of course, I had no contact at all with my family for nearly five years. Leave was obviously a problem for me. I had nowhere to go for such a long time.

Staying aboard *Rodney* while others went home was far from ideal, especially as he faced some truly dreadful cuisine.

Life in Rodney *was as good as possible under the circumstances, and the food was generally quite decent. Let me put it this way, we did not starve, but sometimes you had to draw the line, such as the time they served us sheeps' hearts. The smell was so bad that it all went into a bucket and then was tipped over the side.*

On 16 September 1942, with her men returned from leave, *Rodney* was moved to a buoy in the Firth of Forth, the next day beginning to take on board ammunition. Sailing on 20 September, the battleship carried out sea trials on the way, reaching Scapa Flow at 8.00 am on 23 September. However, she didn't stay long, as Cdr Parker noted:

> *Sailed 10.30 for secret destination. Arrived port HHZ 14.30. 5 hours to secure.*

The codename HHZ was used for Loch Cairnbawn, to disguise the exact location of the training area. The ordinary sailors and marines in *Rodney* had not much of an idea about why their ship was anchored in a loch in the remote north-west of Scotland, although the significance of what they saw around them – the booms and submarine nets – would later make sense.

> *We were netted in there with all the defences which were ostensibly around* Tirpitz *although we were told nothing at the time.*[1]

The Royal Navy's 'human torpedoes' were created in a remarkably short space of time. In early December 1941 the Italians had provided an object lesson in how to wrest the initiative from a seemingly invulnerable enemy when they sent human torpedoes in to Alexandria, dropping and attaching charges under the battleships *Queen Elizabeth* and *Valiant,* the subsequent explosions causing severe damage and, at a stroke, fatally weakening the British position in the Mediterranean. The full severity of the damage to the two battleships, along with the loss of *Barham* to U-boat attack around a fortnight earlier, was kept secret, preventing the Germans and Italians from capitalising on the situation. The *Queen Elizabeth* did not return to front line service until June 1943, while *Valiant* was operational again by spring 1942. Taking the Italian human torpedo strike as its inspiration, the Royal Navy, at the urging of Winston Churchill, set about creating its own version of the weapon used so effectively at Alexandria. Achieving the same with *Tirpitz* would be a fantastic achievement.

The British were already working on midget submarines but not human torpedoes, although as far back as the First World War someone had proposed just such a weapon, only to have the idea rejected as unfeasible by the Admiralty.

By late summer 1942, the Royal Navy's Chariot human torpedoes were in service and the charioteers who operated them were carrying out successful mock attacks on the brand new battleship HMS *Howe* at Loch Cairnbawn. There was only five hours life in the battery of a Chariot but it was marginally faster than the Italian variant, capable of reaching almost three knots. It would still need to be transported to almost within sight of the *Tirpitz,* by then in the Asenfjord, an offshoot of the Trondensfjord, allegedly confined there due to damage caused by a torpedo fired by a Russian submarine. The Italians who attacked Alexandria transported their human torpedoes within shelters – caissons – on the submarine *Sirce,* but a better option against *Tirpitz* was felt to be the fishing vessels already operating covertly in Norwegian waters. The *Arthur,* commanded by Leif Larsen, a member of the Royal Norwegian Navy's special service unit, seemed ideal for the job. Larsen had already suggested using a Norwegian trawler to attack the enemy battleship, but he envisaged ramming *Tirpitz* rather than using human torpedoes. The *Arthur* was duly taken in hand and modified internally and externally: a secret compartment to carry the four Charioteers and their two support staff; mooring gear to enable the Chariots to be slung underneath the vessel and towed; chocks on the upper deck where the Chariots would rest, hidden under tarpaulins for the majority of the journey; a reinforced derrick to lower them over the side.

The *Arthur* arrived at Loch Cairnbawn not long after *Rodney*, and immediately committed a faux pas, as she came alongside the depot ship that was home to the charioteers, failing to acknowledge the battleship's interrogatory light signals. Larsen was told off for not responding to *Rodney*, but it did little to rein in his casual attitude to authority.

The *Arthur* headed back out of the loch to a bay down the coast and picked up the Chariots, which were hoisted inboard and placed on their chocks. The trawler sailed back towards Loch Cairnbawn and, in the dead of night, when still several miles beyond its entrance, lowered the human torpedoes over the side. The sea was perfect and the two Chariots motored away, the heads of the frogmen just above the surface of the sea. To navigate the charioteers needed sight of their target, which was not easy in anything but a light swell. Against the forested slopes of the loch, even the bulk of *Rodney* would not be easy to see. Having both managed to penetrate three layers of submarine nets, the charioteers attached their dummy warheads magnetically on the *Rodney*'s hull without being detected.

> *... had this not been a mock attack,* Rodney *would have been deep in a Scottish loch.*[2]

Several more practice attacks were carried out at night and all succeeded except for one, when a shaft of moonlight broke through the clouds and chanced to fall on a Chariot and its two operators, which had broken the surface due to a mistake in trimming ballast tanks. At Alexandria just over a year earlier, two of the Italian frogmen had been spotted by sentries patrolling the upper decks of the *Valiant* and captured. While they were being interrogated in the battleship, steel hawsers were put under *Valiant*'s hull and pulled along, in an attempt to knock off any charges attached.[3] This technique was used on *Rodney*, but it was by no means effective – at Alexandria the Italians had dropped their charge underneath *Valiant* and, while there was one attached to *Queen Elizabeth*, the hawser snagged on her hull and so was not passed along the underside properly.[4] Arthur Kavanagh, recovering in the sickbay from his toe ailment, was woken in his bunk by *Rodney*'s attempt to secure the bottom of her hull.

> *... you could hear the rattle of the chains as they tried to knock off any limpet mines.*

Aside from sentries on her upper deck, there were sailors in *Rodney* listening on hydrophones for any suspicious noises – but the electric motors of the Chariots were incredibly quiet and their operators stealth personified.

Petty Officer (Coder) Les Sadler took a break from working in the ship's wireless office, going out onto the upper deck for a breath of fresh air but received a shock.

> *I had a bayonet shoved in my jumper and was told by the eager sentry that nobody was actually allowed onto the upper deck while the mini-submarines were thought to be coming up the loch. Throughout this whole rehearsal business for the Tirpitz attack we were closed down, with not even any mail allowed out to the ship.*

Furthermore, he recalled, *Rodney* was so large that she had to be towed both in and out of position by tugs, due to the narrow loch entrance, which was host to dangerous rocks.

Bearing in mind the success rate both against *Rodney*, and during the earlier mock attacks on *Howe*, it all seemed to bode well for the actual raid on *Tirpitz*, which was to be launched on 31 October, from Scapa Flow. The idea was that *Arthur*, seemingly just another Norwegian fishing vessel going about its business, would sneak as close as possible. However, having got to within five miles of *Tirpitz*, on the brink of launching the attack, rough seas led to the Chariots, which had been put over the side, breaking their tows and disappearing into the depths. The *Arthur* ended up being scuttled, the Norwegian and British sailors attempting an escape overland to Sweden, during which there was a gunfight and a Royal Navy officer was wounded. After being given treatment in hospital and interrogated he was shot by the Nazis. The others escaped.

The *Rodney* had departed Loch Cairnbawn late in the afternoon of 29 September, arriving back at Scapa around midnight. From 2 October to 9 October, she was involved in exercises, preparing for something, although no one knew exactly what, except that it would be a big show.

On 10 October *Rodney* put to sea for gunnery exercises and that afternoon, after she returned to anchor at Scapa, Winston Churchill came aboard, heightening the sense of anticipation. He delivered an inspirational speech to sailors and marines gathered on the ship's upper deck and they gave the Prime Minister an enthusiastic welcome.

Aside from thanking *Rodney*'s men for all their efforts in fighting the Operation Pedestal convoy through to Malta, Churchill hinted that 'a more permanent solution was to be made to the problem of relieving this heroic garrison.'[5]

Further indications that a big operation was about to be mounted came in the form of white bags brought aboard, which would later turn out to contain sealed orders for the task ahead. On 23 October, after more intensive training, including plenty of gunnery shoots, *Rodney* sailed at 5.00 pm, destined for Gibraltar carrying senior American and British army officers. Shortly before sailing, Cdr Parker visited his opposite number in the *Nelson*, to discuss improving damage control techniques. Clearly some form of action with the enemy that might involve all types of attack – from the air, sea and even shore batteries – was anticipated. By the following day *Rodney* was sailing south into rain and choppy seas, with the destroyers *Penn*, *Panther* and *Lookout* forming a protective screen. Managing a respectable seventeen and a half knots, the sea was calmer on 26 October, *Rodney* putting another half knot on her speed, seeming to indicate the refit may have been a success. On reaching Gibraltar, *Rodney* was kept at short notice to sail; it was obvious by the assembly of warships in the harbour that action was imminent. The battleship's sailors enjoyed a run ashore in pubs and clubs that were home to the usual hostility from the bored Army garrison. In one of these hostelries, Petty Officer Myers took a break from carousing to relieve his bladder and found himself swaying at a urinal next to an American sailor, who beamed at him:

> *We're off to North Africa tomorrow, and you guys are coming with us.*

Myers later observed, more than a little sardonically:

> *So much for security.*

In fact, before November was a fortnight old, the *Rodney*'s guns would be duelling with an enemy familiar to previous ships carrying her name: the French.

Notes

1 Hughes, IWM.
2 C.E.T Warren and James Benson, *Above us The Waves.*
3 Jean Hood, *Come Hell & High Water.*
4 Ibid.
5 Kenneth Thompson, *HMS Rodney at War.*

Chapter Seventeen

THE GUNS OF MERS-EL-KEBIR

The man who would command Allied naval forces during the invasion of North Africa was none other than Admiral Sir Andrew Cunningham, the *Rodney*'s former Commanding Officer from the late 1920s. On 28 October 1942, wearing civilian clothes to avoid attracting attention, he took the train from London to Plymouth. Having known the Devon city well during his time in *Rodney*, he was dismayed by what he saw, as the train snaked its way through devastated areas in its centre and down to Millbay Docks. The Luftwaffe's assault on *Rodney*'s home port, which had caused such anxiety in the battleship's sailors and marines, had by late 1942 ceased, but the process of rebuilding was going to be a long one and Admiral Cunningham was 'greatly shocked by the wholesale destruction wrought by German bombers.'

The devastation was frightful.[1]

As he gazed around him, Cunningham reflected that Plymouth's fate was a good illustration of how hard it had been to stand alone against the Germans.

From Millbay, Cunningham was taken by boat to the cruiser *Scylla*. To preserve the secrecy of Operation Torch, as the invasion of North Africa was known, it was implied to *Scylla*'s men that Cunningham was taking passage to Gibraltar as the first leg in a journey to command in the Far East. *Scylla* reached The Rock on 1 November where Cunningham was greeted with an impressive array of naval hardware, including *Rodney*, all of which he would soon be sending into action. The British admiral and his staff were headquartered deep underground, in offices within a dank and gloomy tunnel, alongside Supreme Allied Commander General Dwight D. Eisenhower, other senior officers and their myriad supporting staffs. Operation Torch would unleash three separate amphibious assaults: all-American landings, under the command of General George Patton, at Casablanca, in Morocco (45,000 troops), and Oran, in Algeria (39,000 troops) and an Anglo-US assault against Algiers (23,000 UK and 10,000 US troops).[2] This would enable the Allies to squeeze the Afrika Korps and Italian land forces between two advancing armies, as Montgomery's 8th Army also rolled them up from the East. Once victory was achieved, North Africa and Malta could be used as launchpads for a thrust up through the so-called soft-underbelly of Europe: Italy.

When Admiral Cunningham and other Allied commanders were planning the Torch landings, they were obliged, wherever possible, to play down British involvement. American units were pushed to the fore, because the Vichy French forces would, in theory, be more likely to capitulate. Bitter anger at Britain's destruction of French warships at Oran in 1940, still burned in French breasts. For her part, *Rodney* was implementing one or two cunning ruses. Petty Officer Myers was called to the bridge, where he was given a pair of binoculars and told to look at the planes arrayed on the flight-deck of the nearby HMS *Formidable*.

At first I thought that they were American aircraft but a closer study revealed that they were British but with American markings. Apparently the object was to convince the natives that this was an American operation and I was told to camouflage the Walrus accordingly. This meant climbing on top of those fabric covered mainplanes to paint out the red, white and blue roundels, a difficult job in harbour, but at sea, with the ship rolling, it was a very delicate operation 40 feet above the deck. We then painted an American star on the side.

The *Rodney* had sailed from Gibraltar on 6 November, at 7.40 pm, and by 4.00 am was heading east with the rest of Force H, in fine and calm weather.

Primary tasking for Force H was to provide distant cover against interference from Vichy or Italian major surface units for both the Eastern Naval Task Force, assigned to attack Algiers, and the Centre Naval Task Force, assaulting Oran. The two naval task forces also had their own integral cruisers and destroyers for close protection. Force H was still under the command of Syfret, whose flagship was *Duke of York*, and, as well as *Rodney*, his striking power resided in *Renown*, *Formidable* and two other carriers, *Furious* and *Victorious*, with a cruiser screen composed of *Sirius*, *Argonaut* and *Bermuda*. Once it was judged enemy battleships and cruisers would not contest the landings, *Rodney*, together with *Furious* and a trio of escorting destroyers, would join the Centre Naval Task Force early on the morning of 8 November.

At 4.45 pm on 7 November, *Rodney* and other ships were harassed by a gaggle of Ju88s, but anti-aircraft fire successfully deterred them from pressing home their attack. The *Rodney*'s Marine Jack Austin recalled a casualty due to so-called friendly fire.

It gave me cause to admire the work of Surgeon Commander Keating, who had been at the marines' recruit depot in Deal where he once put my leg in plaster, and asked me how my leg was when he became Rodney's *surgeon. In November 1942, off North Africa, he was called upon to do brain surgery on a corporal who failed to wear his helmet whilst in charge of a gun mounted on B turret when shrapnel from AA bursts penetrated his skull. Using a carpenter's brace and bit,*[3] *Surgeon Commander Keating removed the shrapnel while still at sea and a few weeks later, after we returned to Gib, the corporal was back on board, his normal self.*

Despite the enemy's failure to sink Allied ships, the discovery of the convoy did not bode well for the morning, when it was expected more aircraft, and probably U-boats, would be unleashed, in a co-ordinated onslaught.

The French Navy, also responsible for manning coastal defences in North Africa, contested the landings in determined fashion, with resistance fiercest at Casablanca. Any French air power that had not been eliminated in airfield hangars or on runways, was destroyed in the air, but shore batteries remained a real menace, firing on Allied vessels, forcing them to keep out of range and delaying landings at Oran.

The morning of 8 November was bright and clear, although with mist clinging to both shore and sea. At 6.45 am *Aurora* got involved in a scrap with French destroyers but, despite high land towering over the bay interfering with gunnery radar, the cruiser and her accompanying destroyers made short work of their opponents. *La Tramontaine* and *La Surprise* were sunk, *La Tornade* beached on fire, while *Le Typhon* retreated damaged into Oran harbour. She withdrew past the rusting wrecks of ships sunk by the British in 1940. To witnesses in *Rodney*, the Vichy French performed with 'real courage and determination'. About two hours after the first melee, *Rodney*'s observers saw *Aurora* surrounded by shell splashes. It was good shooting by the four 7.6-inch guns of Fort du Santon, perched on a 1,000 ft high ridge looming over Mers-El-Kebir, with a commanding view of surrounding waters. *Aurora* requested a fire mission by *Rodney* against the fort but it would prove no easy task. Santon was obscured by cloud clinging to the top of the ridge and visibility was poor, only between eight and ten miles. *Rodney* was, of course, only the latest British warship of the name to play the game of battleships versus shore batteries. In both the Napoleonic and Crimean wars, bombarding *Rodneys* had come off second best, both those earlier ships placed in mortal danger for little, if any, result. However, that form of combat was, from November 1942 onwards, to become the main offensive tasking of *Rodney*. While doing so she made a rather large, slow, if not immobile, target close to shore. Fortunately, from that point on, the Allies more or less established air supremacy wherever they waged war, and anti-submarine warfare capabilities were improving rapidly. Shore batteries had a fixed maximum range, likely to be less than the more mobile battleship's main weapons; the warship could, if need be, move out of harm's way, but land-based guns, being fixed by nature, obviously did not enjoy that defence. Taking her time to weigh up the task at hand – there were a number of settlements in the vicinity of Santon – and, after launching her Walrus aircraft to survey the French, *Rodney* fired sixteen 16-inch shells, finishing at 1.30 pm The French guns chose not to respond but, during the fire mission, *Aurora* reported a torpedo track and *Rodney* was forced to momentarily suspend her gunnery, taking an emergency turn to starboard. Among the battleship's French contingent, Frank Summers experienced more than a little anxiety during the bombardment.

> *It was an uncomfortable time, with my ship firing at French people, especially when I was French-born and an uncle of mine was on the other side. Fortunately, as I later discovered, he was quite some distance away, so he at least was safe.*

At 3.00 pm *Rodney*'s 16-inch guns opened up again and, as with the first episode, Fort Santon chose to remain silent. Unfortunately, the Walrus had been recovered by the time of this second bombardment session, George Thomas relating with some dismay:

> *The catapult was my responsibility at that time and usually the Walrus was off the catapult, which was situated on X turret, during 16-inch gun fire. Unfortunately we were called upon to open fire when the Walrus was on the catapult.*

Bill Myers and the rest of the aircraft's crew, were horrified.

> *Bombardment over, we went out on to the deck to have a look at the Walrus -what a sorry sight it was. The blast from those 16-inch guns had caused havoc – fabric blown in, streamlined rigging wires broken, side windows shattered, ribs broken. It was now getting dark – nothing could be done until the morning – or so I thought.*

During the course of her gunnery spotting duties the Walrus, also known as the Shagbat, had also been hit by French anti-aircraft fire, which so shredded the flimsily constructed plane that she had not appeared fit for flying. Now, of course, she was even worse off. However, her maintainers were determined to get the ungainly old bird back in the air. They loved *Rodney*'s Shagbat even if no one else did.

> *The Walrus has always been regarded as a bit of a joke by the ship's company. Men crowd on to the upper deck every time she is launched, chiefly, I think, with the hope that one day they may see it slide into the drink ...*[4]

Ugly, noisy, slow and neither a pure air vehicle or a boat, she was simply regarded as 'weird' by *Rodney*'s men.

> *... it is not surprising she is not taken very seriously.*[5]

However, *Rodney*'s Commanding Officer valued the Walrus as a key asset, not only for spotting fall of shot, but also in deterring potentially hostile submarines. 'Much later the pilot, Petty Officer 'Hooky' Walker, and myself were called to the bridge,' recalled Bill Myers.

> *The Captain told us that he had received a signal from the C-in-C to the effect that there was a Vichy submarine in the harbour 'in all respects ready for sea' and he wanted our Walrus to patrol the harbour entrance at first light, until he could get adequate forces in the area. Hooky Walker did not hesitate. He said to me: 'Bill, put the Walrus back together, and I'll fly it.' So I started, first going down into the bowels of the ship to collect spare wires and other bits and pieces, then back up onto the catapult. I was not allowed to show any lights, so measurements were taken with pieces of string. Back down to the workshop. Got a shipwright friend to board up the side windows – the windscreen was intact. Got the streamlined wires refitted, had to judge the tension by feel. On a biplane, if you got the tensions in the landing and flying wires reasonably the same, the rigging would not be far out. Repaired the ribs, stitched up the fabric, plastered the whole lot with red dope, and waited for the dawn ... In daylight the Walrus was not a pretty sight but it was in one piece. Started the engine – belted it to full power and back, shut it down and then we fitted a depth charge under each wing. The crew boarded, the* [X] *turret was traversed, catapult extended, all the hands on the upper deck with their cameras at the ready, the engine belting, bang went the cordite and off went the Walrus, like a bird. The Walrus did her job and kept that submarine under surveillance until the anti-submarine craft arrived but then the power began to fall off. There was nothing that could be done about it. The throttle was on its stops and the engine developed a 'negative rated altitude' so they landed on the water. Fortunately there was an A/S* [Anti-Submarine] *trawler nearby who picked them up. The trawler skipper opened fire with Oerlikon guns intending to sink the Walrus, but Hooky whispered in his ear about the two primed depth charges on board – the trawler moved away, quickly!*

That day would see surprisingly good shooting by the Vichy gunners.

> *At half-past eight, as we were still patrolling up and down waiting for instructions, Santon opened fire at us, and came as near to hitting us as anyone has been in this war, the* Bismarck *included.*[6]

Rodney's command team had believed she was beyond the maximum range but were now relieved of that fallacy.

Those on the bridge were under the impression that they [the 7.6-inch shells] *whistled through the ship's rigging.*

Jack Austin, who would have been safely closed up at Action Stations inside one of *Rodney*'s 6-inch guns had there been any prior warning of danger, later reflected:

Steaming through a heavy sea fog and coming out of it close to shore, I remember leaning on the guard rail when one of the shells zipped overhead with a sound like ripping canvas. A dozen marines trying to get through a one-man door back into the turret isn't funny

An hour later *Rodney*, withdrawn to a safer distance and hidden by the mist, took her revenge, with help from a Forward Observation Officer. Len Nicholl was looking on.

We fired one gun salvoes. This spotting officer was saying 'up 50 yards' and Rodney*'s shots were either spot on or over the top, landing on the other side of the hill.*

At 10.50 am, Vichy destroyers again tried to interfere but the cruisers *Jamaica* and *Aurora* stopped them cold: *Epervier* beached on fire to prevent herself from sinking while the already damaged *Le Typhon* was scuttled.

On 10 November three 9.4-inch guns in the nearby Canastelle battery were causing problems for advancing American troops, so *Rodney* moved down to help. However, before the ship could intervene, Canastelle was hit by an air strike or artillery, so *Rodney* turned her attention back to Fort Santon, which was bombarding other advancing American troops with high explosive shells. This was to be *Rodney*'s key counter-battery action at Oran. Captain Rivett-Carnac wrote in his post-action report that it was a very tricky shoot, at a range of 17 miles, with bad visibility in general and the usual cloud cover on top of the ridge. With American troops just 600 yards from Santon, the possibility of a blue-on-blue was considerable, but *Rodney* provided a display of exceptional accuracy, the shells falling within 100 yards of the target. The Captain remarked:

The fort capitulated; it is not known whether due to the bombardment or events ashore, or both; but it is considered in any case that this last bombardment on D + 2 was very satisfactory.[7]

In his pocket diary the engineering department's Cdr Parker noted:

Bombarding batteries with 16" and 6". Oran capitulated during afternoon. Had a bath!

Admiral Cunningham took a keen interest in the bombardments of Fort Santon, making the important judgment that it was not necessarily the accuracy of the shooting, which was decisive. 'Once again this operation proved that naval bombardments, however accurate, do not get direct hits on guns in protected emplacements,' he wrote.[8] Cunningham observed it was the adverse impact on the morale of people operating the shore batteries that gave intensive naval bombardments their effect. That did not mean the shooting shouldn't be accurate, but, in order to force the surrender of a hard nut like Fort Santon, the men inside it had to feel that at any moment they were about to die. Hammer blows falling in rapid succession, gave them no time to recover their senses.

> *As a technical feat* Rodney's *intermittent bombardment for three days of Fort du Santon with 16-inch must rank as a performance of high order.*

Cunningham thought it highly significant Santon 'capitulated shortly after the 16-inch fire was augmented with rapid and accurate fire with 6-inch guns.'

He suggested 'better results can be achieved by firing 6-inch full gun broadsides with a high rate of fire into a small area than by deliberate fire with heavier shell.' Such 'terrorism'achieved the surrender of a gun emplacement 'rather than ... direct hits on small objects.' Admiral Cunningham felt smaller calibres than *Rodney*'s 6-inch would, however, not garner the same results, achieving only 'nuisance value.'

Having met her principal objective of subduing Fort Santon, on 11 November *Rodney* withdrew and rejoined Force H, which cruised up and down the western Mediterranean in fine, calm weather, waiting for the Italian fleet to make a move. Force H soon returned to Gibraltar, but the harbour was so packed with Allied shipping there was no room for *Rodney*. Even then she did not stay long, as Cdr Parker noted on 17 November:

> *Anchored 0300 after steaming about looking for a billet all night. Sailed again 0900!*

Rodney and the rest of Force H arrived at Oran at midday on 18 November, the situation now secure enough for her to moor at Mers-El-Kebir but there was no leave.

> *The harbour was very deep and* Rodney *anchored in the centre to allow the jetty on the seaward side to be used by transports to unload supplies and tanks, etc.*[9]

Over the next two days the battleship's engineering department cleaned out her troublesome boilers and carried out other essential maintenance. By 22 November the ship was back at Gib, facing a long time alongside, kept at two hours' notice to sail. While their fleet declined to come out and do battle, it appeared Italy's commando forces were determined to strike at *Rodney* and other Allied ships.

> *04.00. Human torpedo scare. 2 men captured, raised steam,* [feared] *bottom mines etc! But no explosions. All over by 14.00*[10]

James McLean said an insomniac Royal Marine raised the alarm:

> *We were tied up at the outer wall and he was fishing with a line, etc., over the seaward side, when he saw a black head come to the surface some distance away, and realised it was a frogman. Apparently 3-4 Italian frogmen had come across from Spain armed with limpet mines, to stick on the hulls of our major RN ships. The alarm was raised and we received orders to close all watertight doors, hatches, dead lights, etc., and go to a certain degree of readiness. I heard charges being dropped all 'round the harbour and on the seaward side, where, so I understand, they captured all the frogmen.*

Forty-eight hours later *Rodney* set sail, headed for Oran in company with *Nelson* and *Formidable*, reaching Mers-el-Kebir at Noon the following day. However, that evening there was some excitement, as noted by the indefatigable Cdr Parker.

> *Air raid Red at 20.00! ... upset dinner!*

There was also another limpet mine scare, which, fortunately, turned out to be a false alarm. Meanwhile, far to the north, on 12 December, in France's Gironde River, two Royal Marines who once served in *Rodney* were proving British commandos could also carry out daring raids on shipping. They had both been good mates with Jack Austin.

> *Bert Laver and I had survived the bomb off Norway together, but there was also another Cockleshell Hero aboard* Rodney, *Sgt Samuel 'Mick' Wallace. I remember Bert and I went on leave* [to London] *together, as he only lived one stop on the Underground from me. We were out together scrounging bottles of beer for his engagement party and when we returned to his house there was a red telegram. All it said was: 'Return to warship* Rodney *at once.' As it was late in the day I told Bert I would see him at the station in the morning. The only thing was there weren't a red telegram for me. I asked Mum if she was telling the truth and she convinced me I didn't have one. That was the last time I saw Bert and I never saw Mick Wallace again.*

Both Corporal Laver and Sgt Wallace were among six commandos captured in the aftermath of the famed Cockleshell Hero raid. All would be shot by the Germans in late March 1943.

During her frequent visits to Mers-El-Kebir over the next few months, *Rodney*'s men were finally awarded shore leave, giving them an opportunity to inspect the damage their ship's guns had inflicted. They were gratified to see local settlements unharmed, although roads around Fort Santon had more than a few big craters.

> *We talked to various members of the population who seemed to bear us surprisingly little malice, though it must be remembered that we had fired with extreme care ...*[11]

Unfortunately one of *Rodney*'s shells had demolished a floating crane in the harbour, which was a slight handicap in disembarking equipment and supplies. *Rodney* spent a lot of time at Mers-el-Kebir, waiting for the call to action and, whereas in a chilly Icelandic fjord the monotony was unbearable, here the weather was far better and the scenery more appealing. There were shopping trips to Oran and organised rambles through the surrounding countryside. One of *Rodney*'s senior rates visiting Oran found it to be a pretty shabby place and while cosmetics might be plentiful, there was precious little else for sale, expect for perhaps female flesh. The senior rating gained his entry to a local house of ill repute after giving a local shopkeeper a bar of chocolate for his children and a bar of soap for the man's wife. Responding to this kindness, the shopkeeper invited the *Rodney* sailor to his 'Club'.

> *I thought this might be interesting and it was. His club was a brothel and, as I was his guest, I could have the first choice of the merchandise on view. I thought it was time I returned to my ship.*

Sailors and marines on a run ashore found the only traffic passing along ten miles of road between Mers-el-Kebir and Oran was dozens of Army lorries. James McClean discovered, like many others, that it was considerably easier to get a lift into Oran than thumb one back; the majority of the Army lorries were going where the fighting was and not returning to the port. However, some sailors were not beyond breaking the law, for, with the ship at four hours notice to sail, leave periods were very short and it was best not to court punishment by returning late.

Out of the blue, to our utter amazement, a landau pulled by two horses appeared around the bend. Sat up front holding the reigns was one of our stokers. He stopped and shouted: 'All aboard for Mers-el-Kebir!' So, a crowd of us piled on the landau and set off down the road at the gallop, with the stoker cracking the whip. Everyone was in a jolly mood, singing and laughing without a care in the world; we eventually arrived near the landing steps and disembarked. The stoker tied the horses to some railings and that was that. I often wonder to this day how the stoker came to be in possession of the two horsepower transport and if the owner ever got his horses and landau back!?[12]

Len Nicholl was among those who enjoyed Oran's attractions.

We would get a car to run us in and some of the men bought cosmetics and other exotic goods for their girl friends back home and other items for their families. Our Royal Marine detachment Sgt Major could speak French, which was quite good, but the most I could say was: 'Bier'. We also went for a march along the sea front at Mers-el-Kebir and the people were waving at us as we went along. When we went for a swim they were still waving to us, so they did not seem to resent the damage we had done.

To ensure nobody got lulled into a false sense of peace, there was the ever-present requirement to be ready for a bombardment mission and constant air raid alerts, which fortunately came to nothing. Beyond the harbour, U-boats were taking their toll of Allied shipping and sometimes survivors came to *Rodney* to be looked after temporarily. There were cinema shows aboard ship, both for *Rodney*'s men and the survivors and sailors from destroyers alongside to refuel and get fresh bread, and make use of her workshops. There were inter-departmental sporting competitions and a number of vigorous cross-country runs. Some *Rodney* sailors spent their nights ashore on patrol, to ensure Italian commandos could not sneak across the beach to attack the ships.

'They had a curfew and we had to enforce it, so they gave us sailors a tin hat and a rifle,' recalled Mick Kavanagh.

I had been a pretty good shot with a .22 rifle during training, so I was picked. During the night you would have half a dozen of you walking up and down, trying to find someone to sell you some eggs, which were taken back to the ship.

Rodney also sent out her own boats, with Jim McLean among the sailors involved.

It was decided that regular patrols would be made, mostly at night times, by cutters, dropping 5 lb charges of T.N.T. to prevent frogmen reaching the various naval units, to fix limpet mines on the hull. I was detailed to be responsible for dropping the charges over the side, prior to which I told the coxswain to go full speed ahead, to be away from the upheaval. Then, later, two extra seamen were included in the crew, armed with nets and buckets, so that after the explosion we could turn around and go back to where dead fish, which had been blown to the surface, were floating. They were scooped up and later delivered to the wardroom galley for the Captain and officers, etc.

Two of *Rodney*'s French ratings had relatives and friends living in the vicinity of Oran[13] and they were delighted to be able to see them, but in some cases received a rather hostile welcome from friends less than impressed to discover they were serving in a British battleship. But, a great many former Vichy soldiers, sailors and airmen were very anti-German and couldn't wait to get in the fight against the Nazis, so *Rodney*'s Frenchmen were often hailed as heroes.

By Christmas 1943, *Rodney* was at Algiers, with everyone looking forward to a period alongside, but, as Len Nicholl recalled, an assassination ashore ruined those plans.

Someone decided to kill Admiral Darlan, the Vichy military leader in North Africa, and the Captain decided it was not a healthy place to stay. So, we went to sea and had pork chops instead of turkey, as we did not get a chance to get a hold of our festive supplies before we departed. Nothing happened and we spent a lot of time travelling between Gib, Oran and Algiers. It was an extremely boring period and it looked like the war would never end. In Gib people were killing themselves in the barracks.

After spending New Year at Gibraltar, where it snowed (something unheard of), *Rodney* set sail at 2.00 am on 2 January, called at Algiers on 3 January, but by sunset had sailed for Mers-El-Kebir. She was joined by *Nelson* (flagship), *Formidable*, escorting destroyers and also some new additions to her crew, including Boy Seaman Allan Snowden, who received his baptism of fire during the voyage out from the UK.

I was a seventeen-year old Boy Seaman in 1942, from Crieff in Scotland, and carried out my training on the Isle of Man. I had volunteered rather then being called up, because I'd wanted to join the Navy since I was a kid and actually sat the first examination on my birthday, in February 1940. My father was ground staff in the RAF at the time and my family were quite happy to sign the papers for me to join the Navy. The training establishment on the Isle of Man was called HMS St George *and it had been a holiday camp before the war, although I didn't have much of a holiday there! After that I went down to Devonport for a few weeks more instruction in barracks. Then, towards the end of December 1942, we received orders to join our Devonport Division ships, in my case the* Rodney. *However, I had to find her first. The first leg of my long journey involved heading for Londonderry, so I caught the train up to Stranraer, on the west coast of Scotland, then took the ferry across to Larne in Ulster. It was a cattle boat and the Irish Sea was so rough even the cows were being sick. At Londonderry I picked up a ship called HMS* Exe, *a River Class corvette, with the aim of taking passage in her out to Gibraltar. She was a fairly small ship and the sea was quite rough as we battled on, escorting a convoy. There were several attacks from the air and we also did depth-charging of enemy submarine contacts. It was exciting, as far as we boy sailors aboard a warship for the first time were concerned. I guess the older men, who had been at it for some time, took a different view. One of my jobs on* Exe *was to set the depth at which the depth-charges would explode. Fortunately, we had been well trained in doing that job on the Isle of Man. Aboard* Exe *with us was the well-known* Daily Express *reporter, and historian, Alan Moorhead, and he later wrote a very exciting account of our voyage. During one incident, I got to fire an Oerlikon anti-aircraft gun at some enemy aircraft but I think they were well out of range. It took us ten days to get to Gib, where we expected to pick up* Rodney *but she had already departed. Instead I went aboard HMS* Nelson, *as she was bound for Mers-el-Kebir where* Rodney *already was. The* Nelson *and the* Exe *were as different as night from day – I immediately noticed* Nelson *was far more solid beneath my feet. I wasn't given any job in* Nelson, *whereas the* Exe, *as a small ship, had been grateful for all the hands she could muster; but* Nelson *was obviously a flagship with plenty of bodies. During the voyage to Mers-el-Kebir I just looked around the* Nelson, *seeing what it was like living in a big ship. On arriving at Mers-el-Kebir we saw* Rodney *at anchor and those of us going to her were ferried over by one of* Nelson'*s boats. And that is how I reached the battleship in which I was to spend the next two years.*

Force H returned to Gibraltar on 5 January, *Rodney* next deploying at 2.30 pm on 12 January, the following day finding her off Mers-el-Kebir, where she stayed for the next three days. And so the clockwork mouse routine continued through the early months of 1943, with no real enemy threat until 23 March, when enemy human torpedoes attempted a night attack on Force H at Mers-El-Kebir. Spotted before they could drop their charges, the Italian frogmen were fired on by marines and sailors patrolling the breakwater and also by armament belonging to *Formidable*, which was berthed alongside. Thinking better of it, the Italians made good their escape. Finally, on 7 May, *Rodney* was released from her purgatory, setting course for Plymouth, the ship's first return to her home port since 1939. She was to receive stop-gap repairs and modifications to her ever troublesome steering. *Rodney* would also have her bottom scraped to increase her speed plus extra anti-aircraft weapons fitted. Clearly, a means of docking *Rodney* down at Devonport had been created. The ship was finally able to give home leave every night, something many of her sailors and marines had been dreaming about since the early months of war. By May 1943, plans were being made to rebuild Plymouth as a city fit for heroes, with startling super-modern architecture and a grid layout in place of the old, narrow streets levelled by the Luftwaffe's blitz. The Plymouth area was also by then home to American troops, who would spearhead the Allied invasion of north-west Europe, an event eagerly anticipated but which had, as yet, no fixed date. The city would also become home of the biggest US Navy base in Europe. It must have been a strange experience for *Rodney*'s men, coming back to a home port transformed in so many ways other than just architecturally. Women did many of the jobs that men used to think of as theirs, such as operating dockyard boats; unmarried sailors and marines had to compete with better-paid and better-dressed American servicemen for the favours of local girls. In their few weeks in Plymouth, there was a lot of catching up to do. Marine Nicholl, a Plymothian born and bred, finished his time in the *Rodney* and was delighted to be able to walk out of the dockyard gates and be reunited with his family later the same day. Eighteen-year old Midshipman Tony Robinson, an Australian who had arrived in Britain on 1 July 1942, joined *Rodney* while she was still in dock. Over the next few days he received an introduction to battleship life, including familiarisation with the main armament, from turret to the magazines deep below, also visiting engine rooms and climbing up to the ADP. On the morning of 27 May, Robinson and other midshipmen were taken down into the dry dock, beneath the ship, to inspect her rudder and propeller shafts as well as obtaining a rare look at the underside of the hull. That afternoon the dock was flooded, in ten-foot stages, Midshipman Robinson speculating in his journal that it was 'to see if the ship was leaking at all.' The following day, Robinson and three of his fellow midshipmen were sent ashore for a fire-fighting course, which included classroom work on various damage control devices they would find aboard *Rodney* and a walk through smoke filled compartments wearing special helmets, giving them an idea of what it might be like to tackle a blaze in the confines of a battleship.

On arriving aboard HMS *Rodney* as part of the new draft of sailors, twenty-one year old Ordnance Artificer Tom Brock was put straight to work, helping with installation of more Oerlikon 20 mm guns, which would prove very useful in deterring enemy aircraft in the months to come. Brock, a Plymouth lad, from Lower Compton, had already seen what air attack could do during his four-year naval apprenticeship. In 1941 the Luftwaffe bombed oil tanks at Torpoint and also hit the training base HMS *Raleigh*, both locations close to the Royal Naval Artificers Training Establishment *Fisgard*, where Brock was under instruction. Thirty-eight sailors lost their lives in the HMS *Raleigh* raid.

By the afternoon of 28 May, *Rodney* had been extracted from dock and was moored in the Hamoaze. The ship took aboard ammunition throughout 29 May into 30 May, when *Nelson* arrived in Plymouth, the next day making her way through the Sound and Devil's Narrows to Devonport, going into the same dock for her own spell of essential maintenance. *Rodney* put to sea early on 1 June and set course for Scapa Flow, escorted by the destroyers *Piorun*, *Onslow* and *Inglefield*. Signalman Bill MacKinlay, from Glasgow, recently drafted into the Navy, had joined *Rodney* from HMS *Drake*, the barracks at Devonport.

> *My four older brothers had done their bit for the war effort in the marines, air force and army. When I was 18 years of age and five months I started my training to be a Signalman at HMS* Scotia *in Ayr, Scotland. After six months of intensive training, I received my first posting: HMS* Rodney. *I knew of the ship and some of the engagements she had been involved with. The encounter with the* Bismarck *was of great interest to me. My main duty at that time was signalling by flags from the flag deck to all other ships. This was called visual signalling, as opposed to the Telegraphist who did his by morse code. As Signalmen we were also required to signal by morse code, by light and semaphore. The station required a minimum of four Signalmen and a Petty Officer, who was in charge from sunrise to sunset, as opposed to a watchkeeper Signalman who worked four-hour shifts. My first day at sea, on my 19th birthday, we were sailing from Plymouth to Scapa Flow, and, while en route I had my first scare. From one of the destroyers we received a signal that enemy submarines were detected ahead. Being a capital ship escorted by three destroyers, we immediately altered course to avoid any confrontations.*

On the way north, as *Rodney* and her escorts made their way through the Irish sea, several mines were spotted, probably drifters ripped free from their moorings by rough weather. Just in case, *Rodney* streamed her Paravanes as a counter-measure.[14] Arriving at Scapa on 3 June, both *Rodney* and *Nelson*, the latter reaching the Orkneys a few days later, were involved in a series of complex exercises, which included 16-inch bombardment practice, all of it a rehearsal for Operation Husky, the forthcoming invasion of Sicily. Foggy weather conditions, with so many battleships, cruisers and destroyers in close proximity, made some of the training evolutions rather tricky, as Midshipman Robinson recorded in his journal entry for 9 June.

> *Suddenly* Valiant *and two destroyers appeared on the port bow about half a mile away.* Valiant *was steering an opposite course to us, she promptly did an 180° turn to starboard followed by her destroyers – the last one of these passed about two hundred yards away. Soon after this we ran out of the fog. We went into Action Stations at 20.10 and proceeded with a reduced charge 16-inch and 6-inch shoot. Visibility was bad, the*

target 10,000 yards away – shooting was fair, but the range was really too short for the 16-inch to do their best. About 21.00 a destroyer having done an 180° turn came past us on our port side about two hundred yards away. Her steering gear had jammed and she was completely out of control. She missed our stern by a hundred and fifty yards and came to stop a half a mile away. She soon rectified the trouble and rejoined the screen, but we were extremely lucky she was not steering a point more to port, otherwise she couldn't have missed ramming us. We closed up to action stations again at 00.45. We had two runs on a target firing starshell, 6-inch and 16-inch. The visibility was bad – about 5,000 yards, so things didn't go too well. We did not fall out till after 04.00 – by this time everybody was thoroughly fed up, as a great deal of time was wasted in going 'round and 'round in circles waiting for a merchant ship, which should never have been there in the first place, to clear the range.

When *Rodney, Nelson,* the carriers *Indomitable* and *Formidable,* with escorting destroyers, left Scapa Flow they were heading for Gibraltar, on arrival becoming part of an expanded Force H. The harbour was packed with Allied shipping, including the veteran bombardment monitors *Abercrombie* and *Roberts,* armed with 15-inch guns, together with dozens of Landing Ship Tanks (LSTs) stuffed with military vehicles and stores, in addition to around thirty destroyers, frigates and corvettes.

To cover the invasion, British capital ships were split into three divisions: Division 1 – *Nelson, Rodney, Indomitable;* Division 2 – *Warspite, Valiant, Formidable;* Division 3 – *King George V, Howe* (theses two battleships also known as Force Z).

Malta was HQ for the invasion and Cunningham was back as commander of the Mediterranean Fleet, while retaining his post as Allied naval forces supreme commander. Vice Admiral Bertram Ramsay was the amphibious assault commander, with Montgomery the Allied landing forces boss.

In an attempt to confuse the enemy, the capital ships would initially be sent in various directions: *Howe* and *King George V* to Mers-el-Kebir; *Valiant* and *Warspite* to Alexandria ; *Rodney* and *Nelson* to Mers-el-Kebir and then Algiers by 4 July.

Rodney only stayed five-and-a-half hours before putting back to sea.

The captain spoke to us at 18.00 – he read us a message from the C. in C. Med. and told us that this was what we had been waiting for ... We are bound for the Ionian Sea to cover landings – actually where as yet we know not – and to attack the Italian fleet – if it comes out.[15]

In *Rodney*'s starboard for'ard engine room's *Shake Book* – a notebook in which the times that sailors needed waking, to start their watches was recorded – some wag wrote on the page for 10 July:

02.30, call Mussolini.[16]

Rodney, Nelson, Warspite and *Valiant,* with *Indomitable* and *Formidable,* assembled south of Malta, along with more than 2,000 troop transports and other invasion vessels. As the soldiers went ashore the following day, both *Rodney* and *Nelson* were in the Ionian Sea, watching out for the Italian fleet. Early on the morning of 11 July, they moved closer to Sicily, *Rodney*'s log recording: 'Mount Etna in sight.'[17]

However, for *Rodney* the episode was to be a big disappointment, her guns remaining silent. The Italian Navy chose not to come out and the majority of enemy bombers that made a run towards the battleship were shot down. Enemy submarines attacked other Force H ships but not *Rodney*. She headed for Malta, dropping anchor outside Grand Harbour, but she was back on patrol in the Ionian Sea the following day. Again action eluded *Rodney* – she came close to bombarding Catania, but *Erebus*, as she was nearer, got the job instead. An eager Midshipman Robinson noted:

This was rather unfortunate as it would have been a change to have some real fun.

However, on 14 July, to *Rodney* fell the honour of being the first British battleship to enter Malta's Grand Harbour since *Warspite* in December 1940.

Not long after *Rodney* dropped anchor, a small boat carrying a beautiful young woman was rowed out to the battleship, her appearance greeted with great curiosity by the many sailors lining the handrail. With the Officer of the Watch absent on some errand, *Rodney*'s chaplain was sent down the ladder to talk to her.

... she was inquiring for her husband who she believed to be on board, and whom she had not seen for several years.[18]

It transpired her man was indeed in *Rodney*'s complement, a veteran of service in the Mediterranean Fleet's destroyers who had sailed away from Malta in 1939. Twice he was drafted to a ship with orders to call at Malta, each of which was sunk on the way, and he'd also seen action in convoy runs to the battered island, catching sight of it but never able to get ashore. On being drafted to *Rodney* he imagined all hope of seeing his wife again was lost, for battleships did not call at Malta ...

Now the incredible had happened and his wife was actually alongside.[19]

The chaplain ran along to see the captain, who readily agreed to the sailor in question being given special permission for a night ashore. However, on seeing any sign of the ship getting ready to sail he must immediately return.

Rodney's short break lasted barely more than a day before she rejoined Force H, just in time for an intensive air raid on the night of 16 July. The *Indomitable* was hit by a torpedo and at least one enemy plane came dangerously close to *Rodney*. Bill MacKinlay, looking on from the signalling station, was amazed his ship escaped unscathed, but in the darkness it was probably an error on the part of a Luftwaffe pilot who didn't see *Rodney* until the last moment, his aircraft passing over the ship's bows at no more than 100 ft.

During *Rodney*'s frequent visits to Grand Harbour over the next few months there were numerous air raids, one involving at least 50 aircraft coming in waves, but, against the terrific barrage put up by land batteries and ships, it failed to score any successes. *Rodney* played an enthusiastic part in seeing off 'the Hun', as the Germans were routinely referred to. Allan Snowden, by then qualified as a Torpedoman, was also required to assist in keeping anti-aircraft guns firing.

The raids were quite exciting. Usually they happened at night when I pulled duty as an ammunition supplier to one of the pom-pom close-range anti-aircraft weapons. You could see the German aircraft every now and then when they were caught in the searchlights, flashing in and out as they made their runs at us. I used to rush out with some more ammo for the gun but was more at risk from our own shrapnel falling down than enemy bombs. It came pitter-patter down, caused by our ship's AA shells, or those of other vessels, exploding overhead. Strangely, I never heard of anyone being injured. You had tracers every fifth or sixth shell so it was quite a light show too and it was very noisy. We had received a lot of extra anti-aircraft weaponry aboard and the idea was that a ship put up a curtain of steel.

At 3.00 am on 20 July, Malta's anchorages were subjected to 'a spectacular air raid'[20] with an estimated fifteen enemy aircraft actually managing to fly over the warships, three bombs falling close by *Rodney*; in neighbouring French Creek a near miss on the *Nubian* killed seven of her sailors; *Indomitable* was straddled, suffering minor damage. Because *Rodney*'s men spent most of the night trying to shoot down German raiders, the following day they were given a 'make and mend' to regain their strength. A raid duly came at 2.30 am on 22 May, but fortunately lasted only half an hour. Like many other members of *Rodney*'s complement, Midshipman Robinson was now sleeping on the upper deck because it was so hot inside the ship. If a raider suddenly flew over, hundreds of half-clad men would gather up their bedding and sprint for the nearest hatch, to avoid being caught in a shrapnel shower. On the night of 25 July there was another big raid, Midshipman Robinson writing:

It began at 03.00 and went on till nearly 05.00. There was a considerable amount of gunfire – mostly blind barrage. I saw one plane caught in the searchlights – nobody fired at it for nearly ten seconds – by then it was nearly out of range. No bombs fell near us this time. We heard later that six planes were shot down; three by A.A. fire and three by night fighters.

Towards the end of July, Mussolini was deposed and imprisoned, prompting great hopes Italy would lay down its arms. After three weeks of sitting at anchor, *Rodney* went to sea on 5 August for gunnery exercises, which ended all too soon and by 3.30 pm on 6 August she was back at anchor in Malta.

Aside from runs ashore, during which *Rodney*'s men explored the island's bars, there were also opportunities to enjoy sport, in order to ensure both mind and body remained healthy and sharp.

Junior rating Robert G. Jackson, who joined *Rodney* back in March 1941, had played league cricket in England prior to the war and now experienced a rather salty encounter with a senior officer.

Our Jimmy the One[21] *got a cricket team together and one thing I remember well is I was subsequently picked to play for the Navy against the Army and Air Force. Our team captain was Rear Admiral Bisset*[22] *and we had to call him Admiral on the field. About the third ball of my first over the ball went to the Admiral's hands and he dropped it. Of course, as it was hot, I said: 'Bloody Hell!' He replied: 'Sorry, Jacks.' Was this the first time an Admiral had said sorry to a lower decker? Anyway, I had nine for twenty-seven runs and we had a good party afterwards.*[23]

Teenage Signalman Stephen Fordham, from Hackney, sustained some knocks and bruises playing football on pitches that were very far from being the green grass of home – in fact there was no grass at all, just pitted bare earth and rocks. Together with his shipmates he also explored the catacombs of Malta, finding it a rather creepy experience. Having suffered a dearth of fruit back home, Fordham was disappointed to discover the only thing that seemed to grow on the island was pomegranates.

At the end of August, *Rodney*, *Nelson*, the cruiser *Orion* and a screen of destroyers made a daring foray into the Straits of Messina, called Operation Hammer, which aimed to bombard targets on the Calabrian coast as part of the softening up process for an invasion of mainland Italy.

Rodney put to sea at 7.00 pm on 30 August, the captain addressing the ship two hours later, revealing that, finally, the ship's guns were going to show what they could do, by bombarding a pair of 8-inch batteries at around 10.00 am the following morning. Having closed up at Actions Stations by 5.00 am, just in case the enemy launched a dawn air attack, *Rodney* stood down for breakfast at 6.30 am, with Sicily in sight by 8.00 am

Two Ju88s made a run at the bombardment force but, on being greeted with a stiff barrage, turned around. During *Orion* and *Nelson*'s shoot, the Italian shore batteries fired back, shells falling amid the destroyer screen. Overhead Spitfires were spotting fall of shot and, when *Rodney* fired shortly after 10.20 am, the pilot of one exclaimed over the radio:

> *Slap in the middle!*[24]

While this was not strictly protocol, *Rodney*'s gunners took it to mean their shells were hitting the target. For a grand finale, one 16-inch shell did indeed land 'slap in the middle' of an ammunition dump, setting off a spectacular explosion. Looking on from inside his 6-inch gun turret Jim McLean was suitably impressed:

> *It was absolutely huge, with an enormous mushroom cloud.*

For teenager Bill MacKinlay, it was an awesome experience but, as usual, *Rodney* did more than a little damage to herself.

> *Seeing the huge 16-inch guns fired was incredible; the recoil caused the ship to roll with each salvo but there was internal damage, such as deck plates needing attention.*

Midshipman Robinson was helping to plot the fall of shot, listening to the enthusiastic RAF spotter and marking off where the shells fell, *Rodney* firing a total of 25 salvos. His verdict on the action:

> *I learned later that we had successfully obliterated our target and that the fires were burning for several days. And so ended my first offensive action – the thing for which I joined the Navy – to fight and hit the Italian and the Jerry and not to sit in harbour doing nothing. At last, I had done it.*

Allan Snowden calmly went about his business, seemingly oblivious to events.

> *During such bombardments I used to be on the upper deck and go around with my wee bag of tools. The noise was terrific and the recoil of the guns used to shake everything up. Off Regia de Calabria, you could see the splashes as their shells hit the water about a quarter of a mile away from us. Even to me on the upper deck, as I went around making sure various electrical bits of equipment were ticking over, it seemed remote, which I suppose was due to our confidence in our capital ship being able to keep well out of range of the enemy while still hitting them.*

Even *Nelson* was impressed enough with *Rodney*'s shooting to send a signal of congratulations. When the Eighth Army made its crossing of the Straits of Messina on 3 September, the invasion ships were not molested by the Italian batteries, British troops finding them shattered and deserted. *Rodney*'s next action would be covering Operation Avalanche landings in the Bay of Salerno, south of Naples, with D-Day set for 9 September. Sailing from Malta on 7 September with the rest of Force H, the following day, when approximately 60 miles to the south-west of the island of Capri, a concerted series of attacks by German torpedo-bombers was fended off. The same day the Italians surrendered, but the Luftwaffe assault was ample proof that war in the Mediterranean was far from over. German torpedo-bombers usually liked to strike in the dark, for maximum protection, and they preferred moonlit nights like that of 8 September. *Rodney* and the other warships put up the, by-now familiar, blind barrage, using radar to detect the sector of the incoming attack. With plane after plane lunging out of the black, *Rodney*'s guns fired almost continuously over a two-hour period.

> *We saw one Hun come down in flames, and later discovered that several others had been shot down ... There is a dead silence just before the attack, except for the sounds caused by the lazy movement of the ship in the sea – then the Air Defence Officer's voice comes over the warning telephone, saying: 'Blind barrage in Sector five commence,' and immediately the 6-inch, 4.7-inch, and pom-poms go into action.*[25]

The order to cease-fire was issued and 'invariably at least one gun fails to hear the pipe, and goes on steadily pouring shells into its allotted section.'[26] The gunner, so deafened by the sound of his own weapon, would have to be banged on the top of his helmet to get the message. Despite their best efforts, the Germans could only manage near misses on *Warspite* and *Formidable*, but some 60 torpedoes were dropped.[27] Midshipman Robinson expressed satisfaction at seeing a German plane crash and burn:

> *One of the destroyers succeeded in shooting a Jerry down in flames – a lovely sight – he hit the water with a great crash and burned for several minutes before he finally sank.*

The *Rodney*'s official Admiralty history registers satisfaction with the anti-aircraft performance of Force H, recording 'at least three of the enemy aircraft were seen to crash and three more thought to have been destroyed.'[28] Force H kept a watching brief off-shore; providing an AA barrage and fighter cover umbrella for troop ships and supply vessels off the beachhead. Once Allied air forces were operating from airfields in Italy, the carriers and battleships withdrew to Malta. The British sailors and marines were amazed to find the Italian fleet at anchor, it having surrendered two days earlier. In celebration, the order to 'Splice the main brace' – an extra tot of rum for everyone of drinking age in the ship – was issued.

For *Rodney*'s recently appointed assistant supply officer, Lieutenant Commander Ian Hamilton, the sight of the Italian warships – four battleships and eight cruisers – in the bay just outside Valetta had special significance. Back in June 1940, he took part in one of the first naval actions in the war against Italy, while temporarily serving in the cruiser HMS *Gloucester*, when British and Australian warships bombarded Italian positions on the Libyan coast. As someone charged with decoding and encrypting signals traffic, Hamilton had handled a signal telling British and Commonwealth units to commence hostilities with Italy. Now he was back in the

Med when the signal bringing hostilities between Britain and Italy to an end was sent by one of *Rodney*'s former Commanding Officers.

> *To my mind Cunningham's signal to the Admiralty in London – 'Be pleased to inform their lordships that the Italian Battle Fleet lies at anchor beneath the guns of the fortress of Malta' – is worthy of a place alongside Nelson's 'England Expects'.*

A former *Rodney* officer had encountered the Italian fleet on its way into activity, during one of those rare moments of poetry in war. Since leaving the ship in 1940, Commander John Boord, *Rodney*'s former gunnery officer, had been on many adventures around the Mediterranean with naval landing parties, including participation in Allied landings in North Africa. He had just played a major part in seeing assault forces ashore at Salerno and was taking a ride back to Tripoli in a motor patrol boat.

> *As we approached the Straits of Messina, I remember it was dawn, I was sleeping on the upper deck, on the bridge, on a camp bed, and I looked up and saw in the distance a line of battleships. It was two of our battleships, the* Valiant *and* Warspite, *leading the Italian battle fleet en route for Malta.*

Boord suggested to the Cdr RNVR in command of the flotilla that his patrol boats should form up in line ahead and give three cheers as they passed the battleships. Their salute was returned by the venerable *Warspite* and *Valiant*. A little while later Boord advised the patrol boat's CO to stop engines near some fishermen and try to get some fish, which they did, dining extremely well that evening.

> *On arrival in Tripoli I found a signal waiting for me to say I was appointed to HMS* Rodney *as the executive officer and I was to join her forthwith.*[29]

Meanwhile, the situation for Allied troops at Salerno had become desperate, a German counter-attack threatening to push the invaders into the sea. Just in case some heavyweight fire support was needed to retrieve the situation, both *Rodney* and *Nelson* were ordered to sail for Sicily, to be close at hand. *Nelson* departed Malta at 3.45 am on 15 September, *Rodney* following fifteen minutes later, but a late turn on the way out of harbour led to the battleship's stern snagging an anti-torpedo net, which wrapped itself around the rudder. The net was ripped to shreds by the battleship's props and the rudder set free, but in the process *Rodney* managed to hit the mole, causing a two-inch dent in the ship's side. After double-checking her steering was okay, *Rodney* followed *Nelson* to Augusta, which both battleships reached mid-morning that day. In the end, timely naval gunfire support for the besieged troops was provided by *Warspite* and *Valiant*, so by 17 September *Rodney* and her sister were back at Malta. Commander Boord joined the ship on 20 September, arriving at Malta aboard a transport aircraft. Delighted as he was to be going back aboard *Rodney*, in his Combined Operations uniform he stuck out like a sore thumb.

> *They were all very smart in their white uniforms and he* [Cdr Ronnie MacKay, the man Boord was replacing] *was horrified when I arrived onboard in khaki shorts and khaki shirt. It was the only uniform I had. I remember he remarked to me: 'You can't possibly be the Commander of* Rodney *without proper uniform.' I said well, I am very sorry but I haven't got any, I left all mine in Cairo.*

While he waited for his things to arrive from Egypt, Cdr Boord went ashore to make a call on Gieves, the celebrated naval tailor in Valetta. They had a number of uniform suits three quarters completed, especially to help out officers temporarily separated from their luggage. Gieves fitted him in the morning and that evening a finished uniform suitable for a battleship Executive Officer was delivered onboard.

On the night of 25 September, Rivett-Carnac, recently promoted Rear Admiral, handed over command of the battleship to Captain the Honourable Robert Oliver Fitz Roy. The new man at the top made a speech, which 'as usual ... held very little interest, as he told us nothing that we didn't know already.'[30]

Rivett-Carnac then said his farewell, which was rather better received. As a picket boat took him away from the starboard side of the battleship, Rivett-Carnac was 'cheered by the crew all the way.'[31]

The new Commanding Officer was eldest son of Edward Fitz Roy MP, Speaker of the House of Commons since 1928, and the Viscountess Daventry. Fitz Roy entered the Royal Navy in 1906, aged twelve, receiving his naval education and training as an officer at Osborne and Dartmouth, and subsequently serving throughout the First World War. In the 1920s he served in *Barham* and HM Yacht *Victoria & Albert* before being appointed captain of the sloop *Crocus* in the Far East. During his inter-war career Fitz Roy was Executive Officer of the cruisers *Frobisher* and *Dragon* and commanded the destroyer *Witch* on the China Station. When war broke out in autumn 1939 he was captain of the minesweeper HMS *Hebe*, in command of a minesweeping flotilla. Remaining in that specialisation, he was Director Mine-sweeping Division in the Admiralty between April 1940 and June 1943, when he was appointed to command *Rodney*.

Joining *Rodney* in mid-September was Roger Morris, who had begun his journey from Londonderry, in HMS *Pelican*, a sloop of the Egret Class.

> *I had been determined to join the Navy and, after three years training as a cadet, aged seventeen-and three-quarter-years-old, I was a lowly Midshipman. I was on leave at home in the Midlands when I received a phone call advising me I was to join* Rodney. *My dad went up with me in the train to Stranraer where I was to catch the ferry to Ulster. At the time I didn't give it a thought, but it must have been terrible for him, waving goodbye to his teenage son, thinking he might never see me again. For me, of course, it was all a huge adventure, starting with the* Pelican *escorting a troop convoy to Algiers, with me doing my bit by assisting on the bridge, a gofer for the officer of the watch. At Algiers, on 28 September, I and some other midshipmen joined HMS* Glengyle, *a troopship, and two days later dropped anchor at Malta. I looked around Grand Harbour for the* Rodney *and could not see her but I was not disappointed when I did. The massive 16-inch guns were awe-inspiring – glimpsed above a huge bow from the pinnace taking me to the ship.*

As Midshipman Morris arrived in Malta, there was trouble ashore, with truculent dockyard workers going on strike, the situation becoming so tense, *Rodney* was required to land two platoons of men as riot squads. Some in the battleship were disgusted that, now the siege was over, the Maltese felt free to take industrial action, even as British servicemen were dying elsewhere in the Mediterranean. However, having endured a horrific aerial bombardment due to the island's key role in the British war effort, the yardies probably felt they finally deserved decent working conditions and pay. *Rodney* continued to land seamen and marines on riot control duty for several days.

During the customary familiarisation tour, Midshipman Morris got to see the 16-inch guns at close quarters, his feet rooted to the spot as he peered down the muzzles of weapons that destroyed *Bismarck*. He wrote in his journal:

> *I just stared for about five minutes, quite awe struck by these great monsters of war.*

In mid-October, two of *Rodney*'s stokers were killed while working in B Space, in the double bottom of the ship. It had not been opened for a long time and, with fuel oil swilling around its bottom, was full of toxic fumes, which soon overwhelmed one stoker, who fell into the bottom of the compartment. His mate went to get some help, and on returning went straight back into the space where he too was overcome. A funeral service was held ashore, attended by many of *Rodney*'s men. With the Allies having secured almost absolute domination of the sea and air in the Mediterranean, the need for Force H was felt to no longer exist and it was disbanded, leaving the Mediterranean Fleet as the main Royal Navy formation in theatre, as had been the case pre-war. On 26 October it was time for *Rodney* to quit the Mediterranean, setting sail in company with *Nelson* and destroyer escort that afternoon, heading for an overnighter in Algiers. The *Rodney*'s air defences were closed up all the way as it was thought likely the Luftwaffe would, possibly, attempt to use glider bombs to kill a capital ship.[32] Young Midshipman Morris found himself in the port 6-inch gunnery director, where his job was to estimate course and speed of any enemy surface vessels daring to make an appearance. On the afternoon of 27 October *Nelson*, which was lead ship, made a potentially fatal error. '*Nelson*'s navigator must have inadvertently laid off his course incorrectly, as we suddenly found we had blundered into an Italian minefield off Cape Bon,' wrote Midshipman Morris.

> ... *a signal* [was] *hurriedly dispatched to* Nelson, *who replied 'thank you' and quietly altered course out of danger, followed by* Rodney ...

Both battleships departed Algiers on 29 October and by 1 November *Rodney* was passing through the Straits of Gibraltar, but not due to call at The Rock as her steering and engines were giving trouble; she therefore had an urgent appointment with a UK dockyard. As *Rodney* passed supposedly neutral Spain, lights of towns and villages twinkling all along the coast, she was lit up by a searchlight. This sinister event was recorded by Midshipman Morris:

> *I have since gathered that there were five U-boats lurking in the narrow channel waiting for us. Fortunately, we got through without being attacked and three of the U-boats have since been destroyed...*

Zig-zagging, *Rodney* set course for the Clyde, arriving on 5 November. Meanwhile, four days later, at the Admiralty in London, her old captain, Admiral Sir Andrew Cunningham – called home from the Mediterranean to become First Sea Lord – wrote to the First Lord of the Admiralty, A.V. Alexander, about modernisation programmes for the Royal Navy's battleships. The only new battlewagon under construction was *Vanguard*, armed with 15-inch guns, and due for launch in November 1944. The war was expected to drag on for several more years at least, so it was essential capital ships already in service had their lives extended. To that end, Cunningham told Alexander it was necessary to modernise not only all four King George V Class ships, but also both *Rodney* and *Nelson*. Cunningham envisaged asking America to carry out work on *Rodney* and her sister, but cautioned 'it is very improbable that they will be able to undertake either ship.'[33]. He went on:

> *If* Rodney *is to continue in service a short refit is essential soon, but she cannot be taken in hand before the King George V Class* [refits] *are completed.*

Cunningham pointed out that Britain's problem was too many ships in need of modernisation and too few of the right, skilled workers. Halting ships under construction to switch manpower would not solve it, as skills needed to modernise *Rodney, Nelson* and the KGVs were fundamentally different to those used in refitting. The First Sea Lord concluded:

> *Our refitting resources are so stretched that the only possibility of refits at present is for ships which are damaged. If they are in hand for that reason long enough, modernisation may be put in hand.*

The *Rodney*'s good luck was also her misfortune, because although she was badly in need of modernisation, she seemed to lead a charmed life in the Second World War, with nothing coming close to harming her since April 1940. Therefore, she had not received a truly major refit throughout the war, not even in Boston. *Rodney* would, ultimately, have a curtailed service life, due to perennial, and neglected, deep-seated steering and propulsion problems. But, between late 1943 and her end of days, she would add more lustre to her already glorious name.

Notes

1 Cunningham, *A Sailor's Odyssey*.
2 Carlo D'Este, *Eisenhower*.
3 For those unfamiliar with carpentry terminology, a brace and bit is a hand tool/drill, usually employed to bore holes in wood. In all likelihood the Surgeon drilled a hole, extracted the shrapnel and at some stage a plate was probably fitted in the skull.
4 Kenneth Thompson, *HMS Rodney at War*.
5 Ibid.
6 Ibid.
7 Ibid.
8 Quotes from Cunningham's Oran bombardments taken from *The Cunningham Papers, Volume II, 1942–1946*.
9 James McLean, in a letter to the author.
10 Parker, RNM.
11 Kenneth Thompson, *HMS Rodney at War*.
12 Jim McClean, writing in *The Rodney Buzz*, April 1995.
13 Kenneth Thompson, *HMS Rodney at War*.
14 Paravanes, or PVs, were underwater vehicles – which bear a resemblance to a kite – trailed on long cables either side of the ship. The theory was that the cables would hit the mooring wires of mines pushed aside by the bow wave, swept along them to the PVs, which were fitted with cutting 'jaws'. The mine would be cut free at a safe distance from the vessel and disappear astern without causing harm, at least to the vessel trailing the PV.
15 Robinson, Midshipman's Journal.
16 Kenneth Thompson, *HMS Rodney at War*.
17 Quoted by McCart in *Nelson & Rodney*.
18 Kenneth Thompson, *HMS Rodney at War*.
19 Ibid.

20 Robinson.
21 Naval slang for First Lieutenant.
22 Rear Admiral A.W. La Touche Bisset, at the time Rear Admiral Escort Carriers in the Mediterranean Fleet and, with his flag flying in *Warspite*, soon to take the surrender of the Italian fleet at sea.
23 Related in a letter to the author.
24 Kenneth Thompson, *HMS Rodney at War*.
25 Ibid.
26 Ibid.
27 Robinson.
28 HMS *Rodney*, Official History.
29 Boord, IWM Sound Archive.
30 Robinson.
31 Ibid.
32 A sobering sight not far from *Rodney* at Malta in autumn 1943 was the *Warspite*, which had limped into port on 19 September, after nearly being sunk off Salerno by a German glider bomb.
33 *The Cunningham Papers, Volume II, 1942–1946*.

Chapter Eighteen

FORGING THE HAMMER

A magnificent sight presented itself in the mouth of the Clyde on 9 November 1943, in the graceful form of the legendary liner S.S. *Queen Elizabeth*, which *Rodney*'s Midshipman Robinson thought 'never ending'. Nearly 1,000 ft long, with a displacement of nearly 84,000 tons, she had just concluded her latest transatlantic crossing, carrying 10,000 troops from the USA. It was just one more sign of the accelerating build-up for the long-awaited invasion of north-west Europe. On 6 December three Army officers came aboard *Rodney*, to receive training as Bombardment Liaison Officers during forthcoming gunnery exercises. However, before *Rodney* could let her guns roar, heavy fog set in, Midshipman Robinson recording a comedy of errors, in his journal.

> *Fog still hung around about us as we weighed anchor at 08.00 this morning* [7 December]. *At 10.50 we anchored somewhere off the bombardment range. At this moment we were completely lost. A boat was to be sent inshore to find out where we were, but fortunately the fog lifted a little and we were able to get a fix. By 14.00 visibility had improved enough to enable us to do a 6″ bombardment – at anchor. We learned afterwards that of the eleven shells we fired seven failed to explode. Not so good!! At 15.00 we weighed anchor again and returned to Dunoon. We dropped anchor at 17.30 – the fog was as bad as ever and as a result no leave was granted.*

Rodney sailed into Scapa Flow on the afternoon of 17 December, her sailors and marines settling down to a bleak festive season. In the early hours of 29 December *Rodney* set sail destined, for a mock duel with a Free French battleship, Midshipman Robinson explaining:

> *At 07.00 we had a night encounter exercise with* Richelieu. *We fired starshell both sides. Port side was poor. Starboard quite good. All other shoots were cancelled due to the weather. We were taking terrific seas over the bows. These seas smashed up Oerlikon guns, bending their shields like paper. Several ready use lockers were carried away. One of the whalers came adrift and, finally, 'A' breakwater tore away, splitting the upper deck right across. Several of the longitudinals cracked and the deck collapsed several inches. Still we stayed at sea, despite the fact that water poured in through the fractures. Finally, a submarine was sighted by* Richelieu. *At this we turned around and headed for the Flow.*

Big things were in the wind for *Rodney*, Captain Fitz Roy being called to London for meetings. Back aboard ship other officers went to a lecture on the recent Battle of North Cape by Admiral Fraser, *Rodney*'s old friend from the Pedestal convoy. Fraser's Home Fleet flagship, *Duke of York*, led the pursuit and destruction of the German capital ship *Scharnhorst* on Boxing Day 1943. Rear Admiral Robert Burnett, *Rodney*'s former Executive Officer of the late 1920s, had commanded the cruisers in the action and also gave a briefing.

Because she was still leaking rather badly, on 8 January *Rodney* was deliberately listed to port for repairs to hull plating. In fact, she was in such a poor condition, that on 11 January, having returned from his meetings in London, Captain Fitz Roy revealed over the public address system that 'the ship was being paid off immediately to three fifths complement, after which she was to de-store and ammunition and go into dock for a long refit – a thing many many years overdue.'[1] While two fifths of the crew went on leave, the remainder prepared the ship for her voyage to a dockyard, Midshipman Robinson detailing *Rodney*'s ailments:

> *At the moment she leaks 1,000 tons an hour, apart from 800 tons which has leaked into tanks that cannot be pumped out. Our forecastle is concreted across the upper deck and, in the split in the sides, of all things, putty has been used to patch it. On good authority I have been told that the ship is certainly unseaworthy. So this dock business is not before its time.*

Perhaps the refit was regarded as the perfect opportunity for the First Sea Lord's modernization plan. It could be that Cunningham was intending to keep *Rodney* out of the forthcoming invasion of Europe in favour of using her in the Pacific theatre after her extensive refit. *Rodney* began the process of de-storing on 13 January, a good proportion of her stores assigned to other ships. It continued until 15 January and at 10.30 pm on the night of 16 January, escorted by two destroyers, *Rodney* left Scapa Flow and headed south. So many people had been sent on leave there were not enough sailors or marines to man her 6-inch guns during cruising stations, so only 4.7-inch secondary armament and close-in weapons were ready for action. To ensure there was no damage to her topmast, it was struck just before *Rodney* went under the legendary Forth Bridge, her radar gear also dismantled for safety's sake. The battleship went to anchor some two miles upstream from the bridge, just off the dockyard, but news came aboard casting doubt on *Rodney*'s deep refit.

> *The draft* [for leave] *following the first fifth has for some unknown reason been cancelled – buzz has it that the old tub still has something more to do before she's given a chance to rest.*[2]

Clearly, the Admiralty had done its calculations and realized it would be better to commit *Rodney*, despite her mechanical flaws, to supporting the forthcoming invasion of France, rather than a KGV, which might be better employed countering *Tirpitz* or out in the East Indies and Pacific.

Winston Churchill, keeping tabs as ever on principal naval units, on 31 January wrote to Admiral Cunningham, noting his approval of *Warspite* being assigned to shore bombardment duties. He went on:

> *I hope also the* Rodney [will be used] *as part of our bombarding fleet ...*[3]

On 11 February, *Rodney* was moved from a buoy in the river to a basin and put alongside its northern wall. Five days later a draft of nearly seventy new men arrived, a definite signal that, far from drawing her complement down to a skeleton crew for a long refit, the battleship was preparing again for war. Among them was Phil Lancett.

> *I chose the Navy because my family lived in the centre of the country, half way between Hereford and Llandrindod Wells. When I first saw* Rodney *at Rosyth, the only*

previous experience I had of the sea was a short trip in a tourist boat at Aberystwyth. When I saw this huge battleship I was very much in awe of her and that is putting it lightly. Rodney *proved to be a fantastic ship. I was very pleased to get to sea following six months at Ayr in Scotland, where I had trained as a Naval Telegraphist, which was the longest course in the Navy. I finished it in late 1943 and joined* Rodney *in the battleship's Mess 44. I took it all in my stride, including sleeping in hammocks. Most of the fellers in the Navy who joined in WW2 were Hostilities Only ratings who had been called up. None of us were living in the lap of luxury before the Navy, so we found conditions aboard ship to be good. It was so exciting and we all had a job to do, didn't we?*

On 28 February *Rodney* was moved into Rosyth's Number 1 dock and, on having the water emptied, the ship's very dirty bottom – covered in speed-reducing weeds and crustaceans – was revealed; fish and eels slithered on the dry-dock floor. The list of work was long: *Rodney* lost her troublesome torpedo tubes, which were covered in; the forecastle was repaired, the split in its side filled with something more substantial than putty; wing tanks were also given a detailed inspection and repairs; in attending to her propulsion problems, both propellers were taken off.[4] The ship also lost her long derided Shagbat.

For D-Day the Spitfires took over spotting for the fall of shot. There was really no job for the Walrus on HMS Rodney, *so in the end, in February '44, they took* [off] *the catapult.*[5]

On 29 March *Rodney* received orders to sail for Scapa, much to the disgust of Midshipman Robinson, who regarded the Orkneys fleet base as 'the hell hole of the Navy'. Midshipman Morris had departed on leave at the end of February and, on returning to the ship in mid-March, found *Rodney* newly painted, but still in dock. While she might be looking sharp on the outside, inside he found a state of chaos:

The whole ship is topsy-turvy, dirt everywhere and dockyard maties swarming like flies wherever one goes. Our bathroom has been dismantled and is in a filthy state ... During the week I explored various parts of the dock, walking under the ship from one end to the other. It is rather terrifying at first, as one always has the feeling that it is going to collapse and crush you at any moment. I was annoyed to find the whole of the bottom is as flat as a pancake. This no doubt will explain the heavy rolling we experience at sea, not that I can say that with much experience to back me up.

There was ammunitioning throughout 20 March but, in a most unorthodox fashion, for it was performed while the ship was still in dock and being worked on. This posed all manner of potential hazards, including 'people smoking and red-hot rivets floating around.'[6]

Fortunately, *Rodney* did not suffer from an accidental detonation and, on 27 March, the dry dock was half flooded, a good sign the major maintenance period was nearing its end. The next day a hurried series of checks for leaks in the hull plating was carried out and dock gates opened at 3.00 pm The ship emerged, hauled astern by two tugs and, when clear, another two were put on the bow. All worked to swing *Rodney* around until she was in line with the basin entrance. Now the ship got underway on her own power, eased clear on her starboard side but touching for'ard on the lock corner. No damage was sustained but a tug only narrowly avoided being crushed. Moored to a buoy in the Forth, on 31 March, at 5.00 pm, *Rodney* slipped it and headed down river, once more sliding under the bridge, and out to the open sea. Heading north to Scapa, she met *Nelson* in company with five frigates, bound for Rosyth and her own period in dock. Arriving at Scapa early on 1 April, *Rodney* had the honour of securing to the Flagship buoy, for the Home Fleet was not, in fact, at home. Both *Anson* and *Duke of York*, together with a powerful, six-strong aircraft carrier force were on Operation Tungsten, an attempt by the resurgent Fleet Air Arm to seriously damage, or sink, *Tirpitz*. The strike was urgently needed, for repairs to the damage inflicted on *Bismarck*'s sister by the previous year's midget submarine attack were almost complete. With the invasion fast approaching, it was important to eliminate this potentially serious threat, to both free up capital ships, such as *Rodney*, for bombardment duties, and to prevent *Tirpitz* being brought south to the Baltic. From there she might threaten the invasion operation. Despite heavy defences in the Kaa Fjord, on 3 April the Fleet Air Arm's Barracuda dive-bombers managed to hit *Tirpitz* fourteen times, killing three hundred German sailors and causing widespread damage. However, while *Tirpitz* was effectively out of action for some months to come, her armoured deck had not been penetrated. There was every possibility she would live to fight another day, even if it was not to strike at the Allied invasion fleet. While great events unfolded many miles to the north, at Scapa Flow *Rodney* carried out post-refit cleaning up. Ahead lay a very intensive programme of gunnery practice, in one instance Swordfish, Skuas and Rocs playing the part of attacking enemy aircraft

Fog continued to hamper exercises and in mid-April even prevented ships from getting back into the fleet anchorage. 'The weather was rather hazy but good enough . . . ,' explained Midshipman Robinson, in his journal entry of 14 April, but soon mechanical gremlins struck, in the middle of diesel generator trials.

> *Our steering motors failed at 10.45 and the stern of the ship plunged into darkness. However, they soon repaired it. The weather cleared and at 13.30 we passed Hoxa gate to go and do a 16-inch shoot. 'Schoolie'*[7] *told the captain that he wouldn't get back that night – the captain didn't believe him. The visibility decreased, but we managed to get in a 16-inch and 6-inch shoot . . . The 6-inch shoot was interrupted by an Air Raid Red over the Orkneys and Shetlands.* [The] *air defence armament closed up. Two groups of planes approached within eight miles and things were getting pretty tense, but they pushed off and we high tailed for home. However, 'Schoolie' was right – the fog came down and we spent the night cruising up and down outside the entrance. We were told to keep a good lookout for a Spitfire pilot who had been brought down and was floating around the sea in his dinghy. We didn't see him and, as far as I know, he was never found.'*

In the morning, another warship came close to colliding with *Rodney*, shooting past her bows with only 300 yards separation.[8] The fog remained clamped down until mid-afternoon, when it finally lifted enough for ships to enter Scapa safely.

The threat from E-Boats, which were likely to be numerous and among the most aggressive enemy units during any invasion of Europe, was plainly occupying the thoughts of Allied planners. *Rodney*'s 6-inch gunners were intensively rehearsed in how to tackle them, Royal Navy fast craft pretending to be the enemy vessels. On the evening of 19 April, *Rodney* set sail for yet more bombardment training, carrying out a 16-inch shoot against Stack Skerry, a small volcanic rock island, to the west of the Orkneys, which is normally home to thousands of nesting seabirds. The Royal

Marines' X turret, mistakenly used high explosive instead of solid practice rounds, achieving some spectacular, if unintended, results.

> *Several hits were obtained and large showers of rock splinters could be clearly seen falling into the sea near the rock.*[9]

By the end of April, *Rodney* was at Greenock, where it appeared a substantial assault force was assembling: half a dozen minesweepers; the elderly, but still powerful, American battleship *Texas*, with ten 14-inch guns; specialist British bombardment monitors *Roberts* and *Erebus*, each packing two 15-inch guns. Midshipman Robinson observed, with grim humour, that newer, more valuable ships were notable by their absence:

> *This looks like the invasion fleet here – all old and therefore 'expendable units' – how nice!*

On 26 April, *Rodney*, in company with *Erebus*, *Ramillies* and *Texas* carried out shore bombardment practice, during which the American battleship rather overdid things, as recorded by Midshipman Robinson in his journal entry for the following day:

> 'Texas' *fired full charge instead of reduced charge and overshot the range by several miles. One landed close to a main road and failed to explode – the other landed half way up a hill and started a fire, which burned for three hours. The villagers are a little frightened* [and it made] *headlines: 'Argyll Villagers Don't Want to be Shelled Again' and are to protest to the authorities. Somebody one of these days may inform them that there's a war on and things like this are a rather unfortunate accident resulting from this.*

On 1 May, *Rodney* suffered a hit from an experimental magnetic torpedo fired at her during development trials. Having been set to run deep under the battleship, it hit the seabed and rebounded, striking *Rodney*'s port screw. Fortunately, it did not cause any damage but the torpedo sank to the bottom, a casualty of mock war. Two days later *Rodney* took aboard 398 high explosive shells for her 16-inch guns, provoking another round of invasion speculation. The same day, as if to provide further proof, the ship got her first issue of a new variety of anti-aircraft shell designed to explode when it came within 50 ft of an aircraft. Having been used in other ships for some four years, Midshipman Robinson noted rather drily:

> *... good ole* Rodney, *better late than never.*

New supplies of cordite were brought aboard and all across the port other ships also received ammunition, despite bad weather making the seas rather choppy for the tenders. *Rodney* set sail shortly before 1 pm on 6 May, but instead of heading south, her men were dismayed to realize she was northward bound, back again to dreary old Scapa Flow, for yet more exercises and hanging around.

A key question in the mind of the command team was: what would happen if the ship was hit by one of the dreaded glider bombs, such as *Warspite* had barely survived? Therefore, on 8 May, during the forenoon, *Rodney* was listed ten degrees to port and the hands went to general quarters for a damage control exercise, which aimed to ensure they could stabilize the ship. The exercise was very useful because it pointed up a number of errors and showed people where they had to improve their performance. Anti-aircraft gunnery exercises now also included shoots against glider targets simulating the dreaded weapon. On 9 May, General Montgomery visited *Rodney*, Monty's theme being that *Rodney* would do superbly, yet again, in supporting a victorious invasion force.

On the afternoon of 20 May, *Rodney* put to sea with the destroyer *Meteor*, in order to again test her defences against E-Boats, this time firing at splash targets, the 6-inch guns recording some good hits but the pom-poms proving ineffective. Next came the glider bomb targets, which, according to Midshipman Robinson, were 'shot to pieces'.

> *This was followed by a terrific air attack. We met up with four more destroyers at 19.00 and these formed our A/S screen. At 21.00 we were attacked by twelve Barracudas – flown by the pilots who hit the* Tirpitz *– and by fifteen Spitfires, all at once. These attacks were followed by glider bomb attack – the bombs being represented by Martinets diving on the ship. The whole exercise was highly successful ... This was followed at 01.00 by an E-Boat night encounter exercise with four Motor Launches* [playing the enemy]. *Starshell was fired by all ships, which lit up the whole sky. It was quite a spectacular performance.*

Captain Fitz Roy left the ship on 21 May, heading down south, his departure sending the ship's rumour mill into over-drive. Telegraphist Phil Lancett found he was a popular man.

> *My job was to handle the signals and I worked down in the wireless office. You knew a lot more than most people, so I regularly had men coming up to me and asking what the latest was, as I was regarded as a man with the inside news. The view was that we Telegraphists knew things before even the skipper. But, everything was coded – you knew the general trend but not the exact details. Although we were coders as well as Telegraphists, so we could code and de-code things, the actual de-coding was done by other people. But, the D-Day invasion was clearly imminent and everybody knew it. Actually, one good sign our departure date was close was when we were sent ashore at Rosyth to pick up radio batteries, which were to be stand-by power in case we got hit.*

When Fitz Roy returned on 25 May, he was carrying sailing orders for the ship's part in the invasion of Normandy. Hitler's most fanatical troops would soon come to loathe the name HMS *Rodney*, for it spelled their doom.

Notes

1 Robinson, Midshipman's Journal.
2 Ibid.
3 Winston Churchill, *The Second World War*, Vol V.
4 Robinson, Midshipman's Journal.
5 Wilkey, IWM Sound Archive. This was not the Walrus so sorely treated by *Rodney*'s guns off Oran in late 1942. Bill Myers had been tasked with going to procure a replacement from a hangar in Gibraltar and, after some haggling, came back with a brand new plane, which was now removed from the ship.
6 Morris, Midshipman's Journal.
7 Education officer, who also specialized in meteorological matters.
8 Robinson.
9 Morris.

Chapter Nineteen

D-DAY SAVIOUR

The fly boys of the Fleet Air Arm were determined to embarrass the surface warships, with Barracudas, Seafires and Sea Hurricanes hurtling down in deadly earnest, simulating the kind of determined, furious attack the Luftwaffe would surely mount against the invasion fleet. It certainly filled Midshipman Robinson with trepidation.

> *... they came in on the starboard side in great numbers and, had they been real enemy planes,* Rodney *would no doubt have vanished there and then in a cloud of smoke and spray, with little or no survivors.*

With just eleven days to go before the projected D-Day[1] for Operation Overlord, as the Allied liberation of north-west Europe was code-named, *Rodney* had departed Scapa for a final air-defence exercise, in company with *Howe* and the destroyers *Wakeful*, *Wager* and *Meteor*.

While *Howe*, not destined to take part in the invasion, headed back to Scapa, *Rodney* carried out a 6-inch gunnery shoot and then set course for Greenock, although nobody was admitting her destination. Midshipman Robinson found the secrecy excessive:

> *For some unknown reason we are not being told where we are going – we used to be told where we were going as soon as we left harbour ... Why I can't imagine, as one of the things the ship's company looks forward to is being told what's happening, and there is no possibility of information being given away once we're at sea.*

On 28 May, *Rodney* came close to colliding with a troop ship leaving the Clyde but 'by good luck we managed to turn in time and avoid her, but it was pretty close.'[2] Had the two ships made contact, the battleship would possibly have ended up in a dockyard under repair for months, and so missed her crowning glory. With the ship safely dropping anchor off Greenock, Midshipman Morris gazed in awe at the assembled naval hardware:

> *The anchorage is very full of H.M. Ships including* Ramillies, Warspite, Frobisher, Dragon, Danae *and* Mauritius. *This is quite an impressive fleet and looks this time as if we really mean business and will soon be 'on the job'.*

Late in the afternoon of 29 May *Rodney* and other warships departed for an invasion rehearsal. Midshipman Robinson was down in the engine room, helping to control the ship's momentum as she deployed to sea.

> *I operated the throttle, which was quite good fun, especially as the Captain didn't seem to be able to make up his mind what he wanted and we started and stopped several times. We closed up at 20.30 for an hour during which we were attacked by Beaufighters ... At 00.01 we closed up for night action control parties and an attack by 'E-boats'. We did our usual two hours wait – one just accepts this as a matter of course now. At 02.45 the Motor Launches arrived and we had some quite good runs.*

All the ships fired starshell and the targets were well lit up. We fell out at 03.25. At 04.00 the ship went to action stations. The whole fleet closed on the 'enemy' coast, the way being led by the 40th Minesweeper Squadron who also laid the mark buoys in the position from which we were to bombard. Each ship fired two shells from its main armament – ours fell within a hundred yards of the target. We all withdrew then to a small harbour some half hour's steaming away. During this time we had breakfast at action stations, consisting of one spam sandwich. We fell out for a half hour for a wash. At 08.30 came the warning Air Raid Red and off we went again. We had two attacks made by Hellcats, Avengers, Blenheims and a Beaufighter. This was followed by blind barrage practices – one round from each gun and a pom-pom burst at each alarm of which we had four. At 11.30 we fell out at last, after spending nearly 16 hours closed up. During the air raids we exercised 'Operational Alert' – against human torpedoes. At 12.00 we weighed anchor and in company with Frobisher, Danae *and a couple of frigates returned to Greenock.*

For the next three days the ship was frantically taking aboard stores. On 2 June some warships departed, but *Rodney* did not, Midshipman Morris hoping she wouldn't be held back long.

We are expecting to leave at any time now and are getting rather keyed up waiting to see what we are going to do as we seem to be an independent force and may have to do one of these death or glory stunts.

Rodney's assigned consorts were capable of countering not only the range of threats it was anticipated the capital ship would face off the Normandy coast, but also acting to protect other vessels.

As an anti-aircraft cruiser, the *Sirius* was armed with ten high-angle 5.2-inch guns, but had also seen plenty of surface action in the Mediterranean and Adriatic. Her job in the summer of 1944 was to take out German planes before they reached the battleship. The Captain Class frigate *Riou,* tasked with both eliminating E-boats and countering the underwater threat, packed a punch that included three 3-inch guns and nine 20 mm cannons, plus possessed the ability to drop and hurl depth charges. *Westcott* was an elderly, but rebuilt, First World War-era V&W Class destroyer, a veteran anti-submarine ship, with orders to destroy U-boats and human torpedoes. For this task *Westcott* was fitted with the formidable Hedgehog system, which enabled her to launch anti-submarine bombs. As the first British destroyer to use Hedgehog in action, she had claimed *U-581,* in early February 1942. *Westcott* was also armed with three 4-inch guns, which could be used to attack other surface vessels or carry out shore bombardment. As *Rodney*'s task group sailed out at 1.00 pm on 3 June, the flag officer at Greenock flashed a pugnacious message:

Good Bye, Good Luck, and Give 'em Hell.

Midshipman Robinson observed:

... this confirmed any doubts we may have as to our mission – we were off to the Invasion for which we had all been waiting so long.

At 7.00 pm Captain Fitz Roy addressed *Rodney*'s men via the tannoy, telling them she was stand-by bombardment vessel, ready to take up the job when other ships ran out of ammunition or were damaged. He also informed them that *Nelson*, which had by then joined *Rodney*, would be held even further back in reserve, something that no doubt gave his sailors and marines great satisfaction.[3] What Captain Fitz Roy didn't tell them was the invasion was likely to be postponed due to poor weather. He kept details to a strict minimum, so he would not have to keep everyone aboard in quarantine if the ship returned to the Clyde. Midshipman Morris scanned the grim horizon and came to his own conclusion:

The sea appears to be getting up and the visibility decreasing. In fact it rather looks as if the weather experts have picked the wrong time for their invasion ...

At 8.00 am on 4 June, as *Rodney*, *Nelson* and escorts approached the Smalls Light in the St George's Channel, confirmation of a postponement came through. *Nelson* sailed on for Milford Haven, but *Rodney* turned around and loitered off the Isle of Anglesey.

Weather is very bad, Gale Force 5 and blowing – low clouds and rains and a heavy swell ... making any prospect for a landing hopeless, as any small landing craft would just be smashed to pieces by such a sea.[4]

The weather improved slightly, raising hopes it would be good enough by 6 June for the invasion to proceed, *Rodney*'s group turning south again on the morning of 5 June. Now it was the turn of her men to hear a familiar, but no less pulse-quickening, order signifying action was close: 'Shower and put on clean underwear.' This was necessary to minimize infection if men were hit, for fragments of material would be driven into their wounds; it was best to have clean clothes at the outset of any action. As the ship sailed back through the St George's Channel Able Seaman John Frankland just had time to write some notes.

Today, Monday 5th June, all washing has to be completed, clean overalls and underwear has to be worn. The padre has just spoken ... We had a short prayer for the boys who were making the first assault, the parachutists, and for the others who would go after them. Also, one for our warship and all who sailed in her. Everything has to be secured for battle and I am now getting everything ready for going to Action Stations: biscuits, chocolate, chewing gum, for we may be closed up for days, sleeping beside our guns.[5]

Frankland scribbled his notes on the back of a sheet of paper upon which was published an address from Supreme Allied Commander, General Eisenhower.

Soldiers, Sailors and Airmen of the Allied Expeditionary Force! You are about to embark upon the Great Crusade, towards which we have striven these many months. The eyes of the world are upon you.

But, Eisenhower warned:

Your task will not be an easy one. Your enemy is well trained, well equipped and battle-hardened. He will fight savagely.

The Allied commander concluded:

I have full confidence in your courage, devotion to duty and skill in battle. We will accept nothing less than full Victory! Good luck! And let us beseech the blessing of Almighty God upon this great and noble undertaking.

That afternoon, Midshipman Morris and other young officers were allowed into the War Room, a space in the ship given over to maps of Normandy, which was also home to the Bombardment Liaison Officer (BLO) and other key players. The BLO explained how the invasion would unfold, the assault taking place on a 50-mile front, stretching from Ouistreham in the mouth of the Orne River down to the eastern side of the Contentin Peninsula. There were five sectors, from east to west, assigned to the different nations contributing the main effort in those areas: Sword (British), Juno (Canadian and British), Gold (British), Omaha (American) and Utah (American). The BLO explained troops would go ashore after intensive bombing by Allied air forces. Particular attention would be paid to big guns around Le Havre, with 1,000 RAF Lancasters alone devoted to pummelling them. There would also be bombing of trench and bunker networks beyond the beaches and likely enemy troop concentrations further inland. The BLO explained that a large number of British and American airborne troops were to land just after midnight. They would aim to capture bridges, knock out any surviving guns and seize key towns, villages and crossroads. The airborne troops would also resist any early German counter-attacks. H-Hour, when the first landing craft would touch the beach, was to be 7.20 am. Shortly before troops and tanks went ashore, there would be a massive naval bombardment. The BLO forecast good progress right from the start:

> *It was expected that we would be some 3 miles inland at the conclusion of D-Day and that our beachhead would be well established. He told us that the general plan, which would cover some 3 months, was for the British and Canadians to advance to the south of Caen forming a flank along the River Orne and attempt to draw the main weight of the German armour, hence allowing the Americans to advance quickly, take the Cherbourg Peninsula and then push southwards, taking the whole of Normandy in so doing. This operation having been completed, the whole front was to be consolidated and a mass offensive started, with Paris as the final objective.*[6]

The BLO revealed there might be another landing in the south of France. Together with the offensive in Normandy, Italian campaign and Russians closing on Germany from the east, the Nazis 'would then be quickly annihilated.'[7]

The briefing left Midshipman Morris feeling 'optimistic about a quick defeat' for the enemy. However, it all seemed but a dream, a far away event, even then, as *Rodney* sailed past the tip of south-west England, home waters she knew so well, but which she had rarely visited during the long years of conflict. For Midshipman Morris, who, during his last summer holiday, at Cornwall's Sennen Cove in 1939, watched the Home Fleet sail by on its way to war, it was a magic time.

> *During the afternoon the sea abated and the sun shone down from an almost cloudless sky making the rocky coastline of Cornwall glint like diamonds.*

Rodney and her consorts kept tight in to the coast and, as the battleship came around Land's End, at 7.00 pm, *Riou* made a suspicious contact off Wolf Rock, dropping two sets of depth charges. The fountains kicked up completely hid the frigate from observers in *Rodney* and Midshipman Morris was not surprised to hear *Riou* had suffered shock damage to her engines. He thought the frigate was chasing shadows.

> *No results were observed, but she insisted that it was a definite sub contact.*

The *Westcott* was running low on fuel, so handed over to a Hunt Class escort named HMS *Bleasdale,* while she headed for a port to take on oil. *Bleasdale* soon reported a potential contact, but judged it more likely to be a wreck than a German submarine.

The invasion armada was being funnelled from the various embarkation ports towards a point off the Isle of Wight dubbed Piccadily Circus, where a swirling mass of shipping was got into order before making its crossing to the Bay of the Seine. The 6,740 support and transport vessels were protected by nine battleships, 23 cruisers, 104 destroyers and 71 corvettes. Fulfilling her role of heavyweight bombardment reserve, *Rodney* trailed behind the first wave, but was still in defence watches, everyone closed up at their guns from dusk, for the sun setting in the west would perfectly silhouette vessels for attack. The preliminary aerial bombardment got under way, with hundreds of aircraft flying over the ship. Soon Midshipman Morris saw 'low on the southern horizon ... great flashes lighting the sky at frequent intervals ...'

During the night, the moon peeped from between the clouds and one could see train after train of aircraft crossing the gaps silhouetted in the moonlight, the sky almost appearing to be choked with them. Those were no doubt the paratroops and airborne troops on their way to carry out their dangerous mission in France.

By 2.30 am *Rodney* was off the Isle of Wight and Midshipman Robinson also marvelled at the spectacle of war presented by the Allied air fleets.

They all burnt their navigation lights until they were half way across the Channel, making the sky appear to be full of long lines of lights. A light flashing dash-dash-dot on the Isle was their guiding light, both streams flying straight over the top of it. Altogether some 1,000 transports were seen passing overhead during the middle watch.

By 3.00 am, *Rodney* was among the troopships and landing vessels. Allan Snowden was standing by one of the searchlights on the upper deck, just in case something went wrong and his electrical skills were needed to get it running again. What he saw around him almost defied description.

It is indescribable ... there are so many ships, all going towards Normandy. The mind cannot take it all in.

At 4.00 am the ship went to dawn Action Stations. Enemy aircraft were expected out of the rising sun, the gunners of escort ships potentially blinded by its rays. But, rather than an enemy on the attack, there was another awesome display of overwhelming Allied military might.

At the break of dawn we could see hundreds of heavy bombers heading for the enemy coast ...[8]

Next came dozens and dozens of Marauders, speeding across at lower level and, as the sky lightened, formations of fighter aircraft wheeled overhead. The attention of one *Rodney* officer was attracted to the skies by gunfire:

We could see no hostile aircraft and soon realised that they were merely testing their guns.[9]

D-Day dawned fair, with a strong swell, but few clouds in the sky and a gentle breeze, which was only enough to put 'white caps on the waves which glinted brightly in the morning sun.'[10] It seemed too good a day for war.

Unlike many in *Rodney*, Lieutenant Commander Ian Hamilton, as the battleship's deputy supply officer official battle observer, was in a perfect observation position.

From the time I joined in 1943 my job was keeping a record for the official reports for submission to the Commander-in-Chief at Portsmouth. I got the job because I was one of the few who could write shorthand. I would spend some time on the bridge, where I would be at Action Stations, with a board taking notes, using a stop watch, recording the time of the ship's change of course, or orders given to the guns and what was coming from observers in planes, that sort of thing. I had more information probably than anyone else. I was either on the bridge or diving into the chart room, where they kept the plot, to get information on our location.

As the battleship neared the Normandy coast, Hamilton clearly felt the hand of history on his shoulder.

I am not anxious. I am not even nervous. On the contrary, I am elated. I am privileged. At this moment I would not change places with anyone. I am standing on the bridge of HMS Rodney *as we steam towards the coast of Normandy ... I see unfold before my eyes one of the great events in the history of our time.*

Hamilton felt 'nothing to equal it is likely to happen again.'

We are about to break the Atlantic Wall!

He felt sorry for those who would not see the spectacle, closed up at their Action Stations deep within the ship.

Their horizon is limited to the bulkheads of the compartments in which they are closed-up and having to rely for reports from time to time over the P.A. system, given by the Chaplain, on what is going on outside the confines of their own little world.[11]

As he scanned the vista laid out before him, Hamilton probably reflected on the fact that he may well know many of the young men in the landing craft. Prior to being appointed to *Rodney*, he had been on the training staff of a Combined Operations school in Scotland, where the raw material selected to command many of the landing vessels was knocked into shape, or rejected as unsuitable. The principal instructor there was none other than Commander Charles Richard Benstead, who had served in *Rodney* during the early 1930s and wrote the book *HMS Rodney at Sea*, about the battleship's first two commissions.

The Germans had laid extensive minefields off the Normandy coast and channels had been swept clear at both the eastern and western ends of the invasion front.

Rodney entered the eastern swept channel 'marked by gaily-painted buoys with little flags on top'[12] heading for Sword sector.

Groups of landing craft continued to cross our bows, causing us to make violent changes of course. These changes seemed only to lead us into further danger of collision. Eventually Captain Fitz Roy declared: 'We'll keep our course. They will have to take their chance!'[13]

The battleship could not expect freedom of manoeuvre until she reached the more open areas, off the actual invasion beaches. Midshipman Robinson recorded *Rodney*'s approach to Sword sector:

> *At 10.50 we went to A.A. action stations in preparation for going into the beaches to see what was happening – about this time a tremendous number of Fortresses and Liberators flew over bound for the Continent, a magnificent sight. We were approaching the entrance to the swept Channel when a signal arrived telling us to return to Portsmouth – disappointment? – but no, the Captain ignored* [it] *and we went on in ... As far as anyone who asked was concerned the signal arrived after we entered the* [swept] *Channel! The Channel was the easternmost one which passes within seven miles of Le Havre – only last night a 16-inch gun and a battery of 5.9-inch guarded it – now they no longer exist and we passed safely down into the area Sword.*

Midshipman Morris was closed up in the port fore 6-inch gun director and therefore had a good view via powerful optics.

> *I was excited at the prospect of seeing France ... naturally enough I was nervous and had a funny feeling in the pit of my stomach as one usually gets before a First XV rugger match or a boxing match at school.*

This, however, swiftly disappeared.

> *We encountered a floating mine as we neared the enemy coast and the Gunnery Officer fired several rounds at it, hitting it twice but it failed to explode and floated astern of us for somebody else to have a bang at. By this time we were getting quite near and I could see literally hundreds of ships all anchored close together in different positions almost as far as the eye could see. On approaching nearer we could pick out the warships all together in a group,* Warspite *prominent with her high bridge and large funnel. She appeared to be firing in a southerly direction at some target or other.*

Allan Snowden, again working on the upper deck, was thunderstruck.

> *The sheer volume of noise ... the blast of the guns, was incredible and you could feel it through your body even if you were quite a distance from the gun actually doing the firing. A bit nearer the coast were these rocket ships, which were like huge landing craft. When they fired it was like Guy Fawkes' night and you would see their rockets whooshing off into the air. You couldn't help feeling a bit sorry for the guys on the receiving end.*

Adding to the cacophony were the roaring engines of wave after wave of Allied fighter aircraft zooming overhead, including formidable British ground attack Typhoons and American Thunderbolts, armed with under-wing racks of rockets. Each rocket could split open a panzer.

Exiting the swept channel, *Rodney* shouldered her way through the landing vessels, causing them to scatter in alarm. Seeing the huge, and unexpected, bulk of *Rodney* nosing in among the confusion of shipping, the commander of the Eastern Task Force, the plain-speaking Rear Admiral Philip Vian, flashed a signal from the cruiser *Scylla* to *Rodney*, ordering the battleship to 'get the hell out of it.'[14] *Rodney* and her group were told again to sail for Portsmouth. Turning back into the swept channel, she passed some landing craft escorted by a frigate, being shelled by a shore battery situated near Le Havre, a couple of 5.9-inch shells falling short. The frigate made smoke, so the frustrated German gunners turned their attention to *Rodney*. Jim Wilde, a Royal Marine serving in one of *Rodney*'s port 6-inch turrets, was gazing at the landing craft crossing to and fro.

> *All at once a huge plume of water appeared right in front of P-1 and the look-outs reported the same to starboard. We were a sitting duck for the 15-inch* [sic] *guns on the Le Havre battery.*[15]

This attempt to hit his ship was also observed by Midshipman Morris.

> *... they dropped one shell over and one short. Action stations were sounded off and we fired two rounds of 16-inch armour-piercing in the general direction of the battery. No further fire ensued and the newspapers later reported* [wrongly] *that it had been silenced by two shells from HMS* Nelson*'s 6-inch guns.*

As Royal Marine commando Stanley Blacker went ashore from his landing craft, *Rodney*'s shells screamed overhead, making a noise 'which almost shattered your ears.'[16] However, the swept channel did a dog-leg and this prevented the ship from continuing to bring her guns to bear. Writing in his journal that night Midshipman Robinson gave his own verdict on why the enemy was silenced:

> *I presume that the morale* [sic] *effect of having 16-inch guns firing back at him was too much and he gave up. But we had fired our first shots in anger at the invasion which pleased everyone tremendously.*

Rodney anchored at Spithead around 7.00 pm, but *Riou* was sent over to Normandy, to tow back a Landing Craft Tank damaged on the beaches. *Westcott* was not long in *Rodney*'s company either, suffering from condenser difficulties, which she went off to get fixed. When they came up onto the upper deck, *Rodney*'s men discovered they were surrounded by dozens of landing vessels and transport ships packed with troops and equipment, all waiting to go across. The battleship was placed in strict quarantine, with no one allowed on and nobody allowed off. Confined to the Gun Room, Midshipman Robinson decided to write up his journal.

> *And so ended D-Day – the most eventful day in history. Two questions puzzled us seriously: where is the Luftwaffe and where are the E-Boats and U-Boats? – both of which we expected great doings from and both of whom, so far, have failed to put in an appearance.*

They had, of course, tried to interfere with the invasion, but were ineffective due to the almost total Allied domination of the air and sea.

An oil tanker came alongside as soon as *Rodney* dropped anchor and she was put at short notice to sail. Aboard ship, sailors and marines tuned into the BBC World Service, eager for news on how the landings were progressing. It appeared Allied divisions were managing to advance inland, with both troops and supplies pouring across the beaches.

The *Rodney*'s stay at Portsmouth was short, for in the early hours of 7 June those not on watch were roused from their bunks and hammocks, the ship weighing anchor at 2.45 am She made her way past the Isle of Wight to the open sea, with *Bleasdale*, *Sirius* and *Riou*, the latter only just returned from towing the LCT back. As the battleship went out, she jostled for sea room with dozens of other vessels and, in such crowded waters, it was almost inevitable there would be dreadful accidents, especially in the hours of darkness.

> *... an L.C.T. shot across our bows. The one following was hit by us, we went clean over the top of him and he went straight to the bottom. Almost immediately a third hit us – rammed us bow on, on our port bow. Sparks flew in all directions and he retired with a bashed in bow, after putting a nine foot-long gash in our bows. We threw nets into the water and turned on searchlights to enable the survivors to get onto them. Why on earth they did it I can't imagine, as we had right of way and everything else besides, due to our size. Anyway they got the blame for it. We had to leave them to it – there were plenty of other small ships around to pick them up.*[17]

Roger Morris was in the Gun-Room and felt the ship 'heave and lurch.'

> *I thought we had gone aground, so I rushed up on deck and was just in time to see a capsized craft float down our starboard side with the men struggling in the water and some of them screaming for help. A scrambling net was quickly lowered over the side but was of little use.*

Royal Marine F. Longworth was helping to haul in *Rodney*'s quarterdeck ladder, on the ship's starboard side, when he felt a bump.

> *The landing craft was scraping along the ship's side and the screams of the men being sucked into* Rodney's *screws was* [sic] *horrific.*[18]

Sirius also turned on a searchlight, but by the time its probing beam swept over the sea there was no sign of wreckage or people. The mighty battleship had simply given 'a slight bobble' and 'the landing craft and her crew, were gone forever.'[19]

The *Rodney*, together with her three consorts, reached waters off the American beaches at around 9.30 am and, after passing through rows of landing ships, ahead lay the US Navy bombardment group – *Texas, Nevada* and *Arkansas*, along with the cruiser *Tuscaloosa* – 'all firing like fury'.[20]

There was a keen wind, the sky was overcast and rain squalls occasionally obscured the view of Omaha sector, where the Americans had suffered heavy casualties for little territory gained. The shoreline was different from the flatness of Sword sector with its resorts. Cliffs topped with woods were in places directly above Omaha's beaches, affording excellent cover for the defenders and giving them a commanding view. From *Rodney*, shells could clearly be made out exploding in the trees. The battle had plainly moved only a little way inland, with flashes of gunfire flickering and smoke clouds billowing. As she progressed east towards the British and Canadian beaches, *Rodney* passed landing craft mounting guns blasting away. She encountered Royal Navy cruisers in Gold sector, including *Ajax* and *Emerald*, pouring fire inland and then *Belfast* and *Diadem*, some of the latter's shells actually passing over *Rodney*. The litter of war was strewn all along the invasion front.

> *We could see numerous landing craft washed up on the beaches, some with broken backs, some capsized and some completely smashed. Almost the whole way along, the German steel obstacles could be clearly seen, but many gaps, where craft were busy landing supplies, had been made in these. What few houses we saw on shore were badly damaged or total wrecks.*[21]

As the battleship progressed east, Cdr Hamilton, on the signal bridge, noticed it had all become too much for one young sailor.

I remember a Signal Boy, horror-struck yet fascinated, peering through his binoculars at bodies floating past, some headless, then going to be sick in a bucket in the corner of the bridge. Hundreds of dead cuttlefish and squid floated past, killed by the concussion of shells exploding in the water. The scene around was quite astonishing.[22]

Reaching Sword sector, *Rodney* dropped anchor, not far from *Warspite* and cruisers *Frobisher*, *Mauritius*, *Dragon* and *Danae*. By 1.00 pm the weather cleared and it became a pleasant summer's afternoon. While *Rodney* awaited the call for her first official bombardment, those of her complement able to see what was going on gawped at the theatre of war, Midshipman Morris using a pair of binoculars to get a close-up view of fighting in Ouistreham.

We could see machine gun fire coming from several houses covering the beach and numerous Landing Craft Assault were fired at while I watched. They soon took cover behind larger craft further out and refused to venture back. Nearly every house on the shore was damaged in some way and several of the church spires appeared to have been hit, and the town looked as if it had suffered some very fierce fighting on D-Day.

The stream of soldiers going ashore from landing ships appeared never-ending. Initially looking 'like a disturbed anthill, [it] was now more like columns of warrior ants snaking away inland.'[23]

By late afternoon four destroyers were slowly steaming up and down, in line ahead, providing direct naval gunfire support, targeting German positions that refused to capitulate. Elements of the British 3rd Division may have reached three miles inland, but they had not managed to mop up properly behind them, such had been the urge to press on for Caen. 'We saw several of the shells pass right into the buildings and sections of them were removed,' recorded Midshipman Morris.

... but even on direct hits they refused to collapse completely, probably because they had already been strengthened by the Germans for use as strong points ...

Some shells fell short, causing casualties among British troops. Having hung around and watched other ships do their bit, *Rodney*'s men were becoming impatient to join in. Their chance came in the evening, the ship opening fire at 6.30 pm with both her 16-inch and starboard 6-inch guns against a target some two miles north of Caen. Fifteen minutes later, having turned about, *Rodney* let rip with 16-inch guns and port 6-inch. To Midshipman Morris, his ship's gunnery was by far the most exciting so far witnessed.

We fired rapid salvos the whole time and it must have looked very impressive from outside as all the other bombardments up to ours had been so slow and deliberate.

That day the 12th SS Hitler Jugend Division had lunged at the British and Canadian armies. Fighting was fierce, but then a terrifying new sound was heard overhead by the teenage stormtroopers: the 16-inch shells of *Rodney*, often likened to an express train and falling like Odin's hammer blows. The Germans suffered heavy casualties. Tanks were knocked out, hurled aside like toys; panzer grenadiers ripped limb from limb or buried alive by the earth thrown up. One of the 12th SS divisional staff officers who survived *Rodney*'s bombardment that day later said it was 'a lesson in what was to be our fate in the coming weeks.' He continued:

> *... the whistling of the approaching heavy shells and the explosions as they struck had a devastating effect.*[24]

At sea, Midshipman Robinson recorded with satisfaction that *Rodney* had fired ninety-nine 6-inch shells and also 132 16-inch.

> *Some idiot of a reporter ashore reported that the* Nelson *was at the beaches instead of us – a crashing mistake. The Captain sent a signal asking to have this rectified as soon as possible as it was detrimental to the morale of our crew – everybody was extremely annoyed at the mistake – they really couldn't have done worse if they'd tried.*

As 7 June closed, reports of the fighting ashore were mixed. The British and Canadians appeared to be making better progress, clawing their way inland and capturing Bayeux, while the Americans were involved in heavy fighting, finding it extremely hard going despite facing lighter forces. That night *Rodney* moved west to Juno, dropping anchor among transport ships, well shielded from air attack and any prowling E-boats. There were several air raid alerts, something Midshipman Morris found scary, as he could not make out if the bangs were *Rodney*'s anti-aircraft barrage or enemy bombs. However, none came anywhere near the ship, although it was reported intruders dropped mines nearby.

D + 2 (8 June) began as a fine summer's day, with hardly any cloud, the sun bright and warm and *Rodney* got to work early. The port 6-inch guns fired 20 rounds against enemy troop formations near Caen at 9.00 am, with a further shoot – this time the starboard 6-inch guns – at 2.00 pm, against 'a fortified farm'.[25] Controlled by a spotter aircraft, a number of enemy vehicles were reported destroyed. In the afternoon, with the weather becoming overcast, the Luftwaffe decided to launch a concerted attack, using low cloud cover, but only managed two near misses on *Frobisher*. One enemy bomber fared better when attacking a petrol dump ashore, Midshipman Morris among those looking on as a spectacular conflagration took hold.

> *The smoke cloud was colossal and through glasses I could see the soldiers trying to get the fire under control, which in spite of their efforts was spreading rapidly and enveloping all the buildings in the neighbourhood.*

In one incident, a German Me109 fighter was chased right over the Eastern Task Force by a Spitfire. Well aware of blue-on-blue dangers in such circumstances, due to her experiences on Malta convoys, *Rodney* held fire. Other warships did not and the RAF fighter was accidentally shot down. However, a pilot from a Fleet Air Arm Spitfire, spotting the battleship's fall of shot, did claim to have been a victim of *Rodney*'s AA gunners. The unfortunate pilot could not get his cockpit fully open as the aircraft spiralled to Earth and, in desperation, fed some of his parachute through a small gap. The rushing air inflated it, ripping open the cockpit, pulling him from the plane just in time. He narrowly avoided landing in the blazing wreckage of his Spitfire, which had crashed on the beach, but his parachute snagged a mine on a post, which detonated. The pilot's luck held, as he suffered only a sprained ankle. Limping off the beach he found a field aid station in some buildings where the doctor who treated him sympathized, for the slates on the roof above were forever being blown off by the shockwave from *Rodney*'s guns.[26]

Joining naval block ships in forming harbours off the beaches were old merchant vessels, including one that provided a rather macabre home for a Royal Marine who had served in *Rodney* until a few months earlier. The young bootneck officer was in command of 'a motor boat squadron, running what appeared to be a kind of taxi service. He had taken up residence in the partly flooded hold of one of these merchant ships,' recalled Cdr Hamilton.

> *When the tide rose a body floated up from a corner of the hold to join him. As it receded the body disappeared, to rejoin him with the next tide.*

During the night of 8 June, the Luftwaffe launched a series of air attacks against the invasion armada, one of the enemy flying at *Rodney*, dropping four bombs. Fortunately, they missed, falling on the battleship's 'seaward beam'.[27]

Rodney's anti-aircraft gunners had to be careful they didn't cause a friendly fire incident, as one of their number, Alan Sharp recalled.

> *Sometimes the German planes were flying so low between the ships you couldn't fire at them for fear of hitting one of the Allied warships or landing vessels.*

There was intelligence enemy warships would also that night mount an attack on Allied ships. In an attempt to detect them, Royal Navy destroyers and cruisers sent up starshells at regular intervals over the Seine estuary. But the attempted enemy breakthrough came nowhere near *Rodney* and, around 1.00 am, the ship relaxed her alert state. At 3.15 am she received a call for fire from troops ashore and over the next twenty minutes *Rodney* fired seventy-eight rounds of 16-inch HE, while on the move. She then conducted another bombardment run of around the same length of time, firing a further seventy-five. This shoot was against enemy troops and tanks in Caen, the spire of the church of St Pierre, a gothic masterpiece in the centre of the city, becoming a casualty of *Rodney*'s guns.[28] The razing of Caen, in which *Rodney* played such a leading part, was not something her men could take any pleasure in, but the overriding sentiment of the time was grim determination to drive the enemy out. The men of *Rodney* were certainly well aware of the destruction likely to be wrought in Caen,[29] for battleship big guns remained the most powerful man-made destructive force on the planet, until the advent of the nuclear bomb. Midshipman Morris observed that *Rodney* contributed to the process of 'reducing Caen to rubble.'

> *Reports received later said that fires were still burning in the centre of the town and one, from an American Thunderbolt pilot over Caen at the time, said he had never been so frightened in his life, as he saw trees, houses and buildings melting away in terrific explosions that rocked his aircraft, as he flew over the town.*

However, the punishment meted out by *Rodney* on 8 June was unduly severe due to a misreading of the request for fire. She was meant to fire fifteen shells rather than seventy-five. Communications rating Les Sadler was on duty in the Wireless Office when it arrived.

> *A signal was received in plain language from HMS* Newcastle, *the Gunnery Control ship at the beachhead. She was responsible for calling up whatever kind of fire was needed, from the ships at the disposal of the Senior Gunnery Officer. The signal*

read: 'Fire 15 rounds H.E. 16-inch shell at position ...' Firing commenced and then a signal from Newcastle *was later received, quite to the point: 'CEASE FIRE'. The Sparker* [Telegraphist], *when questioned, gave the answer to his questioner: 'I always write my ones in that way.' At the inquiry afterwards, the Leading Telegraphist and I both corroborated the sparker's explanation, and after spending time in the brig, he was exonerated. He shall remain anonymous.*[30]

Near the end of the bombardment the senior British naval officer off Gold Sector had demanded:

Report why you have fired so many rounds?[31]

Receiving this, Captain Fitz Roy, 'who was enjoying himself'[32] asked:

How many rounds have we fired?

He was told:

Sixty-eight, Sir!

Fitz Roy responded:

We might as well complete the seventy-five. Carry on firing!

Ian Hamilton gave his version of how the mystery was solved:

When we completed the firing, we puzzled over the Flag Officer's signal. The signalman was summoned: 'Did you get that signal from Flag Officer Gold, correctly?' The signalman looked at his pad: 'Yes, Sir. Fire fifteen rounds of 16-inch H.E. shell at AFV concentration, map reference ...'

It was pointed out that the signal appeared to say:

Fire seventy-five rounds.

The Telegraphist (signalman) replied:

No, Sir. Fifteen rounds. I always make my one's with a tick at the front.[33]

The use of so much 16-inch ammunition by mistake was a serious error, as Midshipman Morris confided in his journal that night.

This of course sadly depleted our stock of valuable 16-inch HE shells of which there were only 900 left in the country.[34]

The morning of 9 June found *Rodney* off Sword sector again, where the Germans were pressing hard on the eastern flank held by the Paras and Commandos. At 9.00 am, as an enemy counter-attack came rolling in, *Rodney*'s 6-inch guns responded to a call from a commando forward observer, calling for a 'blind shoot'[35] against a wood where Germans were massing. The ship's gunnery director staff were able to see shell bursts in the trees, the commandos sending back a satisfied report. A similar shoot was carried out by *Rodney* later that morning, against enemy troops and vehicles close to Caen. *Rodney*'s guns were also wreaking havoc aboard ship, the blast destroying one of her picket boats and otherwise making a mess of her aft upper works.

While Germans gathering themselves for counter-attacks might be one problem, the enemy's coastal guns were another, holding out despite the poundings they received. When *Frobisher* could not crack a battery at Benneville, *Rodney* unleashed seven rounds of 16-inch armour-piercing, making direct hits, after which that particular gun emplacement fell silent. In the meantime, the battleship's 6-inch guns were asked to fire against a battery at Houlgate, which had been lobbing shells at Allied destroyers. *Rodney* worked without a forward observer or spotter aircraft, as the target could be clearly seen from the ship. Correcting her own fall of shot, the enemy battery was well plastered. With poor weather in Britain, there was no fighter cover to intercept incoming enemy air attacks, but fortunately the Luftwaffe mounted very few. However, at 4.00 pm, a dozen Me109s and Fw190s swooped down on *Rodney*, unleashing a clutch of bombs, but, such was their haste to get away, they missed the battleship by a wide margin, instead straddling the monitor *Roberts*.

Once the raid was over, *Rodney* weighed anchor and set course for Britain in company with her faithful attendants, *Riou* and *Bleasdale*, plus the cruiser *Dragon*. Captain Fitz Roy came on the tannoy, telling his sailors and marines the ship was heading for Milford Haven, to take on board more ammunition. He warned they would be expected to work through the night with no break. The voyage was without incident, aside from the ship's anti-aircraft guns firing on a RAF Sunderland flying boat that neglected to switch on its IFF.[36] The crews of the 6-inch guns were also sent to Action Stations, as E-boats in packs up to 30-strong were reportedly looking for prey.[37]

No time was wasted at Milford Haven.

> *On arrival the ammunition lighters came out to meet us and were alongside almost as soon as we had anchored, the ammunition derricks having been rigged during the forenoon whilst still at sea. Work started in under half an hour and before the end of the dogs* [watch] *we had embarked over 600 6-inch HE and quite a lot of 16-inch.*[38] *Work proceeded throughout the night and by 11.30 the next day everything was completed, a really excellent job done in record time.*[39]

Jim Maclean was one of those working hard to bring the ammunition aboard.

> *We worked all night in different watches and, in spite of the blackout, the ship was fully illuminated, to allow a safe and clear way to the magazine hatches. It must have been a revelation to the people ashore to see the blaze of light in the centre of the harbour and no doubt to see what was going on. My part was that of relief crane driver. The crane's electrical resistors and other parts got so hot the covers were removed to allow the crane to be used hour after hour.*

Some Wrens ashore were overawed by having a battle-scarred battleship in harbour and, despite regulations banning the sending of frivolous signals, flashed one anyway:

> *This signal is illegal, but we wish to have the honour of signalling to P.T. 29.*[40]

Midshipman Robinson remarked:

> *Imagine anyone wanting the 'honour' of all things of signalling to us. I guess they must have thought that the hole forward was a shell hole.*

Of course it had been made by one of the unfortunate landing craft that came to grief a week or so earlier; it was patched up at Milford Haven, a steel plate welded over it. When *Rodney* set sail on 11 June she was well loaded down, with 260 16-inch HE rounds, 610 16-inch AP and 2,400 6-inch shells, the latter of both AP and HE varieties.[41] The 16-inch shells were the last to be had anywhere in Britain and it would be some time before another batch was made.

As *Rodney* made her way back around Land's End, there was a gladness in the hearts of her men, eager and happy to be going back to do their bit in the liberation of Europe. The weather was superb despite a thick, early morning fog, which had delayed departure. The afternoon yielded wonderful summer cruising weather, 'the sea a beautiful deep blue with the occasional white caps here and there.'[42]

Rodney even managed to exceed 20 knots, a remarkable turn of speed for the old battlewagon. Having passed a troop ship convoy off Land's End, she pressed on, her escorts constantly vigilant for threats. At 9.00 pm *Riou* detected a potential submarine contact and carried out a depth-charging run, the violence of which damaged her engines, forcing a withdrawal to Plymouth.

Having expected to go straight back into the fight early on the morning of 12 June, *Rodney* was instead ordered to Portsmouth, crushing everyone's hopes.

Reaching Spithead at 7.30 am, *Rodney* remained at Portsmouth for the next five days, with nobody allowed off for leave, rendering the ship's company 'very annoyed and rather impatient.'[43] Deck games and a band concert could not banish the frustration. Finally, early on the morning of 18 June, escorted by British destroyers *Scourge* and *Fury* and the Royal Canadian Navy Tribal Class destroyer *Algonquin*, *Rodney* set sail once again for Normandy. Heading across the Channel she passed *Ramillies* and US Navy battleships coming out to get ammunition.

On nearing the French coast, *Rodney* met her old rival *Nelson*, reportedly unhappy at being pulled back to Portsmouth after only a short time on the gun line. However *Nelson*'s gunners could console themselves with having killed the commander of the 12th SS Panzer Division and a good many of his staff officers, a bombardment mission often erroneously attributed to *Rodney*.

Rodney dropped anchor off Juno and, once night fell, there were the usual air raids, during which an illumination flare was dropped near the ship, floating down the starboard side, lighting her up quite well.

> *Luckily no enemy planes could have been in the vicinity at the time, or we would undoubtedly have caught quite a packet.*[44]

While supremacy achieved by Allied air forces through sheer weight of numbers was key, the real ace in the pack was the ability of code-breakers in the Government Code and Cipher School (GC & CS), at the Admiralty-run Bletchley Park, in Buckinghamshire, near London, to provide insight into enemy intentions. The work of the decrypters at Bletchley enabled air attacks against the Allied armada to be snuffed out before they developed. For example, a German wireless transmission was intercepted on 14 June and decoded within 24 hours, indicating the Luftwaffe was to mount a daylight glider-bomb assault on the Allied invasion ships within the next few days.[45] On the evening of 16 June the airfield where the relevant German aircraft were based was bombed, so preventing the attack from being launched. Two days earlier German E-boats assembled at Boulogne and Le Havre were obliterated during RAF heavy bomber raids. *Rodney*, back on the gun line would surely have been a prime target for these enemy air and sea forces. On her return *Rodney* came under the command of Vice Admiral Dalrymple-Hamilton, commander of bombarding ships off the British beaches, with his flag flying in the cruiser *Belfast*. Also in a senior position with the naval forces off Normandy was another former CO of *Rodney*, Rear Admiral Rivett-Carnac. With these two men in charge, *Rodney*'s officers and men were optimistic they would get some plum assignments.

By 6.00 am, on 19 June, a severe, Force 8 gale had begun, bringing with it low cloud and rain, blowing from the N/W 'straight onto the beaches'.[46] An offensive by the British and Canadians against Caen was postponed due to the dreadful weather, which continued into 20 June, growing worse. The Allies were deprived of badly needed ammunition and other stores, without which no serious attacks could be mounted, while reinforcement divisions could not risk coming ashore.

> *... unloading* [of troops and equipment] *was undoubtedly held up all day due to this and damage must have been pretty severe on the beaches. We dragged anchor rather badly and had to let go a second anchor. We are now the only battleship over here ...*[47]

Astern of *Rodney* was an LCT, carrying a cargo of eight Churchill tanks, which soon found itself in trouble. *Rodney* put across wires to secure it astern, but when these parted a thick cable was used, which was soon also under severe strain, as the LCT bucked and twisted. In the early hours of 21 June, with the storm still raging, a trawler was in collision with *Rodney* but, while the battleship shrugged it off, the smaller vessel suffered a mangled gun platform and Oerlikon AA weapons bent out of shape.[48]

By 22 June the wind had reduced to 25 mph and at 6.00 am, the LCT indicated she could manage on her own. 'She signalled us later that, of twenty-three L.C.T.s which came in her convoy, she was the sole survivor afloat,' wrote Midshipman Robinson.

> *The rest had been driven ashore. We could see some of the effects ... large numbers of L.C.Ts were pitched up on the beach heeled over on all sorts of angles – some had been flung right off the beaches into the fields beyond – however, with luck, they should have been able to get the material out of them. A couple of dead bodies came floating by during the forenoon – one decapitated with the head floating some distance behind. It was the first time I'd seen a dead man close to. It was rather nauseating.*

At midday an American mass bombing raid, composed of Flying Fortresses and Liberators, passed overhead at 10,000 feet, headed to pound an enemy airfield near Paris. Not long after, almost at wave-top height, came seventy Bostons and Marauders on their way to attack enemy positions around Caen. *Rodney*'s men watched flak filling the sky, the aircraft flying on without altering course, and then a massive cloud of smoke rose from where they must have dropped their bombs. Later a single Boston limped past, one of its engines knocked out and a Flying Fortress crashed just behind the beaches, a huge fireball going up and only four parachutes coming down, signifying six of the plane's crew had died.

By 23 June the weather had improved, with troops, their equipment and supplies once more flowing into Normandy. At 11.30 pm that night a Ju88 dive bomber made an attack run on *Rodney*, but, running into a curtain of steel, decided to attack other ships. However, an hour and forty-five minutes later another Ju88, with a more courageous pilot, swooped down and released two bombs over *Rodney*. Fortunately, they exploded harmlessly in the sea. The vibration of the explosions was keenly felt throughout the ship. Le Havre-based E-boats also made a foray but were beaten back by Allied destroyers and there were various other air intruders throughout the night, *Rodney*'s gunners claiming at least one, which, according to Midshipman Robinson, 'crashed in flames in area "Gold" and bounced on the water for some time.' *Rodney*'s blind barrages consumed one hundred-and-twenty 4.7-inch shells, thirty 6-inch and a thousand 2pdr pom-pom shells in one night alone.[49]

The most deadly weapon deployed by the Germans against Allied ships was the mine, claiming an ever-increasing number of victims. A trawler sank in 15 seconds off Sword, with not many survivors, while a troopship not far from *Rodney* was broken in half by a mine explosion, its bows left poking above the surface. The cruiser *Arethusa* was so badly damaged by a mine she had to be towed back to England. Most feared was the so-called Oyster, which lay on the bottom and was detonated by the difference in pressure created by a ship passing overhead. By 28 June a number of other British warships had also detonated mines in the English Channel and off the beaches, with varying degrees of harm, including battleships *Warspite* and *Nelson*, cruiser *Scylla*, destroyer *Fury*, hospital ship *Dinard*, together with several merchant vessels. It was estimated by Allied intelligence that on some nights up to 50 aircraft would attempt to infiltrate and mine waters off the invasion beaches. With *Rodney* sitting in the same place for several days, the Luftwaffe must surely have her exact position marked, Midshipman Robinson remarking:

> *... the mine menace has become very serious – we are mined in and cannot move even if we want to.*

While she waited for the call to fire, the battleship played an important part in supplying smaller vessels, such as destroyers and LCTs, with everything from fuel to food and medical assistance, taking aboard casualties for treatment in the ship's hospital. *Rodney* also offered shelter to the Royal Navy's Motor Torpedo Boats and Motor Gun Boats, which could secure to the battleship to avoid wasting fuel prior to patrolling among Allied shipping. Unfortunately, *Rodney*'s 4.7-inch guns on one occasion fired at British MTBs, mistaking their engines for low-flying Luftwaffe bombers, but, thankfully, they missed.

On 26 June, with the British 2nd Army making a concerted effort to take Caen, *Rodney* could make a significant contribution to the battle on land.

In the days before Operation Epsom, *Rodney*'s men listened to the rumble of the artillery bombardment and saw the flashes. Now it was their turn to weigh in, along with the *Roberts* and *Diadem*, supporting, among other British Army formations, the 43rd Wessex Division, which drew some of its units from *Rodney*'s home city of Plymouth. *Rodney*'s guns opened up half an hour after 60,000 British troops, supported by 600 tanks and 700 artillery pieces, began their advance. Epsom sought to envelop Caen by driving out wide to the south-west, across the Odon River through Hill 112, where, unfortunately, the II SS Panzer Corps, consisting of the 9th and 10th SS Divisions, both veterans of fighting on the Eastern Front, lay in wait. *Rodney*'s role was to pin down the 12th SS Division, to the east of the British thrust, so it could not advance and cut it off. 'At 08.00 we fired our big guns for the first time since we arrived here over a week ago,' wrote Midshipman Robinson in his journal on the night of 26 June.

> *We fired ten rounds in an hour and a half – harassing fire – at Carpiquet aerodrome. This fire is designed to make the Germans keep under cover – we fire a round then wait ten minutes or so, fire another – wait, fire say two in quick succession so that he never quite knows when the next one is coming – and we know that the Germans loathe more than anything else this long range bombardment by heavy naval guns – it has proved most effective ... At 12.30 we fired another ten rounds in a similar style to this morning's effort at the same target.* Roberts *was firing at the same time as were the army ashore – the whole air was vibrating with the concussions. We heard later that, directly due to our bombardment, the army had advanced 3,000 yards and over the day over 6,000 yards had been covered. This attack shows possibilities of developing into a major push.*

The toll from mines continued, *Rodney* still vulnerable and hemmed in, but she remained a lucky ship even if others were not, two mines exploding on 27 June, nearly sinking a trawler and sending a Q-boat (an armed merchant ship) to the bottom. On 28 June a dozen mines were detonated off Sword, a liberty ship claimed, sinking off *Rodney*'s port side. Intelligence reports stated that on the night of 29 June there would be an E-boat or torpedo-bomber attack on *Rodney*, so thirty-seven LCTs were gathered around to act as her shield, positioned in places four deep on either side. Better to sacrifice them than the only battleship off the beaches, especially when she was doing such good work.

Between 30 June and 7 July the battle for Caen became bloodier, as the follow-up offensives to the failed Epsom drew more and more soldiers from both sides into the meat grinder. Between D-Day and the end of June, British and Canadian armies alone suffered 25,000 casualties.[50]

Rodney conducted a 16-inch gun shoot against two villages on the Orne River, spotting carried out by Army Air Corps aircraft, which experienced 'some difficulty owing to flack [sic].'[51] The RN, of course, also worked with special squadrons of Spitfires and they, together with the Army's intrepid Auster spotter aircraft, flying only 1,000 ft up over the front line, had to dodge shells fired by ships they were working with. Midshipman Morris greatly admired their work.

> *Such spotting aircraft worked with what is known as a weaver, that is another aircraft to keep a lookout for any enemy fighters that may appear. During the first* [16-inch] *attack the actual spotting aircraft was hit in the wing and had to make a forced landing behind our lines, leaving the weaver alone. This plane was soon substituted for by another who told his 'oppo' to 'keep weaving fast' and fared little better, having a large piece of his wing removed* [by AA fire] *after flying a few minutes over the target area. He managed to struggle to one of the landing strips and got home safely ... The third aircraft was more successful but the weaver this time had engine trouble so the project was abandoned. Several hits were reported and good results obtained – one's attention was immediately drawn to the fact that German flak in the beachhead area was very heavy and caused our aircraft considerable trouble. One could see it quite clearly from the ADP and on several occasions we had seen a Lancaster explode in mid-air and fighters spiral into the trees ... One thing that occurred at frequent intervals was the attack by rocket-carrying Typhoons* [Each rocket was equivalent to a 4-inch shell] *on German tanks in the area about Caen. We could see these planes quite distinctly from the ship as they dived down, a brown puff of smoke*

> *marking the firing of the missiles and then large clouds of smoke rising from behind a ridge of trees. The planes would then wheel away, re-group and head for home to re-load their deadly cargo.*

The shoot on 30 June commenced at 2.00 pm, lasting for an hour, *Rodney* firing 18 rounds 'harassing fire' at the two villages where German armour was assembling, the distance from the ship being approximately 18 miles.

> *... we managed to hit the first target with the fourth shot and the second target with the very first shot.*[52]

General Paul Hausser, commander of the II SS Panzer Corps, was forced at the end of June to tell his higher commanders that a 'murderous fire from naval guns' together with concentrated fire of British Army artillery had 'destroyed the bulk of our attacking force in its assembly area. The few tanks that did manage to go forward were easily stopped by the British anti-tank guns.'[53]

But Hausser and the other German commanders were unaware the 'guns had been alerted by a very timely Ultra decrypt.'[54] Bletchley Park's repeated penetration of wireless and signals traffic handed the Allies a decisive edge. Even without decrypting the wireless transmissions, via the Traffic Analysis method Allied commanders were able to identify both the location of a signal's origin and which unit it was from.[55] Decrypts, combined with Traffic Analysis, explain why the Allies often knew the exact intentions of German commanders and were able to strike with naval gunfire and artillery while tanks and panzer grenadiers were gathering for an attack.

Carpet bombing by the Allied air forces often inflicted destruction on empty woods and fields, whereas naval guns and Army artillery could be directed with far greater precision against tank hides and bunkers. Nevertheless, the psychological impact of bombardment from the air, combined with the guns of the Navy and Army, inflicted hell on earth upon the enemy, some of whom were literally driven insane and even resorted to shooting themselves, rather than endure a moment more. In one episode where Bletchley's decrypters played a vital role, some 50 out of 127 German tanks massing for an attack were wiped out.[56] The UK's official naval historian chose to highlight *Rodney*'s remarkable fire mission against German troops and tanks of 30 June, but at the time of writing (1960), was not able to do more than hint at the remarkable advantages the Allies enjoyed.

> *... the* Rodney *astonished the Germans by planting her 16-inch shells squarely on tanks which were massing for a counter-attack 17 miles inland from the 'Gold' beaches. Again and again did such ships earn the warm appreciation of the soldiers, and the frequent lamentations of the German army commanders also testify to the effectiveness of the naval gunfire.*[57]

After Operation Epsom, the Germans launched their big counter-attack, the preparation for which generated a huge volume of signals traffic. However, the shelling and bombing brought down – including *Rodney*'s 16-inch shells, 'put an end to the last German hopes of ejecting the Allies from Europe.'[58] Regular briefings in *Rodney* revealed to her men that enemy counter-attacks were determined, involving increasing numbers of Waffen SS soldiers, although 50 per cent of 'German' troops taken prisoner were actually 'of foreign blood', including Poles,

Czechs and Russians. The *Rodney*'s men were immensely pleased to hear their ship's bombardments shattered enemy morale, one German soldier allegedly saying as he surrendered:

We'll fight you. We'll fight your tanks, but those naval guns are too much.[59]

It was a bombardment by *Rodney*'s 16-inch guns that opened a Canadian assault against Carpiquet called Operation Windsor, on 3 July, her shells smashing numerous buildings. However, despite such efforts, the enemy remained in partial possession of the airfield.

On 4 July *Rodney* received three very distinguished visitors: Vice Admiral Dalrymple-Hamilton, Rear Admiral Rivett-Carnac, and, most exciting of all, General Montgomery, who lunched with the senior officers, and spoke to the ship's company. The Allied land forces commander provided details of how he saw the campaign, predicting the Germans would be defeated by October. Monty revealed 'that he had a bet on it ...'

... and advised us to put some money on it as well.[60]

Monty said Allied soldiers were fighting well and he provided an anecdote to illustrate the fanaticism of some enemy troops, probably the Waffen SS.

He told the story of a wounded German soldier who, when offered a blood transfusion, asked if it was British blood and, on getting an affirmative reply, answered: 'No British blood for me.' He was told he would die if he refused it but he still said no and he died.[61]

After the traditional three cheers from the assembled men, Monty went to *Rodney*'s ward room to give another lecture, this time aimed solely at the officer level. Using maps, he explained what had happened since D-Day when the Americans faced extremely bitter resistance at Omaha. He paid tribute to the 'grim determination and heroic courage' of the US troops who then pushed inland. Montgomery revealed moves to take Caen would pick up pace over the next few days and he hoped to finally have the city firmly in the Allied hands by 10 July. For Caen, some 50 miles closer to Paris than the American end of the invasion front, was key to a successful breakout, acting like a hinge around which the Allied armies could swing. Montgomery's plan was to draw the majority of the enemy's best divisions, particularly the Waffen SS panzer units, onto the British and Canadian armies, while the highly mobile Americans would break through to the south and slam the door behind the Germans, trapping them for final destruction. Monty promised more targets for *Rodney* to shoot at, claiming the Allies had won the battle to establish a beachhead, so far getting 3,000 tanks and 750,000 men ashore, together with many thousands of artillery guns. He admitted that, due to the storm of mid-June, the British and Canadians had failed to consolidate gains, suffering from a lack of supplies. But now, said Monty, the Allies were gaining, and holding, the initiative. However, when the big push on Caen as outlined aboard *Rodney* was unleashed, the British and Canadians suffered terrible casualties and for a time there were severe doubts about Montgomery's strategy working.

Fast asleep in the front row of seats during Monty's talk was Commander Boord, but there again, he had already heard it all before during a trip ashore to visit officers in the 1st Guards Brigade. Montgomery knew Boord from his time in command of the Portsmouth garrison and it was the *Rodney* officer who had asked him to visit the ship. Boord gave a humorous account of Monty's visit.

> *Admiral Dalrymple-Hamilton was delighted with the opportunity of meeting the general because his wife owned a chateau in the enclave* [beachhead] *and he was anxious that it shouldn't be lived in by the troops and he offered it to the general as his headquarters and the general said no he preferred his caravans. And Freddie Dalrymple-Hamilton said ... 'Oh, but it has a moat you know. It is very easily defended.' And the general still wasn't impressed and then the Admiral said: 'It's got peacocks.' And the general said: 'I'm very fond of birds but I don't like cats and I don't like dogs but I had roast peacock the day I landed in Sicily.' And Admiral Dalrymple-Hamilton then picked up the menu card in front of him and showed it to General Montgomery and said: 'You are in luck today, sir, canary pudding.' I don't think the general saw the joke. After lunch I took the general to the wardroom. It was a very hot day ... and he asked if the ventilation could be switched off, as he couldn't shout above the noise of the electric fans. We switched the thing off and the result was it was very hot and very crowded in the ward room ... and, not having been to bed for several days, I am afraid that, having introduced the general to the officers and got the blackboard correct, and all the pictures correct, and the lighting correct, and the noise correct ... in fact, I nodded off in the middle of it sitting in a big armchair in the front row. I came to just as the general was finishing his lecture and I was able to get up and thank him and comment on the lecture because I had heard it before. Then I escorted the general down across the quarterdeck to the Captain's quarters and he took me by the arm and said: 'Jack, you are the first officer I have ever noticed go to sleep in one of my lectures.' He forgave me.*

The next day *Rodney* received a visit from officers in the 1st Guards Brigade, who were given a tour of the ship. Midshipman Robinson was one of those who heard an amazing tribute to the *Rodney*'s lethal reputation and ability to shape the land battle.

> *They had seen a number of German prisoners who had been under our bombardment. One wounded German told one of them that he knew what it was that hit him – a 16-inch shell from* Rodney. *He said that the troops in the line had known for some time that we were lying off the beaches and that there was nothing that they could do about it. He said he had been in England when she* [Rodney] *was built and he didn't like her then – he hates her now. We had blown both his legs off!! So, I don't blame him.*

Ian Hamilton heard more tributes to the effectiveness of *Rodney*'s mighty guns.

> *Even without making direct hits, the blast from our exploding 16-inch shells was fearsome enough to knock a 45-ton Tiger tank over on its side and obliterate personnel not (protected) behind armour. We were hammering, without any possibility of response, tank concentrations as far inland as Caen. It must have been devastating to the morale of the German tank crews.*

When the visitors left, they took with them much-prized gifts that would help to alleviate hardship for the troops ashore. Hamilton saw 'a Guards officer, immaculately dressed, leaving the ship with two newly baked loaves, wrapped in tissue paper, under each arm.' Front line army rations offered only dreadful brown bread, so the virgin, white crusty loaves produced by *Rodney*'s bakery were truly manna from heaven. Hamilton recalled the Guards were not the only ones who could turn themselves out in pristine fashion, despite being in a state of war.

Our Supply Officer, Commander Greswolde Ozanne Davis, a small, wiry Channel-Islander, wearing steel-rimmed glasses, was not to be deflected of his custom of thirty years by a small matter like a Second Front. While the rest of us in the Wardroom wore white overalls and rank shoulder-boards, he dressed for dinner each night.

The Supply Officer would don a freshly ironed shirt and put on a bow tie in his cabin, then walk a short distance to an office that housed the ship's safe. Within was his pristine mess jacket, which he pulled on and then went to the ward room for an aperitif.

He also had his very own Oerlikon guns. Whether he had ever had to go to 'Action Stations' in his Mess Dress, I do not know, as I would be otherwise engaged. It would make an incongruous spectacle, someone in Mess Dress manning an Oerlikon gun, repelling a German air attack.[62]

Despite vastly inferior maritime assets, the Germans were still seeking to gain the initiative at sea and, in the early hours of 6 July, *Rodney* was informed human torpedoes and midget submarines were trying to infiltrate Allied anchorages off the beachhead. *Rodney* was their prime target, the warning prompting her to raise steam with all speed, Midshipman Robinson describing the ship as at 'panic stations'. There had already been several false alarms.

Someone saw bubbles appearing from the ship's side. Suspicious of a limpet mine being placed on the hull, the alarm was sounded and a small charge dropped over the side. Investigation proved that someone had left a pump from a bathroom sump running, and after clearing the water it was pumping air out![63]

Unlike the British variant, which used a detachable warhead, the German V3 human torpedo consisted of one that its pilot rode with another torpedo slung beneath, which he fired when lined up with a target. *Rodney* was such a prize, because not only would removing the British battleship relieve pressure on German divisions being slowly ground into dust by Allied firepower, it would also hand the Nazis a much-needed propaganda victory. Cutters were sent out to circle the ship, their crews tasked with dropping small explosive charges at a regular interval to deter frogmen. Motor Launches joined in, dropping their own. This failed to kill any enemy but threw up plentiful supplies of fish, eagerly scooped up by sailors in various ships, including *Rodney*. In the meantime, a Polish Navy ML had captured a V3 and its pilot. Under interrogation the German frogman 'confessed that there were 50 of them operating from ... a small town just beyond our eastern flank.'

... at 19.00 approximately we [Rodney] *opened fire ... the target being numerous factory buildings believed to be those used for operating the enemy torpedoes. Sixteen rounds were fired and repeated hits were scored, this being followed by another shoot at 19.15, only four rounds being fired, as the target was observed to have been destroyed ...*[64]

On 7 July, Midshipman Robinson discovered he was among eight officers from *Rodney* who were to be official guests of the Guards ashore.

Leaving the ship at 9.20 am, the battleship's officers, together with a number of junior and senior ratings, were met by their hosts, transport provided by three covered trucks, one open top truck and a jeep, in which Midshipman Robinson rode. Meanwhile, Roger Morris and another *Rodney* midshipman were also ashore, as guests of the 8th Beach Group. After leaving the *Rodney*'s boat, they were not met by any specially laid on transport and had to use fresh loaves from the ship's bakery to buy lifts in various Army vehicles to Berniers sur Mer where the 8th BG was headquartered. The young naval officers were soon on the move, in a jeep driven by one of the 8th BG's officers, taking them to the 2nd Army headquarters at Creully and from there to look at the front line. They were driven east along the fast Bayeux-Caen road, through a land in which Morris saw signs of war, but where a centuries old rural rhythm was becoming ascendant again.

During the journey we passed along roads through numerous cornfields, with aircraft strips cut through them, and signs of 'Danger Minen' with a black skull and cross bones on them planted by the German armies as a hoax and, in some cases, the truth. In parts they were cutting the hay ready for ricking and soldiers told us that several bodies had been found ... some of them over three weeks old and, by that time, rather high. Soon the terrain changed from open flat fields to high trees and shrubs, completely screening the road and forming a sort of avenue through which streamed the yellow rays of the bright morning sun. We passed rich pasture land with old farmhouses surrounded by orchards, the trees laden with the young fruit that had only recently formed from the blossom and cattle quietly grazing in the nearby meadows. It was, in fact, the same typical country scenery that one sees in southern England, the only difference being the quaint Normandy architecture of the farmhouses. Everywhere looked surprisingly undisturbed and any signs of battle were very few and far between in this district. Except for the occasional knocked out tank or wreck of an aircraft one would never have believed that it had been the scene of heavy fighting only a week previous.

At the 2nd Army Headquarters the two midshipmen inspected an apparently undamaged Panther tank abandoned by the Germans. They climbed inside and played with it, training the turret and elevating the gun, marvelling at how cramped the panzer's turret was compared to those of their ship. Inside a war room at the HQ the young officers inspected detailed maps of the battleground and gained a distinct impression a decisive bid to capture Caen was imminent.

Climbing back aboard the jeep, *Rodney*'s midshipmen were driven to a village where they gave their sandwiches to soldiers, who were overjoyed at some real food after a month of field ration biscuits. Going west, they hit the main Bayeux-Caen road again, heading at high speed for the front line, the jeep halting at a village near Carpiquet, only 500 yards from the fighting. 'This information didn't exactly make me anxious to continue beyond the village,' wrote Morris.

Luckily we turned left and headed along parallel to the fighting zone, coming out on a ridge by a main crossroads overlooking the valley, with the town of Caen away in the distance. We could see the smoke and flashes rising from a group of trees in the fields quite close by and were informed that those were the advanced British infantry units breaking through to allow the massed armoured divisions of tanks to follow. Our guide said that he would have liked to have taken us down a small road to our left but, as we were already under enemy observation, it would be inadvisable to approach nearer the front line as we would most certainly be fired on by artillery or mortars.

Behind them a battery of 25 pdr field artillery guns carried out a fire mission, shells arcing overhead and plunging down to explode in the valley, making bright yellow flashes. The midshipmen and their guide drove on, turning back towards Creully, passing another battery of 25 pdrs, embedded in a ridge, and Canadian tanks lined up one behind the other, waiting for the call to advance. They also passed hundreds of lorries parked under hedgerows, camouflaged to hide from enemy forward observers. They saw Auster spotter aircraft on airstrips and also a jumbled mass of captured enemy artillery and self-propelled guns dumped in a field. After lunch the 8th BG officer dropped them off at St Aubin sur Mer where the midshipmen were able to buy cheeses, which they secreted in their haversacks. They then made off at the trot for Mike White beach to get the boat back out to the *Rodney*. They waited for a while in the drizzle but the boat did not arrive and so hitched a ride to Courseulles sur Mer to do some more shopping. Morris bought a cardigan for his sister and each of the midshipmen purchased a bottle of wine. They also hid these at the bottom of their haversacks and then headed back to the beach.

Unfortunately we were picked up by a marine MP who questioned us for a long time and then said he would have to report the matter as we had been buying cheese in an out-of-bounds shop. Luckily he did not search our haversacks and, feeling rather scared, we hurried on, boarding an RAF lorry and ended up once again at the pontoon where we knew we were safe.

Midshipman Robinson's tour of the battleground courtesy of the Guards Armoured Brigade had also included an inspection of the Panther tank, but thereafter his excursion convoy headed to Tilly, notorious for heavy fighting, with severe casualties on both sides, in which the Germans lost the village and re-took it several times before the British seized and held it for good.

... but we were stopped about a mile outside by an M.P. He told us that the Germans were shelling the road and village and no traffic was allowed down it. At this stage we were about a mile from the front line – we passed a notice saying 'Achtung – Jerry – Dust brings shells, Be Careful', so we had to turn around.

The next stop was Bayeux and on the way, during a picnic lunch by the side of the road, Midshipman Robinson and others from *Rodney* picked poppies to take back to the ship, which they intended to press as mementos of their battlefield tour. Before the trucks hit the road again, one of the senior ratings even managed to harvest a good crop of strawberries. 'Bayeux was supposed to be out of bounds, but not many people took notice of this – we didn't,' Robinson wrote in his journal that night.

First we went to a shop where we bought some cheese. Here, I also collected some invasion money – special notes printed in England and issued to the D-Day troops. Then we went to see the Cathedral – a lucky shower drove us into the place from our rather exposed jeep. It is a lovely building, I liked it much better than any church I've seen in England. In a room off the main chapel was spread out the famous Bayeux Tapestry. I spent some time looking at it. It is very well made, but, like most famous things, it was not nearly as impressive as I thought it would be ... Bayeux annoyed me!

The shops were full of clothes, luxuries and jewellery. Food is unrationed – you can buy as much cheese, butter and meat as you want – tea and coffee are a little short, but the invasion and the food we'll send over should get over this. The place is untouched by the war – except for the uniforms, one wouldn't know there was a war raging fifteen miles away. The women and men are well dressed as well, if not better, than British people. The women – at least the ones I saw – were rather good-looking and not in the least way starved. Maybe this is only Normandy, where agriculture is the main thing, and things will be more like our propaganda reports further inland. Anyway, it was quite an eye-opener.

As the convoy passed close to the front line, it came across a knocked out Tiger tank.

The turret had been wrenched from the body of the tank and lay in the grass some distance away . . . A lonely little row of crosses marked where the dead had been buried, and we paused to pray for the repose of their souls.[65]

The *Rodney* convoy returned to the beach via the same route, but by now the roads were clogged with traffic and long columns of troops marching towards the front. Midshipman Robinson found the beach no less congested.

Here the landing craft were unloading gear at an incredible rate – the amount of stuff coming ashore was amazing. A sudden crack surprised me and I looked around for the gun, which had fired. Seeing nothing I looked out to sea just in time to see us [Rodney] *fire – 16-inch. Several seconds later the noise arrived with a loud crack. It was a very impressive sight.*

While they had been away, *Rodney* bombarded a crossroads north of Caen, near Hill 112, laying down forty-nine 16-inch shells, hoping to persuade the Germans it was not worth holding. Later, there was a second fire mission, against enemy troops and tanks, with the usual spectacular results. Chief Engine Room Artificer Ken George recalls that *Rodney*'s attitude was altered, to ensure she could hit targets deeper inland, in and around Caen.

The ship was tilted, by moving oil through the tanks, for the guns' trajectory [to be increased] *in order to attack Rommel's panzers. The range needed was provided by aircraft.*

As the *Rodney* tourists waited for their boat ride back out to the battleship, an endless stream of trucks and tanks passed, heading for the road at the top of the beach. Many of the troops coming ashore paused to look at *Rodney* as she continued hammering the enemy, giving the waiting sailors and marines an immense feeling of pride.

Clouds of black smoke covered her as she opened up, and then we heard the sound of an explosion, and sometimes we heard the scream of the shells passing overhead. The smoke drifted away, and she lay quiet and still for a little while before she hurled herself once more at the enemy.[66]

That night the RAF mounted a raid by more than 500 Lancaster bombers against Caen, to soften up the Germans for a big offensive called Operation Charnwood. Midshipman Morris witnessed the dreadful spectacle.

At about nine o'clock pm large numbers of Lancaster bombers began to pass over the ship, flying quite low and in staggered, loose formation, appearing as if by magic from the clouds high above the channel. They came in an endless stream like a huge flock of birds winging their way homeward, as the last rays of the sun filled the sky with a rich, deep red. The drone of these planes could be heard for some 20 minutes, as they came on, heading straight for the target. I wondered at first whether the attack was to be deeper in the heart of France or just on the beachhead area. However, I was not disappointed, as I saw the leaders bank away and steady on a course almost due west. Through the binoculars I could see the flak coming up good and thick but none of the planes faltered an inch. They just flew straight on regardless of their peril and let their deadly loads go. By this time the dull rumble of falling bombs had reached our ears and one could see huge columns of smoke, and flashes appearing from behind a bank of trees over in the Caen sector.

Then another wave of 'black sinister craft' came over, bent on the same mission of destruction, greeted again by a storm of fire.

... this time one of the planes must have been hit in some vital spot, as it went into a sudden dive and, with a shattering roar, exploded in flames just off the beach, uncomfortably close to several small ships.

Parachutes blossomed and RAF rescue craft went to pluck survivors from the sea.

This attack was the most amazing spectacle I had ever witnessed since the war began.

The ship vibrated due to concussion caused by the mass bombing raid, Midshipman Robinson giving his perspective in the journal entry for 7 July:

We saw two planes come down, one hit inshore, the other came down about half a mile away from us. It was an awful sight ... we saw four parachutes billow out followed soon after by another one, then the plane turned over and dived straight into the sea, where it burst into flames. The men were soon picked up. I presume the others were already dead before the plane hit the water. They [the Lancasters] *took over half an hour to pass over. All through the night a large fire could be seen ashore and clouds of smoke rolled over the countryside. This was, in company with an army bombardment, the initial phase in a big push to capture Caen – the push that Monty told us about.*

The bombers dropped their loads back from the German front line to avoid killing Allied troops on their start lines, which meant the bombs failed to destroy many enemy positions, although Caen itself suffered dreadfully. The RAF were bitterly opposed to mounting the raid, seeing it as a distraction from their campaign against the industrialised heart of the Nazi war machine, in the Ruhr. Air Marshal Harris, who had travelled to America with his family in *Rodney* some three years earlier, made scathing comments about the RAF making up for the poor performance of the Army.

Reducing Caen to rubble did not make clearing out the Germans any easier, as the ruins made good cover, the aerial bombardment rendering many streets in the city impassable for Allied armour. The raid was dubbed 'one of the most futile air attacks of the war'.[67] The RAF's true vital role in the beachhead, like the Navy's, was in direct tactical air support for fighting troops on the ground, using aircraft like the Typhoon. Harris nonetheless claimed that while heavy bomber raids might not always be effective in destroying enemy troops and equipment physically, they had a severe psychological impact. Furthermore, the constant bombing of the French rail and road network prevented German reinforcements from reaching the front in time to make a difference or in any fit state to fight effectively. Of course, neither air power nor naval guns could win a battle on their own – the Germans could only ever be beaten by ground troops taking them on and defeating them face-to-face. The war would not end until Allied armies took the battle right to the heart of the Reich.

Like air power, naval gunfire support, and *Rodney*'s guns in particular, formed the great equalizer in the Normandy campaign. Commander Michael Chichester, on the staff of Admiral Dalrymple-Hamilton aboard *Belfast*, described *Rodney*'s 16-inch guns as 'striking terror into the hearts of those Germans unfortunate enough to be at the receiving end of one of her salvos.'[68]

The British Army saluted *Rodney*'s intervention as a 'Victory Salvo', such was the devastating effect of 16-inch guns on the battlefield. One infantry battalion commander referring to it as 'a great solace', describing how his Brigade Headquarters would contact *Rodney* via radio during the night and ask for just such a 'Victory Salvo'.

> *Over the Channel a great flash, like lightning, would suddenly light up the sky, followed shortly afterwards by a rumble overhead like a tube train emerging from its tunnel.*

Next the sound of the battleship's guns firing would reach the ears of the expectant soldiers. Finally, 'a series of loud clumps' would be heard, as the shells hit their target near Caen.[69]

The wider impact of naval bombardment, beyond reducing gun emplacements above the invasion beaches, is poorly appreciated. While numerically the Germans, as each day passed, were at an increasing disadvantage, the quality of their tanks, the skill of their best, most experienced, troops, and their strong, reinforced positions aided by the tenacity of the landscape, gave them every chance of pushing the invaders back into the sea.

The *Rodney*'s ability to intervene many miles inland, literally wiping out fortifications, neutralizing whole battalions of soldiers at a time and hurling battle tanks about, or smashing them to pieces, surely saved hundreds, if not thousands, of lives on the Allied side. For example, small numbers of German Tiger tanks, well-armoured and powerfully armed, were able to stop British offensives in their tracks. In one episode a single Tiger of the Waffen SS used its 88 mm gun to destroy 24 British tanks and armoured vehicles together with a pair of anti-tank guns, all within a ten-minute time frame.[70] The Sherman and Cromwell tanks of the British and Canadian armies, with their pathetic guns and comparatively thin armour, were, with the exception of the Sherman Firefly, no match for Tigers or Panthers. The fact that a bombardment by *Rodney* could churn up an entire wood or fortified village where panzers or 88 mm anti-tank gun batteries lay in wait with their grenadiers was a huge boost to the morale of the attackers and undoubtedly meant many Allied infantrymen and tank crews lived to see another day. As we have seen already, such overwhelming firepower filled the Germans with impotent fury and fear, explaining why the remnants of the Luftwaffe and the Kriegsmarine made repeated efforts to sink *Rodney*.

On 8 July *Rodney* was again in action, opening fire at 8.00 am, pummelling an enemy armoured formation at a crossroads with fifty rounds of 16-inch.

> *We followed this by another fifty rounds at an eight gun mobile battery – we knocked the lot out.*[71]

Ashore, the 3rd Canadian Division, 2nd Canadian Armoured Brigade, plus the UK's 59th and 3rd Divisions, were fighting their way forward in the teeth of determined German opposition.

In the afternoon there were two shoots, the first against enemy trucks and the second on a group of thirty-five enemy tanks, both bombardments highly effective. By 7.00 pm the ship heard that British and Canadian troops were 'within half a mile of the centre of Caen.'[72] While German mine-laying aircraft may have given up, the Luftwaffe's bombers, as if in a last ditch attempt to stop Caen from falling, decided to make a renewed effort to sew chaos and destruction off the invasion beaches, Midshipman Robinson writing in his journal on 9 July:

> *About 02.00 they made a very determined attack on the anchorage for a change. Most of the planes were over the beaches – a terrific barrage went up at them. Several flew over us, one dropping a stick of five bombs, which fell about three hundred yards off our starboard bow, shaking the ship. A large number of flares were dropped down in Sword area but none near us. I loathe the flares – one feels so awfully naked as they drift about overhead and there is nothing we can do about them. A barrage balloon was shot down at the height of the activities. It was reported that there were one hundred and fifty enemy planes over us altogether – more than we've ever had before in a single night.*

Come the morning, *Rodney* – the only battleship providing fire support to Operation Charnwood – was still firing, still hurting the enemy's panzers and troops, still being loudly cursed by Germans vainly burrowing their way into the earth to escape her shells or putting their tanks in fast reverse. When the Germans heard big naval guns, they knew it was *Rodney*. They knew it was the crack of doom and fled.

> *At 08.45 we fired fifteen rounds at some enemy tanks. We knocked out two before they got out of it. This was our last effort for now, on our twenty first day. We are leaving.*[73]

On 5 July the millionth Allied soldier had gone ashore, so ending Operation Neptune, the amphibious assault phase of Overlord. The Allied armies had more than enough artillery now and, with Caen on the brink of liberation, the campaign would move into a new phase, breaking out into the flat, wide open country towards Paris. The warfare would become fast moving, eating up miles of countryside every day, rather than just thousands of yards for hundreds of lives. The battle would soon be beyond the reach of even *Rodney*'s 16-inch guns.

Therefore, it was no surprise she now had orders to head home. Because room was tight, and for fear of straying into mines, two tugs helped turn the great battleship. While *Rodney* was edging her way out slowly through the swept channel, the young officers watched a movie in the wardroom, *In Old Oklahoma*, in which

John Wayne played a buccaneering oil wildcatter. The ship was under tow for the next eight hours and doing a mere two knots, so that she would, hopefully, not detonate bottom mines or hit floaters. Following her out were *Bleasdale* and the destroyer *Kelvin*, with only one heart-stopping moment during the exit process.

> *We had a scare at one time when a destroyer dropped a depth charge, everyone thinking the ship had been mined.*[74]

Once she had freed herself from the tugs and was in safer waters, *Rodney* wound up her speed to between fifteen and twenty knots, heading for Spithead, arriving there at 10.00 pm. Midshipman Morris concluded of the ship's role in the D-Day invasion:

> Rodney *herself had played an important part, with the accurate firing from the 16-inch guns causing many German armoured troops to surrender under the terrible blast from the huge shells. The army welcomed our support and said they loved to hear us firing, as the demoralizing effect of our fire on the German troops was really astounding.*

Now the ship was safely at anchor in Spithead, Midshipman Robinson could abandon sleeping in his uniform.

> *... lovely – pyjamas, sheets, a pillow, again. I'd almost forgotten what they looked like.*

He took time to record in his journal how, during her Normandy fire missions, *Rodney* expended the following ammunition: 16-inch – 519; 6-inch – 454; 4.7-inch – 1,200. And the news from Normandy was excellent. Monty's plan had finally paid off, but getting there had been far bloodier and more drawn out than the British general would ever admit, earning him severe criticism from enemies in both UK and US camps. But all that behind-the-scenes politics was way above the musings of a mere midshipman in HMS *Rodney*. 'The war news is very good,' recorded Midshipman Robinson.

> *Caen – as Monty said it would – has fallen, inside the week. In Lithuania, Vilnius has fallen to the victorious Russians. The Germans have been routed and are falling back at a terrific pace. We ammunitioned today 16-inch – from* Nelson['s stock] *– if only she knew! We took on potatoes, vegetables and mail today, which brings us back again to our normal state.*

As *Rodney*'s men, including Cdr Hamilton, listened to the radio, they expected glowing reports of their ship's participation in the capture of Caen, but were sadly disappointed.

> *... we were infuriated when we heard the BBC attribute all our successes and efforts to our arch rival, HMS* Nelson, *who, we grumbled, had spent the last fortnight 'swinging round a buoy at Milford Haven', and there was not a word about* Rodney*!*[75]

But *Rodney*'s big guns, while silent, would receive one more fire mission and it would be against British territory. However, before that curious episode, there would be an interlude in God's own country, for the battleship soon weighed anchor and sailed for Devon. She was going home to Plymouth.

Notes

1 Although the Normandy invasion is generally known as D-Day, the term applied to many other Allied amphibious assaults. It was the cover name used to denote the first day of the assault, the Disembarkation day, hence D-Day.
2 Robinson, Midshipman's Journal.
3 Stephen E. Ambrose points out in *D-Day* that *Rodney* was the youngest of the battleships to supply naval gunfire support for the Allied armies during the invasion.
4 Morris, Midshipman's Journal.
5 Document kept in the archive of the now disbanded HMS *Rodney* Association.
6 Morris, Midshipman's Journal.
7 Ibid.
8 Ibid.
9 Commander Ian Hamilton RN, *Recollections of D-Day and Thereabouts*, published in *The Rodney Buzz*, Christmas 1998.
10 Morris, Midshipman's Journal.
11 Commander Ian Hamilton RN, *Recollections of D-Day and Thereabouts*.
12 Ibid.
13 Ibid.
14 Robinson, Midshipman's Journal.
15 Robin Neillands and Roderick De Normann, *D-Day 1944*.
16 *D-Day As They Saw It*, edited by Jon E. Lewis.
17 Robinson, Midshipman's Journal.
18 His account published in *The Rodney Buzz*, Christmas 1995.
19 Commander Ian Hamilton RN, *Recollections of D-Day and Thereabouts*. Cdr Hamilton also wrote of this incident: 'The identity of the Landing Craft only became known a considerable time later when relatives of her crew began writing to the authorities stating that they were receiving no replies to their letters to the ship's company and asking for information about the ship. It was only when a member of staff of the C-in-C Portsmouth remembered reading in *Rodney*'s "Official Narrative" a report of the sinking of a Landing Craft that this was married up with these reports of unanswered letters.'
20 Morris, Midshipman's Journal.
21 Ibid.
22 Commander Ian Hamilton RN, *Recollections of D-Day and Thereabouts*.
23 Ibid.
24 Quoted by Andrew Williams in *D-Day to Berlin*.
25 Robinson, Midshipman's Journal.
26 Philip Warner, *The D-Day Landings*.
27 Morris, Midshipman's Journal.
28 John Keegan, *Six Armies in Normandy*.
29 Some 6,000 French civilians died in the ruins of Caen, but they still welcomed liberating Allied troops.
30 Les Sadler, in *The Rodney Buzz*, July 1999.
31 Commander Ian Hamilton RN, *Recollections of D-Day and Thereabouts*.
32 Ibid.
33 Ibid.
34 Morris, Midshipman's Journal.
35 Ibid.
36 Identification Friend of Foe, a system to enable units to automatically identify themselves to friendly units.
37 Morris, Midshipman's Journal.
38 Robinson says in his journal that *Rodney* loaded fifty 16-inch shells and 100 cordite cases.
39 Morris, Midshipman's Journal.
40 Quote from Robinson, Midshipman's Journal. 'P.T. 29' – pennant number of *Rodney*.
41 Robinson, Midshipman's Journal.
42 Morris, Midshipman's Journal.
43 Ibid.

44 Ibid.
45 Macksey, *The Searchers.*
46 Robinson, Midshipman's Journal.
47 Ibid.
48 Ibid.
49 Ibid.
50 Mark Urban, *The Generals.*
51 Morris, Midshipman's Journal.
52 Robinson, Midshipman's Journal.
53 Quoted by John Keegan in *Six Armies in Normandy.*
54 Ibid. Ultra was the British codeword for intelligence extracted from German wireless traffic decrypts during the Second World War.
55 Ibid.
56 Macksey, *The Searchers.*
57 Roskill, *The Navy at War.*
58 Macksey, *The Searchers.*
59 Robinson, Midshipman's Journal.
60 Morris, Midshipman's Journal.
61 Ibid.
62 Commander Ian Hamilton RN, *Recollections of D-Day and Thereabouts.*
63 Ibid.
64 Morris, Midshipman's Journal.
65 Kenneth Thompson, *HMS Rodney at War.*
66 Ibid.
67 Max Hastings, *Overlord.*
68 *The Greatest Amphibious Operation in History (And a Great Naval Bombardment)*, by Cdr Michael Chichester, *The Naval Review*, April 1994.
69 Lieutenant Colonel E. Jones, quoted by Jonathan Bastable in *Voices from D-Day.*
70 Andrew Williams, *D-Day to Berlin.*
71 Robinson, Midshipman's Journal.
72 Ibid.
73 Robinson, Midshipman's Journal.
74 Morris, Midshipman's Journal.
75 Commander Ian Hamilton RN, *Recollections of D-Day and Thereabouts.*

Chapter Twenty

TARGET ALDERNEY

The Reverend Gordon Taylor first saw HMS *Rodney* from astern; a magnificent broad-beamed behemoth, moored mid-stream in the wide river Tamar, with Brunel's spectacular railway bridge as a backdrop. His journey to the battleship had been a long one, for prior to *Rodney* the twenty-eight year old naval Chaplain stood more chance of being eaten alive by a lion than coming under enemy fire.

In 1943 I had been appointed Chaplain at the Royal Naval Air Yard at Nairobi in Kenya, over 400 miles from the sea, which is pretty unusual for a naval shore base, but it was a welcome change after almost 100,000 miles of seafaring, mainly in Armed Merchant Cruisers. There were wild animals all around, in a very open setting. Kenya in those days seemed to be a big game reserve right down to the sea. There was no real fence around the aerodrome. It was not unknown for people to be mauled at night. In 1944 I was told I was returning to England, and I got back in July to enjoy brief Foreign Service leave. Then I was quickly re-appointed, to the battleship Rodney, *which I joined at Devonport in late July.*[1]

Rodney had been home for around a fortnight, her sailors hearing they were bound for Plymouth from none other than the architect of Operation Neptune himself, Admiral Bertram Ramsay, when he came aboard at Portsmouth, on 14 July. Gathering the ship's company around him on the upper deck in the pouring rain, the admiral found his views on the war, including the revelation that it was he who had made the bet with Monty about it being over by October, made little impact on *Rodney*'s complement, most of whom could not hear what he was saying anyway. However, news that the ship would be going to her home port caused great excitement. On 15 July *Rodney* weighed anchor at 4.30 am and, escorted by two sloops and a frigate, set a course for the south-west of England, where the battleship was promised a long period alongside. On arrival Midshipman Robinson was unforgiving of bomb-battered Plymouth and there was possibly a feeling of anticlimax throughout the ship.

No cheering crowds greeted us, as was expected, only a dark fog and a few women waving handkerchiefs. After a trip ashore I was convinced that Plymouth is a good place to work for an [signals] *exam – it's deader than Portsmouth.*[2]

Midshipman Morris was more upbeat, commenting in his journal, with evident pleasure, that boats taking men to and from ship were run by Wrens. Every four days a 24-hour leave pass was granted to members of the ship's company, which enabled local married men to spend more time at home.

Midshipman Morris went to a Glenn Miller concert in a cinema, which was so packed he had to stand in the aisles. One afternoon, with some fellow midshipmen, he walked to Looe, a shark fishing town in south-east Cornwall, getting some rather muddy shoes, but taking the train back to Plymouth. He was tired, but refreshed by the glories of the English countryside after so many weeks confined to a big, grey warship. However, on 7 August, Captain Fitz Roy told *Rodney*'s men there would be no more leave, for the ship had been put on notice to carry out a bombardment mission. On 10 August all boats were hoisted in during the forenoon and the ship secured for sea, sailing at 1.00 pm, in company with destroyers *Faulknor* and *Stoord*, the latter a Norwegian warship. Midshipman Morris revelled in the ship's departure.

> *The weather was perfect, the sun making the sea glint like gold, as it shone down from a cloud speckled sky, the rocky cliffs of Devon being visible on our port side.*

Rodney was heading for Portland, on the way carrying out anti-aircraft gunnery live-firing to sharpen up her defences. Arriving that evening, some of the battleship's sailors and marines, including Roger Morris, enjoyed a spot of mackerel fishing. Back aboard ship 'the buzz had it that we were to bombard the island of Alderney on the following day.'[3] The *Rodney* slipped her buoy at 6.45 am, accompanied by her two escorts, plus the Battle of North Cape veteran destroyer *Saumarez*, the latter only for a short while, before being replaced by *Urania*. A trio of escorts was necessary because, in recent times, waters around the Channel Islands had seen pitched battles between German and Allied warships, including engagements in which the Canadian destroyer *Athabaskan* and British cruiser *Charybdis* were sunk. As the only British Crown territories occupied by the Germans, the Channel Islands were highly prized and heavily fortified. Hitler expected there would be a determined assault to liberate them, but he guessed wrong and, like many of the Channel ports on the coast of France after D-Day, the Allies decided it was best to ignore them, merely cutting off their garrisons.[4] In looking at options for the invasion of Normandy, the Allies had considered a direct assault on the Contentin Peninsula, to seize the major port of Cherbourg, but planners felt it would be necessary to capture Alderney, and possibly Guernsey, first, something potentially involving major casualties.

However, during the summer of 1944, with Alderney just over half a dozen miles from the Contentin, its guns were making a nuisance of themselves, loosing a trio of shells every few hours to cause as much disruption as possible.[5]

A strike by bomber aircraft on such a small target was not felt to be practical because of heavy air defences on the island said to include four batteries of the dreaded 88 mm[6], but there was also, possibly, a certain amount of hesitation about levelling a piece of British territory. The American and British 'bomber barons' were also probably more interested in destroying the heart of the German war machine than diverting their resources to its periphery.

The answer was a battleship with a track record of hammering gun emplacements into submission. Fortunately, the majority of the civilian population of Alderney had been evacuated in 1940, when the British government elected not to defend the Channel Islands, to avoid a dangerous drain on military resources. The Germans subsequently established labour camps on Alderney, incarcerating Polish and Russian PoWs, Spanish socialists, together with Jews, the latter selected for elimination once their usefulness had been sweated out of them. These slave labourers constructed the formidable fortifications, including emplacements for the guns harassing the Contentin. The inmates of the camps were evacuated to Germany in June 1944, but not before several hundred people had been worked to death or liquidated by the SS at Lager Sylt, the only fully-fledged concentration camp on British soil. *Rodney*'s bombardment of Alderney was to be the only instance in naval history of a

British battleship firing her guns in anger at Crown territory. Her objective was the destruction of four 6-inch German guns situated in Batterie Blucher, on a hill in the centre of the island, half a mile from the town of St Anne. It must have been a strange experience for one of *Rodney*'s men, Leading Seaman P. LePoidvin, who had been in the ship since 1939, for he was a native of Alderney. He had been consulted on where the remaining civilian population was likely to be and, naturally enough, advised the gunners to avoid hitting St Anne.[7]

Rodney was to work with aircraft from No. 26 Squadron, which specialized in spotting for naval bombardment missions. Aerial photographs dating from March 1944 were studied and a new photo-reconnaissance mission flown on 9 August, with the images produced brought aboard *Rodney* at Portland the following day. On studying the photos, the aiming point was changed, in order to ensure greater accuracy. Meteorological conditions were assessed to see if they were likely to be favourable on 11 August.[8]

There was an experimental side to *Rodney*'s fire mission, with Captain Fitz Roy instructed to determine 'what damage could be expected from the deliberate bombardment by a capital ship at long range of this type of target.'[9]

The results of bombardments against similar gun positions in Normandy had been far from satisfactory and the Admiralty considered the fire mission against Batterie Blucher to be a means of exploring better liaison between ships and spotter aircraft. The weather on 11 August turned out wrong – clear skies, with no cloud cover in which the spotter aircraft could take refuge from flak – and so *Rodney* turned around. On *Rodney*'s return to Portland, which was wreathed in fog, afternoon leave was given but the ship's company was told not to discuss their impending mission with anyone. For all they knew German spies might be at work in nearby Weymouth. The fog cleared to reveal a fine summer's day, the order 'hands to bathe' sounded aboard *Rodney*, her sailors and marines jumping from the accommodation ladder into the sea. As they larked about, all around were Allied landing ships, MTBs, corvettes and destroyers, similarly basking in the sun. However, for senior midshipmen, including Tony Robinson, it was time for the Lieutenant's Exam.

> *It took all day and was quite an ordeal. Afterwards I relaxed by showing a couple of Wren officers around the ship. They kindly invited us to a dance at their hostel which was amusing at times, though rather nauseating due to too much gold braid.*

On 12 August, *Rodney* proceeded to sea at 7.30 am, with destroyers *Jervis* and *Faulkner* providing protection.

> *This time the show was really on and we headed straight for the French coast at full speed ... It was a fresh morning with the wind blowing from the south, white caps on the waves and the sky clouded* [sic], *with patches of deep blue between the breaks. The destroyers appeared to be licking along at a fine rate, rising and falling slightly on the gentle swell, while* Rodney *just ploughed straight on in her usual style.*[10]

Towards lunch the coast of France came into view, the ship going to Action Stations, as return fire from Alderney was expected; the wind dropped and the sky was cloudless by the time Cherbourg was sighted directly ahead. *Rodney* 'turned West and crept up along the coast of the peninsula, dropping anchor at 12.15, a mile offshore about a mile from the tip.'[11]

The intention was to use Cap de la Hague as a shield for the ship, the 16-inch guns actually firing over it. The two destroyers patrolled on the seaward side, just in case any E-boats or enemy submarines tried to intervene.

Lt Cdr Hamilton was stationed on the battleship's bridge, armed with a pair of binoculars, a shorthand notebook and a stopwatch, repeating the observation role he had performed during action off Normandy, in order to produce the 'Official Narrative' of the bombardment for Commander-in-Chief Portsmouth. As he waited for the guns to open fire, Hamilton remarked to someone standing nearby: 'I wish they would get a move on, or we will miss afternoon tea.'[12]

At 1.56 pm the Spitfire lurking overhead reported:

> *Ready to spot.*

The shoot began at 2.11 pm, the first shell falling wide of the mark and demolishing a farmhouse,[13] but, with corrections from the spotter aircraft, the shells were soon straddling the battery, scoring a direct hit sixteen minutes later.[14] According to the legend among the *Rodney*'s company, the Germans were literally caught napping.

> *Because we were out of sight behind the Cherbourg Peninsula* [sic], *some of the Germans were rudely disturbed as they snoozed in deck chairs, sunning themselves.*[15]

Rodney was approximately twenty miles, as the crow flies, from the island and time of flight for each shell to target was around one minute, the spotter aircraft working in pairs over the target for an hour at a time. An Associated Press reporter aboard the battleship reported how she 'shook and shivered' as the 16-inch guns 'spurted flame, smoke and death.'[16]

Midshipman Morris recorded his perspective on how the fire mission unfolded:

> *... a low mist obscured both us and the target. After a short wait, the spotting plane arrived and reported that he could see the target in spite of the mist ... and we opened fire. Three hits were reported during the first ten rounds and firing at regular intervals continued until 75 shells had been sent their way. Altogether three of the guns were reported to have received direct hits, the remaining one suffering a twenty yard miss, that must have dislodged it from its mounting, the* [emplacement's] *control tower being hit nine times! ... During the latter half of the shoot the mist lifted, and we could see the outline of the island behind the mainland. Several bursts could be seen and huge pillars of smoke spiralled up into the sky after some of the hits. Occasional flashes of gunfire could be seen from the island and the sky was dotted with the little black spots of A.A. bursts.*

Whenever the AA fire became too hot the Spitfire darted into cloud, at one stage its pilot instructing the *Rodney*: 'Cease firing – changing position'.[17]

The ship's new Chaplain thought it most appropriate the shoot was taking place on 'the Glorious Twelfth', the opening day of the grouse-shooting season.

> *As* Rodney *was going across the Channel for this duty, a small warship passed us on a reciprocal course, and she signalled: 'And one for us.' I watched the shelling, which took over two hours, from the vacant Admiral's Bridge, where I could almost see down the funnel. I did not have a fixed Action Station, though, if I had had to do so, and there were casualties, it would obviously have been the sick-bay. The bombardment of Alderney shook the ship, for, when a 16-inch gun is fired, it provides great concussion.*

Midshipman Robinson wrote in his account of the episode:

> *The top of Alderney could just be seen from A.D.P. ... We fired one-gun salvos from the right of A and centre of B* [turrets], *with an occasional two-gun one thrown in ... We had expected our fire to be returned and were prepared for damage, but he never knew what hit him and nothing came back. The Spits did a magnificent job with their spotting – flak was heavy to start with, but fell off soon after we'd begun. I guess they all went to ground.*

He added that it was 'a very successful shoot' and the ship's official Admiralty history would later report 'three of the four guns in the battery were reported damaged.' At the conclusion of the bombardment, to avoid *Rodney* being exposed to fire by sailing out from behind the cover of Cap de la Hague, the ship was turned on the spot by a US Navy tug from Cherbourg. During the bombardment this same vessel also ensured *Rodney* did not swing at anchor, maintaining her position broadside on to the target.[18] Turned around, *Rodney* piled on the speed and headed for Portland. Meanwhile, prior to filing his despatch, the AP reporter had been carrying out research into the cost of the bombardment, discovering that each shell cost £250, with £18,750 worth of shells hurled against the German gun positions on Alderney.

As the ship made her way back to Portland, he noted her 'battle ensign whipping smartly in the breeze.'[19]

Meanwhile, on the island of Guernsey, civil servant Louis Guillemette, secretary to the president of the States Controlling Committee during the German occupation, recorded in his diary that he watched columns of black smoke rising from Alderney. Alerted to the sounds of something dramatic happening, other Channel Islanders used secret radios to find out what was going on and heard a misleading BBC broadcast claiming it was the beginning of an Allied invasion.

Despite glowing contemporary Royal Navy reports of the bombardment's effectiveness, and also a widespread belief in its devastating effect aboard *Rodney*, only one gun was actually taken out of action for any length of time, which was transported to Guernsey, repaired and soon returned to its emplacement.[20] There were no civilian victims of the bombardment, although two German soldiers were killed, neither of them belonging to the gun crews, all of whom retreated into bunkers. A trench system around Batterie Blucher received heavy punishment and *Rodney*'s fall of shot was indeed accurate – forty 16-inch shells fell within a 200 metres radius of the battery's centre. But there was no escaping that, overall, results were very disappointing, especially as Batterie Blucher's guns had no overhead protection. Three of the German guns were firing at Allied shipping by 30 August and by November all four were in commission, with plans afoot to resume bombardment of the Contentin.[21] Fortunately, in all their fire missions, the guns of the Batterie Blucher caused few casualties, with only one American soldier losing his life. Among those taking cover from *Rodney*'s hammer blows was twenty-four year old Luftwaffe flak regiment NCO Hubert Wolf, one of 35,000 German military personnel making up the islands' occupation force. For Wolf, the bombardment ended weeks of tense waiting for the Allies to finally turn their ire on the Channel Islands.

> *On the radio we heard that the* [Normandy] *invasion was successful and day-by-day the Allies made progress in gaining territory in France. We realized that Alderney*

> *was in a trap, surrounded by sea and cut off from France, our source of supply. What will the Allies do to Alderney? But nothing happened. Our daily life and routine went on like before D-Day. Waiting to be attacked or not. One day an alarm was given, because* [of] *the British battleship* Rodney, *positioned to the north of Cherbourg and too far away to be reached by our guns ... We were told to stay in our dugouts. One shell landed only about 15 metres away from our shelter – the hole in the ground was much deeper than our shelter. Our life had been saved by millimetres of different firing angle. This event was no fight; we thought that the* Rodney *fired on Alderney as an exercise to show us that war is still on and that we are vulnerable.*[22]

Hubert Wolf ended up spending two years in England as a Prisoner-of-War, returning to Alderney for the first time since the war in 2004, when he was welcomed warmly by its inhabitants and gave a talk on his experiences.

He recalled events surrounding the *Rodney* bombardment, revealing that, with the exception of coming under fire from the British battleship, being posted to Alderney was a godsend. While he had experienced 'conditions that were not so bright' during two years on the island, Wolf avoided being involved in the kind of combat that elsewhere claimed the lives of thousands of young men like him. Hubert Wolf concluded:

> *... it ultimately had saved my life. For this I am very grateful.*[23]

To this day, *Rodney*'s Cdr Ian Hamilton, who was on the battleship's bridge throughout the bombardment, remains convinced *Rodney* inflicted far more damage and loss of life than admitted by the Germans.

> *It is almost impossible to believe – after HMS* Rodney *some few weeks earlier had obliterated a German 45-ton Tiger tank concentration some 20 miles distant – that on a day and time suitable weather-wise for spotter aircraft, firing from anchor, with tugs to keep her from swinging, at a suitable range, at a target recently photographed, and without enemy opposition, firing, in the main, single gun salvos – with the target area about 170 yards by 140 yards, walled but open topped – with the result that the blast from direct hits made the maximum damage, and shells were landing about one every three minutes, that only one soldier was killed and a few injured and there was only damage to one gun which was quickly repaired!? Believe that if you can!*

Having ceased firing at 4.42 pm and weighed anchor eighteen minutes later, *Rodney* reached Portland at 10.30 pm on the evening of the Alderney bombardment, remaining there for the next fortnight, which allowed plenty of shore leave for her men. Having passed his Sub Lieutenant's Exam, it was time for Midshipman Robinson to depart.

> *So, on Friday, 19 August we left the venerable and famous* Rodney. *Despite all the things I may have said and thought about the old ship, I really enjoyed life aboard her immensely and only hope that life in my future ships will be as happy and pleasant as they have been over the past sixteen months.*[24]

Setting sail at 5.45 am on 27 August, *Rodney* headed west, bound for Plymouth, a sloop and two destroyers as escort. Along the way, there was the usual enthusiastic depth-charging of suspected submarine contacts, which Midshipmen Morris told his journal were, as was so often the case, probably wrecks on the seabed. The ship reverberated to each explosion, sounding like she had hit a mine. By 1.30 pm that day she was alongside at Devonport, Captain Fitz Roy ordering clear lower decks for an important announcement. He told the men 'their days of bombarding France were over'[25] and they would each receive 25 days' leave.

This amazing statement brought cheers of appreciation from all the ship's company.

In that late summer of 1944 the feeling that the war in Europe would soon be over was widespread and Captain Fitz Roy echoed that sentiment by telling his men the Allies would within months turn their full attention to the Far East. He said the ship's company of *Rodney* would soon be broken up, with many of them sent to fight the Japanese. He had more information related to this in a signal[26] but needed further confirmation from the Admiralty before he could reveal its exact contents. The lower deck was cleared again at 4.00 pm, but Captain Fitz Roy told the men a mistake had been made; he had discovered *Rodney* would not be taken out of commission. It seemed her fighting life was not yet over and they would, after all, only get five days leave at home each, but with travel time on top. It was crushing news.

No loud cheers![27]

Two days later *Rodney* was moved into Devonport Dockyard's 5 Basin for essential work, with Roger Morris among the first to receive leave, returning to the ship on 5 September. Between 6 September and 13 September, the monotony of maintenance progressed but there was leeway for additional leave, Morris borrowing the ship's motorbike for a day trip to Paignton. On the way back its exhaust fell to pieces, causing it to 'make a loud roar like an aircraft engine.'

...frightening many of the war weary people of Plymouth, who probably thought it was a flying bomb approaching at a great rate of knots.

The Bombardment Liaison Officer, a Captain in the Army, had meanwhile left the ship, a sure sign that at least *Rodney*'s fire support days were over. A problem with one of *Rodney*'s propeller shaft glands had meanwhile been discovered, which had to be repaired with the help of divers.

Once all her men had returned from leave, in the second week of September *Rodney* was moved out of the basin, becoming jammed in the narrow lock entrance. Fortunately a tug was able to nose her off the jetty side, enabling another to tow the battleship out stern first into the Hamoaze. Leaving Plymouth, *Rodney* headed north, on 14 September, carrying out a full 16-inch gunnery shoot in the Pentland Firth. Once in the familiar fleet anchorage of Scapa Flow, she off-loaded her high explosive shells, replacing them with armour-piercing, for *Rodney's* next mission was to ride shotgun on a Russia-bound convoy, ready to do battle with *Tirpitz*.

Notes

1 Gordon Taylor replaced the padre, Kenneth Thompson, who wrote the bulk of the book *HMS Rodney at War*, an affectionate, idiosyncratic insiders' account of the battleship's service in war. All royalties from the sale of the book, which was published in 1946, went to fund a cot named 'Rodney' in the children's ward of a Plymouth hospital. The Rev. Taylor would complete the book, by writing its final chapter.

2 Robinson, Midshipman's Journal.

3 Morris, Midshipman's Journal.
4 In fact, freedom from Nazi occupation would not come for the Channel Islands until after Germany surrendered, in May 1945. The Germans ultimately signed the surrender in Guernsey harbour, aboard HMS *Bulldog*, the warship which had captured an Enigma machine and documents in May 1941, off Iceland. Alderney would not actually be liberated until a week later.
5 *The Guillemette Diaries, Guernsey Press*, Wednesday 4 May 2005.
6 Trevor Davenport and Terry Gander, *Short History of Batterie Blücher, Alderney*, Channel Islands Occupation Review, No. 33, May 2003.
7 Recounted to the author by *Rodney* veteran Alan Sharp during a 2005 interview. LePoidvin is in the crew list for the battleship compiled by Paul Maddison.
8 Robinson, Midshipman's Journal.
9 Trevor Davenport and Terry Gander, *Short History of Batterie Blücher, Alderney*.
10 Morris, Midshipman's Journal.
11 Robinson, Midshipman's Journal.
12 Recounted by Ian Hamilton in a letter to the Channel Islands Occupation Society.
13 Trevor Davenport and Terry Gander, *Short History of Batterie Blücher, Alderney*.
14 Ibid.
15 Recounted to the author by *Rodney* veteran Alan Sharp during a 2005 interview.
16 J. Moroso in an AP report, filed 16 August 1944, entitled H.*M.S. Rodney Bombards Isle of Alderney*.
17 Official RN Narrative of the Alderney bombardment, as written up by Cdr Ian Hamilton.
18 Trevor Davenport and Terry Gander, *Short History of Batterie Blücher, Alderney*.
19 J. Moroso.
20 A fact recorded both by Davenport and Gander in their recent paper on the bombardment and also by the *The Guillemette Diaries*.
21 Trevor Davenport and Terry Gander, *Short History of Batterie Blücher, Alderney*.
22 Hubert Wolf, *Memories of a German flak gunner, Alderney 1943–1945*, The Alderney Society Bulletin 2004.
23 Ibid.
24 See People Appendix for more on Robinson's subsequent naval career.
25 Morris, Midshipman's Journal.
26 Possibly it was an order for *Rodney* to be decommissioned for a long refit, or even to be put into reserve.
27 Morris, Midshipman's Journal.

Chapter Twenty-One

KOLA RUN

Allied victory in the Second World War, while bought with the blood of young men from America and Britain, together with their Western allies, was also purchased at a profligate rate of expenditure in human lives and military equipment on the Eastern Front. In the Normandy campaign some 400,000 Nazi troops fought to hold back a tide of 800,000 invaders, while simultaneously, to the East, even bigger, more wasteful battles unfolded. In late June 1944, the Red Army launched a huge offensive known as Operation Bagration, pitching 1.4 million Soviet troops against 1.2 million Axis soldiers. Inevitably consuming vast quantities of men and material, it made the need for supplies from the West, via not only the Kola Run to Murmansk and Archangel but also the Persian Gulf, absolutely essential. Bagration, which brought the Russians to the borders of Poland and East Prussia, cost the Red Army 180,000 men killed, wounded or missing in action, with nearly 3,000 tanks, close to 2,500 artillery guns and in excess of 800 aircraft destroyed. German losses were even worse: some 550,000 dead and wounded, together with 2,000 tanks and nearly 60,000 motor vehicles wiped out. While, with *Scharnhorst* sunk and *Tirpitz* damaged, there had been a period where battleship cover was not necessarily needed on the Russia convoys, by autumn 1944 the presence of a battlewagon was again essential. *Tirpitz* had been in Norwegian waters since early 1942 and the only time she had so far conducted an offensive operation in which her guns fired in anger was September 1943 when, in company with *Scharnhorst*, she bombarded Spitzbergen, causing little meaningful damage. Having been damaged by charges dropped by British X-craft mini-submarines later that month, sustaining further wounds in subsequent Fleet Air Arm raids, it was believed *Tirpitz* was by September 1944 repaired sufficiently to pose a real threat. To neutralize it, No. 617 Squadron – the famed Dam Busters – and No. 9 Squadron, thirty-nine Lancasters in all, were launched at the German battleship. Twenty-six of them carried a single 12,000 lbs Tallboy bomb, while the other thirteen were packed with mines to be dropped around the enemy warship. The Lancasters would conduct their bombing mission on 15 September, flying from an airfield near Archangel, the raid timed specifically to be in synch with the departure of convoy JW60 to Russia. Hopefully, *Tirpitz* could be put out of action before the ships reached North Cape, close to the Altenfjord where she lurked.

Prior to receiving sailing orders for Murmansk, the big buzz in *Rodney* was that she would shortly take Winston Churchill across the Atlantic for a conference with President Roosevelt. However, when two Russian liaison officers arrived, it was obvious where *Rodney* was really heading. The Soviet Union's huge sacrifice in the great battle against Nazi evil was greatly admired in *Rodney*, filling her complement with 'a rare enthusiasm, and many men on board felt a deep personal affection for the solid dominating figure of Generalissimo Stalin.'

> *The long journey to help an Ally, about whom we all knew far too little, fulfilled the occasional, and surprising, stirrings of romanticism in the heart of the most hardened three-badge man.*[1]

With Scapa Flow so much further north than the departure point for the merchant ships, there was no need for *Rodney* to sail until 16 September. Early the previous morning she had taken aboard more ammunition, her junior commissioned officers guilty of being rather tardy in playing their part in getting shells to their magazines.

> *Owing to the affinity of many midshipmen to their hammocks and, consequently, there being no sign of them at hands fall in yesterday, when ammunitioning was about to start, we all had to turn out this morning* [16 September], *stagger blindly up to the 4.7-inch gun deck and carry out drill at the hour of 7 o'clock in the morning. Some difficulty was experienced by the R.N.R. midshipmen, who had never been near a Q.F.* [Quick Firing] *gun before, one of these catching a shell neatly in the crutch, that laid him out for a little time.*[2]

At 1.00 pm *Rodney* set sail, joining a substantial task group for the first time since D-Day. With her was part of the escort, in the shape of *Striker* and *Campania* (carriers), destroyers *Zambesi, Verulam, Savage, Myngs, Stord* (Norwegian) and *Algonquin* (Canadian). The convoy escort commander, Rear Admiral R.R. McGrigor, flew his flag in *Campania* and intended rendezvousing with the rest of JW60 at 6.00 am on 17 September, but mist meant it was not sighted for another four hours. No attempt could be made to establish contact by wireless, due to the need for radio silence. With the convoy emerging out of the mist, fine on the starboard bow, some of the destroyers around *Rodney* were replaced with a new escort composed of *Milne, Meteor, Marne* and *Musketeer*. The battleship took up station in the centre of the 28-ship convoy, with the vessel carrying the Commodore in charge of the merchant ships at 45 degrees on her starboard bow and the anti-aircraft cruiser *Diadem* on the starboard beam. The two carriers were astern of *Rodney*, so they could turn into the wind, to enable them to launch aircraft at will without disrupting the convoy formation. Because it had to proceed at the speed of the slowest vessel, JW60 made its way north at just nine-and-a-half knots. At 3.40 pm Captain Fitz Roy addressed the ship's company over the tannoy, explaining the purpose of *Rodney*'s presence, namely deterring *Tirpitz*. On the third day out from the UK, the weather deteriorated, a heavy swell making the ship roll and yaw wildly, but *Striker* was still launching aircraft. Among those in *Rodney* initially not enjoying the heavy weather, was junior rating Allan Snowden, who felt very queasy for the first few days.

Then, unlike many in the ship, he got better, with the exception of a rotten tooth, which caused him a great deal of pain. *Rodney* was experiencing the kind of dreadful, mind-numbing, morale-sapping seas that had proved to be such a test of Allied sailors' mettle since the beginning of the Russia convoys in August 1941.

> *The sea was a very dull sage green, lashed into white at the wave tops by the fury of the wind. The swell was quite heavy, and as each water-mountain passed under her keel from the port bow the old girl was rolling away and then back into the trough. Before she rode them, they must have been much taller than the tops of her turrets.*[3]

Even though twenty-year old Signalman Stephen Fordham's duty station was high up in the Octopoidal, the seas still appeared quite terrifying.

> *You couldn't see anything but a wall of water, couldn't even see the sky. When it was cold we really appreciated the daily tot of rum. It was good stuff and when that was not available we used to have hot chocolate.*

Several potential submarine contacts were made, with furious depth-charging but no confirmed U-boat sinkings or even probables. On 21 September, as the ship crossed into the Arctic Circle, the weather got even worse, becoming a huge gale. The ship changed course to south-east, waves now on the beam rather than from astern, making her roll as much as 20 degrees. Midshipman Morris, returning from a bitterly cold watch in the Air Defence Position, found the Gun Room a disaster zone:

> *All the Sub Lieutenants* [who also used it for their mess] *were lying in a sprawled mess on the deck, with food on top of them, the coffee and all the cups swilling around the bottom end of the gunroom and all the Mids food piled on one of the sofas where it had slid from the table. In addition I was narrowly missed by a tin filing cabinet while coming off watch ...*

The weather became very changeable: blowing hard in the morning, yet flat calm in the evening; foggy, with visibility down to 500 yards, then clear with visibility for miles. It was usually starting to become light around 3.00 am with the ship closed up at 4.00 am in broad daylight. This was a realm like no other *Rodney* had sailed in. The sun was low on the horizon all day and during the hours of darkness the sky often became a kaleidoscope of swirling colours, created by the celebrated Northern Lights so evident in that latitude during September and October. But the main characteristic of the journey seemed to be fog.

> *For many days, and generally in a heavy mist, the long columns of ships steamed steadily on. At times it was impossible to see beyond the ships on either beam, but we were aware that, behind the thick blanket of fog, were several miles of shipping.*[4]

When the fog melted away, a strong wind blew down from the north.

> *It was a bitter wind, born in the pack-ice hundreds of miles ahead.*[5]

It was OK for those in the enclosed bridge, but for the anti-aircraft gun crews and people in the equally exposed ADP it was a raw, cutting experience. But then, as the ship came in sight of Russia, the sun broke through. On 21 September, three days after *Rodney* entered the Arctic Circle, and abiding by a tradition that pertains to this day, 'Blue Nose' certificates were awarded to sailors and marines in the *Rodney*'s complement, including Allan Snowden and Tom Brock, for whom it was their first time in the northernmost regions of King Neptune's realm.

By 23 September, a large number of Russian aircraft were milling about overhead, with Red Navy destroyers encountered in the forenoon, a flotilla taking up position on *Rodney*'s starboard beam. Midshipman Morris gloried in the scene:

> *The convoy has now re-arranged itself in anticipation of our approach to the Kola Inlet, where it is to split up. The day was fine with a calm sea, light sun and the wash from the ships sparkling like champagne as they seemed to skim over the surface of the sea.*

For the majority of the complement, closed up inside *Rodney*'s many compartments, and therefore unable to inhale of the glory of nature, convoy escort work could be a dull business in which long months of separation from family and home were more unbearable than ever. Fortunately, the ship's Sin Bosun[6] – the Rev. Gordon Taylor – was on hand to lend a sympathetic ear and help out with advice. He had settled well into life aboard a battleship, carrying out his vital work with vigour.

I had a fine cabin, two actually – day and night – with a scuttle. I did very many different jobs on board, such as being In-Charge of the ship's shop, which is the best way in which a Chaplain can get to know the ship's company; and, of course, I was also a Cypher [code] *Officer, and thereby knew everything that was going on. The more jobs you did on board, the more men you met, and got to know well. You did not have to talk about religion; you found the men did that to you anyway. If someone had a problem, he could always come and see the Chaplain just by knocking on his cabin door. Otherwise he had to see his Divisional Officer, which often took till the 'morrow. The Chaplain was officially regarded as 'the friend and advisor of all on board', and this is the Chaplain's greatest responsibility. It has been wisely said that the Chaplain – who is an officer, but who also holds no rank – has the equivalent rank of whoever he talks to. In the 'dog watches'* [6–8 at night] *I would make a point of being seen on the mess decks, where I would casually meet scores of sailors. Some of the men were having the greatest time in all their lives. It could be tedious at times, but during the war we all knew there was a job to be done, and we got on with it. The war was a fight for survival, and everyone, including clergymen, was involved. There was certainly no conflict between being a man of God and being in the Navy.*

Reaching waters off the Kola Peninsula, half the convoy split off for Archangel, while *Rodney*, along with the carriers, picked up speed to seventeen-and-a-half knots for the fleet anchorage at Vaenga, about twenty miles down the sixty-mile-long inlet and ten from the fishing settlement of Murmansk. A Russian pilot came aboard with an interpreter and the battleship dropped anchor at 7.05 pm. *Rodney*'s anti-aircraft armament would stay crewed because an enemy airbase was only 12 minutes flying time away. Convoy JW60 had been extremely fortunate, seeing no sign of either enemy aircraft, flying out of Stavanger, or U-boats. As for *Tirpitz*, the raid of 15 September managed one significant hit on the starboard side of the battleship's forecastle, which actually passed right through and exploded under the hull. The upper deck was peeled back and bulkheads split open, rendering *Tirpitz* virtually unseaworthy, but the British were not fully aware of the severity of the damage, despite photo-reconnaissance and their sources in the Norwegian resistance. Among those in *Rodney* relieved not to have faced *Bismarck*'s sister was Gordon Taylor, who believed any clash amid vulnerable merchant vessels would have been 'a most bloody duel'.

Midshipman Morris at first sight found Stalin's Russia not hugely welcoming, his 24 September journal entry carrying more than an echo of the diary kept by the Crimean War-era *Rodney*'s chaplain.

The village of Vaenga lies at the foot of some low hills and, from the ship, appears to have only two large buildings and a few houses at the top of the shore on which it is built. The countryside around these parts is devoid of large trees and green shrubbery, consisting mainly of black rock and tiny bushes of a reddy-yellow tinge that can survive the severe winters that befall such a desolate place. The scenery, with its barren islands with no habitation, rather reminds one of Scapa Flow ...

The anglers in *Rodney*'s ship's company, however, liked what they found around the battleship.

The sea is very deep here, but this has not deterred our ardent fishermen from trying their hand and several haddocks have been caught.[7]

On 26 September the charismatic Admiral A.G. Golovko, thirty-seven year old Russian Northern Fleet commander, came aboard for discussions with Rear Admiral McGrigor on further improving protection for the Kola Run convoys and the current situation regarding *Tirpitz*. Golovko was given a tour of the ship during which he 'wondered how we kept everything so clean, when really it was just the usual shambles that we see every day, as the old lady is now over 18 years old.'[8] Golovko probably met with the two Russian liaison officers who, during the voyage from Britain, 'never appeared in the wardroom or on deck together. Presumably there was always one in his cabin clutching the Russian cipher book to his chest. Not surprising, for if there had been any hint of failure in security on their part they would have gone in front of a firing squad.'[9] The Russians put aboard eleven boxes of platinum and twenty-five cases of gold, as part-payment for the war supplies. The trucks that brought the bullion to the quayside were very heavily guarded and it took two men to carry each box down to *Rodney*'s cells, where it was all kept under guard by Royal Marines. As the bullion came aboard, Allan Snowden was going ashore to try and find a solution for his excruciating toothache, for the battleship carried no 'fang farrier'[10] to excise his pain. He soon wished he hadn't.

The locals seemed to be a bit suspicious of us. Let's put it this way ... they did not seem to be over-friendly. The dentist I found was a lady who seemed about seven-feet tall and she sort of leaned over on top of me. They didn't have any anaesthetic, not even a glass of vodka, so they just hauled the offending tooth out. I did a bit of shouting and I believe she must have been saying to me: 'Don't be such a baby.'

Plenty of other ratings, including Alan Sharp, found Russia a grave disappointment on the shopping front.

When the buzz was that we were going to take Churchill to the USA, everyone saved up money and had orders from people back home for nylon stockings and such like – the sort of luxuries available in the States but not in the UK – but there was sod all to buy at Vaenga.

Meanwhile, Roger Morris had heard there were some knives to be had ashore in exchange for sweaters, sweets or cigarettes.

He encountered Red Navy sailors in dirty, stinking uniforms, which, so Morris believed, had not ever been removed. Vaenga was clustered around hospital buildings, with telephones lines and electric cables running hither and thither amid the general squalor. Another village crouched on a nearby hill and in its centre was a large cinema adorned with huge picture of 'Uncle Joe' gazing down benevolently. Midshipman Morris decided to go in and watch the movie, which turned out to be 'Spring Parade', starring Deanna Durbin, a Hollywood musical from 1941, but with no Russian subtitles.

The benches were very hard and the sound was much too loud.

Exiting the cinema, Morris resumed his quest for a hunting knife but was besieged by children who, like all the adults, wore military uniform. They bombarded him with pleas for cigarettes and sweets.

In the end he obtained his knife for two packets of cigarettes – not being a smoker himself at the time, he had taken them just to barter for goods – and four bags of sweets. Also in search of souvenirs was Tom Brock who, on a previous run ashore from *Rodney*, at Augusta, Sicily, had been struck by the sheer exoticism and rich colours of orange groves. He found Vaenga drab and most of the people he encountered were female Red Army soldiers, which perhaps reminded him of his sister who was in the Womens' Auxiliary Air Force back home.

> *I was a keen stamp collector and my main objective was to obtain some Russian stamps, which somehow I did, even in my single hour ashore. I must have bartered something for them, ending up with an envelope full.*

There were two enemy air raids, which fortunately did not come anywhere near the ships at anchor. If they had then, according to anti-aircraft gunner Alan Sharp, there was not a lot *Rodney* would have been permitted to do about it.

> *I was crewing an eight-barrel multi-pom-pom anti-aircraft gun and the Russians wouldn't allow us to fire.*

Soviet air defences were more likely to shoot down a friendly aircraft than one belonging to the Luftwaffe. 'The Russian shore batteries opened up on several occasions at high-flying aircraft, which were probably their own,' Midshipman Morris observed caustically in his journal.

> *... their motto seems to be shoot first and ask questions afterwards. A good example of this attitude occurred just recently when an American Liberator was shot down.*

Already damaged by enemy fire and flying on just one engine, the Liberator contacted a Murmansk airfield, requesting permission to land, but was instead lit up by searchlights, and fired at by a number of Russian anti-aircraft batteries. The crew baled out, with the exception of the pilot, who was killed in the subsequent crash. On landing the surviving airmen were surrounded by Russian troops and, throwing their hands in the air, screamed:

> *Americans!*

This proved no deterrent to being shot at, one of the aviators being hit in the leg, while others were also wounded. Finally getting the message, the apologetic Russians took the American to a nearby hospital, promising not to shoot at them again. After initial treatment the American flyers were put aboard *Rodney* for the voyage back to Britain, tended to by the battleship's surgeons. Early on the morning of 28 September *Rodney* weighed anchor and set sail, following other British warships up the Kola Inlet to the sea, soon reaching 19 knots as it was suspected U-boats might be waiting at its entrance for targets of opportunity. The Russian propensity for attacking erstwhile allies struck again that day, when a Swordfish on anti-submarine patrol was attacked by Soviet aircraft, prompting *Campania* to scramble her Wildcat fighters. The Russian aviators realised their mistake and backed off. *Rodney* met a convoy from Archangel (RA60) in the forenoon and on the second day out, the ships reached the point of the voyage closest to the Norwegian coast. Enemy submarine activity had recently peaked, with a number of U-boats previously operating from French Atlantic ports migrating north. Two of RA60's merchant ships – the *Samsurva* and *Edward H. Crockett* – were hit by torpedoes from *U-310* and left in such a poor state they had to be sunk by friendly gunnery. The usual frantic depth-charging was carried out to gain revenge, but *U-310* slipped away. However, the following day Swordfish from *Campania*, armed with depth-charges, sank *U-921*, which was lost with all hands. On 1 October the Canadian destroyer *Sioux* came alongside *Rodney* and a doctor and a sick berth attendant were transferred to her. The two battleship medics were taken to a merchant ship where someone was seriously ill and needed an operation. Passing close by the Altenfjord, where *Tirpitz* still lurked, condition unknown, Action Stations were very tense. *Rodney* sat at the centre of the convoy, ready to meet the enemy capital ship threat.

> *... any attack if it was to come could be expected now. Luckily nothing happened and the ship reverted to the usual cruising watches.*[11]

Not long after, a Swordfish reported a U-boat on the surface, which fired on the British torpedo-bomber, possibly damaging it. Contact was lost and aircraft were launched from *Campania* to try and bring the Swordfish home, but no trace was found. *Rodney* increased speed to 16 knots after leaving the convoy at 7.00 pm on 4 October.

> *The ship creaked and groaned her stately way through the waters. She was getting on in years now and was rather proud that she could add North Russia to all her other journeys.*[12]

Reaching Scapa Flow at 7.30 am on 5 October, four days later the battleship cleared lower decks to practice the ceremony of becoming Home Fleet flagship. After the parade rehearsal, Captain Fitz Roy told assembled sailors and marines 'that he hoped we would grin and bear it, when large numbers of additional personnel arrived with the C-in-C [Admiral Henry Moore], making life rather crowded and hectic for us.'[13]

Leading Signalman Harry Farmer joined *Rodney* with the rest of the C-in-C Home Fleet's staff, transferring from the previous incumbent ship, HMS *Duke of York*, which went to the Far East to become flagship of the British Pacific Fleet. The contrast between *Duke of York*, only in commission for a few years, and the old *Rodney* was not as great as Farmer might have imagined.

> *Actually, the* Rodney *was a very comfortable ship to work and live in, for, although built pre-war, she was still very modern by Navy standards. Accommodation below decks was very spacious.*

Compared with other episodes in his sea-going life – Farmer witnessed the destruction of the German battlecruiser *Scharnhorst* during the Battle of North Cape – his time in *Rodney* proved to be a complete anti-climax.

No one in *Rodney* really wanted her to be flagship and it was especially wearing to face months swinging at anchor in Scapa, especially when the prospect of 25 days leave had been dangled prior to the convoy run. With some of them recalling Montgomery telling them the war would be over by October, it was clear to many of *Rodney*'s men that it would drag on into 1945 and the battleship could expect a long, cold, boring winter in northern waters.

In mid-October the ship sailed down to Rosyth Dockyard for maintenance, including attention to her troublesome steering and propulsion, returning to Scapa by the end of the month. However, in his journal entry for 30 October, Midshipman Morris was able to record what appeared to be excellent news.

> *Forced to leave her hideout at the Altenfjord and steam southwards hugging the Norwegian coast, by the threat of Russian armies advancing into northern Norway,*

> *and already crippled by seven previous attacks,* Tirpitz *was sheltering off Haakoy Island, near Tromso, Norway, when she was attacked by Lancaster aircraft of the Royal Air Force.*

Hopes that it might finally have ended the *Tirpitz* menace proved false, for only a single near miss was achieved and the Nazi warship still floated, remaining a notional threat, which had to be countered by *Rodney*'s presence in the Orkneys. To ensure she remained sharp for any contest with *Tirpitz*, the *Rodney* set sail for a gunnery shoot on 8 November. Four days later the RAF sent thirty-two Lancaster bombers against the German battleship, hitting her three times with 12,000 lbs bombs, and achieving two near misses, causing *Tirpitz* to turn turtle. Of her complement of 1,900, in excess of fifty per cent were killed. Absolute confirmation of the RAF's destruction of *Tirpitz* did not reach the Home Fleet flagship until 27 November, with officers in *Rodney* able to inspect reconnaissance photographs that clearly showed *Tirpitz* floating keel up. Winston Churchill later noted of this achievement:

> *All British heavy ships were now free to move to Far East.*[14]

With the exception of the remaining U-boats, which would continue to harvest their victims until the last moments of the war, the German Navy had effectively ceased to be an effective fighting force. While more and more Royal Navy people and ships were now going to the Far East, neither *Rodney* or Midshipman Morris would be among them. Destined for more Russia convoy work, in the destroyer *Scorpion*, Morris concluded the portion of his journal devoted to *Rodney* by reflecting:

> *I will be leaving the ship in the near future and in conclusion I should like to say that I am very much looking forward to my destroyer time, but nevertheless will be sorry to leave the old ship, in which I have found so many friends during the past sixteen months of my midshipman's time.*

Roger Morris would spend many more years at sea in the Royal Navy and also as an officer in the British merchant fleet. He preferred to remember *Rodney* in her glorious realm, her natural environment; a battleship at sea, guns roaring during the 8 November 1944 practice shoot.

> *The sun, low on the horizon, made the snow-capped mountains of Scotland glint in the morning rays and at one time the view in my glasses was typical of many a Christmas card, with the cruiser* Euryalus *steaming one way, a tiny fishing vessel going the other and a Sunderland aircraft above, with the background of rugged Scottish highlands with their snow-capped hills and rocky cliffs. Suddenly this picturesque panorama was blotted from view by a howling snow storm, which we had run into and which fortunately did not last long.*

As ever the old battlewagon parted the waves majestically, her long forecastle, dominated by the trio of awe-inspiring 16-inch gun turrets, which turned from side to side, seeming to sniff out targets as she ploughed on. On that spectacular winter's day, in the final months of her war service, the twilight moments of her long life, *Rodney* acted as a target for *Euryalus*. The cruiser's puny 5.25-inch shells deliberately fell astern, as the smaller warship carried out a throw-off shoot, in which her targetting was adjusted to miss by a certain margin. It was richly ironic, and no doubt a source of some humour to *Rodney*'s men, that it was a Royal Navy warship coming close to hitting a survivor of so much enemy action. She had shrugged off *Bismarck*'s shooting before delivering her own killer blows, evaded many attempts by enemy aircraft to sink her – including the near-disaster off Bergen in 1940 and the Pedestal convoy run to Malta – even weathering near misses from French guns off North Africa. With *Euryalus* completing her shoot, and her own 6-inch guns having spat fire, *Rodney*'s legendary 16-inch guns roared, hurling their one-ton shells towards a jagged, rocky range at Cape Wrath. Falling silent, the last wisps of gun smoke dissipating, *Rodney* turned her great bulk around, towards Scapa, as ever slow to answer the helm. To anyone looking on from ashore or in *Euryalus*, the battleship's menacing, instantly recognizable, outline, clad in its drab war paint, no doubt still inspired a feeling of pride and awe. For she was the very symbol of tenacity in the face of adversity. By late 1944, the Royal Navy's position as the supreme safeguard of the seas was rapidly fading, but it had written another illustrious chapter in its long and glorious history. Battleship *Rodney*, silhouette melting even now into the far horizon, carved her name with pride among the battle honours.

Notes

1 Thompson/Taylor, *HMS Rodney at War*. 'Three-badge man' is naval slang for a veteran rating, with three stripes ('badges') on his sleeve, each one of them symbolizing five years' service.
2 Morris, Midshipman's Journal.
3 Thompson/Taylor, *HMS Rodney at War*.
4 Ibid.
5 Ibid.
6 Naval slang for the padre.
7 Morris, Midshipman's Journal.
8 Ibid.
9 Cdr Ian Hamilton, quoted by McCart in *Nelson and Rodney*.
10 Naval slang for dentist.
11 Morris, Midshipman's Journal.
12 Thompson/Taylor, *HMS Rodney at War*.
13 Morris, Midshipman's Journal.
14 Winston Churchill, *The Second World War*.

Epilogue

CODA FOR A FIGHTING LIFE

She lived on, of course, for this was technically not the end of *Rodney*'s fighting life. Old and worn out, without a major, very expensive refit, she was fit for nothing but the scrapyard. With the ascendancy of the aircraft carrier as capital ship, the days of all battleships were numbered, never mind *Rodney*.

For some of her men the dreariness of Scapa Flow was partially relieved by joining the cast of the *Rodney Review*, a variety show that travelled from ship-to-ship. For others, despite ice there was deck hockey to burn off pent-up energy, also boxing contests or rugby and football matches ashore, provided the ground wasn't too hard. For Tom Brock and a couple of shipmates, there were invigorating cross-country runs, but there was still rather too much swinging around the buoy for active young men to tolerate, *Rodney* remaining at Scapa for the first five months of 1945. Across the North Sea, Allied armies recovered from barely holding the line against a last-ditch German attack on the Ardennes and pushed on, finally launching themselves successfully across the Rhine and striking deep into the Third Reich's black heart. Meanwhile, the Soviets swept all before them on the Eastern Front. Sailors and marines in *Rodney* had to content themselves with reading about the titanic struggle in newspapers and listening to BBC radio news broadcasts. During her sojourn at Scapa, *Rodney* went to sea not much more than half a dozen times, and even then only for brief periods. Dramas were few, though at the beginning of March there was some excitement when an American-built helicopter, on loan to the British for trials, crashed into the sea not far from *Rodney*. One of her boats was sent to pluck the aircrew to safety. Then, during an anti-aircraft gunnery shoot at sea, some of *Rodney*'s pom-pom shells hit a Canadian destroyer, killing a young sailor. The war in Europe came to a close on 8 May and three days later the First Lord of the Admiralty, A.V. Alexander, visited the ship, to witness the official surrender of U-boats, which, under orders to sail for the nearest British naval base, streamed into Scapa, their arrogant crews accommodated in the hulk of the *Iron Duke*, a First Wold War-era battleship that was Jellicoe's flagship at Jutland. Some of the German submarines were open to the public, and *Rodney*'s men were no doubt among those who inspected them, finally gaining a close-up look at the enemy's hardware. For their part, German naval officers who came aboard the Home Fleet flagship to surrender were able to gain a much better look at the legendary *Rodney* than afforded by a glance through an attack periscope.

Before the month was out *Rodney* sailed for Rosyth, probably to give her bored complement a taste of civilization. Returning to the Orkneys in July, the ship was pretty soon sailing south again, as if the dawn of peace had released her from confinement. She still had to keep herself 'run-in', all systems turning over, just in case she was called forward and received that deep refit to be sent back into the gun line, in the Far East. It was a *very* remote possibility. *Rodney* was anyway due a visit from King George VI and to receive him needed a new coat of paint all over, with some spit and polish on her bright works. The ship was moored in the middle of the Forth at the end of September, the King and Queen bringing aboard Princess Margaret and Princess Elizabeth, the Royal Standard flying from the battleship's mainmast.

In mid-November 1945, with battlecruiser *Renown* returned from the Far East relieving her as Scapa guardship, *Rodney* sailed for Portsmouth, on the voyage south firing her guns for the last time, during an anti-aircraft gunnery exercise.

At Portsmouth, the flag of the Commander-in-Chief Home Fleet was transferred to sister ship *Nelson*, also recently home from the Far East.

Early on the morning of 28 November *Rodney* left Portsmouth, destined for Rosyth the long way around, passing Plymouth, her old home port, before heading around the south-west peninsula, proceeding up through the Irish Sea and out past the north-western tip of Scotland. The *Rodney* had last received a major refit in 1941, at Boston, since then sailing 156,000 miles, and her engines and boilers were in a wretched state.

It was touch and go whether or not they would hold out during the rather painful, fitful, four-day journey. In the ship bets were being taken on whether or not she would need a tow, but *Rodney* reached Rosyth on 2 December, within the week entering 3 Dock to begin the process of removing ammunition and remaining stores. She was gradually ceasing to be a fully-fledged warship.

In January 1946 Captain Fitz Roy ended his time in command, the complement reducing as the months went by. In the summer Admiral Sir Frederick Dalrymple-Hamilton, by then Flag Officer Commanding Scotland and Northern Ireland, held a farewell dinner in *Rodney*'s ward room for those who had served in the battleship. The admiral probably visited the chart room, where key decisions that brought *Rodney* face-to-face with *Bismarck* had been taken. Many memories of 'The Pursuit' were no doubt rekindled by Dalrymple-Hamilton and guests, gathering for one last time in the ship that killed the pride of Hitler's fleet.

Rodney was laid up in late 1946 to await disposal. The orders sending her to scrap were issued by the Admiralty in January 1948, and on 26 March, she was taken in hand by Messrs. T. W. Ward for breaking up at Inverkeithing, just down the Firth of Forth from Rosyth. It was a bright sunny day, with only a gossamer thin covering of mist, seven tugs shepherding her down river. Looking on from the waterfront was Admiral Dalrymple-Hamilton, the ship of war he once commanded appearing to be going meekly to her destruction, defeated by time and its inevitable decay, already bedraggled and careworn. However, as *Rodney* progressed slowly on the green waters of the Forth, the strong cross current off North Queensferry made it difficult for the tugs to keep control of her. It looked like she might break free, making a last bid to escape an ignoble end. Although she swung away, the tugs won their struggle, nudging *Rodney* back on course, down the middle of the deep channel that ran under the northern span of the famous railway bridge. Either side of *Rodney*'s superstructure were three yawning gaps, like sockets left by pulled teeth, for her 6-inch gun turrets had been extracted. It made the battleship lighter, so her draught was shallow enough to go alongside in the inner berth where she would be torn apart. For the same reason *Rodney*'s rudder was also removed.[1] The topmast and aerials were gone too, enabling her to slide under the bridge, despite riding higher in the water. As *Rodney* did so, one of the bridge's workers may well have climbed down to a platform in the lower part of the structure to take one last look at her broad majesty, having no doubt seen her in a time when she was a living, breathing fighting ship and not an empty shell. In some senses *Rodney* still had the appearance of a dreadnought, for while the secondary armament was gone, her 16-inch guns were still there. However, over subsequent months, as the trains rattled over the bridge, their passengers were able to see her towering silhouette reduced day-by-day.[2]

While metal from *Rodney* was salvaged as part of the process of turning swords into ploughshares, going into the melting pot in order to rebuild a shattered Britain, some remnants were saved for posterity. Admiral Dalrymple-Hamilton was given the ship's crest and large steel letters of her name, the latter formerly attached to the ship's stern. Later, those letters were the property of a Sea Cadet Corps unit at Stranraer in Scotland, appropriately enough named Training Ship *Rodney*. However, by the time of writing T.S. *Rodney* had disbanded but the name lives on in two English Sea Cadet Corps units, based at Skelmersdale and Gosforth. There is a Canadian Sea Cadets unit named *Rodney* in the maritime city of St. John, New Brunswick, not far from the St. Lawrence up which the first ever HMS *Rodney* sailed, back in the 1750s. St. John is also close to Newfoundland, of which Captain Rodney was Governor. The unit has the ship's badge as its crest, its official title being No. 9 Royal Canadian Sea Cadet Corps *Rodney*. Formed in 1928, it took the name *Rodney* as part of a tradition of naming units after Royal Navy ships and admirals. In November 1945 the captain of HMS *Rodney* sent over the ship's crest to use, along with permission for it to become the official insignia of the unit.

The ensign flown by *Rodney* during her battle with the *Bismarck* was hung in a church near Stranraer, as it was where the Dalrymple-Hamilton family worshipped. Items from *Rodney* were still being traded in 2007, via internet auction sites, including a tankard fashioned out of metal retrieved from the battleship. It is appropriate that one of *Rodney*'s ship's bells is currently in the collection of the Merseyside Maritime Museum, close to her build yard at Birkenhead. In the senior ratings mess of HMS *Drake*, at Devonport Naval Base, there remains a display containing various items of *Rodney* memorabilia. With modernization at the barracks – the mess recently moving into what used to be a drill shed – this shrine to surely the most famous of Devonport-based warships has recently reduced in size. It still contains a model of the battleship, some photographs and one or two other small items. Nearby, in the reception of *Drake*'s ward room, there is a large painting of *Rodney* in all her glory, leading the Atlantic Fleet in the 1930s. Like display items in the senior ratings mess, it was presented by the HMS *Rodney* Association. Rather than dusty artefact it was, of course, the men of *Rodney* who were the blood in her steel veins. The HMS *Rodney* Association held dinners on an annual basis to bring her marines and sailors back together. The association also kept the ship's spirit alive via a news magazine *The Rodney Buzz*, which was distributed on a regular basis.

The HMS *Rodney* Association was formed at HMS *Drake* on 29 November 1986, one of many warship associations set up in the 1980s, when the veterans had finally retired and, looking back on their lives, decided they wanted to get in touch with old shipmates.

Among the regulars at *Rodney* Association reunions was Robert Jackson and his wife Diane. He was 87 when he died, on 8 September 2001, having joined the Royal Navy at the age of eighteen, in 1932. By the outbreak of the Second World War he was a Chief Petty Officer in HMS *Rodney*, seeing action during the destruction of *Bismarck*.

Robert Jackson also saw service on the Russia convoys and in the Far East and in the Korean War. He finally left the Navy in 1954, eventually becoming president of the Margate branch of the Royal Naval Association. A postman in civilian life, he was also an accomplished marine artist, a number of his paintings hanging in the *Rodney* pub in Garlinge, which is named after the famous admiral. It was during a *Bismarck* survivors' reunion that Jackson struck up a friendship with German sailor Herbert Jahn, who predeceased him, dying in June 2000. Mrs Jackson wrote to the author during the course of research for this book:

> *I attended all the* Rodney *Association reunions with my husband plus many other Navy events. We often went to Germany to stay with Herbie Jahn and his wife. We attended the sixtieth anniversary of the* Bismarck [Action] *at the Imperial War Museum on 22 May 2001.*

At its peak the HMS *Rodney* Association had 450 members on its books, but, with the march of time, the ranks inevitably thinned and those remaining, most of them in their eighties, found it difficult to travel to the dinners or devote quite the same energy to organizing its activities. The association concluded its business with a grand dinner at the Moat House Hotel, York in September 2001. The association's final gesture in disposing of its funds was making a donation to the Millennium Chapel of Peace and Forgiveness, at the National Memorial Arboretum, Staffordshire in the heart of England, for the planting of an oak tree dedicated to HMS *Rodney*. The association also gave £1,000.65 toward the purchase of a digital hymnal in the chapel.[3]

Despite the association being disbanded, some of the *Rodney* veterans continued to meet and swap stories. Robert G. Jackson, who swore at an admiral during a cricket match at Malta in 1943 (and got away with it) wrote to the author in late 2004:

> *One of my old shipmates, Seaman Torpedo Man 'Knocker' White, who is 95-years old has recently got married again, left Bromley and gone to live in Morecombe. Something has done him good. By the way Don Hutchinson, Eddie Simpson and myself* [all *Rodney* veterans] *meet from time to time in Fleetwood Bowling Club. We always have plenty to talk about.*

Mrs M. Watson, of Aberdeenshire, Scotland, wrote that her late father, Leading Seaman James Thoirs, remembered his time in *Rodney* with great fondness. One of her treasured possessions is a plate emblazoned with *Rodney*'s crest together with her dad's name and number.

Many of *Rodney*'s men inevitably lamented her passing long after she was gone to razor blades, including Frank Summers, who had joined her after escaping his native France during the evacuation at Dunkirk.

> *It hurt my heart a little bit to leave the* Rodney. *I joined her having lost my own family and home due to the German invasion, when I was very much alone. The* Rodney *became my home and my family.*

Summers, who married a British girl and took the citizenship of his adopted country, is to this day deaf in his left ear; in regularly checking one of *Rodney*'s machinery spaces, he had to go back and forth through airlocks, suffering the resulting change in air pressure about 20 times a day.

Former Leading Torpedo Operator James McLean stayed with *Rodney* to the end of her operational life.

After she was paid off at Rosyth, the majority of the ship's company left for Devonport by train. Like a number of others I joined the depot ship HMS Defiance *and after a while I was demobbed and returned to civilian life.*

He took with him so many memories of life at sea in one of naval history's great warships, two of them illustrating the toughness of the old girl and her propensity for casually taking lives.

On one occasion after we had departed Rosyth following a refit, we were in the open sea being escorted by three fleet destroyers when there was a huge explosion ahead of us and the ship jumped. It was dark at the time, being about 7 pm. On the lead destroyer a 300 lbs depth-charge had rolled down the chute on the quarterdeck and by the time Rodney *got near it, having sunk to where the setting on the detonator would activate it, the full T.N.T. charge went off with a bang and we got a blast up for'ard.' Another time, we left Greenock about 6–7 pm in the winter and at the time I was on my Mess Deck, starboard side forward, when I heard a loud scraping down the ship's side. We learned later that, as we passed through the boom defence opening we had hit a patrolling trawler and cut her in two. The ship just shuddered and never lost way and, of course, we never stopped. Some poor devils had evidently lost their lives.*[4]

Allan Snowden departed *Rodney* in December 1944 at Scapa Flow, getting the ferry over to the mainland and then a train down to Plymouth, which took a couple of days. Having requested to be sent on a Leading Torpedo Operator's course he too was sent to HMS *Defiance* in Devonport.

I was there only a couple of hours and was then sent on leave, taking the train to my home in Scotland. After I completed the course I was sent out to the Far East and ended up in the engineering repair ship HMS Mullion Cove, *swinging at anchor in Trincomalee as the war ended.*

The *Rodney* retained a strong hold on his affections.

She was a great ship, and a very, very happy ship. I made a lot of good friends aboard her. I wouldn't have missed it for anything.

In 2004, he decided to visit Normandy, participating in the D-Day 60th anniversary events.

My wife and I went into Caen, which was, of course, one of the targets during Rodney's *bombardments. We had a meal at a restaurant by the cathedral and just along a bit was a newsagent selling postcards. I picked a few of the postcards up, which showed the damage done to Caen, some of which was committed by* Rodney. *It makes you a little bit sick to see what the guns of your ship did to a French town, but, incredibly, the local people do not seem to harbour a grudge. During the visit we stayed in a little village outside Caen and one day went along to the Pegasus Bridge, so called because it was taken by British Airborne troops early on D-Day. My wife and I joined this party of tourists and the guide saw my Normandy veterans badge, indicating I had been present during the D-Day campaign. He went away and came back with a paperweight, which had a picture on it showing the bridge with British soldiers coming over it. He also gave me a book. I was very touched by that.*

Writing from his home in New South Wales, Australia, former HMS *Rodney* Royal Marine Jack Austin recalled that, prior to the Normandy invasion, as a marine with more than two years' service, he was required to return to barracks.

I had a choice of commando unit or dispatch rider, so rather than walking, I chose the motorcycle. I did my NCOs course and ended up leading thirty-six Despatch Riders through Europe with Montgomery's HQ.

But, even after his adventures on land, it was *Rodney* that had hold of his heart.

I spent the first four years of the war, from November 1939 to November 1943 in what I consider the finest battleship ever built. I don't think any other ship in the Royal Navy saw as much action. If Winston Churchill had had his way, the Rodney *would still be open to the public on display in Plymouth, making more money than she did as scrap.*

Some of *Rodney*'s former sailors chose to name their sons after the battleship, among those so blessed being Rodney Marsh, the England footballer, who was born in October 1944, possibly while his father was still a member of the ship's company. A Hastings fisherman, who may or may not have served in the legendary warship, was so impressed with her record in supporting the Normandy invasion he named his son – born on 6 June 1944 – Dee-Day Rodney White. It was very hard for the youngster to live down, complaining to a newspaper reporter on his 50th birthday (which was, obviously, also the 50th anniversary of D-Day):

He must have been pissed or something.

Furthermore, the fisherman's son revealed that for years he had been enduring corny quips from friends and acquaintances, such as:

See you, Dee-Day, after tomorrow![5]

The Fleet Air Arm's Bill Myers would serve in the Navy for many years after *Rodney* had long gone, but his days in the battleship left an indelible impression.

The crew were divided into two basic classifications – 'daymen' or 'watchkeepers'. Daymen, like myself, worked normal hours ... Watchkeepers worked a four hours on, eight hours off routine ... I remember my first night aboard Rodney *– my first time aboard a sea-going ship. Having managed to swing myself into my hammock and seemingly just dropped off to sleep, suddenly all Hell broke loose: a voice bellowing over the tannoy system a series of unintelligible instructions and hundreds of sailors charging up and down the gangways. I looked at my watch – approaching midnight. Then, suddenly, silence. Then, seemingly, a short time later the whole raucous procedure was repeated – I looked at my watch – approaching four o'clock. This I soon found out was the middle watchmen and the morning watchmen taking post. Amazing how quickly one got used to it.*

His memories of *Rodney* would never, ever fade.

It's hard to explain to a civilian one's feeling for a ship in which one has served for several years. You forget the hardships, the discomforts, the monotonous food and the dangers, but you remember the comradeship, the runs ashore, the lower deck, indestructible humour. How can you fall in love with a big hunk of steel? But you do, and you never forget.

Notes

1 W. Gordon Campbell, *HMS Rodney – The Story of a Battleship.*
2 An unattributed newspaper report of *Rodney*'s short journey to the scrapyard was reproduced in *The Rodney Buzz,* February 1989.
3 A digital hymnal is a computerized jukebox of digitalized hymns, enabling visitors to select the music of their choice during an act of Remembrance.
4 This was probably the 19 April 1941 incident when *Rodney* sank HMS *Topaze* on her *return* to the Clyde.
5 Report by Richard Norton-Taylor in *The Guardian* newspaper, 6 June 2004. Norton-Taylor was also born on 6 June 1944, hence his interest in the topic.

A view of HMS *Rodney* in late 1941, as she sits at anchor in a snowy Icelandic fjord. The photograph was taken from the carrier HMS *Victorious* (one of her duffel coat-clad sailors and the nose of an Albacore torpedo-bomber are visible right of picture). Both ships were being held in reserve, in case *Tirpitz* attempted a breakout into the Atlantic. *IWM A6435.*

Appendix 1

RODNEY'S PEOPLE

It is not possible to list the post-*Rodney* story of every player encountered in the drama of the battleship's fighting life, and we have already covered the fate of some in the main body text, but it is worth setting down a selection of snapshot biographies.

As one of only two modern battleships built for the Royal Navy between the end of the First World War and the late 1930s, it was inevitable that promising officers who would find fame and high office in the Second World War, or later, passed through HMS Rodney.

Alfred Ernle Chatfield, who did so much at the 1921 Washington Conference to bring her about, departed *Rodney*, which had been his flagship in command of the Atlantic Fleet, in spring 1930, to take command of the Mediterranean Fleet, returning to the UK two years later on being appointed First Sea Lord. He proved a consummate politician, skilfully squeezing as much as possible by way of naval expenditure out of parsimonious politicians. Chatfield also fought hard to preserve battleships as the key naval striking force and also wrested the Fleet Air Arm from the control of the RAF and gave it back to the Navy. His time as the head of the Navy was twice extended and he did not leave office until August 1938, on being elevated to Baron Chatfield of Ditchling. Moving into politics, he spent time in India reorganizing the imperial armed forces. Returning to Britain in early 1939, Chatfield became Minister for Co-ordination of Defence and fought tooth and nail to force the Treasury to release funds needed to speed up rearmament. Although in the War Cabinet when Chamberlain was Prime Minister, he found life as a government minister frustrating, his influence on conduct of the war being negligible. Chatfield left the Government in 1940 and pursued a life away from the spotlight during which he wrote two volumes of memoirs, *The Navy and Defence* and *It Might Happen Again*. He died in November 1967.

Andrew Cunningham became Commodore of Chatham Royal Naval Barracks after leaving *Rodney* in December 1930. He went on to command the destroyers of the Mediterranean Fleet as a Rear Admiral. By summer 1936 Cunningham was a Vice Admiral and deputy commander of the Mediterranean Fleet. Just over two years later he was back in Britain as Deputy Chief of the Naval Staff, where he played an important role in accelerating the Royal Navy's rearmament before being appointed to command the Mediterranean Fleet in the summer of 1939. It was a key command, as the Suez Canal was fundamental to communications with the Empire and access to oil supplies in the Gulf. During the Second World War, Cunningham won lasting renown for mastering the materially superior Italian Navy, achieving notable victories at the battles of Calabria and Matapan and over-seeing the Fleet Air Arm strike on Taranto. His record made him the most successful British combat admiral since Nelson. However, the advent of the Luftwaffe in the Mediterranean brought black days, culminating in the battle for Crete in May 1941 in which the

Royal Navy suffered grievous losses. Cunningham's fleet was depleted further in late 1941 with the sinking of the battleship *Barham* and temporary loss of battleships *Valiant* and *Queen Elizabeth*, which were crippled. Cunningham was sent to Washington D.C. after America entered the war, subsequently becoming Allied naval forces commander for the invasions of North Africa, Sicily and Italy before returning to the UK to become First Sea Lord. Viscount Cunningham of Hyndhope – he was made a peer in September 1945 and a viscount less than a year later – died in 1963.

Robert Burnett, who was *Rodney*'s Executive Officer under Cunningham, went on to achieve renown during the Second World War, famously leading Home Fleet escort forces during the Russian convoys. Rear Admiral Burnett took command after the notorious disaster of Convoy PQ17 and for the subsequent PQ18 sailed in the cruiser HMS *Scylla*. In late December 1942, Burnett commanded a Royal Navy force, his flag flying in the cruiser *Sheffield*, which fought a fierce action against German surface units, including *Hipper* and *Lutzow*, which became known as the Battle of the Barents Sea. On Boxing Day 1943, flying his flag in the *Belfast*, Burnett commanded cruisers at the Battle of North Cape, in which the German battlecruiser *Scharnhorst* was destroyed. Post-war he attained the rank of Vice Admiral, concluding his career as Commander-in-Chief Plymouth. Retiring from the Navy in 1950, he died nine years later.

Like Cunningham before him, on leaving *Rodney* **John Tovey** became Commodore of the naval barracks at Chatham, in 1935, receiving promotion to Rear Admiral several months later. By the spring of 1938 he was in command of the Mediterranean Fleet's destroyers. Remaining in the Med, as a Vice Admiral he commanded the destroyers and cruisers of the Mediterranean Fleet and was also its second-in-command under Cunningham. Tovey distinguished himself at the Battle of Calabria, in July 1940, flying his flag in the cruiser *Orion*. By the end of 1940, Tovey was commanding the Home Fleet, as an acting full Admiral – he was confirmed in the rank during 1942 – over-seeing the pursuit and destruction of *Bismarck* in May 1941, witnessing *Rodney*'s close-range hammering of the German battleship from his flagship, *King George V*. Never enjoying an easy relationship with Winston Churchill, or First Sea Lord Dudley Pound, Admiral Tovey clashed with them over various aspects of the Russia convoys and also conduct of war in the Atlantic. Handing over command of the Home Fleet to Bruce Fraser in 1943, Tovey was appointed Commander-in-Chief, Nore, and became an Admiral of the Fleet in late 1944, his defiance of authority possibly leading to his consignment to what was effectively a backwater for a man of his proven ability. Tovey co-ordinated naval support for Allied ground forces as they pushed into Belgium and Holland after the Normandy breakout. Retiring after the war, he was made Baron Tovey of Langton Matravers and eventually retired to the Portuguese island of Madeira where he died in early 1971.

Geoffrey Cooke, who together with Tovey helped restore *Rodney*'s morale with good man management after Invergordon, lost his life during the Second World War, when *Barham* was sunk in the Mediterranean. He had captained *Barham* at the Battle of Matapan, in March 1941 and later took her to Durban after she suffered extensive damage due to Luftwaffe dive-bomber attack during the Battle of Crete. On 25 November, off Sidi Barrani, *U-331* managed to sneak into the middle of the Mediterranean Fleet and fired a spread of torpedoes. *Barham* was hit by three, capsized and exploded. Her loss was kept secret for fear of the devastating impact such news would have on morale back home.

During his time as Assistant Naval Attache in Japan after leaving *Rodney*, **George Ross**, who served as Deputy Marine Engineer Officer in *Rodney* during the Invergordon Mutiny, met a representative of the Swiss arms manufacturer Oerlikon at a Halloween party. Ross was subsequently impressed by a demonstration of a new 20 mm anti-aircraft gun, but initially found it difficult to persuade the Admiralty it was worth investing in. It was to the lasting credit of Ross that ships of the Royal Navy – including *Rodney* – were ultimately fitted with 20 mm Oerlikon cannons in large numbers, which proved vital in close-range air defence. Appointed Marine Engineer Officer of the cruiser *Manchester* in 1937, during the Second World War Ross was MEO in *Rodney*'s sister ship HMS *Nelson* in which he saw action on the Malta convoy runs. He ended his Royal Navy career as a Rear Admiral in charge of maintenance and repair of Fleet Air Arm aircraft. He died in 1993.

Frank Roddam Twiss, who served as a midshipman in *Rodney* during the 1920s, ended his naval career as the Second Sea Lord, retiring from active service in 1970. During the Second World War Twiss was taken prisoner by the Japanese after his ship, the cruiser *Exeter*, of which he was Gunnery Officer, was sunk at the Battle of the Java Sea, in March 1942. After surviving a harsh captivity, Twiss returned to the Navy, post-war serving in a number of posts that enabled him to improve the lot of lower deck sailors. Serving as Naval Secretary to the Admiralty and Flag Officer Flotillas in the Home Fleet, both in the early 1960s, he was appointed Commander, Far East Fleet in 1965. Twiss returned to the UK in 1967 to become Second Sea Lord and Chief of Naval Personnel. During his time in office there was a scandal over the level of alleged homosexual activity in the Fleet, which so appalled Twiss that he reportedly declared in 1968: 'Fifty per cent of the fleet have sinned homosexually at some time in their naval career.' The scandal broke at a time when there had been a huge furore in the civilian community over the legalisation of homosexual practices. However, Twiss was of the view that the Royal Navy's operational effectiveness could be adversely affected by a permissive attitude towards homosexual activity. After retirement, Twiss was appointed to the prestigious position of Black Rod in the House of Lords, which he held for the next eight years. Dr Chris Howard Bailey used twenty-three tapes of interviews with Twiss as the basis for the book *Social Change in the Royal Navy: 1924-70*, published in 1997, three years after the admiral died.

William Crawford, who was *Rodney*'s Gunnery Officer during the fight with *Bismarck*, also enjoyed a distinguished naval career, ultimately attaining the rank of Vice Admiral. Post-war Crawford was Captain of the Britannia Royal Naval College Dartmouth, between 1954 and 1956, before moving on as a Rear Admiral to found the Royal Navy's Flag Officer Sea Training (FOST) organisation at Portland, but which is now based at Devonport Naval Base. Today FOST provides damage control and combat training to not only the RN but also a number of foreign fleets. Promoted to Vice Admiral in late 1959, a year later Crawford went to the USA as the Commander of the British Naval Staff in Washington D.C. It is said that because his grandfather had been master of a ship that transported convicts to Australia, Crawford passed on the chance to become Lieutenant Governor of Western Australia. However, Crawford himself, in his unpublished autobiography, *Bill Crawford's Log*, said that he turned the post down due to his wife not fancying the idea of yet more years abroad following the posting to the USA. Vice Admiral Crawford died in June 2003.

James Rivett-Carnac, who was the Commanding Officer of *Rodney* between July 1941 and July 1943, went on to command Force H during the Allied landings at Salerno, in September 1943. For the invasion of Normandy he was appointed Chief Naval Administrative Officer to Admiral Bertram Ramsay, the Allied Naval Commander, Expeditionary Forces and was later Flag Officer British Assault Area, which involved ensuring troops and supplies were safely ferried ashore, plus the repair and salvage of damaged vessels and supply of fuel. He also oversaw the protection of the seaward flank of the beachhead and shouldered responsibility for various other logistical, administration and communication activities. Having visited *Rodney* for Montgomery's talk during the latter stages of the breakout by Allied armies, in March 1945 Rivett-Carnac was appointed to a senior position as a Vice Admiral in the newly formed British Pacific Fleet, as it took the fight to Japan. The BPF was under the overall command of Admiral Fraser, who, of course, had seen action in *Rodney* as an incognito passenger on the Pedestal convoy run, when Rivett-Carnac was the battleship's captain. For his role in the BPF, Rivett-Carnac was based ashore at HMS *Beaconsfield*, in Port Melbourne. He died in 1970.

Frederick Dalrymple-Hamilton, who also returned to *Rodney* off the Normandy beaches, was by summer 1944 in command of the 10th Cruiser Squadron, flying his flag in *Belfast*, and responsible for naval gunfire support to troops fighting ashore. He was also, between March 1944 and April 1945, deputy commander of the Home Fleet. Promoted to Vice Admiral, he was appointed to command Malta, with the additional responsibility of Flag Officer Central Mediterranean. Moving on in April 1945, Dalrymple-Hamilton was until 1948 Flag Officer Scotland and Northern Ireland, during which time, as we have seen, he held a farewell dinner aboard *Rodney* and saw his old ship taken to the breakers. His final job in the Navy was in the leadership of the British Joint Services Mission in Washington D.C. Retiring from the Royal Navy in 1950, Sir Frederick Dalrymple-Hamilton passed away on Boxing Day 1974.

But, what of those who did not achieve quite such an exalted position? The following thumbnail sketches provide a sampling of how some of Rodney's *other men fared.*

Eryk Sopocko chronicled the story of his time in *Rodney*, including the *Bismarck* episode, in a book published in 1942, called *Gentlemen, The Bismarck Has Been Sunk*. Post-*Rodney*, Sopocko was appointed to the ORP *Orkan*, a former Royal Navy M Class destroyer previously named *Myrmidon*, which saw action on the Arctic convoys. Sopocko was killed in October 1943, when *Orkan* was sunk in the Barents Sea, hit by a homing torpedo fired by *U-378*. Only 44 of *Orkan*'s 223 sailors survived, representing the worst loss of lives by the free Polish naval forces in the Second World War. Eryk Sopocko was just twenty-three years of age. Incidentally, among others who at one time or other served in HMS *Rodney*, and who lost their lives in the Second World War, but who are not mentioned elsewhere in this book, were: **Engine Room Artificer Henry Mepham**, lost in HMS *Hood*, 24 May 1941; **Seaman Jacob Rowland**, lost when the submarine *Tetrach* was sunk, probably by an enemy mine, in the Mediterranean on 27 October 1941; **Leading Torpedo Operator Rutland Keast**, missing presumed killed, 26 March 1942, possibly in the destroyer *Jaguar*, the only British warship lost to enemy action at sea on that date, sunk off the North African coast, hit by two torpedoes fired by *U-652*.

Charles Richard Benstead was a quite remarkable man, recalled in vivid terms by *Rodney*'s Commander Ian Hamilton: 'Just before I joined *Rodney* in 1943 I was on the staff at *HMS Lochailort*, a Combined Operations training establishment at Inverailort Castle, not far from Fort William in Scotland. It began training officers to command landing craft in late 1942. The principal instructor there was C.R. Benstead, who wrote *HMS Rodney at Sea*, and I got to know him very well. He didn't take part in the war in Europe [during the First World War] and he was sent to north Russia with the Army. One of his claims to fame was that he had shot up Bolsheviks with his revolver. Then he transferred to the Royal Navy. The Commander at the time in *Lochailort* decided, rather stupidly, that we were saving heat and that the fire in the lounge was not to be lit until 4.00 o'clock in the afternoon. Benstead showed his disapproval by wearing his Arctic gloves up to his elbows and also fur boots.'

Whether or not Benstead was involved in the British intervention against the Bolsheviks in Arctic Russia, he fibbed about his earlier career in the Army, perhaps out of modesty. According to a report in *Time* magazine, published on 14 February 1930, Benstead, whom it revealed was aged thirty-three and 6ft 5-ins in height, garnered a Mention in Despatches and the Military Cross. Joining the Army from Cambridge University as a private he was eventually commissioned into the Royal Artillery. Benstead saw action on the Somme, at Vimy Ridge, the Battles of Arras, Ypres and also in resisting the German offensive of spring 1918. He won acclaim for a novel on this latter episode, called *Retreat : A story of 1918*, which was published in 1930, when Benstead, by then an Instructor Lieutenant Commander, was serving in the battleship *Emperor of India*. However, six years earlier his book *Round the World with Battle Cruisers* told the story of his time in the battlecruiser *Hood* when she took part in a circumnavigation with *Repulse* and escorts. Benstead, who served in *Rodney* in the late 1920s and early 1930s, wrote two books on her. The first was a slim 44-page volume giving a brief history of previous ships to carry the name and also an outline of the new battleship, called *Rodney; the Story of an Immortal Name*, which was published in 1931 especially for sale in the ship's own shop. His second tome on the battleship was a substantial account of *Rodney*'s second commission, called *HMS Rodney at Sea*, which was published in 1932. The prolific Benstead also wrote books on Cambridge University and Parliament, producing other works on the Royal Navy and even writing on meteorological matters. Following his service in the Second World War, Benstead returned to academia, becoming a don at St Catherine's College, Cambridge. A renowned cricketer, Benstead played for the Royal Navy and also Cambridge University. He died in July 1980.

Ian Hamilton, who joined *Rodney* as the deputy supply officer after his time at Inverailort Castle, was also the battleship's official battle observer for the D-Day and Alderney bombardments. When the supply officer was appointed to a job in Australia, Hamilton was made Supply Officer, in the rank of Acting Commander, seeing out the rest of his war in *Rodney*. Staying in the Navy until 1958 he was for a time supply officer of the aircraft carrier *Albion*, the first carrier in the world to have an angled flight-deck. On leaving the Navy he decided that he wanted to run a croft in the Highlands of his native Scotland. Acquiring a ten acre croft, he spent his time looking after 'four Highland cattle and their followers.' Ian Hamilton, in his ninety-seventh year as this book was being completed, lives in his beloved Highlands to this day and occupies much of his time writing military history.

Deputy Gunnery Officer **Peter Wells-Cole** left *Rodney* at the beginning of 1943, going to Whale Island, where he qualified as a fully-fledged gunnery officer, thereafter spending some time on the school's training staff. He was then appointed to the destroyer HMS *Milne*, in the 3rd Flotilla, and she went to the Mediterranean. Staying in the Navy after the war, he served in the destroyer *Saumarez* at the time of the notorious Corfu Incident, in which he was injured, suffering a fractured skull. Subsequently seeing service in the ill-fated Suez Campaign of 1956, in its aftermath Wells-Cole was made a temporary civilian aboard a Royal Navy landing ship assigned to the United Nations effort to clear the Suez Canal of wreckage created during hostilities. During this period he saw the statue of Ferdinand de Lesseps – the French diplomat who oversaw construction of the Canal – taken down by jubilant Egyptians. Leaving the Navy in 1960, Peter Wells-Cole worked for a few years in industry before gaining a position with the Lincoln Diocesan Trust. Now retired, Peter Wells-Cole retains an abiding interest in naval history and to this day meets with his brother John, who was a midshipman in the battleship, once a week, for a pint at their local pub in Lincoln.

Rodney's final Chaplain, **Gordon Taylor**, today lives peacefully in retirement in a picturesque Hampshire village not far from Portsmouth. He ended his wartime service with the Royal Marines at Chatham, and after demobilisation had to find himself a parson's job. After a couple of years teaching at Eton, he married and was appointed Rector of St Giles-in-the-Fields in London, near Tottenham Court Road, serving there for just over 50 years before retiring in 1999. Another keen student of naval history, Gordon Taylor is the author of a splendid chronicle of naval chaplains entitled *The Sea Chaplains; a history of the chaplains of the Royal Navy*, which was published in 1978, with a foreword by Prince Charles.

Australian **Tony Robinson**, who joined *Rodney* as a young midshipman at Plymouth, in May 1943, left the battleship at Portland in August 1944. That September he was posted to the Canadian destroyer HMCS *Algonquin*, operating from Scapa Flow, on five occasions escorting aircraft carriers during Fleet Air Arm raids on targets along the Norwegian coast. He recalls: 'We also escorted a large convoy of merchant ships and oil tankers on a 18-day return voyage to Murmansk in Russia. We lost three ships to submarines on the return trip.' After training ashore on the Sub Lieutenant's course, in May 1945 Robinson was appointed as Gunnery Officer in the Hunt Class destroyer *Mendip*. That September he volunteered for training as a Fleet Air Arm pilot, less than two years later embarking on operational training, flying Seafires from St Merryn in Cornwall. In late October 1947 he completed flying training, including eight deck landings in a Seafire on HMS *Illustrious*. Returning to the Royal Australian Navy, he retired in the rank of Commander. By the early 1970s Robinson and family were running a 100-acre farm and a trout fishing lodge at Bibbenluke Lodge, south of Canberra. A decade later Tony Robinson and his wife retired to Tura Beach, near Merimbula on the coast of New South Wales. Today he lives in Canberra and, as this book was being finished, told the author (via e-mail): 'I am 83 now and hope to live long enough to see your book published!'

Roger Morris, who joined *Rodney* as a young midshipman in September 1943, at Malta, went on to serve not only in the Royal Navy but also the Merchant Navy and

Royal Fleet Auxiliary. After leaving *Rodney* in late 1944 he saw more service on the Russia convoys, but in the destroyer *Scorpion*. More than sixty years on he recalled of his time in her: 'My most vivid memory of *Scorpion* was getting punished for returning on board drunk at Polyarny in the Kola Inlet. I was sleeping when another officer poured a bottle of beer over me. Stripping off, I was attempting to dry my pyjamas on the electric fire when the captain entered from the cabin next door, to behold this midshipman starkers, drunk and holding a pair of pyjamas that were on fire. He was not amused.' Morris ended his war in a mine-sweeper working off the east coast of England, out of Harwich. He spent the next fifteen years at sea, but the prospect of a desk job persuaded him to come out of the Navy and for some years he ran a pub with his wife. By the late 1970s, Morris was a deck officer in the Denholm Ship Management Company. One voyage took him to Tokyo in the *Caledonian Forest*, a bulk carrier cum timber ship of 35,000 tons. In 1979, he transferred to the Royal Fleet Auxiliary, gaining promotion to Second Mate. This phase of his sea-going career included service as Watchkeeper and Ops Officer in the supply tanker *Pearleaf*. Roger Morris later returned to the Royal Navy as a Commander, and while based in the UK played an important part in logistics support for the Falklands War task force, for which he was awarded the OBE. He finally retired in late 1982 and today lives in Plymouth, with painting among his hobbies. **Bill Myers** stayed in the Navy after the war, ultimately retiring in the rank of Commander. Having left *Rodney* in early 1944 he was drafted to 794 Naval Air Squadron at RNAS St Merryn, next going to sea in the carrier *Ocean*, which took him back to the Mediterranean. Promoted to Warrant Officer in 1948, Myers served at various naval air stations and air bases, receiving his commission and ending his career in 1970, as Engineer Commander on the staff of Flag Officer Naval Air Command. After leaving the Service, Bill Myers pursued a career in industry before retiring at the age of sixty-three, when he moved back to his native Devon, settling at Brixham and writing his autobiography, published privately for his family to enjoy. *See Sources.* He died in 2004.

Tom Brock left *Rodney* at Rosyth Dockyard on 2 April 1946, following her decommissioning. He went down to Devonport and then was sent up to Glasgow to stand by *Dunkirk*, a Battle Class destroyer being completed on the Clyde. By 1953 Brock was back at Devonport, where he helped look after the Reserve Fleet moored up the Tamar. Five years later, after more service overseas, Brock had been commissioned a Sub Lieutenant, subsequently joining the carrier *Bulwark* and going with her to the Far East and then serving in the destroyer *Defender* before returning to the UK. He was appointed as First Lieutenant of the HMS *Raleigh* training establishment at Torpoint in 1968, retiring from the Navy in 1973. However, he was soon back in uniform, joining the engineering artificer's training school HMS *Fisgard*, next door to *Raleigh*, as Establishment Officer (a retired officer's post but still in uniform). He served in that post until *Fisgard* was closed in mid-1983. Finally out of uniform, Tom Brock was Torpoint town clerk until 1993. He was also mayor of Torpoint 1979/80, continuing to enjoy his retirement in the same Cornish community, just across the Hamoaze from Devonport.

After some time ashore in barracks, Royal Marine **Len Nicholl**, who saw the *Bismarck*'s destruction through the open port of his 6-inch gun turret, helped the home front war effort by doing a spot of spud picking for local farmers near Plymouth. He was subsequently trained as an anti-aircraft gunner and drafted to the carrier HMS *Victorious*, in early 1944, seeing action in her during Japanese kamikaze attacks off the island of Okinawa at the end of the war. Demobbed in late 1945, he found employment in the aviation industry and today lives in his home city of Plymouth.

After his time on the flag staff of Force H, seeing action on the Malta convoys, and during the Allied invasions of North Africa and Sicily, by D-Day **Tommy Byers** was serving in the destroyer *Icarus*, which patrolled off the landing beaches, not far from *Rodney*. By VE Day, Byers was serving in a mine-sweeper working off the Isle of Man and then went out to the Far East in the same ship. Finally getting leave home to Ireland in 1950, he soon found himself in a ship ordered to lay mines in Belfast Lough against a feared Russian invasion, an operation that was called off. Invalided out of the Royal Navy in July 1952 as a Chief Petty Officer, Byers worked in the aviation industry and then in security at Heathrow Airport. After retiring, Tommy Byers went home to Ireland, at the age of 70 becoming a local independent councillor on Ards Borough Council. Tommy Byers died in March 2002.

Engine Room Artificer **Ken George**, who sneaked a look at *Bismarck* as she burned, is a native of Cornwall, born at Porthleven in 1911. He served an apprenticeship as a Fitter and Turner, at Holman Bros. Ltd., Camborne, Cornwall from 25 January 1927 to 16 March 1932. The following July he joined the Royal Navy at the HMS *Drake* naval barracks in Devonport. Prior to being drafted to *Rodney*, in September 1938, he served in the battleship *Barham* and cruiser *Apollo*. Promoted to Chief ERA while still serving in *Rodney*, he didn't leave her until 26 February 1945. Returning to *Drake*, he was sent to stand by the Landing Ship Tank *Broganza*, from 6 July 1945 until 22 September 1945, at Belfast. Demobbed in January 1946, Ken George served in the Royal Fleet Reserve until late October 1956. Today he still lives in his beloved Cornwall.

Arthur 'Mick' Kavanagh first saw *Rodney*'s home port of Plymouth in May 1943, her first return home since the beginning of the war and, like the rest of the battleship's complement, enjoyed his run ashore, which he later described as 'a high old time'. On 1 June, the twenty-one year old Irishman, who had gone from boy to man during his four years in *Rodney*, was drafted back to Chatham naval barracks, having passed for Leading Seaman but not yet made up in the rank. He put himself forward for Torpedo School, ending up in HMS *Cyclops*, a submarine depot ship off the Isle of Bute, Scotland. While there he met two of his uncles, who were in the Canadian Army, busy training for the D-Day invasion and did some sight-seeing with them in a borrowed jeep. In November 1944, Kavanagh was drafted to the British Pacific Fleet, soon finding himself serving in the destroyer *Quadrant*, which joined the action as the Allies closed in on Japan, escorting the carrier *Implacable*. During a typhoon in July 1945, Kavanagh recalled his ship 'standing on one end'. *Quadrant* went to Hong Kong where, with other sailors from her ship's company, he supervised the destruction of Japanese kamikaze speedboats, which were run aground at Picnic Bay, Lamma Island. By early 1946, he had left *Quadrant* and was in India, helping to contain an Indian Navy mutiny. Post-war Mick Kavanagh saw service in the Palestine patrol, not leaving the Navy until 1953. He last saw *Rodney* at the breakers' yard in the late 1940s, as the ship he was serving in passed under the Forth Bridge to the open sea. In civvy street Mick Kavanagh worked for a few months building inshore mine-sweepers for Thornycroft, at their yard on the Thames. He then got a job with the British Tabulating Machine Company, which had manufactured the Bombe mechanisms used by code-breakers at Bletchley Park during the Second World War. Staying with the same employer for thirty-four years, until he retired, today Mick Kavanagh lives with his family in Kingston upon Thames.

Allan Snowden left *Rodney* in December 1944. Sent to the Far East, at Trincomalee he joined HMS *Mullion Cove*, a floating hull repair workshop, supporting the Royal Navy's warships in the dying days of the Second World War. The converted merchant vessel's purpose was to go forward with the Eastern Fleet and offer battle damage repair, but, in Snowden's words, 'she never saw a shot fired in anger, and we ended up swinging around an anchor for seven months.' Returning to the UK in spring 1946, he soon found himself in Malta, where he was drafted to the sloop *Mermaid*, but was invalided out of the Navy in late 1947. For more than three decades Allan Snowden worked as an electrician with the National Coal Board, but for 15 months in 1960/61 returned to sea aboard the MV *Roland*, which was in April 1961 embroiled in the notorious Bay of Pigs invasion fiasco. 'The ship had been chartered by the Russians to carry sugar between Cuba and the Soviet Union,' he recalled. 'We came alongside a jetty only to find a long line of Castro's troops armed with tommy-guns waiting for us, to ensure there were no more invaders hidden aboard ship. They searched the *Roland* from stem to stern and found nothing. Earlier, at sea off Cuba, we were stopped by an American destroyer. It was quite an exciting time.' In addition to taking sugar to Odessa, Kherson and Novorossisk, all Soviet ports in the Black Sea, *Roland* also took sugar to communist China.

Allan Snowden maintains his links with the sea and the Navy, through an active membership of the Royal Naval Association, at one stage being chairman of the Scottish Area of the RNA. In October 2007 he was due to revisit one of his wartime haunts, as part of a RNA group visiting the Orkneys to establish a new branch at Kirkwall. He fully intended to walk the shores of Scapa Flow and once more gaze out across the waters where the legendary *Rodney* rode at anchor. 'I'd like to see if the old canteen we used to frequent, is still there. Due to a shortage of glasses they used to give us beer in old bottles that had their tops sliced off. I recall the older hands in the ship used to play us at Crown and Anchor to try and deprive us youngsters of our hard-earned wages.' While in the Orkneys he also intended visiting the Italian Chapel, so-called because it was built by Italian Prisoners of War, in order to pay his respects to those who gave their lives during the Second World War.

Appendix 2

NELSON CLASS

Nelson
Builder: Armstrong-Whitworth, Tyneside
Laid down: December 1922
Launched: September 1925
Completed: June 1927

Rodney
Builder: Cammell Laird, Birkenhead
Laid down: December 1922
Launched: December 1925
Completed: August 1927

Dimensions
Length: 710 ft (overall)
Beam: 106 ft
Draught: 30 ft
Displacement: *Nelson* – 33,500 tons/*Rodney* – 33,900 tons (standard); *Nelson* – 38,000 tons/*Rodney* – 40,000 tons (full load)

Main Armament
9 x 16-inch
12 x 6-inch
6 x 4.7-inch

Final Anti-Aircraft armament fit
16 × 40 mm
48 × 2pdr pom-pom
61 × 20 mm

Propulsion
Geared turbines, turning two shafts (props)
Designed horsepower: 45,000
Top speed: 23 knots

Fuel
Oil (max capacity 4,000 tons)

Fuel consumption
16 tons an hour at full speed.
2.7 tons per hour at cruising speed of 12 knots

Complement
Normal: 1,314
As flagship: 1,361
War complement: 1,640

Appendix 3

HMS *NELSON*

A sister ship at war

BATTLE HONOURS

Malta Convoys 1941–2
North Africa 1942–3
Sicily 1943
Salerno 1943
Mediterranean 1943
Normandy 1944

HMS *Nelson* in the Mediterranean, mid-1945 on her way to the Far East. *Goodman Collection.*

Named after the most famous British fighting admiral of all time, Horatio Lord Nelson, the *Rodney*'s sister assumed the duty of fleet flagship from her first commissioning. She retained that honour throughout the 1920s and 1930s and rarely relinquished it. HMS *Nelson* was always better maintained than *Rodney*, receiving preferential treatment when it came to major refits. Also involved in the Invergordon mutiny of 1931, *Nelson* memorably ran aground in January 1934 on Hamilton's Shoal, just beyond the entrance to Portsmouth Harbour. This misfortune inevitably prompted ribald comments about Nelson being on top of Hamilton again. *Rodney* stepped in as relief Atlantic Fleet flagship for a cruise to the West Indies, at least until *Nelson* was extracted from her embarrassing predicament and could follow on.

Beginning the Second World War as the flagship of the Home Fleet, operating from Scapa Flow, the *Nelson*, like *Rodney*, saw her first action on 26 September 1939, during the rescue of submarine *Spearfish*. The latter had been damaged during an earlier encounter with the enemy off Norway and was limping home on the surface, the Home Fleet sallying forth to escort her home and coming under attack from Luftwaffe bombers, *Nelson* evading damage. However, the battleship was not so fortunate on 4 December that year when she detonated a magnetic mine, laid earlier by a U-boat, *Nelson* entering Loch Ewe at a speed of 13 knots. One of the larger houses by the entrance to Loch Ewe belonged to the godmother of *Rodney*'s Lieutenant Commander John Boord and her bathroom window overlooked the water. 'She was having a bath and looked out of the window and saw the *Nelson* approaching the harbour and to her alarm she [*Nelson*] was mined on the way in,' recalled Boord some years later.

> *... she was alarmed that only the* Nelson *was there and not the* Rodney. *She thought my ship must have been sunk, because usually the* Nelson *and the* Rodney *appeared together.*

According to Boord the *Nelson*'s First Lieutenant, Lt Cdr Terence Robinson, had both his legs broken, as he had been standing in the eyes of the ship, right over the explosion. Another casualty was the *Nelson*'s heads.

> *... all the china bowls were broken and suddenly the enormous ship's company found themselves without any lavatories. Future ships had metal lavatory pans not china ones as a result of this.*[1]

Some fifty of the *Nelson*'s sailors were injured and the below water damage was critical enough to require six months in dockyard hands at Portsmouth.

The repairs were almost complete by early June 1940, but the German invasion of Holland, Belgium, Luxembourg and France provoked fears of an enemy amphibious assault on southern England, so *Nelson* was moved to the Clyde. When she put to sea on 6 June, to ensure she did not fall victim to mines again the battleship was preceded by mine-sweepers. This precaution swiftly proved its wisdom, for the mine-sweepers 'exploded two magnetic mines laid on the battleship's course.'[2]

Returning to duties as Home Fleet flagship, the *Nelson* on 6 September led an anti-shipping sweep off the coast of Norway. The elderly carrier *Furious* launched aircraft to attack two enemy vessels, sinking one and forcing the crew of the other to abandon ship. Two months later *Nelson* and other ships of the Home Fleet, including *Rodney*, stationed themselves in the Iceland-Faroes gap, in a vain attempt to catch the German surface raider *Admiral Scheer*. In late January 1941, *Nelson* similarly failed to intercept the *Gneisenau* and *Scharnhorst* when they made their breakout into the Atlantic. A further fruitless search for a German surface raider came in February, before in early March *Nelson*, the brand new battleship *King George V* and other units of the Home Fleet watched over the Lofoten Islands commando raid in which some of *Rodney*'s men participated. The remainder of the month was occupied with yet another attempt to intercept German surface warships, plus providing cover for a mine-laying operation between Iceland and the Faroe Islands and escorting a troop convoy heading for the Middle East. *Nelson* reached Cape Town on 16 April but six days later sailed for Durban's dockyard where she was to receive essential maintenance. Leaving Durban on 10 May 1941, the battleship escorted the carrier *Eagle* to Freetown in Sierra Leone, eighteen days later receiving orders for Gibraltar, to provide escort for another convoy. With the pursuit and destruction of *Bismarck* by sister ship *Rodney* and other Royal Navy vessels complete, the process of hunting down German supply ships was initiated. The latter were waiting at various places in the vast Atlantic, in order to rendezvous with the Nazi battleship and sustain her war on commerce. In company with the cruiser *Neptune*, on 4 June *Nelson* intercepted the supply vessel *Gonzenheim*. The German crew attempted to scuttle their ship, but this failed and *Neptune* sank the *Gonzenheim* on 5 June, to remove her as a danger to shipping. In early July *Nelson* was sent back to Gibraltar to join Force H, as flagship for its charismatic commander, Vice Admiral Sir James Somerville.

Nelson's first run to Malta was Operation Substance, a convoy transporting people, weapons and supplies at the end of July. Another similar run was undertaken by Force H before the month was out, under the codename Operation Style. There was a change in focus towards the end of August, with *Nelson* and the carrier *Ark Royal* spearheading an attack on enemy positions on Sardinia, called Operation Mincemeat. The need to keep Malta supplied and properly defended pulled Force H back to mounting protection for a convoy that ferried additional fighter aircraft to the island. Joining sister ship *Rodney* for the Operation Halberd convoy run to Malta, *Nelson* was badly damaged when an Italian air-launched torpedo hit her bows. After temporary repairs at Gibraltar, she sailed for Britain, going into dock at Rosyth in late November. A major refit was carried out, with *Nelson* ready for front line operations again by the end of April 1942, sailing north to Scapa to rejoin the Home Fleet. On 31 May, *Nelson* sailed with convoy WS19P, which was headed initially for Freetown in Sierra Leone. Together with *Rodney*, she provided the heavy escort for troop ships destined for the Middle East and Asia.

Nelson made the return journey to Scapa in company with her sister ship in July the same year and both were assigned to protect the Operation Pedestal convoy to Malta, with *Nelson* once again flagship of Force H. Returning to the UK in late August, she went to Rosyth for further repairs, which took until mid-October to complete. Assigned again to Force H, but too late to take part in supporting Allied landings in North Africa, *Nelson* began her voyage back to the Mediterranean on 16 November, sailing from Scapa Flow and heading once more for Gibraltar. Like *Rodney* she experienced an uneventful few months, waiting in vain for the Italian fleet to emerge and do battle.

Both *Nelson* and *Rodney* received much-needed maintenance at Devonport Dockyard in May 1943, before beginning preparations to participate in further amphibious operations in the Mediterranean.

During the Allied invasion of Sicily in July 1943, *Nelson* was once more flagship of Force H, providing support to troops fighting ashore and escorting carriers, again waiting more in hope than realistic expectation for the Italian navy to make a move against the invasion armada.

Taking part in Operation Hammer on 31 August, alongside *Rodney* and the cruiser *Orion*, the *Nelson* pounded fortifications on the Italian mainland, unleashing her 16-inch and 6-inch guns against two coastal gun batteries, a valuable precursor to the Allied invasion a few days later.

Based on Malta, *Nelson* led Force H when it sailed from the island fortress on 8 September to provide cover for the subsequent Allied landings at Salerno.

With the disbandment of Force H, *Nelson* was released to return home in early November for a timely refit, in order to restore her to full fighting efficiency to play a role in supporting landings in the Bay of the Seine.

Emerging from refit in mid-May 1944, *Nelson* was assigned to the reserve bombardment force, arriving off the Normandy beaches on 11 June, to relieve *Rodney*. On 14 June, *Nelson* gained the distinction of claiming the scalp of a senior Nazi combat division officer. A British spotter aircraft detected activity at a chateau, indicating it may be a German military headquarters. This turned out to be a correct assumption and the shells began to fall just as the HQ staff of the 12th SS Hitler Youth Panzer Division were breaking for lunch.

> *... all thoughts of pea soup with sausage were banished as with a mighty roar ... The first salvo hit the ground beyond the chateau; it was odds-on the next would be more accurate.*[3]

As Brigadefuhrer Fritz Witt, the commander of the division, sprinted for a trench, *Nelson*'s 16-inch shells hit the chateau square on, spraying masonry and shrapnel. Witt and a number of his officers were killed.

Having delivered the decapitation of the Hitler Youth division, *Nelson* was relieved on 18 June. She had notched up twenty bombardments during her week off the invasion beaches, but on the last day detonated two large magnetic mines, which damaged the plating of some exterior hull compartments, causing flooding that gave *Nelson* a minor list to starboard.[4] With UK dockyards working full out on other projects, the *Nelson* on 22 June set sail for a major refit in America. While *Rodney* was so worn out she could expect limited war service by this time, the *Nelson* was in a generally much better state and was now destined to switch to the Far East. Departing American waters at the end of January 1945, *Nelson* headed for Portsmouth Dockyard where her refit would be finished, including important enhancements to anti-aircraft weapons. With the completion of sea trials, *Nelson* sailed for Malta and embarked on operational work-up in the now peaceful Mediterranean. As *Nelson* was being put through her paces in early May, Germany surrendered. The battleship was soon passing south through the Suez Canal, heading to join the Royal Navy's East Indies fleet in action against the Japanese. Between 24 and 26 July, she was part of a task group conducting air strikes and bombardments against enemy targets in the Malay Peninsula. *Nelson*'s sailors and marines got a taste of a deadly new enemy weapon.

> *During this operation she took on board seven officers and 87 ratings, survivors from M/S* [Mine-Sweeper] *VESTAL which was sunk by the first suicide attack by Japanese aircraft on any unit of East Indies Fleet.*[5]

There was also a familiar foe, with twenty-four Japanese mines swept by the task group's vessels, *Nelson* fortunately evading her third mining of the war.

The battleship, using Trincomalee as her operating base, soon returned to waters off Malaya where she provided heavyweight protection for Operation Jurist, the liberation of Penang. With the Japanese agreeing to abide by an unconditional surrender on 14 August, a fortnight later, *Nelson* hosted senior Japanese officers, as did the cruiser HMS *London*, but at Sabang. Undertakings that there would be no attacks on the East Indies fleet were signed. Japanese military leaders returned to *Nelson* on 3 September, signing the formal surrender of Penang. Five days later the battleship set sail, to take part in Operation Zipper, the liberation of western Malaya. By 12 September, *Nelson* was at Singapore, where the official surrender of all Japanese forces in South-East Asia was taken. Heading home via the Mediterranean, with a call at Gibraltar, *Nelson* reached Portsmouth that November. Within a few months *Nelson*, which had initially taken over Home Fleet flagship duties from *Rodney*, had been reduced to a training battleship role. She was decommissioned in February 1948 and, after being used as a target during bombing trials, was sent for scrap in March 1949, at Inverkeithing, being taken apart in the same boneyard as *Rodney*. The name *Nelson* still blesses a 'ship' in the Royal Navy, only a stone frigate, for today's HMS *Nelson* is the main naval barracks at Portsmouth.

- *For further details of HMS* Nelson*'s career see the main narrative of this book.*

Notes

1 IWM Sound Archive.
2 *HMS Nelson, Summary of Service 1939–1948*, S.7515.
3 Rupert Butler, *Hitler's Young Tigers*.
4 Neil McCart, *Rodney and Nelson 1927–1949*.
5 *HMS Nelson, Summary of Service 1939–1948*, S.7515.

Appendix 4

LIEUTENANT RICHARD EVELYN COLTART

Lieutenant **Richard Evelyn Coltart**, who in his midshipman's journal painted both *Nelson* and *Rodney*, served in the former from 5 September 1929 to 27 April 1931. Dick Coltart went on to join the Submarine Service and won the Distinguished Service Cross during the Norwegian campaign in the Second World War, while

Above: HMS *Nelson* (foreground) following HMS *Rodney* around as they lead the Atlantic Fleet, in a painting by Lieutenant Richard Evelyn Coltart. Right: HMS *Nelson* when flagship of the Atlantic Fleet, painted sometime during the period 1929–1931.
Coltart Collection.

Looking war-fatigued, HMS *Nelson* follows sister ship HMS *Rodney* (in the distance, far left) out of Gibraltar harbour in early July 1943, both battleships destined to provide firepower cover for the invasion of Sicily. *US Naval Historical Center.*

serving in the crew of the submarine *Taku*. Showing great leadership promise, he was appointed Commanding Officer of submarine *H49*, a small First World War-era boat, which had even been decommissioned and placed in the Reserve Fleet as recently as 1938. Taking her out from Harwich, to prowl the North Sea in search of likely targets, on 16 September 1940, *H49* fired a pair of torpedoes at a merchant ship off Texel in the occupied Netherlands. However, on 18 October *H49* met her end, while on a similar patrol in the same area. She was caught by German anti-submarine vessels and subjected to intensive depth-charging. Only one member of her crew survived: Stoker George Oliver, who had no recollection at all of how he escaped death and his shipmates did not. Dick Coltart's paintings of *Rodney* and *Nelson* have been published for the first time in this book, with kind permission of his family, forming a remarkable record of the sister ships in a time of peace before the war that, sadly, claimed the artist-sailor's life.

Appendix 5

TWO *RODNEYS*

HMS *Rodney* brig-sloop, 1782

On the day after the surrender of the British colony of Demerara to a French invasion force, in February 1782, Lieutenant Tudor Tucker was 'released' from HMS *Rodney* with the following note from Lt John Brisbane, the sloop's master and commander.

> *Tudor Tucker served as Lieutenant under my command onboard of His Majesty's Sloop The* Rodney *from the 28th Day of July 1781 to the 3rd Day of February 1782 (the Day of surrendering the said sloop, by Capitulation, to His Most Christian Majesty's Forces) during which times he complied with the general printed instruction. Given under my Hand on board the said Sloop this 4th Day of February 1782. J.D. Brisbane.*[1]

HMS *Rodney* battleship, 1933

In early 1933, Captain John Tovey, Commanding Officer of HMS *Rodney*, signed off Commander Ross from his time in the battleship.

> *This is to certify that Mr George Campbell Ross has served as Lieut-Comdr (E) & Commander (E) in HMS* Rodney *under my command from the 12th day of April 1932, to the 10th day of January 1933, during which period he has conducted himself to my entire satisfaction. A very capable Engineer Officer, who should do well in the higher ranks of the Service.*
>
> *Jack. i. Tovey Captain HMS* Rodney[2]

Notes

1 NMM, ADM/L/R/46 Navy Board Lieutenant's Logs *Rodney* 1781–1782.
2 IWM Department of Documents, Rear Admiral G.C. Ross. For more on the career of this officer, see *Rodney*'s People appendix.

Appendix 6

CLIFFORD WOOLLEY AND A BATTLESHIP *RODNEY* WEB SITE

Clifford Woolley as a Royal Navy Petty Officer during the Second World War.
Maddison Collection.

Paul Maddison, who contributed images and some background information for this book, has created an excellent web site on HMS Rodney. *Here, Paul explains how his life-long interest in HMS* Rodney *was inspired by the example of his grandfather, Clifford Woolley, who served in the battleship.*

My earliest awareness of HMS *Rodney* dates back to when I was a young boy of seven. We had emigrated to Canada from Britain in 1963 and my grandparents came over to spend some time with us during the summer of 1968. I remember my grandfather discussing his time aboard the ship. My brother Dave and I were in our bunk beds, and he had come into our room to say goodnight. I'm not sure how we got on the topic, but I remember he mentioned how the concussion from *Rodney*'s 16-inch guns caused the injury of many shipmates. He said one crew member had been decapitated, as a result of walking too close to the guns as they were fired. I also remember a story about my grandfather shooting down an enemy plane that was attacking *Rodney*. Whether he had told us the latter, or a relation did, I don't remember. In the summer of 1971, our family made a return trip to visit relations in Britain. We spent a number of days in Hatch End (a suburb of London), with my grandparents. It was during this visit, that my grandmother opened a leather-bound book containing numerous photographs my grandfather had obtained during the Second World War. Being ten-years old, my interest was just a matter of being polite. I didn't have a great deal of interest in looking at old black and white photographs in a musty-smelling book. However, one of these pictures made an impression. It was an aircraft carrier on its side. I never really thought much more about it, but the image of the sinking ship had made an impact. In November of that same year, I remember a phone call received from overseas stating my grandfather had passed away. Many months after his death, my grandmother discarded some items. Unfortunately one of these items was his uniform, but his medals and the leather-bound book were retained. In 1985 my fiancee and I made the trip back overseas and stayed with my grandmother who had moved to Portsmouth. We both took great interest in the Navy tours and monuments of the city. I asked about the book that I had seen many years earlier. It was brought out and the three of us went through it with great interest. I found the photograph of the sinking aircraft carrier. The caption written under the picture written by my grandfather said:

> *HM Aircraft carrier* Eagle *sinks in seven minutes after being hit by four torpedoes.*

The book was now of great interest to me, a valued family heirloom. Over the many years that followed, I established a career in the computer industry. With the invention of the internet, I learned HTML script and created a few personal web sites before turning my attention to creating a site based on my grandfather's photographs. I thought the pictures, along with his Service history and additional facts about the ship would make an interesting site. I spent some time scanning his photographs, then created it in the spring of 1997. In May of 1998, I re-architected the site and began further research of my grandfather's Service record. I learned that he was in HMS *Rodney* for a majority of the Second World War, as an Ordnance Mechanic. I requested his entire Service record from the Royal Navy, only to find that many of the records were lost in a fire many years ago. The UK Armed Forces Personnel Administration Agency responded with a listing of his Service placements and stated his character assessment was: 'Very Good'. Contained in my grandfather's book was a small newspaper clipping with his photograph, from the *London Gazette*, dated 28 November 1944. The article was labelled 'Mentioned in Despatches'. It turned out that my grandfather had been decorated with an Oak Leaf for action he had taken during the Italian Campaign. Apparently he had left his post after the aft gun crew had been taken out, using their Oerlikon anti-aircraft gun to shoot down a German bomber. The Oak Leaf, along with the other medals he earned, are proudly displayed with his photograph in my mother's home. Since the spring of 1998, I have received numerous e-mails from people regarding their memories of the great ship. Some of them even took the time to contribute photographs to the site. On 3 July 1999, I received a short e-mail asking me to respond if the message was received. It was from Derrick Pearce Hon. Sec. HMS *Rodney* Association. I eagerly responded to the e-mail. With Derrick and the association's help, the web site grew immensely. By the fall of 1999, the site had increased to over 100 photographs, specifications of the ship, a crew listing, and many models and drawings. In May of 2001, I attended an HMS *Rodney* reunion to commemorate the 60th anniversary of the sinking of the *Bismarck*. I brought along a complete printout of the site, which drew considerable interest from the veterans who were there. A few years later Derrick Pearce pointed Iain Ballantyne, the author of this book, in my direction, as he felt my site contained some very worthwhile material that would help Iain with research.

If it wasn't for my grandfather's efforts in creating a scrapbook of his wartime service, it would never had sparked an interest in a young boy that one day led to him in adult life creating the web site. Sadly, the HMS *Rodney* Association is no more, but I am proud to say that through the web site, and now this book, the great battleship is remembered.

HMS *Rodney* Web site address:
http://www.geocities.com/Pentagon/Quarters/4433/

BIBLIOGRAPHY

Acworth, Bernard, *The Navy and the Next War*, Eyre & Spottiswoode, 1934
Ambrose, Stephen E., *D-Day June 6, 1944*, Pocket Books, 2002
Baddeley, Allan, *Royal Navy*, Frederick Muller, 1942
Ballantyne, Iain, *H.M.S. London*, Pen & Sword, 2003
—— *H.M.S. Warspite*, Pen & Sword, 2001
Barnard, John E., *Building Britain's Wooden Walls*, Anthony Nelson, 1997
Bastable, Jonathan, *Voices from D-Day*, David & Charles, 2006
Bekker, Cajus, *Hitler's Naval War*, Macdonald, 1974
Benstead, C.R., *H.M.S. Rodney*, Sellicks, 1931
—— *H.M.S. Rodney at Sea*, Methuen, 1932
Bercuson, David J., and Herwig, Holger H., *Bismarck*, Hutchinson, 2002
Berthold, Will, *The Sinking of the Bismarck*, Transworld, 1960
Bonner-Smith, D., and Dewar, Captain A.C., ed., *Russian War, 1854 Baltic And Black Sea official correspondence*, Navy Records Society, 1943
Bowen, Frank C., *Wooden Walls in Action*, Halton & Co., 1951
Brodhurst, Robin, *Churchill's Anchor*, Pen & Sword, 2000
Brooke, Geoffrey, *Alarm Starboard*, Pen & Sword, 2004
Brown, D.K., *Warrior To Dreadnought*, Chatham, 1997
—— *The Grand Fleet*, 1999
Brown, Malcolm and Meehan, Patricia, *Scapa Flow*, Pan, 2002
Brower, Jack, *The Battleship Bismarck*, Conway, 2005
Burt, R.A., *British Battleships 1919–1939*, Weidenfeld Military, 1993
Butler, Rupert, *Hitler's Young Tigers*, Arrow, 1986
Callender, Geoffrey, *'Sea Kings of Britain, Vol. 3, 1760–1805,* Longmans, 1939
Chatfield, Lord, Admiral of the Fleet, *The Navy and Defence*, Windmill, 1942
—— *It Might Happen Again*, Windmill, 1947
Chesneau, Roger, *Hood*, Cassell, 2002
Churchill, Winston, *The Second World War, Vol I–VI*, Cassell, 1948–1954
Clarke, John D., *The Men of HMS Victory at Trafalgar*, Vintage Naval Library, 1999
Clowes, William, Laird, *The Royal Navy*, Vol II–VII, Chatham, 1996
Collard, Ian, *Cammell Laird*, Tempus, 2004
Connell, Brian, *Knight Errant*, Hodder and Stoughton, 1955
Corrigan, Gordon, *Blood, Sweat and Arrogance*, Weidenfeld & Nicolson, 2006
Cunningham of Hyndhope, Viscount, Admiral of the Fleet, *A Sailor's Odyssey*, Hutchinson & Co, 1951
D'Este, Carlo, *Eisenhower*, Weidenfeld & Nicolson, 2003
—— *Decision in Normandy*, Harper, 1994
Dewar, Captain A.C., ed., *Russian War, 1855 Black Sea Official Correspondence*, Navy Records Society, 1945
Dinardo, R.L., Syrett, David, ed., *The Commissioned Sea Officers of the Royal Navy 1660–1815*, Scolar Press, Navy Records Society, 1994
Divine, A.D., *Destroyer's War*, John Murray, 1942
Divine, David, *Mutiny at Invergordon*, Macdonald, 1970
Doherty, Richard, *Normandy 1944*, Spellmount, 2004
Fraser, David, *And We Shall Shock Them*, Sceptre, 1988
Gardiner, Robert, ed., *The Line of Battle*, Conway Maritime Press, 2004
Gray, Edwyn, *Disasters of the Deep*, Pen & Sword, 2003
—— *Hitler's Battleships*, Pen & Sword, 1999
Grenfell, Russell, Captain, *The Bismarck Episode*, Faber and Faber, 1949

Grove, Eric J., *The Royal Navy*, palgrave, 2005
Hall, Christopher D., *Wellington's Navy*, Chatham Publishing, 2004
Harris, Sir Arthur, Marshal of the RAF, *Bomber Offensive*, Pen & Sword, 2005
Haythornthwaite, Philip, *The Peninsular War*, Brassey's, 2004
Hastings, Max, *Overlord*, Pocket Books, 1986
Heathcote, T.A.,*The British Admirals of the Fleet 1734–1995*, Pen & Sword, 2002
Herman, Arthur, *To Rule the Waves*, Hodder, 2005
Hibbert, Christopher, *The Destruction of Lord Raglan*, Penguin, 1985
Holmes, Richard, ed., *The Oxford Companion to Military History*, Oxford, 2001
Hood, Jean, *Come Hell & High Water*, Conway, 2006
Hore, Captain Peter, *The Habit of Victory*, Pan, 2005
Horne, Alistair, with Montgomery, David, *The Lonely Leader*, Macmillan, 1994
Humble, Richard, *Before Dreadnought*, Macdonald & Jane's, 1976
—— *Fraser of North Cape*, Routledge & Kegan Paul, 1983
Jameson, William, *Ark Royal*, Periscope Publishing, 2004
Jane's Fighting Ships of World War II, Studio Editions, 1996
Jenkins, Roy, *Churchill*, Pan, 2001
Keegan, John, *Six Armies in Normandy*, Pimlico, 1992
Kemp, Paul, *British Warship Losses of the 20th Century*, Sutton, 1999
Kemp, P.K., *Victory at Sea*, Frederick Muller, 1957
Kennedy, Ludovic, *Nelson and His Captains*, Fontana, 1976
—— *Pursuit: The Chase and Sinking of the Bismarck*, Cassell, 2001
King, Cecil, *Rule Britannia*, The Studio, 1941
—— *H.M.S. (His Majesty's Ships) and Their Forebears*, The Studio, 1940
Le Fevre, Peter and Harding, Richard, *Precursors to Nelson*, Chatham, 2000
Lewis, Jon E., *D-Day As They Saw It*, Robinson, 2004
Lewis, Michael, *The Navy of Britain*, George Allen & Unwin, 1948
Lyon, David, *The Sailing Navy List*, Conway, 2001
Macintyre, Captain, Donald, *Narvik*, Evans Brothers, 1959
—— *The Battle for the Mediterranean*, Pan, 1970
McCart, Neil, *Nelson and Rodney 1927–1949*, Maritime Books, 2005
Macksey, Kenneth, *The Searchers*, Cassell, 2003
McLynn, Frank, *1759, The Year Britain Became Master of the World*, Pimlico, 2005
McMurtrie, Francis, *The Cruise of the Bismarck*, Hutchinson, 1942
Mearns, David and White, Rob, *Hood and Bismarck*, Channel 4 Books, 2002
Messenger, Charles, *The Commandos 1940–1946*, William Kimber, 1985
Moreman, Tim, *British Commandos 1940–46*, Osprey, 2006
Moynahan, Brian, *Comrades*, Little, Brown, 1992
Mullenheim-Rechberg, Burkard, Freiherr von, *Battleship Bismarck*, USNI, 1980
Neillands, Robin and De Normann, *D-Day 1944*, Orion, 1994
Pack, S.W.C., *Cunningham The Commander*, Purnell, 1974
Padfield, Peter, *Rule Britannia*, Pimlico, 2002
Parkes, Oscar, *Ships of the Royal Navies*, Sampson Low, Marston & Co., 1936
Parry, Ann, *The Admirals Fremantle 1788–1920*, Chatto & Windus, 1971
Pears, Commander Randolph, *British Battleships 1892–1957*, Putnam, 1957
Peillard, Leonce, *Sink the Tirpitz*, Granada, 1975
Phillips, F.L., and Sainsbury, A.B., *The Royal Navy Day by Day*, Sutton, 2005
Phillipson, David, *Roll on The Rodney!*, Sutton, 1999
Ponting, Clive, *The Crimean War*, Pimlico, 2005
Poolman, Kenneth, *Ark Royal*, NPI Media, 2000
Preston, Anthony, *The World's Worst Warships*, Conway, 2002
Rhys-Jones, Graham, *The Loss of the Bismarck*, Cassell, 1999
Robinson, Derek, *Invasion, 1940*, Constable & Robinson, 2005
Roskill, Capt S.W., *The Navy at War 1939–1945*, Wordsworth Editions, 1998
Royle, Trevor, *Crimea, The Great Crimean War 1854–1856*, Little, Brown and Company, 1999
Schofield, B.B., *The Russian Convoys*, B.T. Batsford, 1964
Shirer, William, *The Sinking of the Bismarck*, Sterling, 2006

Simpson, Michael, ed., *The Cunningham Papers, Volume II, 1942–1946*, Navy Records Society, 2006
Skwiot, Miroslaw Zbigniew and Prusinowska, Elzbieta Teresea, *Hunting the Bismarck*, The Crowood Press, 2006
Smith, Peter C., *Pedestal*, Crecy, 1999
Smyth, Admiral W.H., *The Sailor's Word-Book*, Conway Maritime Press, 2005
Sopocko, Eryk, *Gentlemen, The Bismarck Has Been Sunk*, Methuen, 1942
Spillsbury, Julian, *The Thin Red Line*, Cassell, 2005
Steiner, Zara, *The Lights That Failed*, Oxford, 2005
Stephen, Martin, *The Fighting Admirals*, Leo Cooper, 1991
Sturton, Ian, ed., *All The World's Battleships*, Conway, 1996
Talbot-Booth, E.C., *The Royal Navy*, Sampson Low, Marston & Co., 1939
Thomas, David A., *Malta Convoys*, Leo Cooper, 1999
—— *A Companion to the Royal Navy*, Harrap, 1988
Thomas, Roger D., and Patterson, Brian, *Dreadnoughts in Camera 1905–1920*, Sutton, 1998
Thompson, Kenneth, and members of the ship's company, *HMS Rodney at War*, Hollis and Carter, 1946
Tracy, Nicholas, ed., *The Naval Chronicle, Volume IV, 1807–1810*, Chatham Publishing, 1999
Trew, Peter, *Rodney and the Breaking of the Line*, Pen & Sword Maritime, 2006
Twiston Davis, David, ed., *Daily Telegraph Book of Naval Obituaries*, Grub Street, 2006
Urban, Mark, *The Generals*, Faber and Faber, 2005
van der Vat, Dan, *Standard of Power*, Hutchinson, 2000
Warner, Oliver, *Cunningham of Hyndhope*, John Murray, 1967
Warner, Philip, *The Daily Telegraph Book of the D-Day Landings*, Pen & Sword Military, 2004
Warren, C.E.T., and Benson, James, *Above us The Waves*, Pen & Sword, 2006
Wasley, Gerald, *Blitz: Account of Hitler's Aerial War Over Plymouth*, Devon Books, 1991
Watts, Anthony J., *The Royal Navy*, Arms & Armour, 1994
Wellings, Joseph H., Rear Admiral, *On His Majesty's Service*, Naval War College Press, 1983
Williams, Andrew, *D-Day to Berlin*, Sceptre, 2005
Wilmott, H.P., *Battleship*, Cassell, 2002
Winklareth, Robert J., *Naval Shipyards of the World*, Chatham, 2000
Winton, John, *Carrier Glorious*, Cassell, 1999
A Seaman's Pocket-Book, June 1943, Conway, 2006
The Autobiography of Elder Joseph Bates, Southern Publishing Association, 1970

SOURCES

Imperial War Museum Department of Documents
The papers of:
Brown, E.L., 95/3/1
Conning, G., P424
Ross, Rear Admiral G.C., 86/60/1
Staveley, Lt Cdr, P.M., 05/63/1
Woolf, Captain D.C., 05/10/1
Chart showing the torpedo action between the battleship HMS *Rodney* and the German battleship *Bismarck* in the Atlantic, 27 May 1941 immediately prior to her sinking, drawn by *Rodney*'s Torpedo Officer, Commander (later Captain) R.C. Lewis in July 1941, Misc 177 (2683)

Imperial War Museum Sound Archive
Alexander, William (Accession No. 9734)
Boord, John (Accession No. 9199)
Cloake, C. (Accession No. 5804)
Craddock, Robert (Accession No. 20284)
Crawford, William (Accession No. 10673)
Fetherston Dilke, Charles (Accession No. 19571)
Harris, Edward (Accession No. 5832)
Evans, Arthur (Accession No. 15746)
Hiscox, T.R. (Accession No. 5834)
Hughes, Richard (Accession No. 25525)
Lewis, Roger (Accession No. 10670)
Moulton, James (Accession No. 6818)
Palmer, Edward (Accession No. 27742)
Repard, David (Accession No. 22161)
Sampson, J.H. (Accession No. 5816)
Smerdon, Gordon (Accession No. 17313)
Thomas, George (Accession No. 15110)
Walters, Leonard (Accession No. 12788)
Walton, Eric (Accession No. 13626)
Williams, David (Accession No. 11291)
Wilkey, Desmond (Accession No. 14150)

National Maritime Museum
ADM/L/R/46, Navy Board Lieutenants' Logs, *Rodney* 1781–1782 [Lieutenant Tudor Tucker, service in HMS *Rodney*].
AGC/5/24, Letter by Private Charles Hankinson, Royal Marines, 1840, to his brother George, dated HMS *Rodney*, 19 January 1840.
LOG/N/R/1, Log of Her Majesty's Ship *Rodney* 1840–42.
LUB/39/10, Midshipman's Log, Hon M.H. Nelson, HMS *Rodney* 92 guns 1845–1846.
JOD/65, Rev. Robert Hinds, chaplain of HMS *Rodney*, diary, Black Sea and Crimea, 1853–56.
RAI/309, Journal of HMS *Rodney*, Captain J.H. Rainier, 1895–97.
CNM/67, Admiral of the Fleet, 1st Viscount Cunningham, newspaper cuttings, HMS *Rodney*, 1930.

Royal Naval Museum
Information Sheet No. 19, George Rodney.
Information Sheet No. 21, John Tovey.

Information Sheet No. 68, *Loss of HMS* Hood *and* Bismarck.
RNM 1978.294 and 1978.295, Manuscript journals kept by Frank Twiss, while serving in HMS *Rodney*, 5 January 1928–24 July 1930.
RNM 2004.27/2, Illustrated journal kept by Midshipman Frank Morgan, HMS *Rodney*, 20 November 1934–20 March 1935.
RNM 2000.32/4, Pocket diary kept by Robert Parker, as Engineer Officer and Commander in HMS *Rodney*, 5 May 1942–7 January 1943.
RNM 2000.32/5, Memo book kept as diary by Robert Parker as Engineer Officer and Commander in HMS *Rodney*, 19 January–15 December 1943.
RNM 2000.51, Crossing the Line Certificate issued to Oliver Scarrot in HMS *Rodney*, c.1942. Unusual design showing Churchill as Neptune being pulled along by Hitler and Mussolini.
RNM 2000.32/6, Printed calendar annotated with ship movements, 1942–1943.

National Archive
ADM 36/15900, muster roll of HMS *Victory*.

Journals & Newspapers
International Herald Tribune, 24 February 1897.
Isle of Thanet Gazette, 17 September 2001.
Navy & Army Illustrated, 4 March 1899.
News Chronicle, Wednesday, 28 May 1941.
Periscope, the newspaper of Chatham Royal Dockyard, July 1980.
Sea Breezes, October 1989.
Ship's Monthly, February 1971, March 1971.
The Belfast News-Letter, 16 June 1930.
The Daily Telegraph, 20 June 2003
The Guardian, 6 June 2004.
The Illustrated London News, 14 March 1846, 3 May 1856.
The Malta Government Gazette, 14 June 1837.
The Rodney Buzz, Newsletter of the HMS Rodney Association, February 1989, July 1996, April 1997, Spring 1998, Christmas 1998, April 1999, Spring 2000, June 2000, November 2001.
The Times, 23 June 1845, 28 June 1845, 7 July 1845, 11 July 1929, 26 May 1941, 2 November 1992.
Western Evening Herald, 15 February 1897, 16 February 1897, 22 February 1897, 23 February 1897, 17, 18 December 1925.
Western Morning News, 7 December 1927.
Westmorland Gazette, 10 May 1991.

Others Sources of Information
Pembrokeshire County History Vol IV. A chapter written by Lawrence Phillips, Vice-President, The Society for Nautical Research, on Pembroke Yard.
Steel's List of the Royal Navy, January 1783.
HMS *Hood* Association, *H.M.S.* Hood *Design Background*.
Notes From Other Sources For Plymouth, 1930s, Goodman Collection. An internal Navy document, giving brief outlines of Navy Weeks at Devonport, 1928–1938.
The King's Ships Under Review, Francis E. McMurtrie, Official Programme of the Silver Jubilee Review 1935.
History of H.M.S. Rodney 1939–1948, Admiralty ship's history. Ref No. S.5775.
H.M.S. Nelson, Summary of Service 1939–1948, S.7515.
The 'Invergordon Mutineer' in Plymouth. Held in the Naval Studies Department of Plymouth City Library, letter from retired naval officer Commander H. Pursey, about the visit of Plymothian seaman, and Invergordon Mutiny agitator Leonard Wincott. Envelope 359.133.
World Ship Society Records, Chatham Historic Dockyard. Ref No. 3971915.
Recollections of D-Day and Thereabouts, Commander Ian Hamilton RN.
The Guillemette Diaries, Guernsey Press, Wednesday 4 May 2005.
Short History of Batterie Blücher, Alderney, by Trevor Davenport and Terry Gander, published in the Channel Islands Occupation Review, No 33, May 2003.

Memories of a German flak gunner Alderney 1943–1945, by Hubert Wolf, published in *The Alderney Society Bulletin*, 2004.
Crew List, H.M.S. Rodney, compiled by Paul Maddison.

Unpublished Documents

The Crime and Punishment of Thomas McSweeney, by Jack Snowden.
H.M.S. Rodney: The Story of a Battleship, by W. Gordon Campbell.
An Eyewitness Account of The Sinking of The Bismarck, by Lt Donald Campbell.
The End of the Bismarck, by Major J.E.M. Ruffer RM.
Per'ardship ad Astra or A Brat Goes to Sea;The Memoirs of Commander William L Myers RN (Rtd).
Transcript of interviews with Tommy Byers, regarding his life and also career in the Royal Navy.
The Sinking of the Bismarck, article by Tommy Byers.
Midshipman's Journal, Tony Robinson.
Midshipman's Journal, Roger Morris.
Somewhere in St George's Channel, notes by John Frankland. Document kept in the archive of the H.M.S. *Rodney* Association.

Internet

For Lord Blayney's Narrative, including the passages relating to HMS Rodney:
http://www.napoleonic-literature.com/Book_27

For information on Admiral Smyth:
http://pinetreeweb.com/bp-admiral.htm

More info on Captain Edward Durnford King:
http://members.cox.net/durnford/famous2.html

For a tribute to Admiral Tovey, written by the unidentified author 'RWP' visit
http://familytreemaker.genealogy.com/users/g/a/r/Ian-D-Gardiner/

For information of radar trials
http://www.rafmuseum.org.uk/milestones-of-flight/british_military/1937.html

For details on the careers of Royal Navy officers' visit:
http://www.unithistories.com/officers/RN_officersR.html

For more on the ill-fated Force Z, go to:
http://www.forcez-survivors.org.uk/

For details of officers in the Victorian Royal Navy and other fascinating information on the British fleet in the age of sail, including the Experimental Squadron cruises, go to the web site of Peter Davis, of Zeist in the Netherlands:
http://www.pdavis.nl

INDEX

Ship names: Those mentioned in the text without the HMS prefix are indexed in italics. In the case of *Rodney* herself, where the ship carries the prefix she is indexed but otherwise not, other than in the context of her lineage. Ships carrying the prefix are listed after 'HMS'. Ships are identified by nationality only where necessary.